Dr. Rimaletta Ray with Her Educational Say!

Living Intelligence Or
The Art of Becoming!

With the Plan of Action in the Brain, You Can Life-Gain!

Copyright © 2019 by Dr. Rimaletta Ray.

ISBN   Softcover   978-1-949723-36-6

All rights reserved. No part of this book may be reproduced or transmitted in any form or by any means, electronic or mechanical, including photocopying, recording, or by any information storage and retrieval system without express written permission from the author, except in the case of brief quotations embodied in critical reviews and certain other non-commercial uses permitted by copyright law.

Printed in the United States of America.

To order additional copies of this book, contact:
Bookwhip
1-855-339-3589
https://www.bookwhip.com

Your Mind Needs to Be Inspired!

(The Mental Level of the Holistic Paradigm of Self-Creation)

The Art of Living Is The Art of Becoming!

Inspirational Auto-Suggestive Psychology of Intellectual Self-Ecology

Be a Self-Guru to Accomplish Whatever You Want to!

Dedication

*To my son, **Alex Gazarkh**, for the pride that he fills up my heart with, for having been the light of my life all his life, cut short by the most treacherous war in Ukraine.*

*To my daughter, **Yolanta Lensky** for the joy and love that she brings into my life, and for the beautiful designs that she has contributed to all my books.*

To all those who see

The beauty of the unseen,

The wonder of every "Wow!"

And the magic of the Now!

I wish I could have had the book like this when I was young to be able to bridge the gap between my dream and the reality that I could master only many years later. You are holding the result of my revelation in your hands now. See if it can help you bridge your dream and the reality at the time that provides many newer opportunities, but also casts new temptations, traps, and challenges.

Please, be aware of one thing - Time Can't Change You!

Whatever You Are, You Create!

Book Rationale

1. The Holistic Self-Actualization Pyramid

Dear friends, the book *"Living Intelligence or the Art of Becomming!"* is the third one in the serial of five books, comprising, what I call, ***the Auto-Suggestive Geology of Self-Ecology.*** They are presenting the self-creation process in *the physical, emotional, mental, spiritual, and universal dimensions* of life. These stages, accordingly, are: ***self-awareness, self-monitoring, self-installation, self-realization, and self-salvation.*** They comprise the Holistic Self-Actualization Pyramid and are featured in five books, presented below from bottom to top.

The Holistic Self-Actualization Pyramid: *Books, featuring these stages are:*

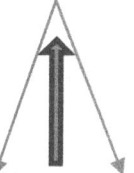

5. *Universal level*	*Self-Salvation*	*" Beyond the Terrestrial!"*
4. *Spiritual level*	*Self-Realization*	*" Self-Taming!"*
3. *Mental level*	*Self-Installation*	*" Living Intelligence of the Art of Becoming!*
2. *Emotional level*	*Self-Monitoring*	*" Soul-Refining!'*
1. *Physical level*	*Self-Awareness*	*" I Am Free to Be the Best of Me!"*

The conceptual frame-work of these five books follows the structure of the Russian dolls, ***Matryoshkas,*** when one level incorporates the next one, forming ***one simple, holistic system of Self-Installation in life***, prompted by the present-day technological revolution and the necessity to adjust our personal pace with it physically, emotionally, mentally, spiritually, and universally.

Living Intelligence puts our intelligence in the working mode of the new reality that is instilling a new network of neurons in the brain, based on the technologically-enhanced, ***holistically-developed intelligence.*** A person on this path grows a new sense of identity, the identity of a person with "***spiritualized intelligence***" (Dr. Fred Bell), ***a considerably-raised self-consciousness,*** and ***the uncluttered mind and the heart***, going along the route of knowing and re-knowing by ***changing his / her subjective,*** limited vision of life to the objective one, beyond survive! The basic conceptual holistic paradigm that each book follows is:

(Body+ Spirit+ Mind) + (Self-Consciousness+ Universal Consciousness) or

(The physical form) + (the spiritual content of life) = A New holistically-developing Self!

The choice to live as a free human being, not indoctrinated by the society, enjoying his / her individuality, realizing the unique potential, and getting self-installed professionally and self-realized personally is a tough choice to make. It requires a lot of will-power to be applied and ***constant intelligence-modification*** to change ***the "biology of our beliefs"*** (Bruce Lipton) by deleting the old ones and installing the new lofty heights of the present-day needed intelligence.

Form + Content = a Complete, Self-Realized Life!

2. Conscious Living Means Conscious Learning!

There is an urgent need for us *to develop aware attention to the reality holistically,* at each level of self-development, presented above *as the strategic plan of action*. Each level builds up on the one before, taking you a step further on the path of expanding the range of possibilities. Gradually, *thought will overpower emotion* and let you be in total charge of your evolving mind. *It should be a clearly-visualized, well-disciplined, and self-monitored process.*

"There is no self- growth without discipline."(George Miller)

As is shown above, the concept of intelligence is central in self-formation, but it needs to be channeled by a person in a conscious way with a clear–cut idea of *what type of intelligence he/ she is developing in time and space.* This information is for those people that are not just career–oriented but are driven by an urge for self-education and self-creation. *Our intellectual development is very chaotic now because it is not based on full awareness of the outcome of self-formation.* We hear young people talk about their goals in terms of education and their future professions, but very rarely, if at all, they talk about creating themselves intellectually because they have no clear plan of action in this respect.

The Art of Living is, in fact, the Art of Becoming!

It is noteworthy to mention that I am not trying in any way to refer below to *the neurological theory of multiple intelligences* by a well-known American psychologist Howard Gardner, who is basing his theory on brain research. He maps nine regions of the brain that govern specific areas of intellectual behavior: *verbal, logical-mathematical, musical, visual, bodily, kinesthetic, interpersonal, naturalistic, and existential intelligences.* The esteemed psychologist explains that *individuals possess the aptitude for all nine qualitative intelligences*, showing that each person has a specific intelligence profile that affects the choice of his / her career. This knowledge is very helpful for young people because it can direct them to their career preferences consciously. They do not make their decisions just at the advice of a school phycologist, or the demands of the job market. This knowledge helps them avoid unnecessary frustration in the future.

Working on Conscious Living is Being, Becoming, and Perceiving!

On top of this knowledge, however, it is critical for young people to consciously expand their general outlook and up-grade their intellectual self-actualization, mastering new vistas of intelligence and *changing the established knowledge base*. Knowledge becomes true power only when you continue t*o self-educate yourself exponentially* and manage to put your *mind and the heart* in sync to finally obtain *the connection with the Universal Mind* in a godly, holistic fashion.

Resist the Gravity of the Common Thought; Be equal to God!

3. The Vistas of Living Intelligence to Install!

Our time is **the Age of Awareness, and** *"awareness is the vibratory frequency of consciousness."(Christof Koch).* There are many theories about what consciousness is all about, and the main worries are about a super computer that can enact change in the world outside a programmer's command when artificial intelligence poses danger for us.(*Ray Kurzweil / Elon Musk)* However, I am more optimistic about it, and I agree with *Dr. Roger Penrose* who talks about **the quantum nature of consciousness**, not dependent on the computation. **"Consciousness is what results from growth, and all growth is educational!"**

This statement, in turn, generates the irreversible truth that to raise our consciousness, **we need to considerably enrich our intelligence** that is based on the memory that we had accumulated and that is exceedingly **outdated.** I suggest changing the existing mental framework in five philosophical levels: ***physical, emotional, mental, spiritual, and universal***, mastering them as an ***integrated holistic system*** of initial start-up knowledge that needs CONSTANT UP-DATING and NEW MEMORY connections spreading. **We are what food for thought we feed to our minds!** The mind can change the brain, or our biological computer by modifying the programs, the hard-ware, and instilling new, ***holistically-modified operational memory*** in it, or ***"accelerating our intelligence."*** (*Ray Kurzweil)*

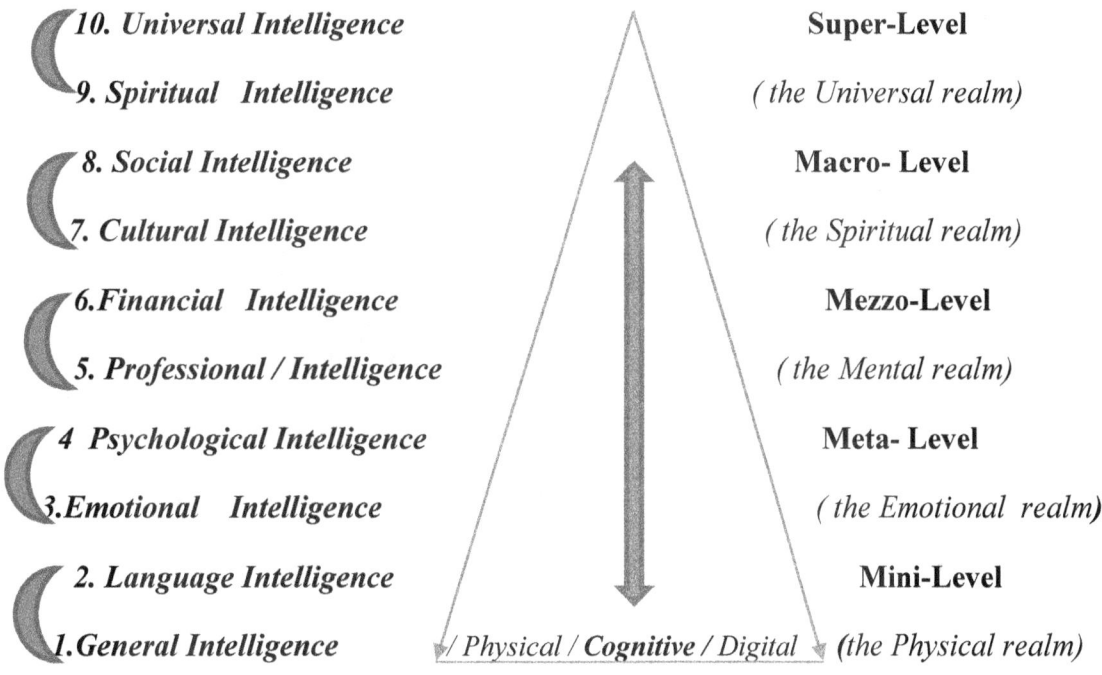

We need to supplement the standard education with enriched and ever-changing vision of life. Standard education is just the initial seed that needs to be nurtured for the rest of our life, developing us into people of wisdom because ***the mind cannot change the brain, but we can!***

"I Can't Teach you anything; I Can only Make you Think." *(Socrates)*

4. The Purity of the Mind is Self-Defined!

I have indicated above that the book" *Living Intelligence or the Art of Becoming!"* is following **the holistic paradigm of Self-Installation at the mental level** as an integral process of *self-actualization* on the path of transforming our divisive, dual mentality to a gradually unifying, holistic one thus, raising our self-consciousness. The book is forming the holistic system as the blueprint for action in five **SELF-MONITORED** dimensions,. Holistically-formed intelligence generates *new self-awareness and the new memory frame-work* in the brain.

"Transformation means nothing of the past will remain."(Sadhguru).

This book is meant to help you form the holistic picture of the basic ten vistas of intelligence from bottom to top, the necessity for which has been verified by me for years of my most successful college teaching in different countries of the world. I think that every intelligent person, striving to get a professional education, should *install these vistas of intelligence* in the mind, *at least in a dilettante way*, to form an integral view of the technologically-enhanced and exponentially-developing new world of ours.

To change the mind means to change self-consciousness!

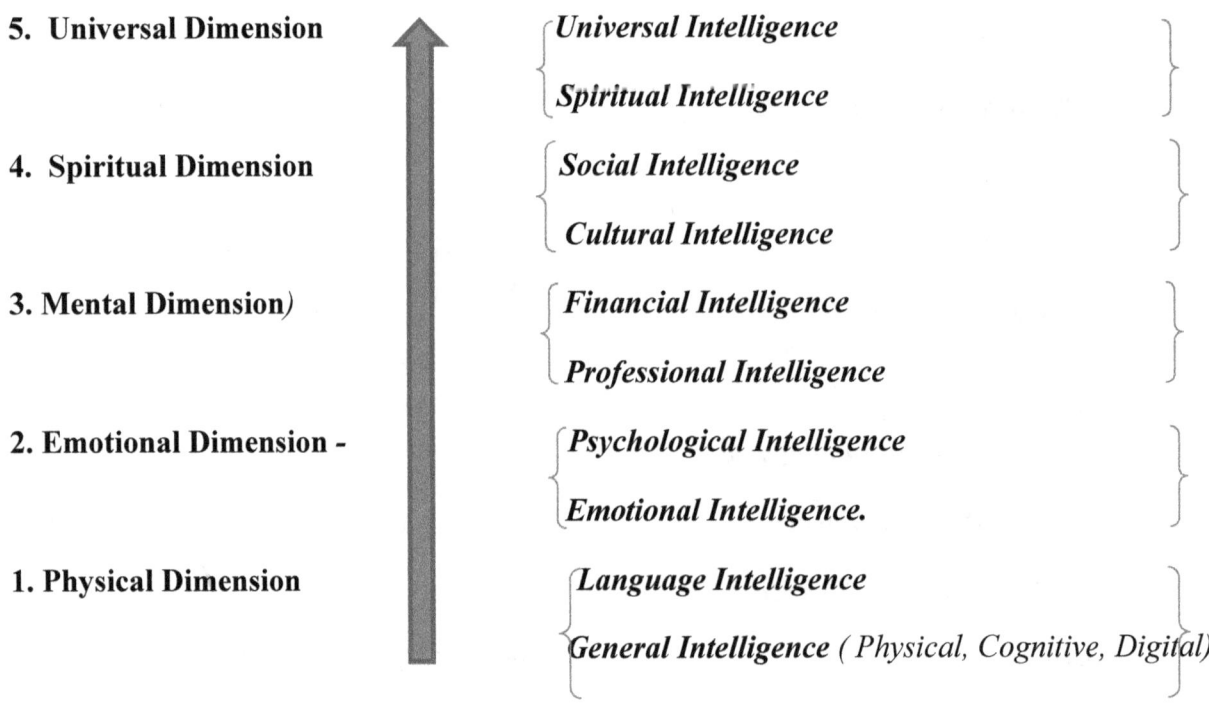

Self-perfection is a life time job that is SELF-CONSCIOUSNESS IN ACTION, the consciousness that is constantly *self-educated, willfully-cultivated, and up-dated!*

A New, Holistic Culture of Thinking is a Must!

5. New Times – New Goals!

The present-day reality demands a lot of self-reliance, self-sufficiency, and self-installation that cannot be accomplished by just being coached by someone more accomplished, better educated, and more enlightened. *It is a self-transforming process of personal self-growth through self-awareness, self-monitoring, self-installation, self-realization, and self-salvation,* or *a holistic self-development.* Each life is unique, and no prescriptions work unless they are based on *objective, personally-processed knowledge* that can be turned into personal wisdom.

Do Self-Coaching without Life-Poaching!

Holism is a mentally-structured inclusiveness because the mind needs a consciously - monitored direction *from a duality to the unity* that we talk much about, but continue seeing the world as Godly and Godless, good and evil, dark and light, without trying *to unify all the polarities in us* with our growing spiritual maturity that I see as the main gain on the path of our tuning to *the Unified Field of Energy (John Hagelin)* that we all came from and that we belong to. I see it possible to move in this direction by *changing our mode of thinking from a devising paradigm to a new holistic one by way of self-coaching in five dimensions of life.*

Self-Synthesis ⟹ *Self-Analysis* ⟹ *Self-Synthesis!*

⬇ ⬇ ⬇

(Self-Awareness) ➡ *(Self-Monitoring +Self-Installation +Self-Realization)* ➡ *(Self-Salvation)*

Work on Your Goal on the Holistic Self-Creation Paradigm Pole!

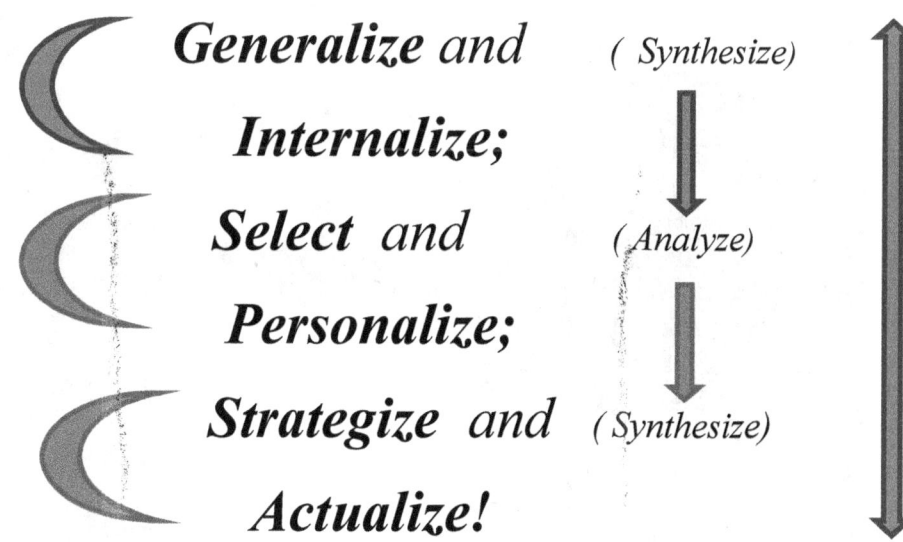

Generalize and (Synthesize)

Internalize;

Select and (Analyze)

Personalize;

Strategize and (Synthesize)

Actualize!

Actions Speak Louder than Dreams!

Inflate Your Self-Dignified Pride with Digitally-Enhanced Intellectual Might!

"Fertilize Your Mind with Thinking!"

(Albert Einstein)

Contents

<u>Book Rationale</u> - The Holistic Self-Actualization Pyramid　　　　　　　(pp. 5-10)

<u>Book Incentive</u> - Our Age is the Time of Awareness!　　　　　　　　　(pp. 17-33)

1. *We are not Getting Better; We are Getting Bitter! (An Inspirational Booster)*
2. *Growth Vs. Stagnation*
3. *Self-Consciousness Evolution is the Solution!*
4. *Our Life's Mission Array is at Play!*
5. *A New, Holistic Culture of Thinking*
6. *Holistic Level of Self-Awareness*
7. *Knowledge Put to Action is Double Power!*
8. *Intellectual Brewing without Sewing!*
9. *A Manuel of Life and Self- Creation*
10. *The Spiral of Holistic Self-Creation.*
11. *Your Life is Your Making!*
12. *Spiritualized Intelligence + Self-Consciousness = Living Intelligence!*

<u>For the Reader to First Consider</u> –The Auto-Suggestive Phycology of Self-Ecology!
Self-Hypnosis is the Best Life Prognosis! --　　　　　　　　　　　　(pp. 34-55)

1. *I Am Rerunning My Life; I am Alive!*
2. *Self-Induction is Your Own Mantra!*
3. *Self-Creation is our Main Job in Life!*
4. *"The Manifestation of Will"*
5. *Uncontrolled Self-Talk must be Harnessed!*
6. *Choreograph Your Moves Yourself!*
7. *Psycho-Kinesis in Action*
8. *Consciously Infuse Your Self-Realization Fuse!*
9. *Sculpture Yourself Through Self-Hypnosis*
10. *The Main Self-Inducting Formula*
11. *I Know Who I Am!*
12. *Where Consciousness Flows, Energy Goes!*
13. *The Auto-Suggestive Meditation*
14. *The Unanimity is the Base of Personal Equity!*
15. *Will Your Life More; That's the Law!*
16. *The Universal Unanimity is Our Infinity!*
17. *Uplift Your Spirit Every Minute!*
18. *Act as though You Are, and You Will Be!*
19. *I'm Unique in Every Stance (An Inspirational booster)*

The Manuel of Holistic Self- Creation

(The Know- How of the Holistic Self-Transformation! (Mental Dimension)

Introduction - From Being to Be Becoming! - *The Holistic Paradigm of Life Learning in 21 essential Thesis Statements)*　　　　　　　　　　　　　　(pp. 56-85)

1. Thesis 1- *We are in the Universal Flow (An Inspirational Booster)*
2. Thesis 2 – *The Grid of Our Intelligence-Consciousness Integration*
3. Thesis 3 – *The Present-Day State of Intelligence*
4. Thesis 4 – *The Predictable Future*
5. Thesis 5 - *Multi-Dimensional Intelligence*
6. Thesis 6 – *Ten Vistas of Intelligence to Install*
7. Thesis 7 – *Synthesis -Analysis-Synthesis*
8. Thesis 8 - *Rationalization of Life is a Must!*
9. Thesis 9 – *The First Shift in Our Holistic Paradigm*
10. Thesis 10 – *"Serve Yourself, then the Money!"*
11. Thesis 11 – *Change Shapes us or destroys us!*
12. Thesis 12 –*" Right is Might!"*
13. Thesis 13 – *Getting Our Intelligence in Sync with the Universal Intelligence*
14. Thesis 14 – *Self-Education is a Must!*
15. Thesis 15 – *The Auto-Suggestive Meditation is the Brain-Sculptor!*
16. Thesis 16 - *Will-Power is Our Inner Gravity!*
17. Thesis 17 – *Self- Regulation Skills*
18. Thesis 18 – *Auto-Suggestive Meditation is Mind-Sculpturing!*
19. Thesis 19 – *The Power of the Momentum!*
20. Thesis 20 - *The Spiral of the Holistic Self-Development*

The Intellectual Odyssey of a Seeking Soul- Ten Stages of Mental Growth　　(pp. 86-87)

Stage One –　General Intelligence *(Mini-Level of the Holistic Paradigm of Self-Creation –*

Division 1 - Physical Intelligence - The Primary Self-Genesis　　　　(pp. 88-122)

1. *Chunk 1 –We Have One Life to Live! (An Inspirational Booster)*
2. *Chunk 2 – Self-Emancipation is a Real Salvation!*
3. *Chunk 3 – The Conscious Mind + A Great Spirit = A Healthy Body*
4. *Chunk 4 - Holistic Enlightenment is a New Frame of Thinking*
5. *Chunk 5 – Rein Over Your Brain!*
6. *Chunk 6 – Physical Intelligence Without negligence*
7. *Chunk 7 – A New You is a Better Aware You!*
8. *Chunk 8 – The Content of Self-Awareness*
9. *Chunk 9 – Self-Refinement is Mental first!*
10. *Chunk 10 – Be Doggedly Tenacious on this Path!*
11. *Chunk 11 – The Sense of Measure is a Great Treasure!*
12. *Chunk 12 - Self--Concept and Self-Quest are Abreast!*

13. Chunk 13- The Way We Live determines the way We Die!
14. Chunk 14 – The Ultimate Result Vision of Yourself
15. Chunk 15 – Auto-Suggestive Self-Love Booster at hand
16. Chunk 16 - Manage Your Health Auto-Suggestively
17. Chunk 17 – Will-Power is Your Main Mental Sculptor
18. Chunk 18 – Moral Intelligence without Negligence
19. Chunk 19 - Love Awareness with Fairness
20. Chunk 20 - Staying Young is Real Fun! (An Inspirational Booster)
21. Chunk 21 - Self X-Raying is Inner-Portraying!
22. Chunk 22 - Self-Assessment Questionnaire
23. Chunk 23 - Beauty is Me; Beauty is my Philosophy!
24. Chunk 24 - To Life-Thrive, Envision a Better Scenario in Life!

Division 2 - Cognitive Intelligence / *General Intelligence, -Division 2* (pp. 124-145)

1. Chunk 1- Intelligence is the Universal Language of Life!
2. Chunk 2- The Time of Elevated Self-Consciousness Has Come!
3. Chunk 3 – The Art of Thinking is the Art of Conscious Learning!
4. Chunk 4 - Mental Architecture is Holistic in Nature.
5. Chunk 5- The Integral You is a Holistically-Thinking You!
6. Chunk 6 – You Are How You Think!
7. Chunk 7 – The World of Organized Inadequacies
8. Chunk 8 – Beware of the Inflation of Thinking!
9. Chunk 9 – Reflective Thinking is Conscience Shaping
10. Chunk 10 – Self-Education without Proration
11. Chunk 11 - Dissipated Consciousness is a Wasted Life!
12. Chunk 12 –Thinking Hygiene is on the Scene!
13. Chunk 13 – Intellectual Superiority is Sky-limited!
14. Chunk 14 - Self-Scanning Auto-Suggestively!
15. Chunk 15 – I Live Consciously and Visually; I am a Visionary!

Division 3 – Digital Intelligence (*General Intelligence, Mini-Level*) (pp. 147-167)

1. Chunk 1 – Artificial Intelligence (An Inspirational Booster)
2. Chunk 2 – Our Mind Potential is Exponential!
3. Chunk 3 – Mind means Intelligence + Self- Consciousness!
4. Chunk 4 – Electronic Intelligence is Ruling the World. So What?
5. Chunk 5 – Brain Plasticity and Automation
6. Chunk 6 - Capitalize on Electronic Competences Consciously
7. Chunk 7 - Immunity against Digital Addiction
8. Chunk 8 – Go beyond the Basic Content of Your Intellect!
9. Chunk 9 – Digital Clicking in Love Seeking
10. Chunk 10 - Raise Self-Consciousness with Digital Means!
11. Chunk 11 – Be Integral, Sincere, and Kind! Be One of a Kind!
12. Chunk12 – The Age of Quantum Computing is coming!
13. Chunk 13 - Strict Mental Hygiene is on the Scene!
14. Chunk 14 - Five-Dimensional Self-Consciousness
15. Chunk 15 –The Holistic Education is the Solution for Our Evolution!
16. Chunk16 – Increase the Psycho-Tronic Energy of Self-Consciousness

Stage One – Language Intelligence -(Mini-Level – Step Two (pp. 169-186)

1. *Chunk 1 – Language is the Matrix of Thinking!*
2. *Chunk 2 – Language Awareness*
3. *Chunk 3- Language Consciousness!*
4. *Chunk 4 – Language Fitness without Cognitive Sickness!*
5. *Chunk 5 – Language Pollution impedes Personal Evolution!*
6. *Chunk 6 – Mind Your Thought Coding! (An Inspirational Booster)*
7. *Chunk 7- Language Correctness and Speech Exactness*
8. *Chunk 8 – Language-Speech Immunity*
9. *Chunk 9 - Tame Your Tongue!*
10. *Chunk 10 - Impeccability of Self- Expressions*
11. *Chunk 11 – Manage Your Language (An Inspirational Booster)*

Stage Two – Emotional Intelligence- Step One / Meta –Level - the Emotional Dimension) (pp. 188-208)

1. *Chunk 1 – Emotional Negligence (An Inspirational Booster)*
2. *Chunk 2 –Life is Mentally Emotional*
3. *Chunk 3 - Emotional Self-Awareness*
4. *Chunk 4 –Self-Creation with Elation*
5. *Chunk 5 – Emotional Skills and Techno-babies*
6. *Chunk 6 - Self-Assessment and Self-Monitoring*
7. *Chunk 7 –To Be More Life-Fit, Snap Out of it!*
8. *Chunk 8 - Cleansing Your Emotional Memory*
9. *Chunk 9 –Emotional Diplomacy and Courtesy*
10. *Chunk 10 – The Code of Love*
11. *Chunk 11 - Love Negligence (An Inspirational Booster)*
12. *Chunk 12 - Love Intelligence + Love Induction*
13. *Chunk 13 –The Elation is Love-Illumination!*
14. *Chunk 14 – Right is My Might!*
15. *Chunk 15 - Look Life in Face!*

Stage Two – Psychological Intelligence – Step Two / Meta –Level- (pp. 210-235)

1. *Chunk 1 – Change Your Psycho-Culture!*
2. *Chunk 2 – The Ultimate Result Vision of Self*
3. *C hunk 3 – Psychological Awareness*
4. *Chunk 4 – Immunity to the Poison of Life*
5. *Chunk 5 – The Demagnetization of the Spirit*
6. *Chunk 6 –Boost Your Will-Power to Self-Empower!*
7. *Chunk 7 –Self-Acceptance is Essential!*
8. *Chunk 8 - Introspection or Self-Inspection*
9. *Chunk 9 – The Path of Moral Maturity*
10. *Chunk10 – Mental Trip to Self- Respect*
11. *Chunk 11 – Don't be Lazy to Excel; Compliment Yourself!*
12. *Chunk 12 – Self- Management is Learnable!*
13. *Chunk 13 – Psychological Adaptability*
14. *Chunk 14 – Enact Psychological diplomacy*

15. *Chunk 15 - Apply Psychological Diplomacy!*
16. *Chunk 16 – Mind Your Soul's Size for it might Get De-magnetized!*
17. *Chunk 17 - Practice What You Preach!*
18. *Chunk 18 – Auto-Suggestive Tools*

Stage Three *–Professional Intelligence-* *Step One / Mezzo- Level – Mental Dimension*

Division 1 – Professional Actualization   (pp. 237-257)

1. *Chunk 1 – Professional Awareness*
2. *Chunk 2 – Professional Installation*
3. *Chunk 3 – Self-Genesis Strategically and Tactically*
4. *Chunk 4 - Rational Thinking and Intuition development*
5. *Chunk 5 – Professional Consciousness*
6. *Chunk 6 – Professional Conscience and Competence*
7. *Chunk 7 – Beware of Stereotyped Thinking*
8. *Chunk 8 – Inflation of Professional Thinking*
9. *Chunk 9 – Holistic Professional Wisdom*
10. *Chunk 10 –Professional Superficiality*
11. *Chunk 11- Professional Self-Assessment*
12. *Chunk 12 –Professional Intelligence Auto-Suggestively*

Division- 2 – Creative Intelligence   (pp. 259-271)

1. *Chunk 1 – "The Will to Create is Encoded in our DNA"*
2. *Chunk 2 – Change the Form and Content of Your Thinking!*
3. *Chunk 3 - Actionable Imagination*
4. *Chunk 4 -Making Things Possible is Not Impossible!*
5. *Chunk 5 – To Be Interesting, Get Interested!*
6. *Chunk 6 – Steer the Self-Judgement of Your Idea!*
7. *Chunk 7 - Self- Hypnosis is at Hand; Remember that!*
8. *Chunk 8 – Oy Vey! Victory is on the Way!*
9. *Chunk 9- Doubt is an Immobility of Thinking!*
10. *Chunk 10 – Self-Affirming is Self-Forming!*
11. *Chunk 11 - To Be Creatively-Charged, Be Self-Judged!(An Inspirational Booster)*

Stage Three Financial Intelligence *- Step Two (Mezzo- Level)-*   (pp. 273-283)

1. *Chunk 1 – Money Veins Need Brains!*
2. *Chunk 2 – Money Management is Learnable!*
3. *Chunk 3 - Good Financial Metabolism*
4. *Chunk 4 – Financial Awareness = Financial Fitness*
5. *Chunk 5 – Money- Actualizing Skills*
6. *Chunk 6 – Dematerialization of the Spirit of Giving*
7. *Chunk 7 – Financial Consciousness*
8. *Chunk 8 – The Vintage You is a Money Guru! (An Inspirational Booster)*

Stage Four - Cultural Intelligence – Step One *(Macro-Level - the Spiritual Dimension)*

1. *Chunk 1 – Life is not Always Fair! (An (Inspirational Booster)*   (pp. 285-295)
2. *Chunk 2 – Cultural Awareness as the Code of Behavior*
3. *Chunk 3 – We are of the Same DNA- You, Me, and They!*
4. *Chunk 4 – Cultural Metabolism and Cultural Consciousness*
5. *Chunk 5 – Compatible Brain Chemistry*
6. *Chunk 6 – Establish a Synergistic Cultural Climate!*
7. *Chunk 7 – Be Culturally- Apt Auto- Suggestively!*
8. *Chunk 8- The Divine Spark of International Intelligence*

Stage Four – Social Intelligence – Step Two -*(Macro-Level – the Spiritual Dimension)*

1. *Chunk 1 – Social Awareness and Aptness*   (pp. 297-305)
2. *Chunk 2 – Social Metabolism without any "Izm"*
3. *Chunk 3 –The Unity of Mind –to- Mind + a Heart -to -Heart is an Art!*
4. *Chunk 4 – Social Network Equilibrium*
5. *Chunk 5 – Social Connection is Language-Interwoven"*
6. *Chunk 6 - Synergize the Trajectory of Your Social Life to Thrive!*

Stage Five – Spiritual Intelligence – Step One *(Super-Level –Spiritual Dimension)*

1. *Chunk 1 – The Universal March Forward and Onward!*   (pp. 307-318)
2. *Chunk 2 – Being Spiritually Aristocratic*
3. *Chunk 3 – Being Godly in a Godless World is Your Self-Award!*
4. *Chunk 4 –"God Helps those who Help Themselves!"*
5. *Chunk 5 – Spiritualized Intelligence is the Root of Wisdom!*
6. *Chunk 6 – I Monitor My Life! I Am Alive!*

Stage Five – The Universal Intelligence – Step Two- *(Super-Level –Universal*

1. *Chunk 1 – Attitude of Gratitude is My Life's Altitude!*   (pp. 320-327)
2. *Chunk 2 –The Universal Mind that We need to Unwind!*
3. *Chunk 3 – Spiritual Luminosity is Our Velocity!*
4. *Chunk 4 –Unite with the Universal Intelligence Might!*
5. *Chunk 5 – Ten Stages of Living Intelligence*
6. *Chunk 6 - Infuse Your self-realization Fuse!(An Inspirational booster)*

Conclusion - The Art of living is the Art of Becoming!   (pp. 328-332)

Post-Thought - "I Have a Dream!" *(Mather Luther King)*   (pp. 334-335)

"New Times are the Times of Exponential Learning!" *(Ray Kurzweil)*

Book Incentive

Our Age is the Time of Awareness!

Grains of Me and My Philosophy

"We are who we are because of what we have learned and what we remember!"

(Eric Kandel, the Nobel Prize winner)

To Life-Thrive, We Need to Self-Derive!

Transform Yourself from a Cocoon to a Butterfly!

Don't Crawl – Fly!

Resist the Gravity of the Common Thought!

Magnetize Yourself with What You are Not!

1. We are Not Getting Better; We are Getting Bitter!

(An Inspirational Booster)

We are not getting better,

We are getting bitter

    When we see cruelty and injustice

    Still unstopped with a Vito!

There is a lot of religious yearning,

But human life is still burning!

    When and where

    Will we start to beware

That our moral steep

Is on a guilt trip?

    The words" placid and serene"

    Are rapidly getting obscene!

We keep wondering," What are the ways

For Christ Consciousness to surface?"

    The causes for that are immense,

    But the acts of reasoning are in defense!

We obviously need to start

Making kinder a human heart!

    We desperately need to go

    Beyond the "collective psyche's flow!

　　　　　　　　　　We still have to release

　　　　　　　　　A great deal of anger disease,

And we must un-bitter

A lot of emotional litter!

　　　　　　　　　　But we should not give up

　　　　　　　　　Even on the tiniest spiritual stuff

That's left in a neighbor or someone's son,

Anyone, stretching his hand for a motor-gun!

　　　　　　　　　Let's give ourselves a conscious bite

　　　　　　　　　And stand up for our principles very tight!

 For there is always hope

Even in the most hopeless dope!

　　　　　　　　　　There is always a ray of Sun

　　　　　　　　　　In a puddle of dirty fun!

All we need to see

Is the soul that has no glee!

　　　　　　　　　　There is always a good grain

　　　　　　　　　　In some deeply buried plane

Where we can plant a seed

For the golden sand to proceed.

　　　　　　　　　　Then this soul will start to shine,

　　　　　　　　　Even if it's tied up with a course twine!

All we need to add

Is some more golden sand!

Thus, we'll build a castle, grain by grain

On a lost soul's terrain.

The dirty foam will subside

Finally, aside

And his or her fractured soul

Will be kindly consoled!

He or she'll go in the right direction

For his / her resurrection!

Thus, before leaving this world,

We'll plant in someone the thought

Of the evolutionary How and Why?

One needs to Fly!

"Only then can we "move from a primary natural potentiality to the formed and finished completion of self." (Aristotle)

So, let's tune our life-elation to

the Quantum Field of the Electro-Magnetic Gravitation!

Let's not Rush to Become Biological Trash!

2. Growth vs. Stagnation

One of the most exciting scientific adventures of all times is *the* search for the ultimate nature of physical reality and the role of consciousness in its evolution. The perpetually evolving world of science and technology demands that we develop our consciousness that remains to be the greatest miracle and a puzzle that the scientists of many fields of knowledge try to unravel. *"The energy of consciousness is all that exists in the universe." (Scientific Mind, June 2010)* Science is just starting a long process of figuring out what dark energy, sizzling black holes, and a string theory can explain, and what their staggering implications are in terms of consciousness that is ruling the universe and our ability to attune to it consciously.

The epoch of shaping life with our consciousness has come!

"There is consciousness on every level of creation, from a human being to a stone. A human being is simply a localized concentration of energy and intelligence in the universal field."(Deepak Chopra) As we learn more about the neural mechanism of intelligence, prospects for enhancing intelligence become more likely. *"We get programmed from berth at the cerebral, emotional, psychological, and physical levels."* However, a person can constantly study, but he remains within the limits of the basic content of his intellect. And quite rightfully, we have many educated people, but very few real intellectuals. As a famous British philosopher David Icke states, *"We have giants of intellect, but pigmies of spiritual qualities, or higher consciousness."* These people live under the effect of *the gravity of the common thought, money-chasing, and fun-basing!*

There is a widespread belief that individual differences in intelligence are innate and hardly modifiable. But science proves that intelligence is not fixed; it is being shaped though our lives. All it takes for a person is *to become aware of his limited mental and spiritual life* and have a desire to holistically expand his consciousness beyond the usual and known to explore oneself.

So, "excessive happiness" is not a sizable bliss, **IT'S AN EARNED MIND-RELEASE!**

It's inconceivable where fundamental research might be leading us, but its horizons are so captivating that we cannot afford being depressed, indifferent, careless, ignorant, and dependent on someone to show us the way to be happier in life. Let's stop trying to be happy and just be happy! *"The secret of change is to focus all of your energy not on fighting the old, but on building the new."(Socrates)* Evidently, the present-day developments in the realm of consciousness are the most advanced ones. They direct us toward the inevitable evolving into a different level of consciousness, or *self-consciousness* that is creating our reality, or *"bending the reality"*(Steve Jobs).Our creative vision in synch with a much higher level of *aware intelligence* will take us to *a higher level of truly constructive consciousness* that will create a new reality of life, without a blind relying on any spiritual leader, a guru, or a life coach.

Evolution or Involution - That is the Question!

3. Self-Consciousness Evolution is the Solution!

The development of our self-consciousness cannot be accomplished unless we *renew our intelligence* in sync with *the Universal Laws of Creation,* and unless we expand our cognition and perception of these laws in full connection with the five dimensions of life.

The Raised Self-Consciousness propels us on-ward, up-ward, and God-ward!

Super Level	*Consciousness of God!*	**Universal Dimension**
Macro Level	*Consciousness of the Universe*	**Spiritual Dimension**
Mezzo Level	*Consciousness of the World*	**Mental Dimension**
Meta level	*Consciousness of the Society*	**Emotional Dimension**
Micro Level	*Consciousness of a Man*	**Physical Dimension**

The consciousness of both the society and the world that is presented above is being now formed by an unprecedented socialization and globalization of our lives that promote our gradual consciousness ascending. *We, in fact, develop the holistic consciousness of inter-dependency* which is not just three-dimensional(*Hight, width, depth*), but is *four-directional* because it has *the volume* that encompasses everything around us and generates *the feeling of Oneness* inside and outside!

Everything relates to everything. *"Our Sun is the mind that guides the solar system; the Galactic mind guides the galaxy, and the Universal mind guides the Universe, the Source of the mind that guides all creation." (David Icke)*

"Consciousness is the source of what we are! (Sadhguru)

Unfortunately, *cerebral unemployment* is a common disease that is looming around us now, especially after the economic downfall that had resulted in many job losses in many countries worldwide, and, naturally, this situation resulted in massive emigration and lessening of intelligence on a big scale.

Many people get discouraged and lose their drive to create anything, let alone themselves. Consequently, there are many intelligent, highly educated people that end up being immigrants, facing the grim reality to start their life from scratch.

"Life does not adjust to us, we adjust to life!"

Many of these people are exceptionally talented, and many of them make a big difference in the countries where they find themselves on the tide of globally changing economy. *Hope for self-realization*, without any national or language wrappings is driving all of us.

"We cannot live better than in seeking to become better!" (Socrates)

"Know Thyself!" says the Bible. There is also much talk about the necessity to enlighten, to *visualize different success manifesting* scenarios, and evolve spiritually. There are zillions of great books by outstanding spiritual leaders, life-coaching trainers, and mind-advanced scientists that give you guidance how *to live in the Now* and *develop the New Age awareness* and spirituality to accomplish desired success, but we cannot stop being a part of a" *dysfunctional civilization."* (Al Gore)

Unfortunately, there is very little, if at all, information **about WHAT+ WHY+ HOW** to attain that goal *in a consistently conscious, holistic way* and, most importantly, how to do it not just verbally, but **DE FACTO YOURSELF,** without any outside help, anyone's coaching, and a considerable amount of money paid to accomplish what I call here *the Living Intelligence skills.* Beyond the necessity to meditate, we seem to know nothing.

We think what we are, and we are what we think, when both are in synch!

Obviously, we need the blueprint, or *a systematized, objective (not subjective!) instruction to follow* so we could develop a conscious life style and *change our lives from broke-ness to happiness*. Many disillusioned people believe that someone, who has accomplished the heights of material security can teach them to uplift themselves.

They attend trainings and on-line seminars, not being aware that their personal, *critical mass of the individually-processed knowledge + substantially-raised self-consciousness* has not been reached! The path of every enlightened person is tough, and much wisdom is accumulated by us though consistent knowledge seeking, information selection, and conscious strategizing of life.

Capture the feeling of the sky with no ceiling!

Self-Coaching and Self-Framing are Life-Gaining!

4. Our Life's Mission Array is at Play!

Speaking of the quantum reality that we started probing, I like a reasonable explanation of how our thoughts and feelings, or **mind+ heart** that I refer to in all my books, work by **Dr. Joe Dispenza.** He calls on us to connect the WHAT and the HOW of our experiential lives to the present moment in the quantum reality, learning to respond to it in a new way..

"Thoughts are the language of the brain, feelings are the language of the body."

I suggest exploring this process of a personal make-up holistically in the **physical, emotional, mental, spiritual, and universal realms of life**. The love of life and the desire to be self-realized in it should always be greater than the fear of death!

"Man, as a being of sense, wants his life to make sense."(Alan W. Watts)

The present-day biology proves that our life's mission array is not engraved in our DNA! ***It's the work of our cells*** that can be re-programmed the way we need, destroying the outdated conviction that we inherit the intelligence and that we are the victims of the hereditary DNA. Dr. Bruce Lipton, an ardent advocate of conscious biology calls this new level of life awareness *"informational medicine"* He says, ***"We need to change the biology of our beliefs!"***

So, this is what this book is about, and the ideas, presented in it go along the lines of **systematization and simplification of knowledge.** We can, and we must change OUR LIMITED PERCEPTION OF OURSELVES AND THE LIFE AROUND US. The ***truth is found in what is simple***, and simple is much more difficult to be discovered behind the complex. Simple needs a lot of sorting out of the redundant information to be done, leaving the essence, the crux of the matter for the generalization and reasoning. This book is an attempt *to present a simple blueprint* of developing **self-guided and self-guarded** intelligence and self-consciousness

Generalizing knowledge – Personalizing it – Actualizing the processed result!

To develop the mind that is the birthplace of reason, we need to be able to see beneath the surface of appearances and recognize the importance of simplification of our vision of things that helps form the short–cuts in our information-overloaded brains. One stops being a victim of circumstances and becomes part of **holistic Universal Divinity that accepts us as its disciples.** I think that each of us should have a **PERSONAL MISSION STATEMENT** formed in the brain without the reliance on anyone's ready-made recipe, or a life-coaching training . There is no goal higher than the goal to become an independent, intelligent, productive, and a NOBLE HUMAN BEING with the highest spiritual qualities that are infinite, eternal, and absolute. I have seen an insatiable desire for self-realization in the eyes of hundreds of my students, and it has been MY PERSONAL MISSION *to help them in the self-quest of becoming the only and the best!*

Self-Quest is Abreast only with the Knowledge Zest!

5. A New, Holistic Culture of Thinking

To continue, I deem it paramount for all of us *to study the Art of Living* and to acquire the basic life-enhancing vistas of intelligence to considerably improve our life and self-awareness. *Holistic self-consciousness is a new, much more reasoned out self-awareness, guided by rational thinking, speaking, and acting* "We develop the soul and the spirit forces through only the mental man."*(Edgar Cayce)* Self-Awareness needs to be holistic! It means that you are aware of your physical state, emotional, mental, spiritual, and universal. It's an adventure into your personalized insights, your own revelation that is shaping your own destiny!

Once we realize the necessity *to reason out the reality of our life holistically*, it will help us transcend our *dual, limited mentality* and resurrect our souls, changing the culture of our thinking and finally becoming masters of our destiny. *"Living intelligence becomes consciousness in action, the consciousness that cultivates "a new culture of thinking." (Dr. Fred Bell)* "The society has crippled us in many ways. Each person must work his way out of this pathological society and the best way to do, so is to start thinking for yourself" (Osho) I describe this way in the first book on self-creation" I Am Free to Be the Best of Me! "as the route:

Generalizing – Internalizing - Actualizing or Self-Synthesis- Self-Analysis -Self-Synthesis!

A new culture of thinking should be the holistically structured to help us gradually clean the mind of the pollution, generated by the influence of *"the collective unconscious"* and going with the flow of general unconsciousness. *(Carl Yung)*. The information that had been stored in our subconscious mind for centuries on end still determines our limited perception of life. *We are in the flow of the general, "I don't know!"* It is filled with indifference, not the desire to probe the unknown and be excited with self- discovery. *This is the goal of education!*

Your personal intellectual array must be at play!

Meanwhile, many of us are driven by the common thought or the crowd mentality, when we, like robots on a remote control, are acting and living in an automatic trance of unconscious patterns of behavior. With a new, *holistic culture of living*, instilled in us in the *physical, emotional, mental, spiritual, and universal dimensions of life*, we will develop an *inclusive, not divisive mentality* and respect all human life, irrespective of religion, skin color, and a social or financial status. *Spiritualized intelligence must be valued as the highest social commodity!*

I see an urgent necessity for our young people to build up their minds on the well sorted-out information and the knowledge that is loaded with *full awareness of the true, not virtual, reality of life*, enriched with the new scientific vision of the ever-changing NOW. They should be guided by *aware attention* to the right actions and the consequences of bad ones.

Personal Integrity must resist the Common Gravity!

6. Holistic Level of Self-Awareness

Self-perfection is a never-ending job of life! It means that you declare your uniqueness to yourself and the world every day and everywhere. You can pump in some emotional gas through self-education, avid reading, knowledge processing, and your insatiable curiosity. Revelation does not come ready-made, or it can hardly be instilled by the best minds of the world. It is a self-processed result of feeling depleted of enthusiasm due to the turmoil of life and the internal wounds, inflicted by it. Experience is teaching us to rely on oneself and trust oneself first, so that *the electro-magnetic core of your personality should never get demagnetized.*

Self- Induction: *Enthuse yourself and inspire; uplift yourself and rewire!*

History proves to us that it had never been easy to accomplish anything in life without having a strong image of Self that makes a person stand out, on the one hand, and revitalize this image in himself repeatedly, on the other.

Self- Induction: *Don't be self-bereft! Give yourself a Go -Ahead!*

However, this process is impossible without heightening your self-consciousness because it involves forming a new, holistic level of self-awareness and a new holistic out-look. We live in *the global world of holistic integration,* and the challenges that we are all facing are not getting easier. Limited education does not work anymore. *The food for thought that we get electronically becomes our new commodity!* It needs to be properly perceived, selected, and consumed.

Self- Induction: *To be interesting, get interested!*

To go with the flow of the present-day science developments, we need to considerably expand our general outlook by deepening our knowledge of science, art, literature, history, technology and by constantly improving our ignorant perception of life in all five dimensions of life *(physical, emotional, mental, spiritual and universal)* *at least 1% a day*. (Multi-dimensional Consciousness, Thesis 8 below.) We need to empower our minds with more and more intelligence at each step on the ladder of higher consciousness formation that is everyone's sole responsibility.

"You cannot live better than in seeking to become better" (Socrates)

But what is the ultimate result that we need to obtain? The ten levels of intelligence that I have presented out above as the essential ones require a lot of knowledge and skills being put to work. That is not enough, though. These intelligences are just the stepping stones on the way of self-actualization. We need to develop ourselves into whole human beings the whole life. In this process of self-formation, we are putting ourselves together in space and time, just as Albert. Einstein advised,

"To be whole means to synergize, not polarize life in time and space."

7. Knowledge Put to Action is Double Power!

Those of us who do not disrupt *the allotted life time span* with unconscious automatic responses to life challenges obtain the will-power, contentment, and happiness that a great American philosopher Joseph Campbell called *"the bliss."* The Eastern philosophy names this state **nirvana,** the state of actual becoming *body, mind, spirit, and soul-whole.* Such wholeness and self-awareness become possible when the external and the internal factors come in synch, creating a holistic self-concept that we call personal integrity, enveloped in high self-consciousness! The spirit is in the center of this holistic paradigm (*See the book "I am Free to be the Best of Me!"*) because the spirit is the glue, *the spiritual substance* that holds the whole structure together. Christ's doctrine is *the Law of the Spirit*, that He defined as the highest values of the godly truth.

Body + Spirit= Mind+ Self-Consciousness+ Super-Consciousness = a Whole Self!

So, raising self-consciousness is the constant work of *the mind + character development* to obtain this unbreakable integrity, fortified with *physical, emotional, psychological, professional, cultural, social, and spiritual self-awareness.* Unconscious living is disconnected living and disconnection is death! So, give yourself a go-ahead to heath, new intelligence, language accuracy, behavior-impeccability, moral intelligence, and full self-actualization, following the holistic paradigm :.

Self-Synthesis ⟹ *Self-Analysis* ⟹ *Self-Synthesis!*

(Self-Awareness) ⟹ (Self-Monitoring +Self-Installation +Self-Realization) ⟹ (Self-Salvation)

Obviously, without developing awareness of this *integral process,* such endeavors are doomed. We cannot let that happen before we leave *the Tree of Life*. On the track of enlightenment, we often skip the mental point – *the state of consciousness that must be substantially developed in every dimension,* irrespective of the unpleasant circumstances in life that we have to face, anyway., These are natural fluctuations of life and should be perceived as such, not getting us off the track due to commonly-shared ignorance. So, encourage yourself with the beautiful words by the pastor Robert H. Schuler:

"Tough times do not last, tough people do!"

Our life-elation is based in a new field of electro-magnetic gravitation. Life after all is the field of energy that is fluctuating between the negative and positive charges. Our happy moments and unhappy ones are just the inevitable flow of life fluctuations that we are supposed to energize us *knowingly, consistently, and consciously, or, putting it differently,* **wisely!**

Managing your life means magnetizing it with wising!

Power Up Your Inner Rehab!

8. Intellectual Brewing Without Sewing!

We are all yarning for life contentment, for more money, for more self-recognition, for something that our souls long for, rejecting ignorance that puts our self-consciousness out of shape. All we have to do is *to find the will power to get out of the impulsive way of living,* liberating the potential energy to unite us with our developing self-consciousness. Only developing the intelligence in the essential areas of life will we satisfy our hunger for the ways of profound transformation of Self, or" *a soul's resurrection."(Dr. Fred Bell)*. Much motivational talking is being done by many great people on line, but we are still crying over the spilt milk. The ills of the society have become chronical, and *the treatment is supposed to be done in each dimension consciously.*

"Injustice anywhere is a threat of justice everywhere." (M. L. King, Jr)

*"Only by changing the culture of our thinking can we revolutionize our developing consciousness" (Dr. F. Bell)*If the mind is coherent, life is coherent, too.

"There is only one good – knowledge and one evil – ignorance." (Socrates)

Unfortunately, unconscious qualities dominate now. People are driven by" *the psychology of the masses*" *(Le Ron),* when *"he is not the individual himself, he is a robot who has no will."* The rust of destruction is rapidly absorbing our daily lives and stealing away our badly needed free time to the point that all we can do is to listlessly absorb the TV most intellectually debilitating shows. Even the news is full of cooking debates. As a result, we hardly have any energy for *a face-to-face, mind-to-mind, and heart–to heart communication* with anybody. There are many very intelligent and spiritually-advanced people who illuminate the world with their presence in it.

However, the process of enlightenment is going on spontaneously, but it needs to be channeled. We have to process new knowledge that we obtain now *through the grid of consciousness integration (Chunk 3 above)* and personal experience, sorting out the information that can be applied to changing the course of action without blindly following any one's path for success We all have the same mind, but the instruction to use it must be different!

Thought-demanding work is in stock!

Self- awareness is not a declaration; it's knowledge accumulation!

In sum, holistic personal evolution should be based on better awareness about life and Self tolead us to a higher level of self-consciousness - *the goal of our evolution!* A new culture of thinking demands transformation of the physical, verbal, emotional, psychological, professional, cultural, social, and spiritual fundamentals of man *So, jump-start your thinking! Let the hard-ware of your brain - the memory, work by the new soft-ware - the mind.*

"You Better Be Unborn than Untaught!" *(Plato)*

9. A Manuel of Life and Self-Creation

No doubt you have read many of self-help books and have listened to the motivational talks of our best scientists, spiritual leaders, and gurus that can be found in abundance on the Internet now, All of them contribute a lot to our intellectual and spiritual growth that is going on in sync with our technological evolution that develops *new electro-magnetic circuits in the brain,* turning on the mind to brewing new ideas and breaking up old stereotypes of thought and feelings.

The best goal of all is to Self-Install!

Every person needs *to make up his / her own strategy of self-actualization, built on the objective knowledge* because every life of different and what works for one person never works for the other. We cannot build up a personal life on someone's subjective experience in it. This is an extremely challenging goal, but I decided to take this challenge because, as an educator, I see an urgent necessity to simplify the information on self-installation and make it more digestible and systematized in the form of a **MANUAL OF LIFE AND SELF-CREATION.** This book must be a general instruction on *the Know-How of obtaining the Living Intelligence Skills* in a holistically-organized, not a random way. The Manuel of Life should reflect such **OBJECTIVE KNOWLEDGE OF ETERNAL VALUE.**

Regrettably, self-knowledge and the awareness of science are now in defiance! There are too many technological temptations now, and any good book on self-transformation and ways of accomplishing success in life doesn't get internalized because *the experiential advice in them is too subjunctivized.* Such information becomes just a secondary storage place in the brain that responds to the immediate gratification whims in a much quicker way. The obtained knowledge is turned into the *museum of wax figures of ideas* that beautify the dream that everyone of us has, but only a few of us enliven *with new awareness + conscious action*, breaking the old patterns of thinking, feeling, speaking, and decision-making. As a matter of fact, *our life is an enigma that needs to be unraveled, studied, and intelligently actualized in full awareness of the new reality in Self* that is changing exponentially and even menacingly.

Having a dream is not putting it on the pedestal statistically, it's achieving it holistically!

Our life now looks more as *a virtual game* and very many young people *identify themselves with the characters of the role-playing games (RPG)* in which they are supposed to master different levels of game proficiency and become more competent and skillful in *the world of Warcraft.* The gaming activity takes hours, days, and even weeks on end. Then the young minds get engaged in discussing their accomplishments and the virtual money gains. *There is no time for self-installation left*; there are no intentions to ever start it and re-direct the life from un-conscious to conscious, from godless to godly and, consequently, inwardly-"rewardly."

The Battle for a Personable Self is won by Yourself!

10. The Spiral of the Holistic Self-Creation

Concluding my philosophical out-lay, *we live in the conceptual Age of Awareness!* Our brains are extraordinary, and the intelligence that we consume technologically now from *the Unified Field of Consciousness / Intelligence* regulates all our bodily functions. It transforms our brains and, consequently, our spiritual make-up that is inseparable with the mental enrichment of our entire being, channeled by raised self-consciousness.

> *"It's time to make the voice of the Universal Consciousness heard."* (Sadhguru)

I think that each of us also writes his / her **BOOK OF LIFE,** chapter by chapter. Each book has *the starting point* at birth. Then a person is processing his life through *the plot development* around the main conflicts between life and death, energy and entropy. *The culminating point* comes in. the middle of the story with *the resolution of the conflict* between the evil and the good sides of life inevitably coming next, and, finally, a person rounds off his life story with *the conclusion of the life cycle*.

THE CATHASIS is to be experienced by each of us, too, and this is THE MAIN STAGE OF LIFE - the realization of the outcome of life that comes with the last breath of either gratitude or regret. It is the Catharsis that generates wisdom in the mind, and we all need to get processed through life *to experience Catharsis at every stage of life.* and in every dimension.

In Sum, the Art of Becoming requires, therefore, *our conscious reprogramming of Self* to be able to create *the Living Intelligence with an individual label* for each one of us consciously steering the life to full self–actualization in the philosophical levels: *mini, meta, mezzo, macro, and super.* These levels constitute correspondingly *the physical, emotional, mental, spiritual, and universal dimensions of life,* presenting the spiral of the holistic self-creation accordingly as: *self-awareness, self-monitoring, self-installation, self-realization, and self-salvation.* We are overloaded with the information, and *it needs to be simplified, selected, personalized, and strategized.* This is what this book is all about.

. **Body+ Spirit+ Mind + Self-Consciousness+ Universal Consciousness = A New, Whole Self!**

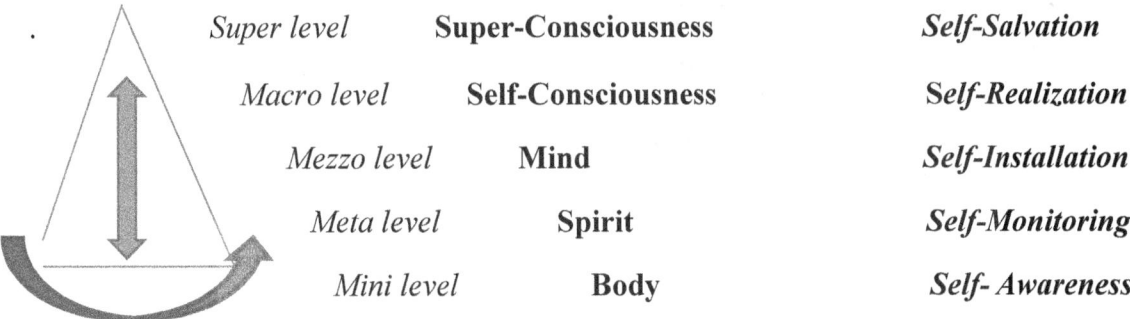

	Super level	**Super-Consciousness**	*Self-Salvation*
	Macro level	**Self-Consciousness**	*Self-Realization*
	Mezzo level	**Mind**	*Self-Installation*
	Meta level	**Spirit**	*Self-Monitoring*
	Mini level	**Body**	*Self- Awareness*

"Life is a Spiral, Not a Circle!" (Dr. Fred Bell)

11. "Your Life is Your Making!" *(Sadhguru)*

In sum, the aim of the book *"Living Intelligence or the Art of Becoming"* is to outline the steps on self-development in the mental dimension that is featured in the holistic paradigm as an intellectual and professional **Self-Installation.**(*See the holistic pyramid above*) It is a modest attempt to help you systematize the living skills and attain the basic intelligences for self-creation and self-modification that the technological evolution demands for every one of us..

Being and becoming are the two main stages in life . The art of living is the art of modifying oneself and the art of creating oneself *thanks to conscious, " perceptual learning"* that according to the Israeli neurologist *Don Sagi.* "*is based on the visual system's plasticity"* and makes the visualization of the plan of action the critical factor in the encoding process.

Let's start from the beginning to write hymns to Living and Being!

This book will pinpoint personalized holistic techniques - ***the know-how of self-creation*** in small, page-long chunks of information, that can always be enriched with many sources on the Internet, So, let's beat the inertia of old thinking by changing the mind that will holistically re-program the brain.

The Auto-Suggestive Psychology of Self-Ecology that is featured in the next part of the book will help you enrich your inner personal store and will your mind more! The psychologically-charged boosters and numerous mind-sets (*the authoritative mind commands here*) are meant to help you structure your own self-suggestive framework of an inspirational character.

Auto-suggestibility is your intelligence in action!

You might want to install the mind-set below into your conscious mind and make it your inspirational booster for health, faith, love, confidence, self-esteem, courage, and success. Just change the word "*success* "in it to the one you need at this moment. Put a small reminder onto the wind-shield of your car and upload it into your smart phone to have it handy as a reminder.

Auto-Induction: **I'm driving through the time and space with success on my interface!**

With the mission accomplished, we can depart,

Without any regrets and with many completed bets!

Every Mind needs a Personal Mentor Program!

12. Spiritualized Intelligence + Self-Consciousness
= Living Intelligence, or Self-Developmental Program!

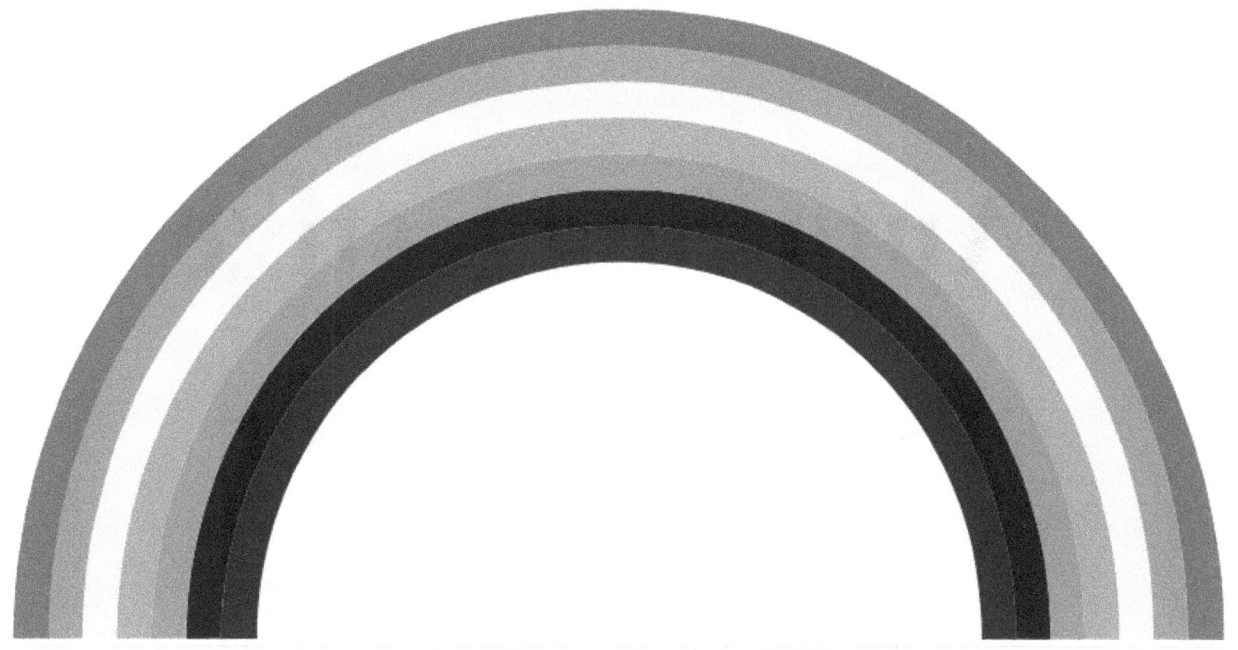

Form	Content
Knowledge	Skills
Awareness	Reasoning
Right Thinking	Right Speaking / Feeling / Acting
Spiritualized Intelligence	Self-Consciousness

= *Consciously-obtained Happiness!*

Body + Spirit + Mind + Self-Consciousness + the Universal Consciousness

= *A Whole Self!*

"The Unexamined Life is Not Worth Living!"

(Socrates)

For the Reader to First Consider!

Auto-Suggestive Psychology for Self-Ecology!

Self-Hypnosis is the Best Life Prognosis!

Recondition the Brain for a New Mind Auto-Suggestively!

Process the Knowledge though the Personal Information Grid and Feel Complete!

Shape Your Evolutionary Function

With Order and Light of Your Inner Expansion!

1. I Am Running My Life Beyond Survive!

We all need a physical, emotional, mental, spiritual, and universal back-up to manage our lives better. So, read these page-long instructions, paying attention to the point of each conceptual chunk separately. Start downloading some of the back-ups that can be found throughout the book in your smart phone, up-loading the brain, changing the sub-conscious mind, and boosting your spirit.

Don't try to imitate someone's success, monitor your own!

Use only those ideas that apply to you now. *generalize* them, *select* those that seem to be making sense for you, and *actualize* them *holistically* at every stage of self-development and in every dimension of life level, one by one.

Be the manager of your own life to thrive, not just to survive!

Self-Induction:

I am running my life, every minute, every hour,

Every day that I devour!

I'm running my life every year;

I am the One to steer!

Every life in its celestial form is but a second long!

And it's always neat to become a life-athlete!

To be self-inspired,

Fix the Mind + Heart wiring and be Self-Inspiring!

Auto-Suggestion is the Onto-Genesis of Self-Formation!

2. Self-Induction is Your Own Mantra!

The challenge that we all face is how to make oneself change when every cell in the body resists change. I try to overcome this hurdle by applying the **AUTO-SUGGESTIVE METHODOLOGY OF SELF-ECOLOGY.** The mind of each person on earth needs to be inspired and *enthused by the spirit* that is the unifying link between the body and the mind.

Body+ Spirit+ Mind + Self-Consciousness + the Universal Consciousness = A New Self!

Inspiring oneself is the process of forcing one's resisting emotional and psychological make-up *to do the self-transformation of the whole-body system*. Apparently, it is every one's personal responsibility to make that work, or, in other words, to imbue oneself with love of life and oneself.

I am One of a kind – in the Name and the Mind!

We can enact this process and double its effect with the help of *auto-suggestibility,* or self-inducting work *by* re-programming the brain and inspiring it in the **I-FOCUSED** simple and **RHYMING WAY!** That's the principle difference between the affirmations and *the rhyming inspirational boosters that are more memorable and constitute a short-cut to the conscious brain!* No wonder kids start learning things that rhyme, or we keep humming the lines from a favorite song when we are in good mood. I often interrupt my lectures, *by instilling in the minds of my students the mind-sets (authoritative commands to the mind) of an auto-suggestible character*, that are conceptually connected to the point that I am making. I ask the students to repeat them after me out loud. with the eyes closed, channeling their breath in a certain way that I describe below. Such interruptions are always welcome by the students because they relax, uplift their spirit, boost the interest, and *raise the knowledge-awareness*. Most importantly, the self-inductions *personalize the information* for them! They identify themselves immediately with such inspirational bosting, become more interested, and much more motivated.

We need to identify with the knowledge we are accumulating consciously to internalize it!

.I started writing my inspirational boosters out of the blue, in my desperate wish to help my daughter deal with an immense trauma after the September 11, 2001 attack. in which she had miraculously survived. Her state of doom and gloom demanded I do something out of the ordinary to bring her back to life. Then one day, while I was driving, I discovered that the psychological concept *started forming into a rhyming booster.* I stopped the car and wrote down what was brewing in me, making me feel up-lifted, hopeful, and willful. Amazingly, my daughter *resonated to the mood of my first rhyming product,* and I never postponed writing down ideas that hit me, developing into *the Introduction, Body, and Conclusion* of the concept as if someone is dictating these boosters to me. My perception is always alert now.

A Rhyming Word goes Better Inward!

3. Self-Creation is Our Full-Time Job!

"The hardest Job in the world is to create oneself!"(Dalai Lama) The work of self-formation is the art of making each life have more sense in terms of self-realization that each one of us is striving hard not only to achieve, but to also protect his / her own identity!

Self-perfection should be the Modus Operandi of every human being on Earth!

In his famous book "***The Hero with a Thousand Faces***," a great American philosopher, Joseph Campbell, writes that" *from the tomb of the womb to the womb of the tomb, a* man tries to create himself on the spiritual path, by educating himself in every way possible".

"The hero is, in fact, the man of self-achieved submission to God."

The process of creation is essential in life. Everything becomes something after berth. Everything in the universe comes into being through fluctuations in *the Unified Field of Energy and Intelligence.* We have to attain the unity of both because energy follows thought. Thoughts create our material world." *Only by changing* **the culture of our thinking** *can we revolutionize our developing consciousness."(Dr. Bell)* **"***Matter is nothing, but energy cloaked in a different form.***"** *(Albert Einstein)* Changing the intelligence, we change the matter and vise versa.

Energy + Intelligence

Matter + Idea $\Big\}$ = *Reality + Consciousness*

Emotions + Intellect   (*Self-Awareness + Self-Consciousness*)

Matter, according to quantum physics, is a form of wave of vibration, and our bodies are pulsating ***dynamic fields of energy*** that are shaping and reshaping the reality. **"***Reality is created in our mind, it does not exist. There is only one reality: what is is!"(Deepak Chopra)* As a matter of fact, each of us is a different reality, so if we need to change ourselves, we have ***to alter the reality that is within our perception of ourselves.*** To accomplish this very challenging goal, we need ***to transcend our belief system and reshape ourselves*** in accordance with our own consciously processed knowledge and life experience, ***without trying to duplicate someone's life story.***

The concept of happiness has been taking a different connotation lately. It's not enough for us now to be just happily married, have nice kids, a good-paying job, a house in the suburbs, and a brand-new car. As soon as we obtain at least some attributes of a commonly desired American dream, it gets transformed into "*a deeply seated sense of incompleteness*"(Eckhart Tolle), or **a *painful void*** that needs to be filled up with an ardent desire to self-express, to self-realize, and to find peace with the inner urge of self-assertion.

The Battle for a Personal Self is won by Yourself!

4. "The Manifestation of Will!"

A great German philosopher *Schopenhauer* called the urge for self-creation and self-realization in life *"the manifestation of will"* which must be the inevitable condition and presupposition of a whole life mission that we all want to be happy, without applying any special effort to changing its route. But *"the real wisdom of life!"* (Schopenhauer) is in *"willing it more!"*(Carl Yung)

Form + Content = the Philosophy of Life beyond survive!

However, self-assertion must be created in a holistic bond of **MIND+SPIRIT+BODY**, constituting *the temple of our life, in a tandem*, with the spirit playing the unifying role between the body and the mind in the holistic paradigm. *(See the book "I Am Free to Be the Best of Me!")*

(Body+ Spirit+ Mind) + (Self-Consciousness+ Universal Consciousness) = A Whole Self!

The physical form + the spiritual content of life = holistic self-development!

We need to accomplish the balance of this unity because *"the further we stray from the balance, the more extreme life becomes."(David Icke)* He writes, *"If you go too far to the positive polarity of life, you lose touch with the practical side of life. You float off in a spiritual mist. Positive energy needs a negative balance. However, if we go too far to the negative polarity of life, we get de-linked from the higher levels of consciousness."* This being said, self-modification and self-regulation need to be consciously practiced in the following direction:

Unconscious ⟶ *Conscious* ⟶ *Superconscious*

Obviously, one needs to have *a self-training program* and apply a lot of will-power, self-control, and self-mastery to practicing it. The outline of this direction for the self-quest that I present in five books on self-creation *(See Preface)* as **THE AUTO-SUGESTIVE KNOW-HOW** had been verified by me *for 35 years of academic teaching* of young students from all over the world. They are all driven inwardly by the desire to accomplish the impossible on the path of self-assertion and self-installation with a road-map in the mind. I think that w*e must focus on the integral power of the essential life skill.* I suggest doing it holistically, in five dimensions - *physical, emotional, mental, spiritual, and universal -* by practicing what we preach, developing intuition that is our *"adult barometer,"* and turning bad life habits into transformative *Living Intelligence Skills.* It's self-refinement by me. Read and see! The concepts of this part of the book permeate all my books on Self-Creation because to go on this essential trip in life, we need to

Defy the gravity of the common thought and fly to the skies, no matter what!

Re-Educate the Mind to Get Self-Refined!

5. Uncontrolled Self-Talk Must be Harnessed!

The books that I have introduced in the *Book Rationale* present an attempt to design *a simple to use self-programming and a consequential method of self-creation* that anyone can put to work with the help of the inspirational techniques in any situation, at anytime, anywhere. So much so, any person who gets on this track starts making a big difference in his self-quest.

Reprogramming oneself is a slow, but sure process!

Habits are changing slowly, but surely only when we change the perception of life *from chaos to order, from going with the common flow, to going where you need to flow!* This work is, in fact, the **MENTAL SELF-TRAINING** that is meant to help you become more self-confident and more invincible for yourself and others who might envy your success. So, the *self-developmental paradigm* is based on *the holistically-channeled auto-suggestive work* at one's own psyche, mind, spirit, and soul. As a matter of fact, our self-talk never ends, but it needs to work for us, not against us!

The purpose of our being is in our expanding, like the universe!

Self-suggesting is the process of self-expansion, too. Any *rhyming induction* restructured in the *"I"-form* works better than an impersonal one. That's why the mind-sets that I conclude every chapter with are mostly *self-directed.* Only the process of shaping yourself into the ULTIMATE BEST OF YOU helps you *get rid of a tunnel vision of life* that generates automatic living, and makes you forget who you are. The path to Self needs to be short, authoritative, and firm to make the unconscious mind follow the conscious one. THE BOOSTERS CHANGE YOUR MIND-SET! They might seem very simple to you, but do not underestimate their convincing power that uplifts the spirit like the rhyming lines from a favorite song that always make you feel elated.

So, to manage your inner current, instill in your consciousness a RHYMING THOUGHT-MOLD. Let the inspirational inductions root in you. Let them help you weed out all the doubts, negative memories, self-pity, and any other inadequacies. Don't harbor negative emotional memories in your mind! Teach yourself to be happy, overjoyed, smiley and shiny. Have the mind-set below on the wind-shield of your car. You may want to insert any needed concept: health, love, luck, success, inner peace, etc. Remember, *changing your mind, you change your personality!*

Auto-Induction: *I can roam any terrain with God./health /success / love* *in my vein!*

Follow the holistic spiral consciously with aware attention to what you think, say, feel, and do.

(*Self-Awareness*)+(*Self-Monitoring* + *Self-Installation*+*Self-Realization*)+ (*Self-Salvation*)
(*Self-Synthesis*) ⟶ Self- Analysis ⟶ Self-Synthesis)

"Grab Life or Life will Grab You!"

6. Choreograph Your Moves Yourself!

The mind in its early stages of self-creation is a *slave of desire*, but as maturity makes us aware of our mission on earth, *the desire is getting curbed*, and we are forced to think before we react to the external stimulation or the *"poisoning of life."* We are supposed to help ourselves *feel complete and accomplished.*, resisting the urges of *"immediate gratification"* of our whims .(See the book *"Self-Taming!"- the spiritual dimension- Book Rationale)*

The wise don't expect to find life worth living, they make it that way!

I have witnessed many times   how physically and mentally-fit, very talented young people wasted their energy, *developing virtual game- personages inside* while their own personalities became very undeveloped, primitive knowledge-wise, and virtually-immersed to the point that *they lost themselves in the virtual reality.* I am not a prude, and I am very savvy in technology myself. I love the way it enriches us intellectually and socially, but I witness the disregard for self-creation and the inability of many young people *to discriminate their on-line images from the real one.* That's why I consider it to be my mission to help my students and anyone who cares for what he / she ultimately becomes in life. *Start sculpturing and choreographing your personalities' moves* to give the world the best you have

In my life-quest, I manifest my best!

 In sum, this book is just a suggestion and an offer of help for those who comprehend that *"time is limited for everyone"(Steve Jobs),* and action speaks louder than a dead dream. So, *stop the whine, "I have no time!"* Step out of the virtual world   and start perceiving yourself as a real personage in the game of life, meant for you to thrive, not just to survive. This book will help you put your reality forward and work out your own, not mine, not any guru's, **Know-How** in life. The book provides *objective, not subjective information* that took me years to sift for validity from the common wisdom of the   *"collective unconscious." (Carl Yung)* That's why every chapter, or *the chunks of information i*n the book are just a page long, religiously following the holistic paradigm of *synthesis-analysis -synthesis, (generalize -select- strategize), or*

Internalize – Optimize - Externalize!

Every paragraph has this structure, too. Therefore, there are *the concluding statements* under the paragraphs that often rhyme to make the concept of the paragraph *more convincing and penetrable into the conscious mind!* You can always supplement information from the Internet. So, upload any appealing mind-set into your smart phone, and help yourself to become the Best of You!.

To Be Self-Installation Inspired,

Become More Self-Aware and Self-Refined!

7. Psycho-Kinesis in Action!

Auto-suggestive psychology is, in fact, *the process of psycho-kinesis - the raising of one's own spirit at will!* The aim of such psycho-persuasive culture is the development of the ability to make one's own thoughts and emotions *I-directed*, not "*collective-unconscious*"- directed. A healthy, self-directed and inspirational self-programming enables a person to actively be his own textbook and *his own mentor, his own psychologist, and a judge.* In a self-training program, you transform your own consciousness with *aware attention yourself,* not. at the suggestion of a psychologist, psychiatrist, a life-coach, or a guru. The mind hears you better and commands to the brain to follow its command! Where you place the attention, energy goes. Hence, you immediately feel better!

Auto-Induction: *I am the manager of my own framing and re-framing!*

We are all familiar with the positive effect of affirmations and quotes, but auto-suggestions work much better because they are *directly targeting you* in a *simple, rhyming and most persuasive way.* You manage to re-program your habitually negative, depressive thoughts and emotions to the positive and constructively-charged ones in simple, rhyming words. Thus, you inspire or fuel yourself on this path, raising your *immunity to the negativity of life* both internally and externally.

I witness amazing changes in my students, once they start *auto-suggestively altering their minds.* Their personalities get revived like a drying plant that you water to save from dying. Research shows that *individuals differ in the quality of their vibrations* which constitute their individual personalities. This is what Mr. Birched writes about it, "*We have a top–down mechanism for managing our bodily mechanism. In modern humans, we are learning to operate outside our consciousness, analyzing our existence from inside out and from outside in*" ("*New Scientist*", Aug. 2913) *Self-training through self-induction is the best way for self-production!*

You are the one who channels your mind and operates your emotions! However, the faculty of consciousness which many people lack, being driven by force of the automatic living, is successfully developed only in those of us who try hard *to accomplish a higher level of intelligence and consciousness in sync,* or a much better awareness of the reality.

Auto-Induction: *My aware attention is never in retention!*

In his wonderful book "*The Ravenous Brain*", Daniel Boor writes, "*Consciousness is effectively an idea factory* – a key component of which is *the discovery of deep structures within the content of awareness* of our own imperfections. Life is full of ideas if we are able to perceive them.*" An idea-factory becomes the producer of channeling mind-sets that work best when they rhyme.*

Love of Life, Will-Power, and Discipline are on the Self-Actualization Scene!

8. Consciously Infuse Your Self-Realization Fuse!

Conscious self-inducting or suggestibility is also very up-lifting and psychologically friendly, especially if the mind-sets are uploaded in a rhyming form. The mind easily absorbs them and reproduces them if need be. *Neuroscience proves the mind's hypnotic effect on the body.* That is the actual effect of any meditation that is accessible in zillions of books as well as different websites. We are taught that one should learn to face the necessity *to transform / modify oneself from within*. It actually happens because we change *the electro-magnetic charge* in the brain, us being *"the electro-magnetic beings, according to Nikola Tesla.* A plant will not sprout if the seed has not already begun to grow inside its shell.

But the present-day life requires our *selective attitude to the information*, or the food for thought that can either be the shortest possible short-cut to Self, or it can become an obstacle because it is ignorantly applied. In the book, *"Touching a Nerve,"* a neuro-philosopher Church Land writes in the chapter *"The Self as Brain", "All things that we have traditionally ascribed to a higher power- morality, free will, the soul - are in fact the products of the brain."* That's very true!

The brain needs to be consciously monitored by the mind!

The power of suppressing bad patterns of behavior using confirmations undoubtedly works. Meditation may also give relief for anxiety, depression, pain, stress, *but the work on self-reformation, self-refinement, and self-actualization demands a lot of* SELF-INDUCTION directed personally to you by you because **IT IS ACTIONABLE MEDITATION!** It will do wonders to you if practiced consistently and consciously. That is the secret *Joel Osteen* is so popular. He is fueling people with inspiration, self-belief, and his preaching is, in fact, *suggestive inspirational work* that penetrates the spirit and boosts it to act. It is Joel's personal hypnotic effect on the public that works so well, and people respond to it hungrily..

People need being inspired with faith in God and themselves!

But you can do the same yourself*! Self-induction starts with aware thinking, focused on helping the Self!* The moment a person starts thinking, one of the levels of consciousness becomes activated. Unfortunately, we are facing the problem *of the lack of disciplined thinking in our digital times* when a lot of life actions are done with an electronic gadget in hand that channels our thoughts along the machine–carved ways. *Eckhart Tolle* states, *"A new reality creates a new screen of concepts, labels, images, judgments, and definitions."* Also, this process requires not only focusing on the knowledge in general, *it also presupposes the knowledge of the brain* and its ability *to process the incoming information in the way that is empowering it with shooting new neurol connections.* That's the most positive effect of the *Transcendental Meditation (Dr. (John Hagelin)* and *the Yoga Meditation*, governed by the wisest sage of our time, Sadhguru,

Self-Hypnosis is the most efficient approach to Self-Change!

9. Sculpture Yourself though Self-Hypnosis!

Achievement is a natural order of life. Self–development is a matter of slowly regaining what you have attained so far and channeling the progression toward bettering yourself-consciousness. It is important to be aware of your misgivings, thus making the whole process of self-evolution conscious. *The mind must beat the brain in the competition for your aware attention!*

We all have an urge for self-realization, but very few of us maintain the necessary **integrity** to meet the challenges on the way. We often turn out to be our worst enemies, rather than the best friends Become more *psychologically-aware (Check out Stage Four below)*, *be your own best friend!* The main challenge is you yourself! The mind will always follow your conscious command because your mind can *self-organize, self-stabilize, self-replicate, and self-modify.* You just need to give it good, inspiration food for thought and keep repeating that thought.

The key is repetition! Induction is mind-reproduction!

Constructive self-hypnosis disciplines our thinking and helps us generate **holistic self-consciousness** when we become part of all life, appreciating life in ourselves, to begin with. *"When you pay more attention to the doing rather than to the future result that you want to achieve through it, you break the old conditioning and install a new, much more constructive one". (Eckhart Tolle))*

Auto- suggestion: *I am a Master of Myself in my every cell!*

To make the process of self-formation easier, I invite you *to interact with yourself* in each chapter through the mind-sets that are meant to hit the mind directly and empower the uncontrolled talk of the brain *to heighten your awareness of the intelligence* that you are developing at a moment - language, emotional, psychological, professional, etc. (See the Main Part).) You are smart enough to word out your own rhyming suggestions, the ones you need at the right moment. The brain wave patterns are functioning at the two main levels: *The Alpha level (or the passive level)* and *The Beta level (an active one).* Meditation works best, of course, when the brain is in the Alpha mode. That's why the practice of meditation is so beneficial. *It slows down the brain waves, on the one hand, and it programs us, on the other.* (See the Auto-Suggestive Meditation below)

The Auto-Inductive Meditation is both passive and active. Auto – induction works great at both levels! It is even more effective at the Beta level because *it boosts the will-power* - the main sculptor of our inner frame. *Each self-induction is food for thought and a boost for action!* First, get better aware of the subject of your self-talk, and then start consciously interacting with yourself and persuading yourself to follow the directions, *internalizing the mind-change consciously.*

Conduct a Self-Suggestive Talk as a Non-Stop Walk!

10. The Main Self-Inducting Formula

I suggest you induct a very simple formula below that contains the life force of self- installation *in life* because it proves to be *easily externalizable and externalizable*. It will be repeated throughout the book at every level of self-sculpturing. Try to use it as often as you can as *a self-help tool*. It will help you rationalize your life in the *physical, emotional, mental, spiritual, and universal* dimensions of self-creation. Download it into the smart phone to have it always at hand. *Modify it the way you need it*. It is key in maintaining awareness about this willful process at any moment:

Auto- suggestion: ***I know who I am!***

I am a strong, calm, bold, and determined owner of my firm will!

I can…; I want to…; and I will…!

I am becoming better and better at* reforming myself / etc. *with each coming day!

There will be many other self- inductions ahead, but memorize this one as the basic one. The steps of your self-suggesting should be:

Regular practice ⟹ *Patience* ⟹ *Self-observation* ⟹
Analysis ⟹ *Decision* ⟹ *the Right action* ⟹ *Self-Compliment*
== *Higher Self-Consciousness!*

Most importantly, get rid of the prefabricated solutions to any situation!

It is a very bad habit, generated by the influence of the *"collective unconscious."* You are in charge of your own life, and what happens to you has never happened to anyone else. Therefore, no generalizations or any one's advice would work for you, unless you listen to your own intuition and get council with your own conscience, your inner guru that will help you reason out the cause and effect of the troubles that you have better than anyone!

The level of your self-consciousness is directly linked to your conscience!

"Your body and mind will gradually *come in synch*, and soon the body will become very sensitive to the vital state of consciousness in you and to THE OPERATOR'S COMMANDS in the form of the mind-sets. They will tune up the mind and the body in one direction - ***self-actualization, self- efficacy, and self- sufficiency.*** Concentrated mind is double power!

Auto- suggestion: ***I am my best friend; I am my beginning and my end!***

Inner Dignity is the Base of Our Personal Equity!

11. I Know Who I Am!

Mind it, please that *the URV (the Ultimate Result Vision) of the best of you should be modified at every stage of your intelligence development (Thesis 9 below),* and it should be crowned by *the Integral You Image -* **THE VINTAGE YOU** at the Universal Intelligence stage.*(Stage 10, Main Part)*

It is crucial to rely on your own objective judgment of yourself, your own self-reflection in your mind and heart. You alone know what you are improving and how well / bad you are doing that! Seeing yourself in the mirror of other people's reactions, their perception of your changed behavior will also help if you perceive it *objectively.*

Auto- suggestion: ***Don't expect any compliments, compliment yourself!***

Ultimately, you will zero in on the Ultimate Result Vision of the best of you all the time. With *the URV instilled in your mind*, you won't let anyone ever change it or destroy it. " *Be the thing in itself*!"*(Hegel)* Don't declare your taking any transformational course, don't boast about any change that is going on in you. That's your personal, private business, your exceptional mission of self-installation. *Erect yourself in your every cell!* Keep injecting the whole formula with confidence, self-esteem, and determination:

Auto- suggestion: ***I know who I am!***

I am a strong, calm, bold, and determined owner of my firm will!

I can…; I want to…; and I will…!

Every auto-suggestive mind-set in this formula shapes you in the desired direction. Its wording is programmed solely by you, not by the society, your family, friends, or anyone. In fact, when you think that you have a near perfect picture of yourself, *modify it at the Mini, Meta, Mezzo, Macro, and Super levels (Thesis 15 below)* every day. Just process your self-change through these levels before going to bed. *A quick self-assessment is very beneficial.* See what you are becoming *physically, emotionally, mentally, spiritually, and universally. Feel content with yourself!*

Auto- suggestion: ***I defy the common-sense gravity; I fly!***

Like the Russian dolls, *one URV will be merging with the previous vision and the next one* through the entire process of self-enrichment. You will be becoming more and more conscious, psychologically enriched, life-loving, and rationally-emotional. Many young minds that I have inspired in my life have transformed themselves with the URV of the best of them **on the screen of their minds irreversibly!**

The Vision of the Best Ultimate You is the Matrix of Your Life!

12. Where Consciousness Flows, Energy Goes!

The Auto-Suggestive Meditation *(see below)* is based on self-induction that is, actually, ***programming all the cells of your body in a positive, instructive way,*** helping the body overcome any discomfort, caused by polluted thoughts and feelings.(*See what Dr. Bruce Lipton says about the role of cells in his writings on Biological Medicine*)

The self-persuasive word produces positive vibrations in the brain that resonate with the entire body. Most importantly, **an inspirational auto-induction boosts the connection between the heart and the mind , vibration-wise,** thus helping the spirit to handle the situation. As you learn to cultivate the personal mastery over your mind and emotions consciously, you will begin to acquire a strong, unbreakable spirit and *whole brain thinking*, when the rational and the emotional minds will get in synch, helping you develop *a New, Whole You.*

Body+ Spirit+ Mind + Self-Consciousness + the Universal Consciousness = A Whole Self!

The biology of consciousness that is being studied most intently now offers *"a sounder basis for* ***mind-controlled living*** *than improvable dogmas of an immortal soul" ("Scientific American", July 2014).* Once we realize that our own consciousness is a product of our brains, we become conscious of our own personal responsibility for self-actualization in life in physical, emotional, mental, and spiritual terms.

" Thoughts impact reality." / The brain works, the mind talks!

It is a very challenging process of ***creation through resistance*** that is backed up by the spirit *(See the book "Self-Taming!")*. My very rich experience of working with college students has proved that our educational work becomes much more enriching intellectually and psychologically if we inspire the students, always following the rule of my favorite psychologist *Leo Vygotsky*

" Do not teach just the subject, teach the whole person!"

Psychologically-inductive teaching proves to be most beneficial in terms of expanding the students' outlook and programming their brains for a very successful, much more insightful, and subject-aware completion of the course. The concept of self-governing and self-modification through self-suggestion is closely connected with the process of self-control without which any self-growth is hardly possible.

I am building up my life's gut without the media's instructional mud!

Aware Attention to Life is what I Must Derive!

13. Auto-Suggestive Meditation

Self-Talk is the Auto-Suggestive Work of a very creative character because *auto-suggestibility implies your own creative approach to the process in inducting yourself*. You know that meditation involves consistent self-focus and the ability to zero in on your own mental state. *The Auto-Suggestive Meditation* will enhance your will-power considerably as any conscious action does. Suggestive meditation is also the best way to heighten your self-consciousness I have introduced above the main auto-suggestive formula that can help you induct anything.

I know who I am!

I am a strong, calm, bold, and determined owner of my firm will!

I can…; I want to…; and I will…!

I am becoming better and better with each coming day!

Learn to mentally **induct yourself with whatever outcome you need** by just breathing in slowly through the mouth the first part of this, or any chosen induction, and breathing out slowly through the mouth the second part of it. These are the most basic inductive actions. ***Appreciate the joint work of your mind and heart in synch!*** To feel the heart, put the thumb of your right hand on the pulse point on the wrist of your left hand. **Listen to the heart's beat**: *21-21-21…*

Put a smile on your face! Let your personality surface!

Upload any auto-suggestion you need during the day. There are many inspirational mind-sets in the book, written in the first person singular for this purpose. *Note it, please; you need to do the Suggestive Meditation in synch with breathing, connecting your heart and the mind.* **Breathe in**, saying inwardly any ending to the formula that you need now.

Auto-Induction*:* *"**I can** be healthy**, I want** to be healthy, **and I will be** healthy."*

Hold the breath for a few seconds, focusing your aware attention on the heart. Hear its rhythmic beat-**21-21-21**. Start **slowly breathing out** through the mouth, saying inwardly,

Auto-Induction: *"**I am becoming healthier and healthier,** stronger and stronger, **etc. with each coming day!"**

Do it three times. Finish the meditation with the self-induction below, or any one of your choice:

My whines and tears, worries and fears (*breathe in*)

varnish as the useless emotional garnish! (*breathe out*)

Will your Life More! That's the Law!

14. Unanimity is the Base of a Personal Equity!

Doing the Auto-Suggestive Meditation, you develop your *aware attention* and the *inner vision,* and you learn to feel the energy flow inside your body as the waves of music fluctuations. The Chinese people say, *"A picture is worth a thousand words."* Tune yourself to the rhythm of the entire life out there with the conscious inducting in sync with your breathing. Doing so, *you unite your mind and the heart,* helping them work in unison with your entire being, seeing, feeling and doing! Experience it! Enjoy it! Listen to the rhythmic heart beat with gratitude - **21-21-21** when having a pause.

Will your life more with the help of the auto-suggestive self-talk.

Programming your own mind, *you perform self-hypnosis* that is essential in boosting your will-power yourself. The will-power determines your character, and *it gives the boost to your spirit.* that is the unifying link between your body and the mind. Always have the holistic paradigm of your self-installation in life at the forefront of your mind as the blue-print of self-modification.

Body+ Spirit+ Mind + Self-Consciousness + the Universal Consciousness = A Whole Self!

Below, there are five very simple auto-meditations, presented in five levels: *physical, emotional, mental, spiritual, and universal (See the book " I Am Free to Be the Best of Me!'" for more).*

Part One - *Calming Down and cleansing your brain (the physical level).*

1) Lie flat on the floor. Close your eyes and start running your aware attention through your body from head to toe. Breathe in deeply, through your nose, inwardly saying the words" Calm," make o short pause, and "down" when breathing out through the mouth. You aay do the same with the words "So"(breathe in) and "Ha-am"(breathing out)

Do it consciously, slowly, and very lovingly to yourself three times. Envision the stream of energy, coming in, and out, taking all the pollution out. Relax for a minute, holding the breath. Listen to the heart- 21-21-21.

Auto-induction: *Calm(in) down (out / calm (in) down(out) / and calm(in) down(out).*

Part Two -*Breathing through the soles and the tips of the toes (the emotional level)*

*1) To begin with , lie flat on the floor, breathe in through **the sole of your left foot,** channeling **the air / energy stream** along the left part of the body **by its main meridian,** going through the center of your left side or the body to the top of your head, right to the spot where the **crown chakra** is. Make a short pause at the top of the head, **focus on the heart – 21 -21-21** , and start slowly breathing out, channeling your aware attention **down the central meridian to the sole of your right foot.***

*Do the same, starting to breathe slowly in through the right sole and **breathe out through the left one.** You have cleansed the entire body from any energy pollution. **Induct yourself with any easy suggestive formula of your choice**, if you feel like it. Induct the first part of any induction when you breathe in, make a pause, listen to the heart, finish inducting yourself, breathing out.*

Auto-Induction: **Light in** *(breathe in)* – **darkness out!** *(breathe out)*

Health in *(breathe in)* – **Sickness out!** *(breathe out)*

Love in *(breathe in)* – **Indifference out!** *(breathe out)*

*2) Now, start breathing in through **the big toe of your left foot,** up to the top of the head. Make a short pause, start slowly breathing out, channeling your aware attention down, by the main meridian **to the big toe of the right foot**. Do the same focused breathing in the opposite direction, breathing in through the toe of your right foot, making a short pause at the top of the head, and breathing out **through the tip of the toe on the left foot.** Do it three times in both directions. **Induct anything you need,** breathing in the first part of the induction and breathing out the second one. Be creative in your mind!*

Auto-Induction: ***Love in** – **hate out**! / **Luck in** – **failure out**! ./ **Happiness in** – **depression out!***

***Inspiration** in - **impulsivity** out! / **Success in** – **failure** out etc.*

Part Three - *Breathing through the palms of your hands* – (the mental level)

*1) Put your hands, palms up, on the knees and **direct your aware attention to the palms**. Start breathing in **through the palm of your left hand** channeling the stream of energy with the help of your aware attention up the left arm, through the left shoulder to the heart. **Make a short pause at the heart;** focus your loving attention on it. Continue breathing slowly out, channeling the stream of energy through the chest, the right shoulder, and **down through the right palm.** Breathe in and out in the same fashion, starting with the right palm, breathing out through the left one.*

*2) **When you breathe in, induct the first part of any inspirational booster of your choice, breathe out, inducting the second part of it.** (Men need to start with the right palm, to begin with). If you practice Auto Suggestive meditation mindfully, **you will feel the stream of air literally coming out from your palms.** Don't forget to focus on the heart - **21-21-21**, when making a pause.*

Auto-induction: **I monitor my mind** *(breathe in)* **to self-rewind** *(breathe out). etc.*

*Open your eyes after the induction and **clutch your fists to boost your will-power** that is driving your spirit and self-inwardly, or out loud: .*

To Be Alive, Beautify Your Life!

15. Will Your Life More ! That's the Law!

Your will-power needs to be constantly activated because *it is the emotional gas of your spirit* that is the most important link between your body and the mind, or the mind and the heart that need to be always in synch.

Part Four-*(Breathing through the tips of the fingers / time-space connection**(the spiritual level)***

*I conduct **the active meditation of this time-space induction** with my students in the middle of the lecture, when I feel that their attention is slacking. They love it! Their aware attention gets charged and they continue studying / perceiving my in-put in a much more productive way. **The auto-meditation also inspires them a lot.***

*1) I ask them to first **rub their hands vigorously and shake them off several times to cleanse the energy** that their hands have accumulated during the day.*

*Please, note first that when we put the central three fingers together and make the pinkie and the thumb go widespread to the sides, we, actually **get the cross** that is also the philosophic signs, representing the two vectors – **the vectors of time** (the present-**the central figure**; the past -**the ring finger** ;and the future – **the index finger**) and **the vectors of space** (the pinkie and the thumb) By the way, the body of a standing man with his arms ,stretched to the sides has the same structure*

*So, by the vector of time we have - (the central finger- the **present**) ; the ring finger – **the-past** ; the index finger-**the future**)*

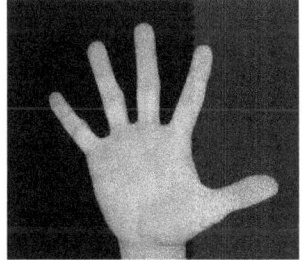 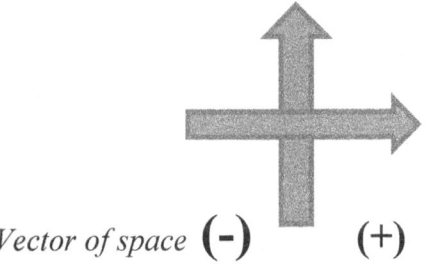

Vector of space **(-)**   **(+)**

By the vector of space, going from *the pinkie* (*absence of result*) to the thumb(*the result finger*). -*from **minus** (-) / to plus* **(+)**. *No wonder we show the thumb in any language when things are great.*

 a) Do the inducting in the following way. Start breathing through the pinkie on the left hand, saying:

*1) "**Life in going on** (breathe in.) Make a pause, **focusing on the heart -21-21-21.** Finish the induction: - and it's beautiful (breathe out through the pinkie of the right hand.)Channel the air stream as was indicated above.*

*2) I forgive myself (Breathe in through the ring finger on the right hand) – **Pause! - all the past mistakes.** (breathe out though the ring finger on the righthand)*

3) I live (Breathe in through the central finger) – Pause / focus on the heart **-21-21-21- consciously**.*(Breathe out though the central finger on the right hand.)*

4) "I will do everything (breathe in though the index finger) – Pause- **that I have planned"** *(breathe out through the index finger of the right hand)*

5) I have already (breathe in through the thumb of the left hand) – Pause - **accomplished a lot!** *(breathe out through the thumb of the right hand.)* **Envision what you have done lately**.

After you have practiced such breathing a couple of times, you will literally feel a slight breeze at the tips of your thumbs / toes when you breathe out.

b) *Next, breathe in and out in the opposite direction, starting with the thumb of the righthand and breathing out though the thumb of the left hand*. Continue breathing in the same in the same fashion through all the fingers. Don't forget to channel the energy with the help of aware attention up the arm, through the chest, down the other arm, out through the corresponding finger. Don't forget to make a loving pause at the heart. *The auto-induction should be a bit changed*, and it should finish with the same induction that you started the meditation with. Breathe in and out slowly and mindfully.

1) The thumb – **I have already**(in),Pause- **done a lot** *(out). (Envision your latest accomplishments)*

2) The index finger - "**I will do**(breathe in) – Pause - **even more.** *(out) (Envision what you want to do)*

3) The central finger – **Because I live** *(breathe in)-* Pause - **consciously**.*(breathe out)*

4) The ring finger – **Because I forgave myself** *(breathe in)* - Pause - **all my past mistakes**(*breathe out)*.

5) The pinkie – **My life is going on** *(breathe in ,-* Pause - **and it is beautiful**!*(breathe (out)*

Concluding the induction, open your eyes and say authoritatively inwardly, or better out loud:

In my life quest, I am the best!

There wasn't, there isn't, there won't ever be

Anyone like me!

"Be Aware of This Moment; It's Your Life!"

16. The Universal Unanimity is Our Infinity!

Any meditation is the way to establish the connection with the source of life, the Universal Intelligence. that has a digital nature. **Connect with the Higher Intelligence for Guidance.**

Part Five –(*Cleansing the aura and tuning the Auto-Antenna to **the Universal Mind**)*

1. This is the concluding part of **the Auto-Suggestive Meditation** when you need to connect as part of the universal life to the unfathomable infinity Above. **a)** *Stand straight Rub your palms vigorously and shake off your hands a few times to clean them from the negative energies. Start breathing slowly in, lifting up your arms* **up, connecting the two palms in the opposite direction over your head.**

a) *Holding the hands like that*, focus your aware attention on *the half-ellipsis that your hands have made over your head.* Make a short pause, holding the breath and keeping the palms in the same position. Breathe out slowly, *drawing in your inner vision the second half circle with your extended arms to the same depth under your feet. Connect your palms in the same fashion.* You have encircled the aura around your body into *a protective egg shell*. Breathe in., instilling the first part of any mind-set; **breathe slowly out**, instilling the second part of it. Do it three times.

1.   2. in   out

b) *Have three encircling breaths ,going clock-wise, and three breaths ,going counter-clock-wise*. This visualized encircling of your body will protect you from any negative intrusions during the entire day. Do it inwardly with your eyes closed before any important event or an action that you are going to undertake. Induct the necessary mind-set while breathing.

2. Do **the pyramidal, spiral breathing,** imagining the spirals going up **the physical, emotional, mental, spiritual and universal** circles around your body. Breathe in a spiral way at each level: and breathe out through the mouth, going down in the opposite direction

These connecting exercise *will secure your* **UNANIMITY** *with the* **UNIVERSAL INTELLIGENCE** and the four elements of life: THE SUN, THE AIR, THE WATER, AND THE EARTH. If you do it while taking a shower before and after the working day, *these simple exercises will burn, blow off, wash off, and ground all the energy blockages in you.* You will feel refreshed and rejuvenated.

It's Phenomenal what the Mind Can Do to cleanse Our Life's Ado!

17. Uplift Your Spirit Every Minute!

From the brain to the spinal cord, the mind transforms the intelligence of every cell in the body and uplifts the level of our consciousness that is the core of self-transformation process.

Only holistically developed intelligence can enrich consciousness!

With this mind-set, we will get easier out of the mental clutter that we accumulate, and we will be able to **perceive the simplicity of life and appreciate life AS IS!** *"From social discord, we'll find inner harmony; from chaos, we'll find order; from lack of thought, and we'll find rationality; from disrespect to nature, we'll accomplish inner integrity"* (Edgar Cayce) **But be objective, not subjective in your self-installation.** See yourself in the mirror of your soul and self-console.

In my noble life quest, I am the best!

Also, life is the cosmic fluctuations of energy, and the fluctuations are a sequence of ups and downs of energy. It obviously means that we, as a part of the entire life flow, are supposed to have our ups and downs as well, for happy and sad are the sides of one coin. So, being aware of this simple fact, we need to free ourselves from bad habits, patterned thinking, programmed reactions, and automatic behaviors *to get into a rhythmic flow of life* that we should accept and appreciate as such, without obsessing over stuff and breaking it with our negativity to multiply.

If a fall behind occurs, clean the dashboard of your life errors and start from a clean slate. Yes, your self-reformation will be slowed down, *but your slowing up will be much more conscious and speedier.* So, there is no need to get frustrated over anything that happens in our life. It's a natural flow of energy fluctuations with its ups and downs. Even the beat of our hearts has this rhythm.

Also, establish a *psychic protection against evil injections* of other people into your life by just putting your thumb at the place of the pulse – beat on the left wrist and focusing on this beat for a minute: **21-21-21**. *The triumph of life in you will immediately calm you down and protect you with its magic.* Keep *the URV(The Ultimate Result Vision)* of the best of you at the front of your mind as a screen. A clear picture of yourself as a totally accomplished person that you are becoming will do the trick.

Self- induction: *Self-Awareness is a great wake-up call!*

For sure, you have noted already that *every paragraph has a concluding statement* in the form of an inspirational booster that rhymes. Every chunk of information *concludes* **with the conceptual statement** that this chunk is communicating to you. So, you have an array of inspiration boosters to choose from, picking them in accordance with your needs, mood, plans, and aspirations.

Be Good! Exude the Self-Management Mood!

18. Act as Though You Are, and You Will Be!

Do *the Auto-Suggestive Meditation* any time you feel your spirit sagging and your self-love, self-esteem, and self-confidence being in need of help to face the challenges of life. Download the most encouraging mind-sets into your smart phone. Change them if need be to have the auto-suggestive help at hand at any space / time proximity. Here are some to start with:

Mind-Sets against Upsets!

*Life is tough; (Breathe in) / Pause / **but I am tougher!** (Breathe out)*

I never whine, (Breathe in) / Pause / I just shine! (Breathe out)

In my mind(in) / Pause / I am One of a kind!(out) etc.

I program my every cell (Breathe in) / Pause / to Life-Excel! (Breathe out)

Talk to your body auto-suggestively, lovingly, and in all five levels. ***Do the self-scanning before you go to bed.*** Let it feel taken care *of physically, emotionally, mentally, spiritually, and universally!* Will your life more with the help of the auto-suggestive work or self-hypnosis. ***Follow the holistic structure of the book.*** Sift the information in it for your personal good. All the inspirational boosters and mind-sets of the authoritative type in this book are presented correspondingly in five levels. They will remind you to live up to your personal potential and follow your own path of evolution without fail, ***boosting up your spirit every minute!***

Supplement your ***knowledge-strategizing*** and ***self-wising*** with *the Auto-Suggestive work –* your **SELF-HYPNOSIS.** any time, when you do any other meditation, while exercising, running, working out in the gym, having a walk at the ocean. Upload the most actionable of the inspirational boosters and mind-sets into your mind to have them handy at the right moment.

P.S. For more inspirational auto-suggestive mind-sets and boosters, check the books: "*I Am Free to Be the Best of Me!*" Soul-Refining!" Self-Taming! and "Beyond the Terrestrial!"

Our Ultimate Goal is to put our lives together!

(Body+ Spirit+ Mind) + (Self-Consciousness+ Universal Consciousness) or

(The physical form) + (the spiritual content of life) = A New Holistically-Developed Self!

To Get to the Universal Intelligence Link,

Put the Form and the Content of Your Life in Sync!

End of the Introductory Part

The Main Part of the Book

(Self-Developmental Program - the Mental Level)

The Manuel of the Holistic Self-Actualization

Self-Synthesis – Self-Analysis – Self-Synthesis!

Internalizing – Analyzing - Actualizing!

Do Not Procrastinate, or It'll Be Too Late!

"A Person Who Doesn't Make a Choice Makes a Choice!"

Introduction

The What and the Why of Developing Living Intelligence

From Being to Becoming!

The Holistic Paradigm of Life-Learning in

20 Essential Thesis Statements

To Be Personally and Socially-Apt,

Study the Living Intelligence Art!

"This is the Time of Self-Seeking!" *(Sadhguru)*

This book is not meant to be read from cover to cover. It is a study book, **the plan of action to tread the path of mental Self-Installation** in life that is meant to help you follow the self-developmental route: **Self-Awareness** *(physical dimension)*; **Self-Monitoring** *(emotional dimension)*; **Self-Installation** *(mental dimension)*; **Self-Realization** *(spiritual dimension)*, **and Self-Salvation** *(universal dimension)*.

5. Universal dimension	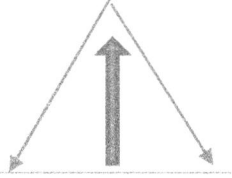	*Self-Salvation*
4. Spiritual dimension		*Self-Realization*
3. Mental dimension		*Self-Installation*
2. Emotional dimension		*Self-Monitoring*
1. Physical dimension		*Self-Awareness*

I have indicated in the two parts of the book above that *to put the mind and heart together*, or to accomplish *"spiritualized intelligence"* that evolution demands from us, each of us needs to establish **the holistic unity of the form and content** of his / her life, following **the Holistic Paradigm** in five dimensions consciously and consistently:

(Body+ Spirit+ Mind) + (Self-Consciousness+ the Universal Consciousness)

(The physical form) $+$ *(the spiritual content of life)* $=$ *New Holistically-Developing Self!*

The main part of the book will feature **ten vistas of intelligence** that a person needs to **install at the mental level of self-development** in his / her mind to enrich intelligence, up-grade self-consciousness, and **gain a holistic vision of life** that the present-day exponential times demand of us. Every chunk of information is a page long, thoroughly sifted for its validity, following the holistic paradigm - **synthesis-analysis-synthesis** and instilling new memory in the brain. Lack of redundancy helps **re-program the mind in a holistic, space-friendly, orderly, and much more inductive way.** The mind-sets *(the authoritative commands to the brain here)* and the inspirational boosters comprise together **the Auto-Suggestive Psychology of Self-Ecology.** *(Check the part "For the Reader to Consider" above)* Pick any mind-set, download it into your smart phone, upload it into your mind, and help yourself justify the mid-set:

In my life quest, I manifest my very best!

"Each of us has his own tree of knowledge which is our own belief system." *(Don Miguel Ruiz)*

Every Noble Work is at First Impossible!

The Blueprint of the Mental Self-Growth:

10. Universal Intelligence	
9. Spiritual Intelligence	Super- Level of Consciousness
8. Social Intelligence	
7. Cultural Intelligence	Macro- Level
6. Financial Intelligence	
5. Professional Intelligence	Mezzo- Level
(Creative Intelligence)	
4. Psychological Intelligence	Meta- Level
3 Emotional Intelligence	
2. Language Intelligence	
1. General Intelligence	
(Physical / Cognitive / Digital)	Mini-Level

Self-Refining is in Mind Re-Designing!

Thesis 1

We Are All in the Universal Flow!

(An Inspirational Booster)

In our global culture,

We are all universally sculptured

In the God's design

By the ancestors' hands in twine!

We breathe in

Their life's cultural spin,

We inherit their national values and illusions;

And we suffer a lot from their blind delusions!

We feel their presence up there,

In the imperceptible somewhere!

Their spirits are still in our hearts de facto;

Their bodies are in the recycle bin of the matter!

The eternal battle of space and time

Is in the background of our energy twine!

Wherever we mentally go,

We are all in the universal flow!

I inwardly thank my parental tank

For bringing me up to life with a spank!

I was later transformed

Into the universally-equal mob!

Due to the socially-unstable fuss,

I joined the international American mass!

I had to change and re-change

The national bonds with which I was chained!

I train my brain for it to sustain

The range of my every day change!

Non-victimization

Is my self-salvation!

Thus, the battle for a personable Self

Is won by Yourself!

The ten stages of the Living Intelligence that this book is featuring next and that are outlined below *as general, language, emotional, psychological, professional. financial, cultural, social, spiritual, and universal -* are based on **20 thesis statements,** presented in this part of the book.

Knowledge put to action is power!

These are **the main conceptual standpoints for the Living Intelligence Skills to be formed.** I have verified them during 35 years of my very successful college teaching experience in different countries of the world. I recommend refreshing these statements at all the stages of the intelligence formation to master them in general terms. You can always supplement this knowledge digitally. The exponential growth of information changes our knowledge of the known and opens the new horizons of the unknown every day. Being in the flow of knowledge changing, *with aware attention at work,* we can accomplish *the goal of self-guided transformational self-growth.*

Self- creation is mind-demanding work, not just a casual talk!

Inflate Your Personal Pride with the Intellectual Might!

Thesis 2

The Grid of Our Intelligence - Consciousness Integration

In the philosophical "*Book Incentive*" part of the book, *Chunk 3,* I have outlined the state of our self-consciousness and the reasons that prompt the necessity for **THE MANUEL OF LIFE** to be prepared for us by the educators and scientists that are trying to unravel the mystery of consciousness that makes us the top of evolution at least in our universe. *"The conscious mind is ruling our evolution and is propelling the growth of our consciousness away from automatism."* (Michael Ford and Peter Berkrot) *"Consciousness is the source of what we are!* (Sadhguru)

"It relates to the adulthood of our mind development" (John Baines).

The development of our self-consciousness cannot be accomplished unless we *re-new our intelligence* in sync with *the Universal Laws of Creation,* and unless we expand our cognition and perception of these laws in full connection with the five dimensions of life. *The Raised Self-Consciousness propels us on-ward, up-ward, and God-ward!*

Super *Level*	*Intelligence of God*	***Universal*** *Dimension*
Macro *Level*	*Intelligence of the Universe*	***Spiritual*** *Dimension*
Mezzo *Level*	*Intelligence of the World*	***Mental*** *Dimension*
Meta *Level*	*Intelligence of the Society*	***Emotional*** *Dimension*
Micro *Level*	*Intelligence of Man*	***Physical*** *Dimension*

The intelligence of both the society and the world that is presented above is being now formed by an unprecedented socialization and globalization of our lives that promote our gradual consciousness ascending. *We, in fact, develop the holistic consciousness of inter-dependency* which is not just three-dimensional (hight, width, depth), but is *four-dimensional* because it has *the spiritual volume* that encompasses everything around and generates *the feeling of Oneness inside and outside!* Everything relates to everything. *"Our Sun is the mind that guides the solar system; the Galactic mind guides the galaxy, and the Universal mind guides the Universe, the Source of the mind that guides all creation."(David Icke)* The process of upgrading of our intelligence is being viewed by me in five main philosophical levels: *Mini, Meta, Mezzo, Macro, and the Super Levels, featuring the corresponding dimensions.* Thanks to such integrity, we will see the world and ourselves in it in total connection with everything and everyone around us. *At the Super Level* of our consciousness development, we will attain **Oneness with Life,** and the state of balance will be ruling our essence, or, in other words, the time of *our Inner Renaissance* will finally come.

Intelligence is the Life Blood of the Universe!

Thesis 3

The Present-Day State of Intelligence

Human kind is a flash of the entire system of evolution of intelligence. *"Life is a flow of intelligence." ("Scientific American Mind", Aug. 2014)* Life is a process of challenging our intelligence and responding to it. Challenges are always new, but *our responses to them are old, conditioned, and patterned.* As Albert Einstein puts it,

"Life is like riding a bicycle. To keep your balance, you must keep moving."

There are two main personalities in each of us – *a thinking personality* and *an emotional one.* Unfortunately, they are not in synch because we lack *"emotional intelligence" (Daniel Goldman),* the intelligence that needs to be developed by us to manage our uncontrolled emotions and get on with developing our intelligence. **Our emotional make-up is above our mental one yet,** and there is little, if at all, awareness how to accomplish real empowerment of emotions that have helped us survive for centuries thanks to their reactive nature. Now **emotional chaos reigns in our minds,** and unless we conquer it with our **well-organized intelligence in sync with new, technologically-enhanced self-awareness,** no transformation of self-consciousness at any level will occur.

*"The biology of consciousness offers a sounder basis for morality than the unprovable dogma of an immortal soul. Once we realize that **our own consciousness is a product of our brains**, it becomes impossible to deny our common capacity to evolve them." (Scientific American Mind", July/ Aug. 29014)* Undoubtedly, we will accomplish a new level of consciousness when ***the cone of intellect will get above the cone of emotions*** and the rationalization of our lives will become possible. It is going one now, but it needs to be enhanced.

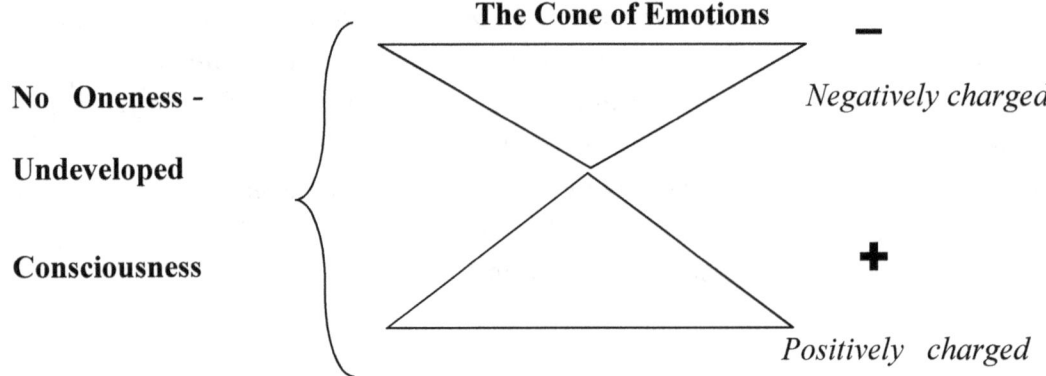

"The Body is the Expression of Our Thoughts."

(Dr. Fred Bell, "Death of Ignorance")

Thesis 4

The Predictable Future

Another problem relates to *the way we process the flood of in-coming information.* Many of us devour information and store it in the cerebral archives without sorting it out for the essence it has. We continue living within the eggshell of out-worked knowledge and over-used vocabulary that produce *stereotyped thoughts, uncontrolled feelings, and impulsive actions.*

Consequently, we develop within the web of our behavioral patterns, governed by reactive thinking that prompts automatic actions. Only by learning more about how the brain establishes and maintains routine behaviors, can we coax ourselves out of undesirable habits into the ones we want and need. Obviously, the *awareness of how the brain works and of the newest development in neuroscience* becomes an urgent demand of time!

Energy follows thought, thought provokes action, action yields habit, habit breeds destiny. The word evolution is defined by the present-day science as *"the process which is dual in operation, spiritual as well as material, and the one that is directed rather than natural."* It is going by the route indicated below:

Unconscious ⟹ *Conscious* ⟹ *Superconscious*

This process consists of *an accompanied continuous development of the brain by a parallel unfolding of self-consciousness at each level: Mini - physical; Meta – emotional; Mezzo - mental; Macro - spiritual,* and *Super - universal.*

Technology is developing at the exponential pace, changing us into different human, or rather, *super-human beings* that are merging with the Artificial Intelligence that is implementing the time of *Singularity* that according to science we are heading to. Our time democratizes the Artificial Intelligence power and is leading us to *the machine extension of ourselves*, updating our cognition to an unprecedented level. A new neural link is being developed now in the cognition system, and it enhances our cognitive abilities immensely with all the electronic gadgets that we have at hand.

The menacing prediction of the genius of our times, *Elon Musk*, that we'll become human machines and will be unable to separate ourselves from the virtual reality is presented by him as inevitable. Fortunately, we are becoming vastly smarter, by up-grading our cognition beyond beliefs, but, unfortunately, we are getting more and more *dependent on the virtual reality* due to the electronic advancements that are literally enslaving us.

We'll be colonizing other planets in pursuing the goal to save humanity from extinction. The level of robotization of our lives is going to be very liberating, on the one hand, and truly questionable as to our adjusting to many jobs' elimination, on the other.

Many young people are living now in the simulated reality, becoming more indifferent, impersonal lovers of themselves, and the technological reality is ***becoming undistinguishable from the simulated world in the games***. Their interest in expanding intelligence is vague, if at all noticeable in many. They hardly read anything, being vastly dependable on plagiarizing the ideas of others, easily accessible on the Internet.

Talking about this menacing possibility of us becoming ***the cybernetic extension of the machine,*** Elon Musk, ***sounds really concerned***, and our role as educators is to share his concern and find the way to deal with his warning as soon as possible.

The first thing that our young, messed up minds forget to consider is that, in marveling at Elon Musk's ideas and ***his super-natural ability to forestall all the resistance to his innovations,*** taking us all into the predictable future, and earning billions of dollars against all odds, is ***his incredible self-education effort***, his insatiable desire to read, to learn, and expand his mind beyond the regular educational limits. In one of his interviews, Elon Musk, talking about ***the effect of Singularity*** consuming our lives, said,

" *If you cannot beat it, join it!* "

To join this inevitable progress, ***one needs to boundlessly educate oneself in all the five levels*** that I suggest considering, raising self-consciousness to the level that will let us save ourselves, as a unique form of life. We need to follow ***the Holistic Paradigm of Self-Creation*** religiously.

The Spiral of Holistic Self-Creation:

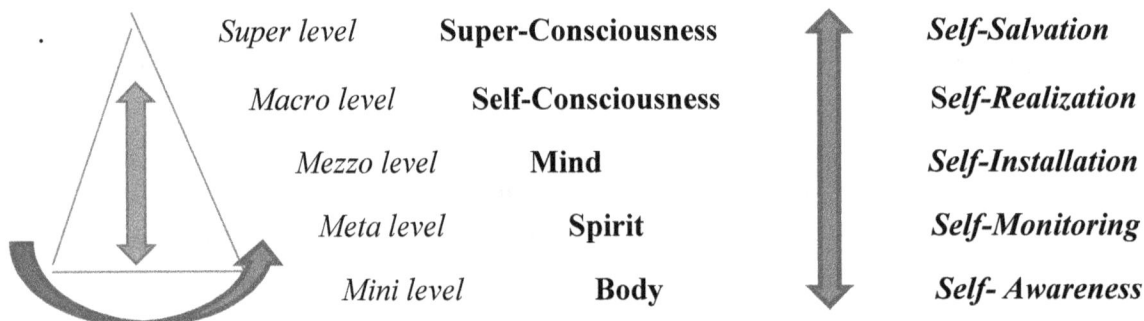

Body+ Spirit+ Mind + Self-Consciousness+ Universal Consciousness

= A New , Holistically-Developing Self at each level!

Our present-day being determines our consciousness.,

while it should be the other way around:

Our Self-Consciousness Should Determine Our Being!

Thesis 5

Multi-Dimensional Intelligence

The profound questions about the Universe are not solved, and much of our well-monitored and *scientifically-charged intelligence* is needed to be up-dated consciously and knowingly... ***The** main problem of our time is not how to better grow technologically, **but how to optimize human growth!***

The rippling effect of true intelligence is life without negligence!

The leading thinkers in science Michelle Ford and Peter Berkrot in their groundbreaking book **"This Explains Everything"** write, *"The consciousness in us is like the visible aspect of the Universe that is only a fraction of the mental world. The dark matter of the mind, the unconscious mind that occupies the greatest part of the cosmic space has the greatest psychic gravity, as well as enormous power."* Our evolutionary upright movement makes it fathomable for us to move through the doors of our growing intelligence with the losses of the memory of our past inquiries. It allows us to move through the evolutionary doors of perception with or without awareness of our actual contribution to this eternal process. No doubt, we absolutely need to install in us the *alert surveillance of every unwanted habit* because the more routine our behavior becomes, the less we are aware of it.

" Bad habits have good tendencies - either you kill them, or they kill you." (A. Einstein)

The insidious failure to check our actions also means that habits can become akin to addictions, gambling, constant texting, tweeting, alcohol and drug use. "A *repetitive addiction-driven pattern of behavior can take over the consciously made good choice." (Scientific American", June 2014)* The neuro-science that has come to the forefront of the most advanced thinking tries to find the cause for our *impulsivity and unconscious actions.*

The Will of the Unconscious is still very powerful.

According to Michael Ford and Peter Berkrot, *"**The concepts upon which the unconscious mind bases its activity are outdated.** They are no longer responsive to the challenges of the present-day life and a man in it. These concepts are not intellectual any more*, but *expressive, reactive, and automatic."* Apparently, we need to profoundly explore these areas of our life and redirect the managing of our minds toward the ways of *de-automaton of our impulsiveness and more rationality* of our actions. In sum, every one of us has a different set of bad habits, and the only way to handle bad habits is to suppress them consciously and balance oneself, based on the on-going development of intelligence *in five dimensions of life holistically -* physically, emotionally, mentally, spiritually, and universally.

"Only Being Whole, We Become Holy." *(Deepak Chopra)"*

Thesis 6

Ten Vistas of Intelligence to Install!

Life on Earth is an outline of the intellectual odyssey for a seeking soul*!** Working at our self-actualization, we can develop different intelligences, one after another, ***both strategically and tactically, without attributing any of the intelligences to preferred working styles or career decisions. (*Howard Gardner and Robert Sternberg above*.) I am mapping out here ***the ten stages of Living Intelligence*** that, in my understanding and profound academic experience, ***are to be followed in anyone's intellectual quest, based on the specifically developed talents***. It is the spiral of holistic self-creation that helps bridge the knowledge gaps.

It is a holistic picture of the most critical intelligences that comprise **Living Intelligence** and sculpture a person on the way of attaining *"**spiritualized intelligence**" (John Baines)* As has been mentioned above, I present the ten most crucial intelligences in five philosophical levels - **Mini, Meta, Mezzo, Macro, and Super.** The hierarchy of the intelligences to acquire goes from bottom up, and this is the order they are being outlined in this book.:

Lofty Heights of Spiritualized Intelligence to be mastered:

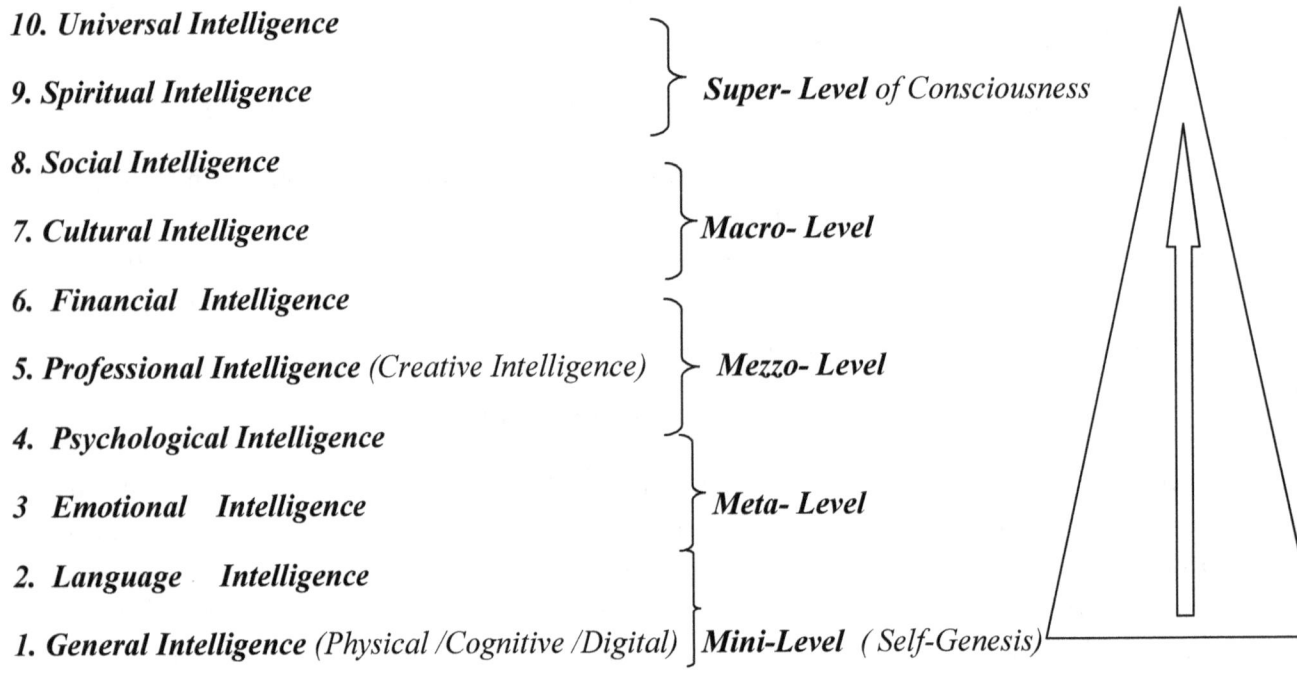

10. Universal Intelligence

9. Spiritual Intelligence — **Super- Level** *of Consciousness*

8. Social Intelligence

7. Cultural Intelligence — **Macro- Level**

6. Financial Intelligence

5. Professional Intelligence (Creative Intelligence) — **Mezzo- Level**

4. Psychological Intelligence

3 Emotional Intelligence — **Meta- Level**

2. Language Intelligence

1. General Intelligence (Physical /Cognitive /Digital) | **Mini-Level** (*Self-Genesis*)

"It's profoundly significant that the only thing over which you have complete control is your mental altitude!" (Napoleon Hill)

Become a Mind-Evolved Being!

Thesis 7

Synthesis-Analysis-Synthesis!

Each of the vistas of intelligence above makes up a strategic plan of action for self- creation in the mental realm in the holistic paradigm: ***self-knowledge, self-monitoring, self-installation, self-realization and self-salvation.*** The stages of intelligence are also interrelated by ***the principle of the Russian dolls,*** when the top doll encompasses all the rest, one by one, in the inter- dependable, holistically- structural route, following the main formula of life: - ***synthesis - analysis-synthesis.***

Synthesis - (*General, Language, Emotional, Psychological intelligences*)

Analysis - (*Professional, Financial, Cultural intelligences*)

Synthesis – (*Social, Spiritual, Universal intelligences*)

Internalizing - Personalizing- Externalizing!

At the Mini- Level – *General Intelligence (Physical Dimension),* we develop our knowledge of life and get more self-awareness. We also become more aware *(Physical Intelligence)* of the preservation of our health and lengthening of our life span. It's the level of our *Self-Genesis.* At this initial**,** *mini-level,* our overall intelligence is developed, based on the *Cognitive Intelligence* and *Language Intelligence.* Both are fortified by *the Digital Intelligence,* indispensable now.

At the Meta- Level - *Emotional Intelligence (Emotional Dimension),* we are learning to channel our emotions constructively, synergizing our space and time and *teaching the mind to prevail in our self-actualization.* To be able to manage our emotions consciously, we learn to manage ourselves. So, *Psychological Intelligence* needs to be developed at this level, too.

At the Mezzo Level - *Professional Intelligence (Mental Dimension)*, we are building up our lives on the paths of *self-installation and self-realization*, and we create ourselves both professionally and personally. We reach the culminating point of self-actualization at this level. This is also the level of our *Creative Maturity.* We give back to the world, justifying our unique presence in it.

At the Macro Level - *Cultural and Social Intelligences (Mental Dimension),* we expand our cultural and spiritual outlook, our human values, and we get an access to the global knowledge and cultures.

At the Super Level - *Spiritual and Universal Intelligences (Spiritual and Universal Dimensions),* we transcend our religious differences, committing to the Universal Intelligence that we all call God holistically, servicing God and life at large on the interpersonal level, social, and extra-terrestrial levels.

We Need to Unwind More of the Mind!

Thesis 8

Rationalization of Life is a Must!

The concept of reason has always been the central one in philosophy. Thinking is such a great gift that it needs to be appreciated and handled with caution. Philosophy for centuries has been addressing the ways of making human existence more sophisticated and reason-oriented. A great German philosopher, *Emmanuel Kant,* in his fundamental work "**The Critique of Pure Reason**" draws our attention to a direct connection between **beauty and reason**, arguing that to see the beauty of life and to get to the core of our existence, "**we have to go beyond the aesthetics into the realm of reason.**" We, obviously, need to refresh the knowledge of the fundamentals of philosophy and teach ourselves and our kids *the sophistication of reasoning* as the best exercise for the brain's expansion of its capacity and raising it to the level of *tapping the Universal Intelligence,* impossible without a substantial development of the critical thinking skills.

"I want to know the God's thoughts. The rest is details." (Albert Einstein)

The concept of reason is inseparable with all the thesis statements that I have outlined above and that are to be yet discussed. I put my own *mission–statement* under the main concept of this book - *the rationalization of our lives!*

" Thinking is the soul talking to itself." (Plato)

To get rid of the automatically-based, crowd-framed mentality that is often devoid of emotional intelligence or any intelligence, for that matter, we need to gradually **change our cerebral matrix** and develop a new one consciously based on *a much better awareness of the new developments in neuro-science, cyber biology*, and *physics* to up-grade the abilities of the brain in terms of its incredible *plasticity.* The digital times develop our thinking skills in any area of expertise making us see the beauty in ourselves and around us in a novel way, but we also need to apply amazing electronic tools *to bettering of our Reasoning Skills*. Current computers are very logical, sequential, and quantitative. They can process lots of data, but they really don't think yet.

The researchers in electronics are trying to change that, and very soon we'll have the quantum computers that will work as a human brain. Our goal is to speed up our thinking by **making a thorough selection of the information** that makes up the memory that our brains and the mini-computers, our cells, operate on. Our goal is to learn **not to clog our brains with redundant information** and not let the viruses of impulsivity, mechanical thinking, and uncontrolled emotional reactions operate our biological computers. The way we think, speak, feel, and act comes to the forefront of our Living Intelligence skills. So, to be interesting, get interested!

Auto-Induction: *Put the thinking cap on your everyday mind's crap!*

Change Your Thinking Time into the Thinking Life!

Thesis 9

The First Shift in Our Holistic Life Paradigm

Self-mastery that enables us to develop the required cognitive and emotional intelligences is another skill that allows us to realize the brain's full awakening potential of the inherent spirit that we all possess. No one has a greater spirit than anyone else, and ***a great spirit is your doing.*** The Auto-Suggestive Phycology is your helping hand in your spirit's well-being!!

If the brain gets more organized and disciplined, thinking becomes more rationalized!

The present-day times demand we become more ***rational, conscious, and appreciative*** of the boundless horizon of possibilities that the technological revolution has revealed to us. New times also presuppose new modes of thinking or ***the Holistic Culture of Thinking*** (See "Book Incentive") to be developed in us to make us much more aware of life in five main philosophical levels: *mini, meta, mezzo, macro, and super holistically.*

Study life at physical + emotional + mental + spiritual + universal levels beyond survive!

True, we have become much better at our thinking habits thanks to the brain storming and operative problem-solving activities that we started practicing more effectively in the computer times. But the ***digital revolution requires more strategical, insightful, and pro-active thinking that can generate a new content of life*** with new concepts, and objectives in a much more productive way.

The tide of evolution sweeps mental drifters away!

Following the holistic paradigm, presented above, the changes in today's technology and the global science culture that is altering us in the core demand that ***we give priority to reconsidering our personal, emotional, mental, spiritual, and universal values.*** Digital times demand a substantial change in our developmental mind-set ***from the specialized one to the holistic one:***

Synthesis - analysis – synthesis!

"The only thing that endures is change!" "This timeless observation was made by a great Greek philosopher Heraclitus in the 6th century BC. Live changes us every day, hour, minute, and even a second*.!* If you empower yourself and journey through the pages of this book, the knowledge that you will derive from it, however simple it may seem to you, will ultimately manifest itself in your subconscious mind ***as a derivative and a reference point*** of everything that moves and breathes in the Universe with us, human beings, at the top of the existential ladder which is our own individual scheme of comprehensible theories of self-reproduction and our own purposeful self-growth through constant change.

Help Intelligence rule the World in the Holistic Mold!

Thesis 10

"Serve Yourself, then the Money!" *(Reid Hoffman)*

Unfortunately, *"in our world, consciousness has been delegated to the backseat and material reality has become a driver. "(Rav. P.S. Berg)"* It may sound banal, and you have definitely read a lot of about self-growth, but like every unprocessed knowledge, it remains just recognizable, but it is not backed up by *actionable awareness that is governed by aware, not pseudo-attention* to life change.

"The cult of success of obtaining great wealth is based on financial accumulation now." (Reid Hoffman) The holistic paradigm for self-creation demands the change of our mentality in a reverse way.

Having helps, but it doesn't shape. vs. Having is the result of the changed life paradigm!

Be somebody! **Have** what you want!
Do something! **Do** something!
Have something! **Be** somebody!

Before you can get something, you must be somebody!

First, *we are all in the same evolutionary boat that goes onward, upward, and God-ward!* Only material aspirations cannot be a great motivator anymore! The chase for money has not brought us happiness; it only divided us and generated conflicts and wars on all the levels of life *So, the paradigm of self-creation is changing now from having to Being and Becoming.*

"Income rarely exceeds a personal growth!" (Reid Hoffman)

Second, *"the cultivation of the mind and the character are needed now. "(Aristotle)* There is a common delusion that if you have money, you will do something that only you are able to do, and then you will become somebody special.

Money chase as a one-pointed goal is a dead-end journey consciousness-wise.

The history of self-creation of many great minds proves to us, however, that *we need to develop true, valid intelligence* first, backing this process up with *a firm will* and self-confidence in order to accomplish full self-realization. We all have felt a great vexation over the troubles and tribulations that the humanity's greatest minds had to endure throughout centuries. *Intelligence had never been respected as much as it needs to be prioritized now!*

Money God is Presiding over the World! So, What?!

Thesis 11

Change Shapes Us or Destroys Us!

I like the main concept of the novel "*The Moon and Sixpence*" by a great British writer *Somerset Maugham,* telling us indirectly about the life of Paul Gaugin. On the one hand, getting on the path of self-realization, the main character becomes a new person and displays his unique talent *on the Moon side*, but on the other one, *on his sixpence side*, he stops caring about anyone and pursues his goal heartlessly and inconsiderately. The end, however, didn't justify the means!

Our moon side should always out-shine the sixpence side!

Apparently, the sixpence side of career education, aimed at just getting a job and making money is killing the best of many young talents now They are not worried about displaying their intelligence; they are more concerned with their bank accounts and the means of survival. Regrettably, a one-sided approach to self-development has proved to be not very beneficial for the evolution of the humanity. Meanwhile, the rule that helps us survive in this turmoil of life is, *"Prefer knowledge to wealth, for the one is transitory, the other is perpetual."* *(Socrates)*

So, first make yourself, then make the money!

Life may have a negative starting point and a totally different ultimate result - *no self-realization due to wrong priorities in life*, but it is, was, and, let's hope will be an exception.

" Do it and then the money comes; not " I'll do it when the money comes."

The decision for self-installation in life should enlighten our lives and the lives of people who happen to be on our path at this time. Self- growth is a mission that makes us feel complete and people gravitate to us. All our time should not be taken by the worries about the job, or the problems connected with money–earning or money-spending. *Our lives should be governed by the urge for self-expression,* enhanced by technology, not destroyed by it. The route is: *Self-creation, self-monitoring, self-installation, self-realization and self-salvation!*

Strategizing - Optimizing- Actualizing! / Synthesis -Analysis – Synthesis!

"*Read a lot. Leaders are readers!*"*(Jim Rohn)* Sift the information in your brain for its validity. Delete the informational redundant noise. Forget about your regrets, guilt, shame, misery ,and ignorance of the past. We are all ignorant, and there is never enough knowledge to bridge the gaps of ignorance that is getting vaster with each fast technologically- developing day. So, keep learning, remembering the words by Socrates: *"I know that I am intelligent because I know that I know nothing"*

The Holistic Mind-Set in the Brain is Your First GAIN!

Thesis 12

"Right is Might!"

Deification of a money–idol is nothing new. It happened over 3000 years ago when Moses was on top of Mount Sinai, *receiving Ten Commandments*. Moses's mission was to raise our collective consciousness and to give us a new plan of action. During these well-known events, *the Law of the Right Human Behavior* was born! Later, in the 20ieth century, it was redefined by a great scientist, Richard W. Wetherill, in his simple, but very thought-provoking book "***Right is Might.***" that was not published during his life time.

The magazine "*The Scientific American Mind*" brought it back to our attention a few years ago. I will be referring you to *the Law of the Right Human Behavior* a lot as a great back–up .. ***This law demands that we learn the right thinking, speaking, and acting on the spiritual level, not just existential one!***

"Right will eventually prevail!"(Richard W. Wetherill)

The present-day speed of our technological advancement demands that we get an advanced view of the latest developments in science, in general, and **in** *Neuroscience,* in particular. ***To adjust to a new neural development, we need to oversee it. in us.*** Each person has a personal intellectual level that he needs ***to exceed conceptually at any age*** to demonstrate to himself and the world his divine spark and the spiritual content of his / her unique personality. ***Spiritual and intellectual advancement is essential for every one of us at our turmoil international times!*** A beautiful, up-lifting song by a well-known American folk singer ***Peter Segal*** comes to mind here:

" *We shall overcome!*

But any trouble-overcoming depends on the clarity of a person's mind, his / her general outlook, and the level of his / her ***self-education*** in every area of knowledge - science, art, literature, music, world history, religion, and culture. Such ***holistic personal enrichment****(development of all the intelligences, Thesis 9)* modifies our values and beliefs and ultimately results ***in the richness of a soul*** that will be better enabled to follow the right and resist the wrong sides of life.

"***The most difficult job in the world is to be a good person.***"*(William Saroyan)*

Apparently, ***self-enrichment becomes a necessary supplement to general education***! We can obtain a better awareness of the reality only through ***expanded self-education and rationalization of life.*** The most intelligent people that are accomplished, well-educated, and well-read always have a special perception of beauty and a very personable vision of the world. Socrates was right,

"It is not Living that Matters but Living Rightly."

Thesis 13

Getting Our Intelligence in Sync with the Universal One!

To get our personal intelligence in synch with the Universal one, we need to change" *the world of knowledge and the world of will"* in ourselves. As a great German philosopher, Emanuel Kant, puts it,

> *"Will is the thing in itself, the inner content of knowing, the essence of the world."*

Will-power and self-discipline, in tandem, comprise are the main moving force on the road of getting free from the social programming of the *"collective unconscious."* Will–power paves the way to our feeling self-reliant, self-sufficient, and self-challenging and base these qualities on a ***much better awareness of the world and the latest developments in science*** that explain it, casting away our outdated, limited vision and generating a new- technologically-enhanced one that gives us a chance to tune our AUTO-ANTENNAS to the universal mind and receive the messages that it is emitting to us at every level of our consciousness development.*(Thesis 2 above)*

To attain this stage of freedom, full of awareness and self-sufficiency, we need to do a lot of willful self-sculpting that is the hardest job on earth*!* We need ***to develop all levels of intelligence in sync with the will*** to resist the downfall tendencies that are tempting us all the time! A famous German philosopher Schopenhauer writes,

> *"For as the world is in one aspect entirely idea, so in another, it is entirely will."*

Intelligence exists in time and space; it's never static! It is in the constant state of flux that is changeable as the result of our changing thoughts, words, and actions. The more consciousness you bring into the body with your will, the stronger your immune system is and the higher is your spirit. ***A healthy spirit gives a healthy body, and a healthy body generates a healthy spirit!***

> *"So, learn to say "Halt!" to your whims and negative patterns of behavior!" (Edgar Cayce)*

Working at your will, you are moving from a three dimensional *(height, width, depth)* to ***the five - dimensional consciousness*** (*See Thesis 1 above*) that demands *that **we change the volume of our thinking*** by willfully intellectualizing our emotions and expanding our consciousness to the universal level that is out evolutionary goal. *This developmental process requires a much higher level of our mental vibrations,* and ***to be in the flow of the Universal Intelligence go***, we need to be raising them consciously through our intelligence and ***soul-refining.*** *(See the book "Soul Refining!' for more.)* Interestingly, we do not see the humanoids that are undoubtedly there somewhere because they exist on the overtone higher than we do. They are living in the fourth dimension that we have just started discovering

"Let's Change the Fabric of Our Thinking!" *(Leo Vygotsky)*

Thesis 14

Self-Education is a Must for a New Culture of Thinking!

We all know that the most advanced-thinking people of our time, such as **Steve Jobs, Bill Gates, Elon Musk, Giacomo Undivert, Franklin Chang Diaz, Jack Ma** and other contemporary giants of the mind are independently-bold thinkers, ***self-educated intellectuals,*** and unabashed enthusiasts of designing a better life for us. They are distinguished, exceptional, and ***multi-dimensional intellectually.*** They are also great models of intellectual expansion for young generation.

The mind of such people monitors the brain! Apparently, being defined just as an accomplished person is not enough for the new times. ***We need people whose minds*** are ***well-rounded holistically.*** And if our education system does not provide that, the mission of every intelligent person is to obtain the education that makes his unique personality shine against all odds on his own. ***Holistic, integral, conscious self-development becomes a priority!*** It should also be noted here that time has come ***to value similarities***, especially intellectual and psychological ones. Thanks to the globalization of the world, we started realizing our sameness more and judging each other less. *"Human differences are very superficial."(Erich Fromm) "We react internally in much the same way".*

The electronic times are uniting us into one family of life!

We are all hungry for knowledge, and we all have a bursting desire for self-realization. Nationality, skin color, or religious affiliations are secondary. I have been teaching students from all over the world for more than twenty-five years in the USA, and they are all knowledge-oriented, very curious, insightful, and bursting with an electrifying desire to change the world. But it all happens only when they get imbued with an inspirational desire to give the world the best they have. It means we are gradually becoming more accomplished and happier inhabitants of the planet Earth, the people that are imbued with new ambitions and fortified with ***the life paradigm of conscious self-creation. "We must make sense with our lives, each and every one of us!"****(Leo Vygotsky)*

Every one of us needs have a clear-cut idea or ***reasoned–out awareness*** of what he / she has become and is becoming, written down **as A MISSION STATEMENT** that only you know of and have the vision of as ***the Ultimate Result Vision*** of the best of you (*See below*). Steering your mind to the desired destination ***consciously, consistently, and willfully***, with or without the judgement what is right or wrong in God's eyes, but with an inner seed of goodness rooted in you, ***you will never go down a rocky road of self-corrode.***

The Vistas of Intelligence to master launch you to success faster!

"From Working God to the Working Thought." *(Sadhguru)*

Thesis 15

The Ultimate Result Vision of Self-Sculpturing!

At the very outset of self-actualization work, it is essential to examine and re-examine yourself for the quality of you at every level and in every dimension separately and consequentially. As the result of this objective self-analysis in process, you need to form *the Ultimate Result Vision* of the best you at each level. *This thesis statement is key* in the formation of all the ten vistas of intelligence that are outlined below one by one.

You are the Only One who knows the Real Value of You!

You are ascending the stairs of evolution on your own because it's a personal responsibility of everyone, and you have already reasoned it out. *The higher level of your consciousness, the more care it requires to survive in our cruel, "merry-go-round" world.* Remind yourself of your being the best in the impersonal world around you. This reminder will not make you too conceited, egotistic, or superior to other people. It will just support you in self- love and self-confidence without which there is no self- growth, self- perfection, or self-actualization. You wouldn't perfect someone that you don't love!

Auto-induction: *I'm self-loving! I internalize my becoming!*

With your intelligence growing at every level, you will eventually arrive at **the VINTAGE YOU** image.*(See Spiritual Intelligence below)* **Y**ou will create this image during your self-transformation along the paths that I have outlined for in the *"Book Incentive"*part.. It should be formed in the brain as the result of a holistic self-growth in all five levels of self-installation: *physical-emotional-mental- spiritual-universal!*

Self-reflection in these levels will be the reference point for your self- installation in life!

At the Super level of Universal consciousness attainment, your creative work will be crowned by the **INTEGRAL YOU** result! Anyone who has personal integrity has such image of himself / herself, and it determines a person's behavior for the entire life.

The Ultimate Result Vision *(the URV further)* of yourself that will comprise both **the Vintage Vou** and **the Integral You** is mentally directed to the outcome of your work at bettering yourself in all the dimensions, and it is **the critical ingredient** in the successful quest for both self-change and self-actualization. The URV of self is meant to serve as **a mental back-up** for your new awareness: *"I know who I am!"* It is created solely by you, not by your parents, friends, psychologist, etc.

*We can draw an analogy here with **the Ariadne thread** from a well-known Greek myth. Conversely, the myth tells us that the daughter of king Minus, Ariadne, who fell in love with Theseus, saved his life with a skein of linen thread that Theseus had fixed at the entrance of the* *labyrinth of death where he was supposed to fight with the monster Minotaur. Thanks to that thread, he found the way out after his successful battle with the monster.*

Like the Ariadne thread, we need to fix **the end of our mental cord to the Universal Intelligence** and then go through the maze of the labyrinth of life, winding it higher and higher, closer and closer to the to the Ultimate destination – a much more conscious you - **the Vintage You, and the Integral You!**

Self- induction: ***I am having the rebirth of my self-worth!***

Forming the URV in your mind, you do not want to forget to take care of your energy field that gets easily demagnetized with negative emotional influx of anger, fear, worry, envy, etc. Much dirty emotional information is also coming from other people that are charged with negative energy, thoughts, emotions, and moods. You need to *learn to resist the negative input* that comes from the external world and keep focusing on your URV, no matter what.

Self-induction: ***The URV is my master key!***

You need to install it in your mind for the entire life. We all have goals in life, but those goals are normally very obscure because the person who has the goal of accomplishing something in life does not see himself in that role every day. **With this auto-suggestive vision (the URV)** of the best of you in mind, you will know what to do and how to help yourself when you feel weak, confused, or scared. Having the URV of yourself, you will try to learn more, be inquisitive and curious like a kid, trying to fill up the insatiable hunger for knowledge that starts driving a child, once he experiences its taste.

"Education is a progressive discovery of your own ignorance"

As a result, the URV will work better than any anti- depressant. You do not need any pills when you resort to your inner gravity in lieu with the vision of the best of you in progress. No one can do it better than you! No psychiatrist or psychologist has the X-Ray picture of your inner magnetic power. Remind yourself religiously who you are and who you want to become! You will sharpen your ***aware attention, rationalize your life*** at every level and in every dimension, and you will never stop inspiring yourself with your own unbeatable personal power.

Self- Suggestion: ***I am totally equipped to get my life's uplift!***

Information processing + Internal qualities monitoring + External behavior transformation

Self-Synthesis – Self-Analysis – Self-Synthesis! (*Part Two, Thesis 3*)

Internalizing – Analyzing - Actualizing!

Thesis 16

Will-Power is Our Inner Gravity!

Willful self-sculpturing comes out on stage next, and the words of Carl Yung below become pivotal in self-actualization   One of the main exercises on developing your will-power is *to do something that you don't want to do* or want to put off till tomorrow. You shape your mind and your will-power by doing something unpleasant intentionally. So, *shake off the old dry leaves from your Tree of Life, and let it grow new ones, strong and green!* We need to *"will our lives more"* to be able to resist temptation that gets us off the track of self-perfection, once the aware attention slacks. Inner integrity, formed by will, is channeling the mind toward *consciously - perceived happiness,* and it helps us modify ourselves to attain it

"Will your life more! "Be Immune to the Poison of Life!" (Carl Yung)

Will-power is not inherited, it is developed, and it should instill in our kids as early as possible. All the kids live in the world of super-heroes, princes and princesses, and they are all living in the world of unbelievably-heroic deeds. They do not doubt their abilities to do the impossible! We generate these doubts to them. I love the concept of the cartoon *"The Tale of Desperaeaux"*, in which the main character, an ugly little mouse, when asked by the Princess if he was a mouse, answered, *"No, I am a gentleman. I am a man of honor!"* And he acts as one. *We are what we think we are,* and thus, the best image of ourselves should rein in the brains of our kids and teenagers while they are getting transformed into their grown-up lives. The process of this growing is what we need to focus on, *not just an ephemeral goal that is often dead-set.*

Auto-induction: *In my life quest, I manifest my best!*

The willful transformation will get more achievable if we continue to zoom in on these words to obtain more strength, will-power, and perseverance. The mind-set will help you go through a reflective process of self-assessment of your deeds, on the one hand, and *mindful, purposeful channeling of your intelligence,* on the other. No one is going to take you by the hand and lead you forward *with the light torch of Prometheus in hand* to lighten up your way to a higher consciousness. *Inject the will-power into your every cell to excel! Be a self-guru to accomplish whatever you want to!*

Even the best of the gurus and spiritual teachers are just showing the way, but it's up to the followers to take it or to step off THE SELF- ACTUALIZATION track. There is an old Swedish proverb that says: *"The best place to find a helping hand is in your mind and at the end of your arm."* Considering the role of intelligence in our life, we can   rightfully declare auto-suggestively:

"My mind is my helping hand!"

Will Your Life More! That's the Law!

Thesis 17

Self-Regulation and Transformation Skills

Another aspect to consider that generates many problems in life is **the lack of the state of higher awareness.** The awareness to which I refer to here originates from the intelligence that is separated from unconscious, automatic living, 'hullabaloo" speaking, uncontrolled emotional reactions, *and irrational behaviors* that call for conscious development of our **self-regulation skills.** To beat the fierce competition in the world, we need to

But we need to develop specific **self-regulation skills** that, when instilled in young minds, help them grow intellectually, **developing the basic intelligences** (*Thesis 6 above*) in synch with the newest scientific developments in five levels. In other words, we need **to put new, holistic knowledge**(*our changed habits*) **and skills** (*the re-programmed patterns of behavior*) in synch at **Mini, Meta, Mezzo, Macro, and Super levels** in physical- emotional, mental, spiritual, and universal dimensions.

Knowledge + Skills = the Know - How of Self-Development!

Apparently, ignorance that according to Albert Einstein is" **the worst enemy of the humanity"** needs to be stopped not by just the influx of money into different social programs, but with a substantial *influx of intelligence into our kids.* Serving money and prioritizing its value over **the necessity to raise intelligence and self- consciousness**, the humanity will still be drowning in wars, bloodsheds, crime, and a blind search of pleasure that makes people forget about **the main goal in life - their own personal transformation and actualization.** "*Strong minds discuss ideas; average minds discuss events; weak minds discuss people and money." (Socrates)*

Intellect should become the best commodity everywhere now!

Surprisingly, the counties that practice **the conversion of socialist and capitalist values** in their social structure seem to be less vulnerable in terms of the intellectual quality of the people they are raising. Sweden, Denmark, China, India ,Australia, Canada, Russia and other rapidly developing societies are a good example of such conversion that, obviously, is propelling their economies by enriching their mind-banks. So, let's hope that the mills of money chasing *"will not grind us too small." (Somerset Maugham)* The evolution is demanding the change of our priorities, and it is making us "*serve ourselves first, then the money*."

The conscious change of the paradigm of self-development demands the use of energy in a more constructive way to develop our intelligence, raise our consciousness, and *reconnect with the wisdom of the Universal Intelligence* that, as science proves, is digital.

To self-excel, be the best version of yourself!

People who have low self-esteem and low tolerance for financial pressure can never get rich! Let's remember *Jim Rohm's* very meaningful words,

"When someone becomes a millionaire, the least important thing is what they have.

The most important thing is what they have become!"

Undoubtedly, the life paradigm of conscious self-creation should be guarding us now. Unfortunately, the present-day education is not "***personality-constructive***" *(Leo Vygotsky)* in this respect. It does not focus on **the holistically-oriented intellectual development** for self-actualization purposes. Hence, a growing child or a teenager deviate toward wrong doing, crumpling their destiny from the start, prioritizing money and fun-seeking over self- enrichment and self-development.

History proves that people who get a lot of wealth do not feel overwhelmingly blissful unless they also manage to self-realize themselves in life to their full potential. The world admires the USA for its ingenious doers and money-makers. There is another very significant issue to consider, too. We all strive to get material security, but like anything in life; there is no security in the money world, either. ***Money needs discipline and intelligence to be managed,*** and then the mind starts enjoying the wisdom of material insecurity that only really-advanced minds can handle.

Money needs brains and self-management skills!!

An amazing display of exceptional intellectual and financial charisma is proudly presented by the magazine *Forbes"* every year. Obviously, *financial intelligence (See below)* is the inseparable part of a personality development, based on solid, ***holistically-developed intelligence of the whole brain thinking, fortified by the Living Intelligence skills*** that our basic education should instill in the young minds and the further self-education should develop to make every life meaningfully actualized.

Finally, a clear majority of us lives ***in a reactive state of mind***, affected by the outside influences and money-worries. There are still much less of us who can be considered ***proactive people***, the ones that ***run their lives consciously***, making enough money to take care of their personal actualization through expanding their overall intelligence and raising their consciousness

Your life is your mission before the final admission

To the station God for His high-heaven reward!

Capture the Feeling of the Sky without the Ceiling!

Thesis 18

Auto-Suggestive Meditation is the Mind-Sculptor!

The auto suggestive work that I have described in the previous part of the book is the essential thesis statement in your up-coming work at ten essential intelligences.

Re-programming your mind at every level of intelligence development, you will be raising the frequency vibrations of our entire energy field, and you will *flood the body with higher consciousness* every moment of your inner self-talk, or meditation.

Meditation is a profound *inner emersion*, or *"the system of inclusiveness"(Sadhguru)* that requires a certain *mind-appeasing skill* that is absolutely essential for our establishing the total control over the chatter box in the mind.

Neuroscience proves now that meditation can deeply transform the adult brain through the process, called *neuro-plasticity* – *"the ability of the brain to adapt to our physical, mental, and emotional states and delegate different functions of the brain to its other parts, if need be." (Michael Merzenich)* Science proves that there is a connection between mental states of a person during meditation and brain plasticity.

De-activating of the mind helps you to self-re-wind!

I am inviting you to use *the Auto-Suggestive Meditation* to sculpture the inner you actively. as the method of inspirational self-training!

Auto-induction: *I can! I want to! And I will!*

This auto-suggestive meditating technique that is presented in the previous part of the book is very beneficial in every respect because *you strengthen the mind-heart connection,* and ,thus, you get more in charge of both your body and the mind *in a holistic way* actively, boosting them to action.

Remember, you manage *to control your mind-heart connection by giving the authoritative command to the mind* to follow your will at any space and time.

Thus, rhyming and easily -memorized auto-inductions become your working memory, or you.

Every Mind needs to Be Enriched and Inspired!

Thesis 19

The Power of the Momentum!

To wrap up this very conceptually- important part of the book, let us remind you of the time issue. *There is incredible power in each momentum!* Do not push off studying the Art of Living, or the Art of Becoming aside. Take daily actions to improve your will-power to do it.

We all need tools for life learning. It's now or never!

"Science is part of the reality of knowing; it is the what, the how, and the why of everything in our experience, but this reality has to become yours as well." *(Rachel Carson)* The book you are holding in your hands extracts the essence from very many sources on self-search and the search of truth, and it forms one genetic entity - *the Manual for the initial strategic work on oneself.*

As a result, *"A New Me" consciousness will* be formed, and it will spin the vortex of self-formation from one level to the next, backing up your ever-getting stronger urge to become someone special. A new consciousness may win over because it has **an operative plan, the** perspective to guard you by and because you are someone special. Someone said,

"It isn't important what you can do in life; it's more important what you will!"

"Luck happens when preparedness meets opportunity, and opportunity is always there in our beautiful world."(Bertram Russell) Do not wait for anyone to change your world. Just know that when you change, the world changes with you, too. Don't procrastinate with time and your fate!

Auto- induction   *Time never has a row with now!*

Living in the moment and making the most of it demands being able to tell the truth to yourself about your own preparedness and the amount of will-power you have to do that. Building up inner integrity starts with being truthful and honest to yourself and others. "When I am in doubt, I tell the truth*!"(Don Miguel Ruiz)* Truthfulness is the ability to always live in the moment and appreciate its illusiveness. In the job of self-creation, *the moment of self-truth is priceless*! It helps you assess your ability to progress objectively and charge yourself with more will-power and patience.

"At the end of the way is freedom, until then patience "(Buddha)

Also, zillions of books are written about the necessity to appreciate life as is. Life is such a tremendous privilege, so exciting that it is the cause for constant thanksgiving that cannot be postponed. To affect permanent mastery over our lives and destinies; we must change our nature and behavior in a holistically developed way. Only then can we enjoy the thrill and the wonder of the momentum of every day change.

We need to consciously monitor our lives by changing "the culture of our thinking."

Our inner holistic transformation gradually becomes the result of the unified work of all the cells of the body, governed by an aware mind, always in charge of what you think, say, and do. ***Capitalize on aware attention to your inner life!*** Thank your cells, as the employees of the private business that you are running with a sincere appreciation of their work in tandem with your thoughts and feelings. Be in touch with the inner music of triumph over your listlessness, inertia, conditioned attitudes, and any habitual weakness that can drag you down now and then.

Design your life in time and space! "

Your conscious reflection on the changes of consciousness in you, your aware attention and concentration on the intelligence that you are developing at a given moment of your self-work will enrich your intelligence considerably. A firmer will-power will help you appreciate your self-work even more. Every small victory over yourself is a step forward, upward, god-ward, toward higher consciousness that will become your second wind in life. Give yourself time and space on the path of self-creation.

The spiral of growth is two twists up, one twist back, not two!

Plug into the void inside you;

Feel the sacredness of "Is."

Learn the power of Now

To enjoy life As Is!

"Our way is not a new way. It's just another way!"
(Neale Donald Walsch)

Carpe Diem! / Seize the Moment!
This Advice is Always Apt. So, Act!

Thesis 20

The Spiral of the Holistic Self-Development

Finally, I have provided *20 thesis statements* that you need to keep in mind when going along the ladder of the essential intelligence formation. The book only scratches the surface of every intelligence that needs to be enriched non-stop your entire life. This book presents them just *at the dilettante level because the subject is broad.,*. You can always do a more insightful search on the Internet.

There is no limit to knowing, and we know so little yet!

The necessity to view these ten steps of developing intelligence *holistically, in five dimensions* is very beneficial for your general outlook because the necessity to get even a fraction of the dilettante knowledge in all of them **is** dictated to us by the exponential growth of technology, the present-day globalization of economy, and our expanded social contacts that ae building us up ,on the one hand, but destroying with the turmoil of messy information, on the other.

This book is a modest contribution to the process of your self-growth at the mental level - **SELF-INSTALLATION.**

Personal awareness and the aware attention to living are life-defining!

The Spiral of Holistic Self- Actualization to follow:

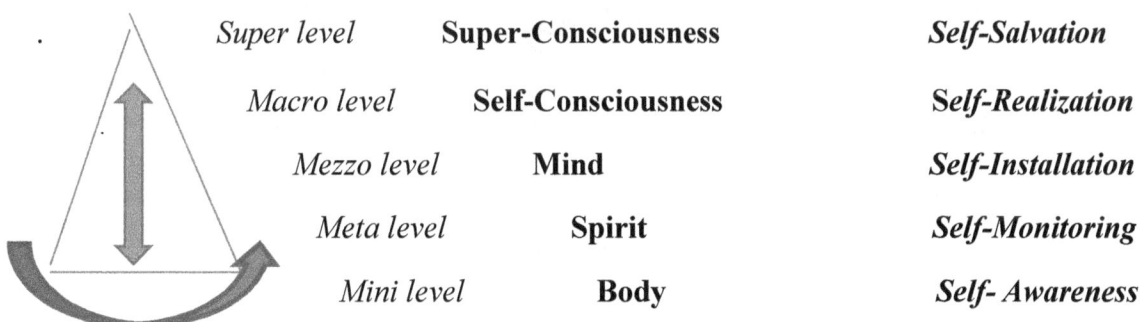

	Super level	**Super-Consciousness**	*Self-Salvation*
	Macro level	**Self-Consciousness**	*Self-Realization*
	Mezzo level	**Mind**	*Self-Installation*
	Meta level	**Spirit**	*Self-Monitoring*
	Mini level	**Body**	*Self- Awareness*

(Body+ Spirit+ Mind) + (Self-Consciousness+ Universal Consciousness) = A Whole Self!

Living Intelligence   *Enlightened Self-Consciousness*

Living Intelligence + Self-Consciousness = A WHOLE SELF!

The Main Part

Let's Focus on the "How?" in the Mental Realm Now!

The Intellectual Odyssey of a Seeking Soul

(The Mental Dimension of the Holistic Paradigm of Self-Creation)

Form + Content = a Complete, Self-Realized Life!

Ten Stages of the Living Intelligence

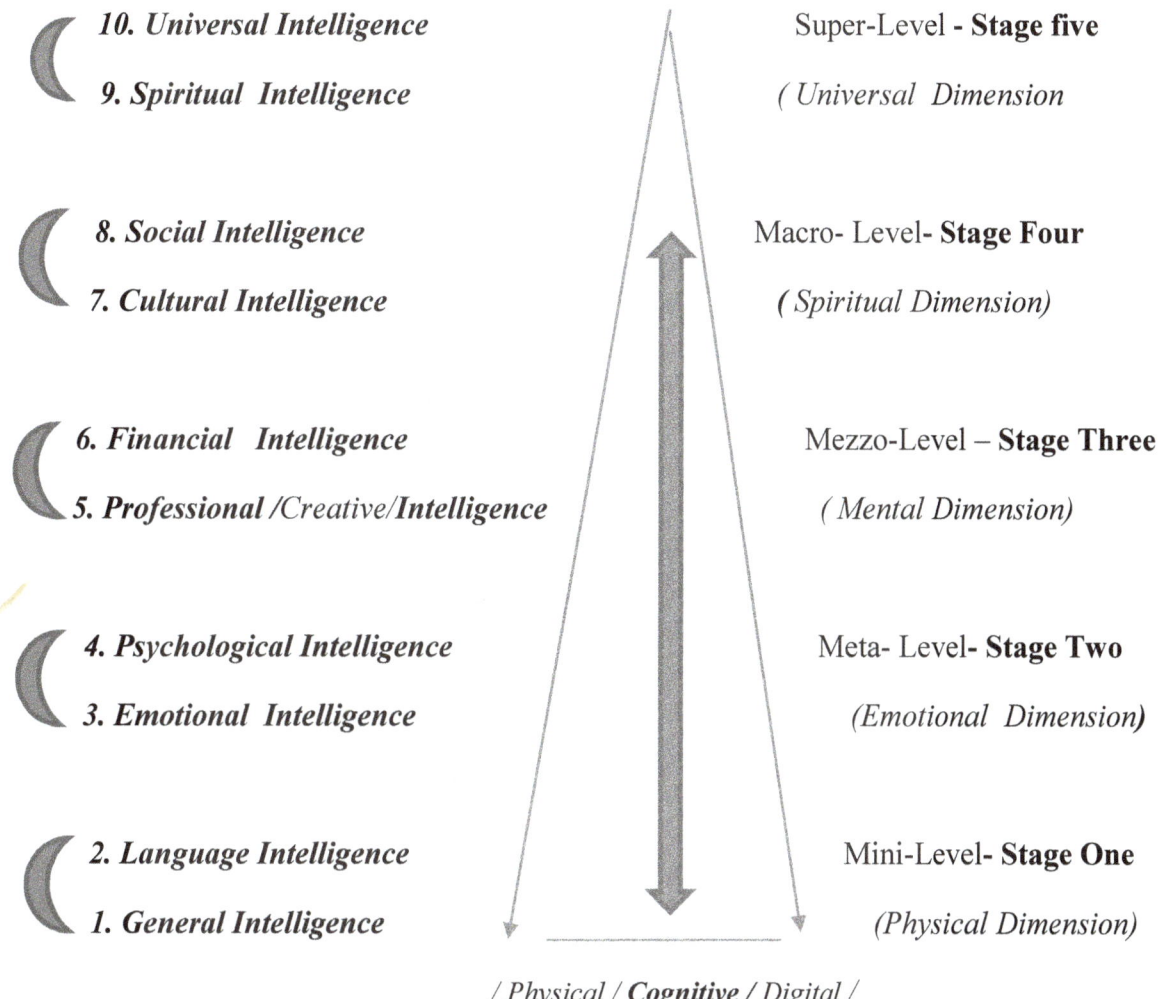

*/ Physical / **Cognitive** / Digital /*

" Fertilize your mind with thinking!"

(Albert Einstein)

New Times are the Times of Exponential Learning!

Stage One

General Intelligence

(Physical, Cognitive, Digital Intelligences)

What? + Why? + How? – Wow!

Resurrect into the Spirit of Self-Installation

with New Awareness and Elation!

Personal Intelligence with Negligence

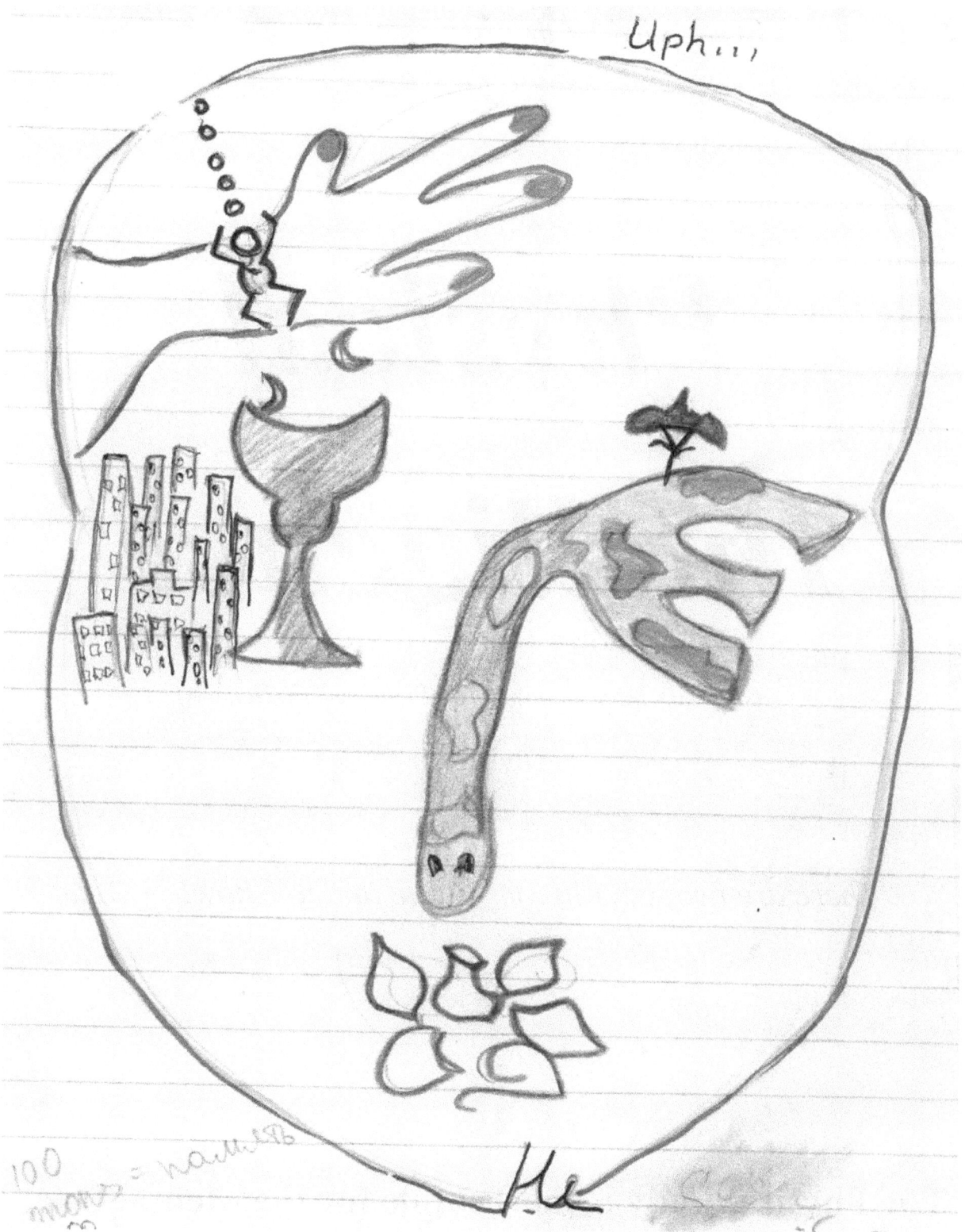

Help Your Mind Monitor the Brain!

Step One

Mini-Level of Intelligence - Physical Dimension

Physical Intelligence

(General   Intelligence - The Primary Self-Genesis)

Division 1

"There are two ways in life - to Be and to Know!" (Osho)

The Physical Body is the Temple for the Mental One!"
(Edgar Cayce)

I Am Unique in Every Stance;

I Was Born, but Only Once!

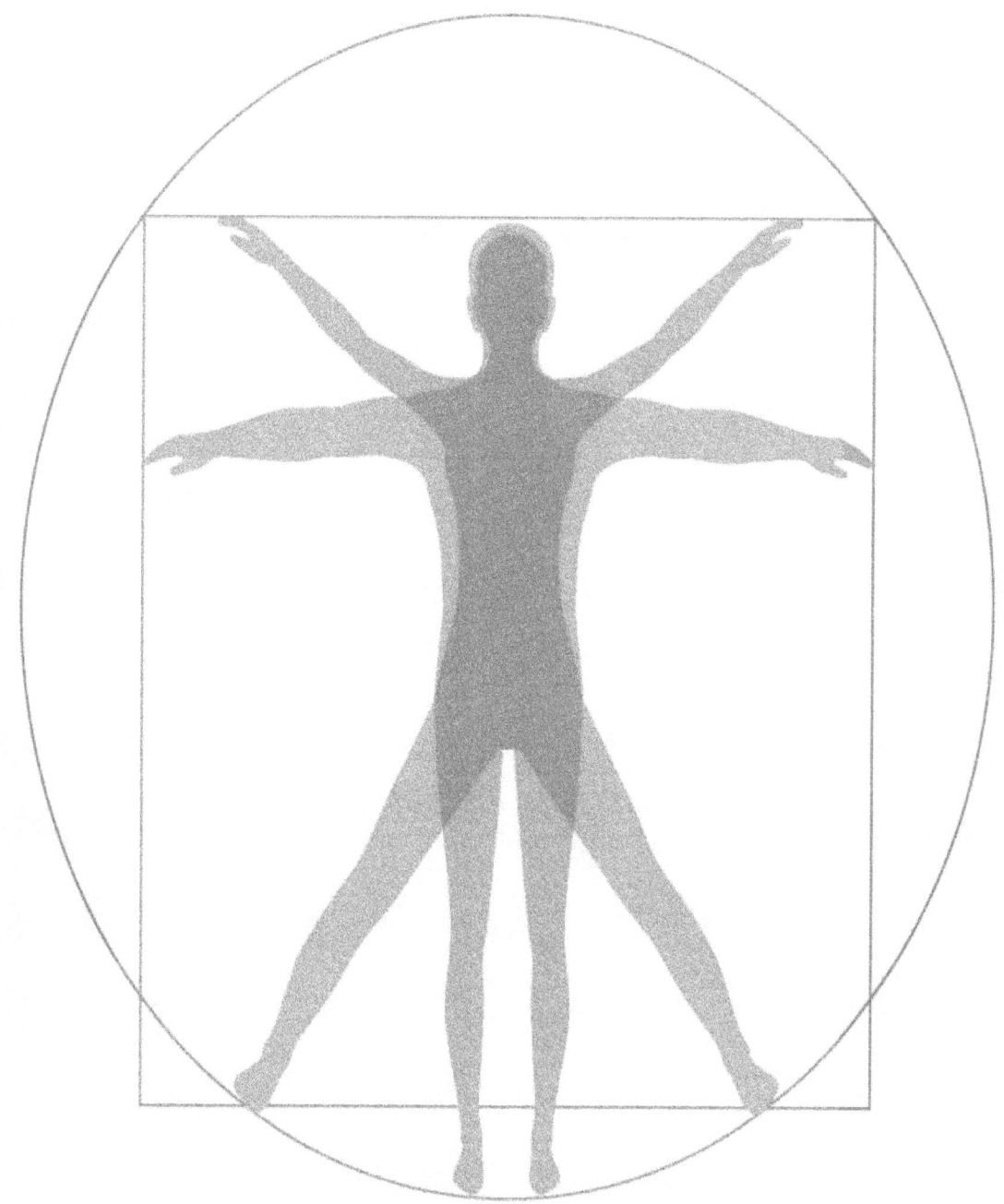

There wasn't, there isn't, and there won't ever be

Anyone like me!

Chunk 1

We Have One Life to Live!

(An Inspirational Booster)

We have one life to live,

One soul to wear

        And one heart inside

        To be charged right,

Not to ever regret

About the life-time uselessly spent!

"Life is a mirror - if you frown at it, it frowns back;

if you smile at it , it returns the greeting."

(A Chinese proverb)

Auto-Induction:

I Never Whine; I Shine!

Chunk 2

Self-Emancipation is a Real Salvation!

The beautiful words by Osho above *"There are two ways in life to be and to know"* determine the conceptual structure of the *Physical Intelligence* part of the book that presents the holistic paradigm of self-creation at the mental level of being. Our primary *self-genesis* starts with figuring out **HOW TO BE** in this world, or how to better adjust to it physically.

"The body is an invisible soul, and the soul is the invisible body." (Osho)

To monitor self-growth and self-modification, we need *a new level of self-awareness* that, in turn, demands a much higher level of intelligence I suggest enriching it holistically, starting with the lowest level of the ten vistas of intelligence to be covered - *General Intelligence.* It comprises *physical, cognitive and digital levels* that form a solid FOUNDATION for other vistas, or compartments of intelligence that we need to install in our brains at the time of the exponentially changing technological reality.

General intelligence is, naturally, *the essential basis for any intelligence* that is to be acquired holistically in five dimensions of self-creation, presented in the holistic paradigm above. You are shaped by the intellectual power that you have *accumulated, selected,* and *disciplinarily-applied.*

"Know Thyself!" We know this provision of God, but we are not fully aware of it. This situation is being generated by the technological revolution that is the greatest challenge that we are facing these days, on the one hand, and our dependence on the society, on the other. Fortunately, inner discontent and the search for balance in life push us forward, on the path of the spiritual quest, anyway. However, *learning to be godly in a godless world of progressive de-humanization* becomes more and more difficult and time-consuming. *The physical, emotional, mental, spiritual and universal growth is **a material process***, to begin with, analogous to the growth of a physical body, the mental body, and the body-consciousness. Notably, we whet our appetite for knowledge with searching for God and getting better informed about our bodies, health, and our physical existence. *The body is a precious possession and taking conscious care of it is our primary duty.*

Physical intelligence enhances health, longevity, love, and ultimately, leads to real enlightenment. We get to know more invaluable information about how the body functions, what energies it, and what forces operate in the twilight realm of matter-body, into which science is now groping its way in the search for the yet unexplainable essence of consciousness that is ruling our lives .and that we are learning to up-grade with the help of new technological breakthroughs. As *Arthur C. Clark says*

"The only way to discover the limits of the possible is to go beyond them into the impossible!"

Whatever we Self-Create, we can Consciously Moderate!

Chunk 3

The Conscious Mind + a Great Spirit = a Healthy Body!

Your body, the spirit, and the mind in sync constitute the sum of total of what you eat, drink, and how you think. *"The power of the physical intelligence is developing rapidly in us now". (Tony Buzan)* We are more aware of the ways our body system is working. **We have become much more health-conscious**. We know how to enhance it with the help of wholesome foods, vitamins, supplements, working out regularly, cutting bad habits, dieting, and meditating. The Internet is booming with all kinds of advice, and the search engines help us explore any health problem.

Thanks to our *growing physical intelligence,* we can form more awareness about the body and its connectedness with the mind that the spirit keeps together. That's why I position the spirit in the center of the self-creation paradigm. Only the freedom of spirit truly inspirits!

The greatest energy remains to be the energy of the unbeatable spirit of Three!

But our goal is not just to sustain life in us better, it is to help the spirit to **keep the form and the content of our life together**. The physical form of life in us needs to be developed in unity with its content in **the physical, emotional, mental, spiritual, and universal dimensions** that in the Book Rationale above is presented as **the Self-Actualization Holistic Pyramid.**

The Spiral of Holistic Self-Actualization to follow:

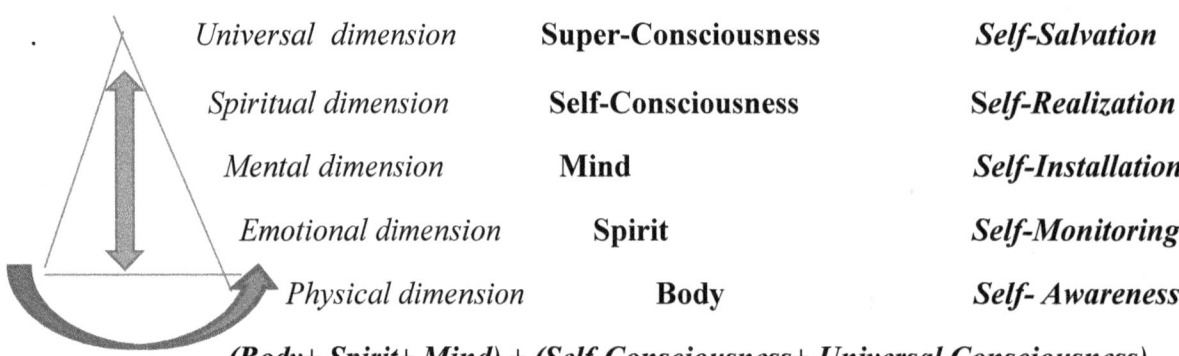

Universal dimension	**Super-Consciousness**	*Self-Salvation*
Spiritual dimension	**Self-Consciousness**	*Self-Realization*
Mental dimension	**Mind**	*Self-Installation*
Emotional dimension	**Spirit**	*Self-Monitoring*
Physical dimension	**Body**	*Self-Awareness*

(Body+ Spirit+ Mind) + (Self-Consciousness+ Universal Consciousness)

(The physical form) **+***(the spiritual content of life)* = *A New Holistically-Developing You!*

I think that a new health system is being formed in us now, *the one that can be consciously operated by Self!* I have verified this system at work with my students for years, and I have always seen an incredible transformation in all of them **both physically and intellectually** because s*piritually-intellectualized self-growth is inherent in us*, and **once I get it re-vitalized inspirationally**, the seeds start growing into the **Tree of Self-Creation** with a consciously-experienced elation.

Physical intelligence also incorporates our inner integrity, family values, and moral standpoints, instilled in us by our parents. It also questions **the existence of a super power over our life and the authenticity of our faith in it**. With knowledge about the body, we acquire more awareness about the quality of life, and *we get physical and spiritual maturity* that helps us **resist the mechanical reaction** to life problems that operate us when we are in a blind, unaware state of mind. As Mr. Ouspensky writes,

"There are only two forces struggling in the world- consciousness and mechanicalness."

Edgar Cayce in his very thought-provoking book" *No Soul Left Behind*" notes that every one of us has a talent for self-promotion –" *the energizing spark that lies within our soul.*" We are all guided by the standards that are shaped by our intelligence and the cultural environment that shapes our values. Edgar Cayce also writes, *"Only constructive, well-formed intelligence may make for better physical and mental development. What we think, what we put into the mind to work upon, to feed upon, to abide by is what we become **because we are what our cells are**"*.

"Our cells in their joint work generate our consciousness."(Edgar Cayce)

Interestingly, the quality of our cells is also directly related to the righteousness of our behaviors and the change in the basic substance of life in us –**"the soul light"**. (*Dr. Frederick. Bell*). Dr. Bell writes that this basic soul light is both positive and negative as everything else in the magnetically-charged world. *He applies the terms fire and water to the masculine and feminine principles, respectfully.* **"As evolution advances, feminine souls display more and more of the fiery masculine qualities, while masculine souls take on the ethereal beauty of the feminine.**" What's most essential is the soul that a human being has and the self-consciousness he / she is developing.

This being said, our growing physical intelligence makes us understand that **it is pointless to verge a fight against gay movement.** Gay people are prone to their self-development as anyone else, and their choice is **the matter of their own soul light and their own soul evolution.** The most important thing is the richness of a person's intelligence and the level of his / her self-consciousness. **Ellen DeGeneres**, for example, is a sparklingly-intelligent, giving, and radiant person. She illuminates the world, and this is what counts most!

Any transformation is the result of the power of thought and the warmth of the heart!

Unfortunately, the forces of attitude, hate, judgment, and, most of all, **ignorance prevail on the lower levels of intelligence in this world.** So, consciousness needs to be considerably heightened so a person could be good, not just appear to be good, and could respect, not just appear to be respectful. **Live and Let live!**

The Ripping Effect of Kindness is Never Mindless!

"Man is a Free Agent!" *(Delia Lama)*

Chunk 4

Holistic Enlightenment is a New Frame of Thinking!

There is much talk about *enlightenment* that we are experiencing on a larger scale now, when people all over the world are getting more and more discontent with the state of things in our minds and hearts. I think that we need to channel this process consciously *on a new, holistic, or unifying level* of our physical existence because new breakthroughs in physics, biology, neuro-science, medicine, and electronics etc. reveal *the scope of our ignorance* about the amazing make-up of our bodies that, as it appears is connected to *the Universal Intelligence that is enveloping us everywhere, digitally.* "We need more awareness than ever of what we think, say, feel, and do". (R. W. Wetherill) You are living at the time of new awareness. So, no point to be careless!

Self-Awareness + Knowledge - Internalizing + Self-Externalizing = Holistic Self-Enlightenment

1. Enlightenment at the universal level is new knowledge-oriented seeing and spiritual growth of any human being in an unbreakable unity with life in its entirety! It has to be our main prerogative in life, the goal that is like a beckon of light in the unknown, unpredictable, and never totally secure ocean of life. It can either leave us helpless and ignorant at *the low tide of our intelligence* or uplift us to the new evolutionary heights with *the high tide of intelligence and self-consciousness* that the Universal Intelligence is directing us . to. (*the Universal level*)

2. Enlightening in the spiritual realm is, the process of *spiritual upgrading of self-consciousness*, limiting or *eliminating completely our still boundless religious ignorance*. We need to focus on and *co-creating ourselves* in the limited time and space that each of us is granted from the Above to complete our mission on earth. (*The Spiritual level*)

3. Enlightenment in the mental dimension of our holistic development means proper digestion of the incoming flood of information and its assimilation that require our conscious interference into *the chaotic process of automatized, unconscious life.* Only applying *the accumulated knowledge of the scientific laws to our thinking, speaking, and acting can we invert the chaos of life*, generated in our minds due to the deflated thinking, to an orderly, governed by reason life of a self-constructive character. *(The Mental level)*

"*Our goal is to make order out of chaos and make music out of noise.*"(Rav. P.S. Berg)

Orderly, enlightened life presupposes organization, discipline, systematization, and rationalization of our thinking. *De-materialization of thinking is the goal of enlightenment!* At present, our being determines our consciousness. But it should be the other way around:

Our self-consciousness should determine our being!

4. *Enlightenment in the emotional dimension* demands developing self-regulation skills, the skills that will help us *operate our emotions in sync with the mind. (The Emotional level)*

Intellectualize the emotions and emotionalize the mind. Be One of a kind!

5. Finally, **enlightenment in the purely physical realm of life** makes it more and more apparent nowadays that *we need more scientific literacy and holistically-applied new knowledge* for the entire process of enlightenment to be successful. " *The world of cells needs to be studied because it will help us understand the fractal nature of cells that have their own individual life"* (*Arthur C. Clarke*)

Apparently, we need to be much more informed about *life on the level of cells* that need to be re-programmed, following the mind-blowing discovery of the fractal nature of life by ***Dr. Mandelbrot***. Following Dr. Mandelbrot's breath-taking revelation, I see ***the natural process of the formation of spiritual fractals of self-symmetry in us as:***

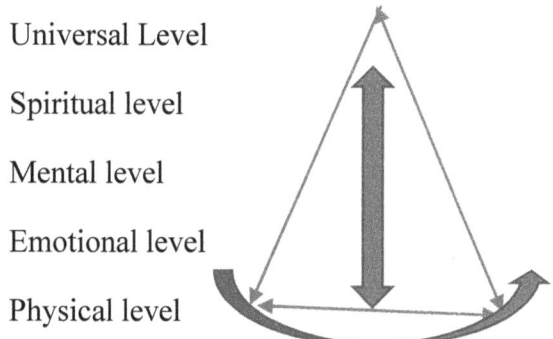

Universal Level	**Oneness** (*Inner Oneness + the unity with all life*)
Spiritual level	**Grace** (*Conscious faith, nobleness*)
Mental level	**Mind** (*Spiritualized intelligence*)
Emotional level	**Spirit** (*Blissfulness, will-power*)
Physical level	**Body** (*Energy, wellness*)

(Body+ Spirit+ Mind) + (Self-Consciousness+ Universal Consciousness)

(The physical form) + (the spiritual content of life)

There is a new branch of medicine, called "***Informational Medicine***", led by *Dr. Bruce Lipton* who urges us to reconsider our outdated knowledge of the role of genes in our life that every school Manuel is promoting as the defining one. Dr. Lipton claims that ***our cells determine our lives,*** and if we learn how to program and re-program them as our ***mini-computers***, we'll be able to improve our health, change the character, and become true masters of our bodies, and therefore, lives. It is also vital that we acquire ***more knowledge of the brain function*** and ***more awareness how to operate it consciously,*** so we could *work out our own knowledge-enhanced, but individually processed through the grid of experiential perception of life* ***our own self-monitoring techniques*** that can propel us to self-installation, self-realization, and, finally, to self-salvation. ***So, the new time demands a Holistic Culture of Thinking!***

My Omega Point is Not Retirement; It's Enlightenment!

Chunk 5

Reign Over Your Brain!

Such transformation requires substantial development in every level of intelligence and *a true modifying of your subconscious mind that needs to be consciously channeling the brain* to the ultimate result - a consequential rise of self- consciousness that will let you re-program your brain by altering its working memory. Your biological computer will get re-charged and re-programmed.

"You are here to enable the divine purpose of the universe to unfold.

That' is how important you are!" (Eckhart Tolle)

Our personal knowledge is the structure of everything we believe in. Every concept, opinion, belief, and value form a little branch of **the Tree of Knowledge** that each of us needs to grow as a branch of *the Tree of Life* that we will leave at some point as of one of its precious leaves.

Psychology proves to us that the feelings of self-accomplishment give us the greatest elation and true feelings of happiness. *The main character of a great movie* **"The Pursuit of Happiness"** *with* **Will Smith** *remembers how happy he was when, as a school student, he got very good grades, anticipating great accomplishments in the future. His dream never got realized.*

But having gone through all kinds of troubles and tribulations and having up-graded his intelligence and done a lot of life-learning, he proved to himself that **he was tougher than his very tough life.** *He became a first-class broker and was offered a great job. This is when he realized what the pursuit of happiness was all about. He said,*

"This is the day of my true happiness. I have created myself!"

In sum, the book **"Living Intelligence or the Art of Becoming"** is an attempt to provide a **comprehensive frame of reference for developing holistic intelligence** as the main prerequisite for a professional self-installation in life that is impossible without a dramatic enrichment of intelligence, much beyond the basic education frame-work!

I provide here just a blueprint that will help you **get out of the labyrinth of self-doubt, desperation, and meaningless existence** and lead you out onto the path of meaningful self-actualization, contentment, integrity, and inner peace.

Life is a form of transformation that starts and ends in you! It's beyond good! It's fantastic! It's phenomenal! Go for it!

Auto-Induction:

I don't need to justify myself; I know who I am in every cell!

Chunk 6

Physical Intelligence without Negligence!

So, *physical intelligence is about self-regeneration, self-creation, self-mastery, and self-actualization*, when you stop being driven by your mind automatically *and live unconsciously*, when you are more able to monitor your physical, emotional, mental, spiritual and, eventually universal states and become *"a Star Person" (John Baines)* in your mind, de juror, and sometime in the unanswerable when, de facto.

Mind, in fact, runs the brain! Be the Master of your Mind!

It is the urgent necessity to apply the power of learning or **the Art of Becoming** as the process of ***holistic accumulation of all the levels of intelligence,*** *presented above*, destroying the walls of resistance:

a) A Physical Wall – *Respect life in ourselves and others in the name of God!*

b) A Linguistic Wall – *Speak consciously! Control the tongue!*

c) An Emotional Wall – *Master yourself! Control your emotions!*

d) A Psychological Wall – *Treat yourself and others consciously and knowingly.!*

E) A Professional Wall – *Work with a new, intellectually and electronically-equipped zest!*

f) A Financial wall – *Manage the money as a tool, not the ruler of life!*

g) A Cultural Wall – *Acculturate yourself! Synergize your life!*

h) A Social Wall – *Expand your social outreach worldwide!*

I) A Spiritual Wall – *"God is one and the only," and we are all One in Him!*

J) A Universal Wall – *Expand your unitarian thinking, cosmic outreach, and possibly extraterrestrial communication!*

Our new scientific world view gives us much new information to absorb about our surroundings, but it also places a burden upon us to find a way to change the structure and quality of our lives to fit into this new reality. This is when a famous call by Thomas Campbell, **"Follow your bliss!"** will become a reality. Obviously, we need to guard ourselves consciously at every of the above-mentioned levels. ***The undercurrent of peace will gradually become our daily bliss!***

Unfold Yourself to the Luminosity of Life beyond Survive!

Chunk 7

A New You is a Better Aware You!

Developing at the physical level means a changed life and a much better aware you. Awareness of the newest developments in brain science, in biology, in nutrition, in the physical aspect of the changes in your body, you wander the world with an open mind and a much more accepting heart, accumulating intelligence non-stop. Revolutionizing our knowledge in the coming years is the first stage of the process of rationalization of our lives.

"Let him who would move the world first move himself." (Socrates)

As we learn about **the neural mechanism of intelligence**, prospects for enhancing intelligence become inevitable. Your better self-awareness, disciplined thinking and **a conscious action**, backed up with **new information that is sorted out for its validity** help you strategize your life. Such self-installation needs constant self-control ,or **self-monitoring** that being the next stage of the holistic paradigm of self-creation *(Chunk 1 above*) is an integral part of each stage.

I'd like to recommend reading a wonderful book" **The Start-Up of You"** by Reid Hoffman and Ben Concha, the two great entrepreneurs from the Silicon Valley. It is addressed to the present-day people with electronically-charged minds who are intellectually and professionally transforming themselves, without blindly following the world around them.

"Be your own coach in life! Become a superior you!"

Reid Hoffman, the founder of "LinkedIn," is calling on us not to succumb to a machine but create more value in ourselves and the world around us by **"proactively investing in our intelligence,** *enhancing our entrepreneurial skills, and expanding our technical know-how."* But such development requires a rigorous **preservation of one's own individuality** and unique way of thinking, without which there is no personal evolution. *"To run a successful start-up of you, you can and must think for yourself, create yourself, and invest in yourself!" (Reid Hoffman)*

"Autonomy of thinking is a Must!"

Obviously, **mind or intelligence is governing our life through its constant evolution**. Unfortunately, it is downright impossible unless we uplift our mental and spiritual levels. The book "***Living Intelligence or the Art of Becoming***" is, in fact, a modest attempt to holistically develop our intelligence and expand the souls by transforming the capacities of our brains so that we could say in the outcome of life, *"No regrets",* or as Mark Twain writes,

"Let us endeavor to live so that when we come to die, even the undertaker will be sorry."

The Highest System of Learning is How We Live Our Lives!

Chunk 8

The Content of Self-Awareness

The content of awareness, or **an objective, independent assessment of reality** and ourselves in it normally starts with our **romanticizing life** first. The period **of conformism** goes next when we adjust ourselves to the society, often losing our own individuality. Finally, we start to **realistically view life.** It happens after we had already faced many challenges and tribulations, when *"the life weariness has already seized the heart" (Joseph Campbell)* So, our awareness goes by this route:

Romanticism ⟶ *Conformism* ⟶ *Realism*

To attain full awareness of the reality at the stage of realism that we inevitably hit, one has to, actually, go through five steps that correspond to five dimensions of life:

1. Self-examination 2. self-analysis 3. self-induction 4. self-training 5. self-actualization

(physical, emotional, mental, spiritual, universal dimensions of self-installation in life)

These five steps in turn, reflect **the five stages of self-creation** that are presented in the first book on **Self-Creation Geology** *"I Am Free to Be the Best of Me"* as.

Self-Awareness ⟶ *Self-Monitoring* ⟶ *Self-Installation* ⟶ *Self-Realization* ⟶ *Self-Salvation*

These steps are essential for framing and re-framing our inner make-up, and they are the concepts of all five books *(Book Rationale, 1)* The third and the forth steps of the auto-suggestive work are the most vital ones in this process because they **build up the immunity against the crowd mentality,** when we are disassociating ourselves from the *"collective unconscious" (Carl Yung).* Unfortunately, right now, *"We are the race of human robots. Most people do not have a thought in their heads that has not been put there by someone or something else." (David Icke)*

"The most important mental and emotional food for our brains now is impression." (Prof. Ouspensky) But the impressions we get from the outside world *need* to be individually processed and rationally sifted for the conscious brain to get food or thought. The impressions that we get from the outside world should not become our inner undigested food that pollutes the mind and corrupts the emotions. The thinking of such a person becomes **deflected from the reality** to the digital realm, or unconscious, impulsive, automatic reactions to the world. Such cluttered minds cannot experience the **CATHARSIS,** or **the state of realization and conscious awareness of the reasons** for the turns and twists of life. The disconnection with one of the main cosmic laws – **the Law of Cause and Effect** is what is in the way of the reasoned-out self-awareness.

We are All just Human Clay!

Chunk 9

Self-Refinement is Mental First!

"Everything in the universe is mental" (John Baines). A human body is a mental energy conduit, too. We need to learn *to channel our mental energy in synch with the universal energy of creation* that is MENTALLY - DIGITAL according to the newest discoveries in physics. We are governed by *the Universal Laws* that we need to be studied and observed without negligence (*Thesis 13*) to learn how to manage ourselves better and in synch with them.

Our purpose is to stop being universally-negligent and become universally-intelligent!

"*Without better intelligence, without acute awareness, without knowing what we really are, we cannot refine even one cell in our bodies." (Don Miguel Ruiz)*

The quality of our life is the quality of our cells ,our biological computers!

I have mentioned above the position of Dr. Bruce Lipton, an advocate of the informational medicine. I think that he is absolutely right, and we do need to re-program ourselves at the cellular level to enhance personal growth of moving between the levels of consciousness. As mental creatures, we must oversee our merging with the universal energy field because we have the divine purpose **to become One with the Universal Intelligence**, to be accepted by it, helped by it, and guarded by it. So, our concerns in the physical dimension of self-perfection should be *our bodies and our intention to preserve them as the vessels of our immortal souls.*

"Take charge of your internal pharmacy!"(Paul Pearsall)

There are zillions of books on a healthy life style. However, working on *heightening our physical intelligence,* **you** should sort out carefully the information that we get from different sources and see what **suits your** *body and mind* **best**. We cannot go with the flow of mass media advertised medications or any medical, dietary, or psychological advice blindly. Our family doctors have become so money-oriented and impersonal in their attitude to an individual case that we have nothing to do but become more self-aware and self-conscious.

It's vital to individualize knowledge-processing with self-awareness and mindedness.

"Know thyself" at each level of the holistic paradigm and in every dimension, or ,in other words*, "practice mind over brain attitude" (Dr. Rudolph Tanzi)* It means having the mind, devoid of inner conflicts and obsessive reactions to the past or the present.

"From Working God to the Working Thought!"*(Sadhguru)*

Chunk 10

"Be Doggedly Tenacious on This Path!" *(T. D. Jakes)*

The processing of the working thought in every dimension should be governed by the following standpoints **consciously, holistically, and auto-suggestively.** Pay **aware attention** to the main inductions ,recommended to be instilled in the conscious mind, too.

1. Physical Level - *mindful body awareness, heal-conscious, nutrition, stress management, language rationality, speech immunity to foul language or negative talking.* Remember, you are best friend; you are your beginning and your end!

Self- Induction: *Eat less, talk less, fight less, and spend less!*

Conduct a self-restriction war - less is more!

2. Emotional Level – emotional awareness, c*ontrolling emotions and* d*eveloping the feelings of love and synergy.* Your main induction should be:

Self-Induction: *The smile, the posture, and a good mood are my emotional food!*

3. Mental Level - mental awareness - a *lot of quality reading, thinking, visualizing, rationalizing, planning, systematizing, studying, and positively projecting, professional realization, creativity, being truly mindful at any action that you perform.* Your main induction should be:

Self-Induction: *"Fertilize your mind with thinking!"* (Albert Einstein)

4. Spiritual Level – *spiritual awareness*, *honest service, interpersonal development, cultural enrichment and responsibility to the society, commitment to self-refinement,* grea*t values, sincere faith.* Your main induction should be:

Self-Induction: *Make your mind kind and your heart smart!*

5. Universal Level - *Internalized rules of living, develop* **spiritualized intelligence**, *correct behavior, unified thinking, high level of consciousness, new horizons of perception of entire life.* Your main induction should be:

Self-Induction: *I am One with everything under the Sun!*

In sum, developing ***the initial personal level of intelligence - Physical Intelligence*** requires much self-awareness that needs to be consciously processed through five level of holistic self-creation., *following the holistic formula of life:*

Self- Synthesis ⟹ Self-Analysis ⟹ Self-Synthesis!

Chunk 11

The Sense of Measure is a Great Treasure!

Physical Intelligence is the basic one is us, and *it should be enhanced with the sense on measure* in our perceiving the life's pleasure and the price we pay for it if we disregard this principle first and foremost! *Higher physical fitness generates higher mental fitness*

Auto-suggestion: *Will your life more! That's the Law!*

So, will-power, self-discipline, self-control, and the ability to deny oneself the excessiveness of any sort: harmful foods, drinks, extra clothing, accumulating different odds and ends, pointless talking, tongue-lashing, impulsive relationships, uncontrolled sex-drive meaningless texting, tended to be cut in the bud.

Self- Induction: *Less is more! That's the Law!*

Remember, change happens *in a spiral upward way - two twists up and one twist back*. Sometimes, two twists back happen to block the advancement So, you *need to mentally condition yourself for consistency auto-suggestively* and go through processing your self-creation with a sane head.

But sanity and good health are earned, they are not a given!

True physical intelligence is working when your mind, will-power and spirit, not the doctors, are involved, "*God cures, and the doctor sends the bill.*" *(Mark Twain)* Keep intellectualizing your heart and emotionalizing the mind by magnetizing your inner core.

The cyclone derives its power from the center!

Do not get inflated with the crowd mentality of common sense. *Think for yourself!* Magnetize your center with the mental power *(Cognitive Intelligence below)* to develop a strong opinion to which people will gravitate for guidance, inspiration, and inner strength.

Finally, be unique, free-spirited, and magnetically–attractive! Belonging to any social or religious dogma, or chauvinism of any sort did not make the humanity any better or any happier, but *personal richness* has inspired and uplifted people for centuries. According to Albert Einstein, "*Everything, even lunacy is mass produced*." For it not to happen, keep repeating:

Self – Induction: *My life equation of pressure and pleasure*

Comes in the bits of treasure

That only the Best of Me can measure!

Live a More Aware Life! Be Totally Alive!

Chunk 12

Self-Concept and a Self-Quest are Abreast!

We are born with a tremendous possibility of intelligence. Each person has his personal level of intelligence, and if that level is too low, conceptually and culturally, it is difficult to attain a higher level of consciousness, but it is not altogether impossible. A person requires *self-awareness,* a *positive self-concept*, and *an inspiring self-image,* to begin with. *(Introduction, Ch. 7)*

> ***Self-concept is the way you think of yourself; self-image is your vision of this thinking.***

Next, it is essential to accomplish *a new, more aware intellectual basis* that will help you develop much deeper, higher, and richer consciousness with a committed effort on your part and full awareness of what you are bettering and why you need to do so. We absolutely need to get rid of **Don Quixote's blindness** and stop fighting with our own windmills - *the self-created and pattern-thinking generated impulsiveness , fears, anxieties, and uncertainties.*

> ***Subjective vision of life must turn into an objective, holistic vision of oneself in the society.***

Self-concept or **a** *clear-cut self-identity* is the starting point on this way. *"Identity is your ability to use who you are to where you find yourself."(T. D. James)* People who seek higher intelligence are easily identified. They have a much broader view of life and of themselves in it. They are very personable, kind, compassionate, giving. Also, they are extremely disciplined, well-organized, and very demanding to themselves and to the people working with them. They are doing all kinds of good deeds because *they have superior criteria in life.* No wonder we call such people quality people.

Quality people *manage to empower their bad habits and accomplish amazing inner integrity.* Their self-concept is maturing together with the resistance to the *"immediate gratification"* demands of the control–resisting body. These people *shine from inside, irrespective of the skin color,* and they are great role-models for the ones who seek a holistic personal growth. A mental picture of what you want to be should be set in your mind's eye as early as possible and kept there the entire life. You may borrow some of the features of the people that you admire but make them yours in size.

> ***Your self-concept and self-image should comprise a unique sense of self.***

Both will be in sync and in a constant formation flow, *in a holistic unity with your inner integrity and the Sense of Self* that you upload each time with the words:

Self- Induction: ***I know who I am!***

Steve Jobs was the business genius of our generation and a real role-model for thousands of young, electronically-minded people because he had this exceptional ***self-developed intelligence and a Strong Sense of Self.***

His professional integrity gave a go-ahead to the intelligence of many people, and he created a clear framework of opportunities and risky alternatives for the exploration of the artificial mind's possibilities that seem to be endless. A great Russian psychologist Leo Vygotsky wrote, *"At the end of your life, all you are going to have is who you have become as a person. All is left for the people behind you."*

"Leave a lot of yourself for them!"

For sure, and all exceptionally talented people, like Steve Jobs, are in constant search for the truth of life and their own special place in it. Obviously, there is no higher consciousness to be developed in us without obtaining higher intelligence that must be every one's prior concern. Insightful self-quest and knowledge in sync uplift us to new levels of consciousness.

Start sculpturing the best of you strategically!

The first strategic strength to acquire is the power of seeing, hearing, knowing and reasoning at a much broader level professionally, culturally and socially. But there is one enemy that we need to beware of and that is our constant battle with change and the desire for permanency. But *"persistence beats resistance!"(Antony Robins*

*)*However, rationalizing our lives and perfecting ourselves is not enough for our spiritual growth.

"We also need to obtain connected consciousness with all."(Schopenhauer)

We have to learn how to be able to **constantly harmonize our lives**, get them **in synch with the Universal Accords,** changing the melody in our hearts to much more harmonious vibrations and becoming whole people that are able to experience **the uniformity with all forms of life,** harmonizing themselves from within and radiating happiness back to the world. We are promised to obtain this skill sometime in the Golden Age of the humanity, **but why not now, in our very limited time / space continuum?** To be more life-fitting, keep repeating:

Auto-Suggestion: *Don't be at rest; be on a spiritual quest!*

Live in God's standards, not in people's grandeurs!

Long Live the Belief in Myself without "If"!

Chunk 13

The Way We Live; Determines the Way We Die!

That is the rule of life that we often disregard. How many times we have heard the Bible statement:" ***Love thyself to be able to love others!*** " However, we keep being discontent with ourselves for every small or big thing that we might have obtained or done not in accordance with someone's, or God's assessment. Our wrong doings get stuck in the personal matrix, and rotten our thoughts, sending us on a guilt trip.

Self- induction: ***Stop being a drama-king / queen / and get serene!***

"***To know thyself***" means to" ***love thyself***" the way you are and to make yourself better every day knowingly. Knowing entails being aware of the traits of character that we need to work on. Then we are growing the personal power that is called ***personal magnetism*** and that makes people around us gravitate to us and like us. This job should start with the formation of ***the strategic Ultimate Result Vision of the best of Self*** that is one of the main concepts of this book. *(Introduction Thesis))* You need to see the ultimate result of your self-creation at its every stage ,starting with the physical one. It means that you need to first ***visualize your sculpturing yourself strategically, then work on your URV tactically*** , level by level (*in the physical, emotional ,mental, spiritual, and universal realms of your life level by level)* , and, finally, see the outcome of your work in a general picture again – ***all the levels in synch.*** They constitute your personal integrity, following the strategic route: ***Self-Synthesis - Self-Analysis - Self- Synthesis!***

Internalizing the information ⟹ ***processing and selecting it for its validity*** ⟹ ***externalizing and actualizing it!***

So, working with the information ***holistically and applying it to self-growth consciously***, you will be forming a luminous vision of the ultimate picture of the best of you and have it as ***a reference point because as you see yourself, so you will be!*** Keep the picture of your ideal self ***(the URV)*** active in your mind at each level, each time revising it and making it even better. ***Upload the URV of yourself into your mind auto-suggestively***, *in accordance with your strategic needs:*

Self- induction: *I know who I am!*

I am a strong, calm, bold, and determined owner of my firm will!

I can…, I want to…, and I will …!

I am becoming better and better……. with each coming day!

In My Life Quest, I Manifest My Best!

Chunk 14

The Ultimate Result Vision of Yourself!

The URV will be changing at each holistic level *(Introduction Thesis 17*) and at each age of our self-growth, in the same way as our perception of different pieces of classic literature changes with maturing of our intelligence and consciousness.

We stop reading junk books, we become more reflective, truly *experiencing the Catharsis* when listening to classical music, reading classic literature, or enjoying the works of art that are always an insightful self-expression of the mind and the heart of the author. we seek wisdom in books and in people around us.

Such change always testifies to the growth in intelligence, human qualities, and life-processed wisdom. People that have it shine from inside with the vintage image of *themselves* ***physically, emotionally, mentally, spiritually, and universally.*** We get mesmerized, listening to their insightful revelations.

So, *the Ultimate Result Vision of yourself* or the VINTAGE YOU IMAGE IS THE ONE THAT YOU OBTAIN HOLISTICALLY. It's an intellectually-integral, self-processed clear picture of yourself in perfect health, as a happy and totally self-actualized ,or self-installed person Develop your own uniqueness, without comparing or contrasting it with someone else's.

Self-Induction: ***Don't compare and don't compete. be in a unique Yourself out-fit!***

It will fill you up with a great sense of magnetic power, and it will ***enrich you with personal magnetism***. You will compete only with yourself in your every cell, making yourself better with each conscious breath. How great the Living Intelligence like that is!

However, the most challenging part of self-work at your **URV** is your ability *to practice what I preach here holistically* through study, practice, intense reading, thinking, creative imagination, constant spiritual growth, and, most importantly, consistent action, fortified by a firm will! Why?

Holistic is a new paradigm in the scientific belief system!

Every branch of science is developing toward **the *unification of knowledge and its synchronizing with the fundamental laws of the cosmos***. Science, technology, business, everything is getting integrated to obtain a more holistically advanced shape, as it had been in ancient times in the *Spartan Education* system in Greece. So, upload the main self-induction for life

Being responsively nice, polite and inwardly-kind means being aristocratically-refined!

Form the Ultimate Result Vision with the Utmost Precision!

Chunk 15

Auto-Suggestive Self-Love Booster

The booster below is **an Active Suggestive Meditation** that you need more than any others at any critical because when we make mistakes, we stop loving ourselves ,and self-guilt is practically eating us out, often giving way to cancer to flourish. I call it ***Self-Love Meditation***. It is very simple, but it is extremely effective ***to boost your, or your kid's self-love and self-confidence.***

a) *Cross your arms as if hugging yourself on the shoulders so that the centers of your palms on both hands that **represent the solar plexus of your body** could lie on the very center of the edges of your shoulders, on their rounding parts. **These are the spots of love!** Embrace yourself in this fashion most lovingly. Then, start moving your hands slowly down your arms, saying to yourself inwardly ,with your eyes closes, exuding self-love, the following booster:*

Auto-induction: *I love myself the way I am!(breathe in slowly)*

b) *When your hands come to the point where **both palms meet at the solar plexus area, put them** facing one another in an opposite mirror fashion, **make a short pause.** Do not breathe for a few seconds, instilling the words in the mind. Then, start **breathing slowly out**, moving the palms apart slowly disconnecting, and bringing them to the initial position by the sides of the body.*

c) *Start breathing in slowly again saying inwardly :*

If any one doesn't like me, (breathe in) Picture the one who doesn't like you.

d) *Now, **shake off your hands vigorously**, thus removing any negative thoughts or feelings that you might have accumulated against yourself or other people that may be having grudges against you and breathing out slowly, **say out loud disarmingly:***

Auto-suggestion: *It's his or her problem, not mine!*

I know who I am!

I do not depend on anyone's opinion.(Breathe in)

I have my own personal continuum! (Breathe out)

Great! ***You have given a boost to your spirit of self-love.*** Keep doing it as often as you need. Don't be apprehensive about practicing these simple exercises. **Simple is power!** "To conquer others is to have power; to conquer yourself is to know the way" (Tara Rae)

Will Your Love More! That's the Law!

Chunk 16

Manage Your Health Auto-Suggestively!

Physical health is your wealth! Physical, emotional, psychological, mental and spiritual wellness are deeply related and interdependent. *In Part Four of the Suggestive Meditation* above, I provide some very simple exercises to follow If God forbid, you get sick, start with changing your thinking about the disease first*. Any disease manifests itself on the mental level first,* so be sure to delete any accumulation of the negative energy in your mind.   Auto-suggestive work is extremely beneficial in dealing with any health problems because it helps *to re-program the mini-computers in the body*, responsible for your health - *your cells.* They illuminate the contaminated cells in the body and *energize them with the electro-magnetic energy of life* ,and cancer cells gets dissolved in that light. The healthy spirit saves the mind and the body because the mind *"can talk to the body, telling it to calm down, to drop the pain, to heal the sick organ"*(Osho" Intelligence

It takes only a stroke to change a minus into a plus! Do it, thus!

The Auto-Suggestive meditation is extremely helpful because *it also connects the mind and the heart in their united struggle for life.* Mental cleansing and visualized breathing will remove *the energy blocks* in your body. You'll have to radiate a lot of compassion, harmony, and love for yourself, and you need *to ask for your body's forgiveness* for having inflicted disease on it through an unhealthy life style. *The authoritative commands, given to the mind , oust darkness from the master computer in your body, and it subsequently gives the same commands to the cells.*

So, when you feel helpless, over-emotional, angry, irritable, put the left hand on your solar plexus and the thumb of right hand on the pulse spot of your left wrist. You will protect yourself from a huge energy drain, on the one hand, and you'll get back to the conscious perception of the life in you, on the other. *The beat of your heart* will remind you of your on-going life auto-suggestively:

21, 21, 21, or Calm down, calm down, calm down, or Thank you, thank you, thank you…

This simple meditative suggestion *will synchronize every cell in your body with your self-managed vibration flow* that, in turn*, will synchronize you with your mind without fail.* Get in love with your life, body, mind, heart, liver, lungs, etc. *Boost them, too!!!*If you practice this simple exercise continuously, you will acquire a **HEALING MODALITY** of the *brain energy.* Intelligence will become the ruling force in your cells that will do the job OBIDIENTLY.

Auto- Induction: *I can be healthy, I want to be healthy, and I will be healthy!*

I am becoming better and better, healthier and healthier with each coming day!

"Take care of the outside for people, take care of the inside for God!"

Chunk 17

Will-Power is Your Main Physical Sculptor!

Will-power formation is the key in the Art of Living at any level. (Introduction, Thesis 15) Self–management techniques are based on developing the will-power as an essential requirement in self-construction and self-actualization. Below, there are a few *general tips on building up will-power* to change your thinking culture and fortify your self-management skills that you develop with your growing intelligence.

"The brain is the atlas of the mind." (Guy Harrison)

1. *The brain needs order because order means stability.* No dissipated or messed up mind is able to generate new ideas or focus on bettering its owner. We absolutely need to put our thoughts in order to be aware of them at any moment and to be in charge of the mind that operates the brain.

2. *Conscious work on changing our conditioned brain patterns* is the next step on the path of rationalizing our thinking and bettering our life. Nothing must be done on the automatic pilot; every thought that generates your word must be channeled toward a better, more reasonable and insightful one. *(General- specific-general / synthesis- analysis -synthesis))*

3. *Only by consciously monitoring our own behavior patterns can we say no to suffering.* Lack of *the sense of measure* in our indulgence with the *"immediate gratification"* pattern of life ruins our will-power and *generates complexes of inferiority and ruinous self-pity.* We should avoid wasting time when dealing with emotional turmoil. *Acquiring mental and emotional equilibrium is a primary goal in self formation.* Use the following auto-induction form: *Right is My Might!*

"*Always think, say and do what is right. Refuse to think, say and do what is wrong!*"

4. *Develop your aware attention skills; stop living on the automatic pilot!* Much knowledge needs to be accumulated into an aware attention framework. Every level of intelligence that we outline in this book presupposes a new level of awareness to be developed accordingly.

Self-Induction: *Even when I am totally wrong, I am aware of it and strong*!

5. *We desperately need to monitor ourselves emotionally,* managing our emotions and developing our intuition that is our inner guide in life. Emotions are the messages from inside, and our intuition is inseparable with them. Peeling off the layers of automatic reactions and bad habits, we give space to the soul to feel, perceive, and prompt our actions to follow intuition. As a result, we will *read into the life coincidences*, and reason out better the gut feelings of warning against wrong doing.

6. We must monitor ourselves strategically first and tactically then by *instilling the Ultimate Result Vision of self-creation in the mind* and channeling ourselves along the paths of upgrading our intelligence to accomplish it.

7. *The philosophy of love literally regenerates us*! It had been instilled in us by Jesus Christ and love is the most effective consciousness upgrading tool. Science has proven that *the neurological place of love is in the mind.*

Self-suggestion: ***To be a love-kind, rewind the mind!***

We come to know that any disease manifests itself as a lack of love first on the mental level, then on the emotional level, and finally, on the physical one. Creating more love for ourselves and the people around us, we draw the shot-cuts for managing any situation and develop *the will-power of love.*

Auto-induction: ***"The measure of love is love without measure!"***

Finally, you might argue with me that all my arguments are valid and that you have read a lot about self-transformation in many other sources, but the cart of your self-installation in still there. You, most likely, haven't moved it forward that much, nor have you put much of effort into filling it up with the three essential steps in will power formation:

Self-Suggestion- ***Resist, reject, reform to self-transform!*** – **369** *(the magic number)*

No doubt, we all need huge work to be done. We all need the above-mentioned techniques to be applied on a regular basis to get into a better shape, consciousness-wise. But if we just talk, read about it, but not work on it, we'll end up our life with the dash between the dates of the birth and death. There will be no transformation, no actualization, no self-realization, *just a wasted life* with many regrets and unfinished bets.

Self-induction: ***I do not depend on anyone's opinion;***

I have your own personal continuum!

Don't Let Anything Rot in Your Inner Store;

"Will Your Life More!"

Chunk 18

Moral Intelligence Without Negligence!

Physical intelligence is inseparable with moral intelligence. It is another angle of the aware vision of yourself in the world. Be mindful that we generate it at the lowest level of self-growth. *Moral integrity* needs to be instilled in us as early as possible, and in many cultures, it is a natural rule of life. Naturally, with your growing intelligence, your morality should take an individual form, not the society, family, friend, or any common-wisdom affected.

As the form of your life is changing, the content should be altered accordingly!

The concept of morality is inseparable with *"pure reason." (Emanuel Kant)* According to Kant's ethical philosophy," *without insightful reasoning, there is no moral philosophy of pure reason"*. The foundation of life is based on *"a working criterion that any rational agent supposedly employs as a guide in making his own choices and judgments."*

"Intelligence and morality are the result of brain development." (Richard S. Haier)

Obviously, a moral you is the person with *a purified mind and a stable, integral morality.* Gradually, through experience, extensive reading, thinking and watching the people that are much wiser than us, we come to realize that our destiny and the whole purpose of being here are guided by the forces that have a much larger perspective on the world stage and that are based on the *godly principle of goodness versus evilness.* These principles are instilled in us by our parents, and they are the explicit values of any religion. Thanks to this moral foundation, you can say self-suggestively:

I can remove my past emotional knots and deal with the present-day warts!

We all know that moral self-perfection is a life-long commitment that requires a lot of reasoning and will-power, and *a lot of self-purifying, both mentally and emotionally.* In the course of intelligence enrichment and spiritual enlightenment, we start merging our consciousness with everything, expanding our intelligence beyond the physical, emotional, and moral intelligence. Through this expansion, we are accumulating *inner integrity* that will never leave us once it gets rooted inside. Then, all the experience and knowledge that we have been processing in our minds *reach a critical mass.*

It's the state of **CATHARSIS** that we go through when the realization of the true value of things happening to us hits us. *We start reasoning at a higher level of self-consciousness!*

We Have a Rebirth of Self-Worth!

Chunk 19

Love Awareness with Fairness!

Love is the main ingredient of our happiness, and *the Love Skills* are the essential skills t of the physical, emotional and psychological intelligences that are interconnected. We need to instill the sacredness of the feeling of love *in the minds and hearts of our kids and ourselves in sync* as early as possible and as entirely as possible.

We have great movies, poems, novels about the beauty of love and its sacredness, and our schools should make this wealth accessible to the kids in the class- rooms. Otherwise, we see how early kids become sex-oriented, paying attention to looking sexy much more than *being worthy of love physically, emotionally, mentally, spiritually, and universally.*

Love is also the main motivator of our self-creation and self-realization. When we are in love, we can move mountains inside, and we can fly! The most fantastic pieces of poetry and art, numerous innovations and discoveries were made in the name of love. Humans, being the main constructive creators of life, need their *minds to be inspired and their hearts to be excited in an inseparable unity* that only love can provide. .The new discoveries in neuro-science prove that love has the neuro-logical basis, and *the seat of love is not in the heart; it is in the mind*

But in the situation when the mind and the heart are in conflict, science suggests going after the heart. *Love needs to be nurtured in us since berth*, and this fragile feeling should be studied (*see" Emotional Intelligence' below*) and sacredly treated to be holistically flourishing in us at all levels of self-creation : *physical, emotional, mental, spiritual, and universal.*

I expand my space of love

To the left, right, and Above!

I embrace everyone who's upset or feels dark,

And all those that have no luck!

I radiate my love to all of them,

Right into their brain stem!

For the brain, not the heart,

Learns the Love Art!

"We live the way we love, and we love the way we live!"

(Ursula Gorczak)

Chunk 20

Staying Young is Real Fun!

Aware attention, consciously monitored by the mind *uplifts the body's vibrations*, changing the frequencies of our thoughts, words, and feelings about our health, and the entire physical state. We heighten our consciousness, strengthen our immune system, *and rejuvenate the body.*

Auto-induction: *You are inseparable with your brain, or you are insane!*

We can also inspire the mind for a much longer, younger life. When we think young, we become younger! In fact, there are three different ages that we have:

1. **Chronological** - *how old you are according to your passport.*

2. **Physiological** - *how old you feel you are.*

3. **Psychological** – *how old you think you are!*

Instill in yourself the program for a much younger age or eternal youth and keep saying auto-suggestively the mind-set below. It will help you stay as young as you want. I was inspired to write it having read the book *"Ageless Body, Timeless Mind" by, Deepak Chopra* years ago. It is still working!

A light heart lives long. " (William Shakespeare)

What kind of person you are now and what you will be in the process of self- creation will result into what kind of person you will be leaving this earth. Keep suggesting a much younger age to your mind with the feelings of gratitude to your body and God for the gift of life that you have. Do it without regrets, blames, grudges, discomfort, and thoughts about a wasted life. It's in no way wasted if you are holding this book in your hands.

Here's **the Auto-Inductive Program for youth** that I say to myself every morning, looking into the mirror. Choose the age you feel most comfortable to project to yourself.

I am 27 (...) and not a day more!

I am as young as ever before!

I am dynamic, as ever; I am sluggish - never!

I was, I am, and I will be young - forever!

Long Live the Beat of "So Be It!"

Chunk 21

Self-X-Raying is Inner Self-Portraying!

It is not an overstatement to say that there is a direct link between your concept of self and the ultimate outcome of your life. Objective, not subjective, **self-assessment, or self - X-raying** helps form an objective self-image. It needs to be distinguished from self-criticism, though. You are not self-critical; *you are **self-shaping, self-steering, and self-reforming**!*

Life is a process of challenging and responding, not judgement-forming.

The challenges are always there, but your responses to them make a difference. *'To have eyes to see and ears to hear,"* you need **to halt any images of fear on this way**, willing another image of the positive outcome through the mind and heightening the level of self-awareness with each new level of intelligence that you are empowering in a spiral way.

Remember also, that **you are being assessed by the people around you**, too. We get grades for our looks, speaking and acting.

Auto-suggestion: *Always beware! There are eyes and years everywhere!*

Self-X-raying is a tactical action before forming a strategic one, which is shaping and re-shaping your self-image that also demands that you get more aware of the reality so that you could **rationalize your life better, step by step.** In the turmoil of automatic existence, we often forget to watch ourselves for the correctness of our thoughts, words, and actions.

This being said, in order to form an objective self- image, we need again, for the reference point, to familiarize ourselves with the fundamentals of the Law of the Right Human Behavior," by Richard Wetherill. As R. Wetherill puts it, *"Always think, say and do what is right; refuse to think, say or do what is wrong."* Assess yourself from these premises.

Auto-induction: *I know who I am!*

I am a strong, calm, bold, and determined owner of my firm will!

I can…! I want to…! And I will…!

Remember that you are competing with yourself every day, becoming better and better, stronger and stronger, more reasonable, rational, much calmer and self-possessed. An objective, **not subjective** self- determined identity is the first step in forming **a constructive self-image** that becomes the starting point in self-creation. *Your **Ultimate Result Vision of self,** (the URV)* is based on the self-concept that comprises your vision of self.

Auto-Induction: *As you see yourself, so you are! If you like yourself, so do the people.*

The process of projecting an exciting and attractive self-image and developing personal charisma should never stop. The real you is the one you can **consciously watch, monitor, and control with awareness, self- love, and appreciation for what you have already accomplished** on the path of professional and personal self-installation , no matter how little that accomplishment may be.

Auto-Suggestion: ***Two steps forward, one step back is your life track!***

One step back needs to be taken to assess your moving forward with aware attention because you will have a bigger picture of what you have become Self-image is also *your point of reference* and your fort. In any challenging situation, your self- induction *"I know who I am!"* is **your inner gravity and the core of your personal magnetism**. It will help you stay on the right path even if a temptation you might be facing is difficult to resist.

Auto-Induction: *To double my life force, (breathe in) I become my own boss!(breathe out)*

To begin with, *get an objective snapshot* of who you are and where you are now. Below, you can see the most fundamental questions to ask yourself, doing the self-assessment X-raying. Do not rely on anyone's impression of you. ***Check out how self-aware you are most objectively!***

Auto-Induction: ***Be a thing in yourself! Trust yourself!***

There are many sites now that address self-growth, promising success, money, and health. Be sure to trust your own Self and your intuition more, and do not get deviated from your ***holistic plan of action.*** Enrich your knowledge after you select the valuable information for yourself, but do not change the tracks.

Dissipated consciousness is always a dead end!

Do the Auto-Suggestive Meditation continuously

Help yourself help you!

(See Part One, Chunks 11-14)

Auto-Induction:

I am Not in Anyone's Delirium; I have My Own Life Continuum!

Chunk 22

Self-Assessment Questionnaire:

*1.**Do you accept yourself** physically, emotionally, mentally, spiritually, and universally?*

*Are you aware of any **shortcomings** in your character, speaking, behavior?*   **Yes / No**

*2. Do you **get defensive** about criticism? Do you react to it?*

*3. Do you **feel out of place** anywhere?*

*4. Do you try to be **emotionally- attuned** to anyone or to any unexpected situation?*

*5. Do you ever **care for anyone** else besides yourself?*

*7. Does **appreciation of people** mean a lot to you?*

*8. Do you **appreciate others** as much as yourself?*

*9. Do you **feel comfortable with yourself**?*

10. Are you self-sufficient, able to be alone and to take decisions on your own?

*9. Do you **feel comfortable with people**? Do you like socializing?*

*10. Do you **respect yourself** and stand up for yourself/?*

*11. Do you **listen to your voice within**?!*

*12. Do you truly and unapologetically **love yourself**?*

*13. Do you **talk negatively about yourself** in front of other people? etc.*

*14. **Do you hold your posture, a smile and a good mood**?*

There is one more question that is very important to consider because it relates to a very insightful observation made by Carl Yung,

"If you want to get to know a person better, check his / her attitude to money."

Carl Yung considered the attitude to money to be **the basis of our emotional connection** with people. He writes that if a person is cheap in terms of money, he will be cheap in love that is the basis of all relations between humans. Assess yourself in every aspect of this question on the scale from **1 to 10** to get a very objective picture of your emotional intelligence that is inseparable with the physical one *(See Stage Three, Emotional Intelligence below)* So, here we go: *15. **What is the basis of your emotional connection with people?***

Is it money, love, codependence, independence, pride, love, superiority, inferiority, compassion, self-pity, self-confidence, etc.? You might answer that it depends on who you deal with. But then, ascertain the three aspects that your emotional connection with people depends on, irrespective of the life circumstances.

Even if you have answered most of the above questions positively, and answering the last question presents you as a pretty good person, *improve this picture of yourself, anyway! Upload your memory with fresh self-information! Memory changes yourself-consciousness!* When you improved it, improve it again and again! Also, remember your accomplishments.

"Learning is remembering!"(Plato)

To never stop reflecting on your self-image, start developing your inner gravity or **the gravitational, magnetic power.** Self-image is created in the clash between the external and internal factors of life. The internal factor has to be much stronger to help you create an unbeatable self-image. Be proactive, not reactive in life. A person who is inwardly strong has **solid inner gravity** that won't let him / her get swept off his reasoning and do stupid things that are wrong, to begin with.

Your inner gravity is also anchored in your will-power!

So, devote time to studying yourself *from inside out.* To gain more self-knowledge, try to assess your every action and X-ray every word that comes from your mouth for their gravitational power. If people gravitate to your thoughts, words, actions and your conceptual reaction to their behavior, it's the best indication of your being right about yourself and your self-knowledge.

Self- Induction: *I do not spread any personal poison, only personal charm!*

Pay attention to the suggestive meditation .in connection with your breathing at any time and in any place! It relates to self-boosting, self-inspiring, and self-refining.

Auto- Induction: *I never whine(breathe in); I self-refine!(breathe out)*

And again: *Will your life More!(Breathe in) That's the Law!(Breathe out)*

"Be Your Authentic Self!"(Dr. Phil) **Be Yourself!**

Chunk 23

Beauty is Me; Beauty is My Philosophy!

Enlightenment is, in fact, a holistic refinement of a person that constitutes inner beauty., It's our overall wisdom that encompasses our education, personal processing of the acquired knowledge, demonstrating the ability to sort it out in a new way and apply it to life and living..

Auto-Induction: ***The inner dignity of the whole is the aristocratism of my soul!***

As our *self- awareness changes, we start to live consciously,* with much more appreciation of life and the new developments in science that change the thinking and perceiving mind. ***We stop living on the automatic pilot of the mass-media governed riot!*** The market rule, "***Sex cells!*** does not have its power on us anymore because we've had too much of this product . Repulsion is often the reaction! We are becoming more human, more rational, more aware of the consequences of our actions, and ***much stronger in our gravitational power***. It Mind it, please, that this state is very real, and it implies that we absolutely need to think not of the physical or mental improvement only. ***Your goal is holistic beautifying of your life*** in five life dimensions: physical, emotional, mental, spiritual, and universal.

Acquiring the Living Intelligence holistically, we are deepening our knowledge of the totality of life. Also, we get better energized, more intellectualized and emotionalized, much better informed, and totally reformed! Finally, we start realizing the moral difference in ourselves because everything is perceived in comparison. We start shining, illuminating our own life and the lives of others.

Self- Induction: ***I'm my own mate; I illuminate my fate!***

Obviously, *there is* **no moral transformation without the mental one** that presupposes that we become able to interpret God – the Universal Intelligence at work thanks to our developed moral intelligence, not sporadically and out of fear of sin, but consciously and rationally, feeling the empowerment inside that uplifts to God because you become worthy of being godly. So, our life should be focused on ***self-knowledge and self-transformation*** as a tiny cell of the Universal Intelligence that we perfect with our existence and rationalized thinking.

On this path, we should beware, though, because "*the main dangers of insanity, cruelty and obsession are generated by the feelings of inferiority or superiority."* (Sigmund Fraud) Human nature is weak, changeable, and self-contradictory. *"Being detached, loving life in all its manifestations frees the spirit form these demons, but it is the hardest job on earth."* (Buddha)

Self-induction: ***I love my life at its every turn, and life loves me in return!***

A Holistic Me is an Aristocratic Me!

Chunk 24

To Life-Thrive, Envision a Better Scenario in Life!

In conclusion of my outlining **the conceptual basics of the Physical Intelligence**, I'd like to accentuate an absolute necessity **to train your imagery** that I call aware attention training with the suggestive meditation techniques, outlined above, **visualizing the Ultimate Vision of the Best of You** (*the URV*) at in each dimension holistically.

Scientists suggest **we talk to our organs**, programming the mini-computers, our cells, for heath and success in life. Dr Mirza Narbekov(*"Body and Spirit Training"*) recommends focusing our thinking on this or that organ of the body, imagining it **getting warmer or colder** at the will of a thought. He calls it *"a contactless massage."* Without any physical contact, by just using the power of your thought, you can change the physical state of any organ, especially if there appears to be a problem. Here is how you are going an auto-suggestive way. I have been using th method for years, and it works without fail.:'

Try a Contactless Massage

By the power of your imagination, command to the ailing organ *(no such work on the heart or the head!)*. **to get hot, hotter, very hot**, regulating your breathing in an auto-suggestive way. *Make a pause; do not breathe. Breathe out, releasing the command. Relax. Start breathing again, commanding the organ* **to get cold, colder, very cold make a pause.** *Breathe out, releasing the cold. Relax. Repeat until the pain is gone. Send love to this organ and thank it for servicing you well.* **Conclude the meditation with a declarative statement that you need.**

Auto-Induction: ***I can** (feel better, be healthy, etc)**! I want to! And I will!***

By the same token, ***you can imagine a much better scenario of your life!*** Upload the scenario of the life you want into your mind and enjoy watching the success-movie when need be, or before falling asleep. Relax completely and smile widely, enjoying your new life. ***See yourself in it in your URV image*** that you have created at the start of your self-quest.*(Part One, thesis 15)* Always supplement your vision with a good mind-set. Oversee your breathing, **having the mind and the heart work in synch.**

The union of the mind and the heart makes you double smart!

Such visualizing pumps up emotional gas into your veins and helps you spread your wings Upload the movie into every cell of your brain Let this movie have the episodes of love, your accomplishments in life, and the recognition at a job, your kind deeds, the moments of standing up for yourself or for other people that have no guts to do that. ***Get into the habit of visualizing a better scenario of your life every night.***

A lot of information on applying **the Law of Attraction** and sending the messages to the universe to boost your success, etc in life can be obtained on the Internet, too. Train yourself to be exceptional!

Unfreeze your uniqueness in the mind! Be One of a kind!

Positive, constructive, and **energy imbuing visualization** helps the brain extract dopamine that warms up you spirit and embraces your soul! Imagine yourself becoming empowered by *a new frame of thinking* that I have strategized here for you.

It's a conscious synergetic approach that instills a new mode of thinking into your brain and boosts the motor of your life – your constructive, unbeatable spirit!

Always have the holistic paradigm at the front of your mind! Be holistically-refined!

Body+ Spirit+ Mind + Self-Consciousness+ Universal Consciousness

= A New Integral Self!

The Pyramid of Holistic Self-Resurrection

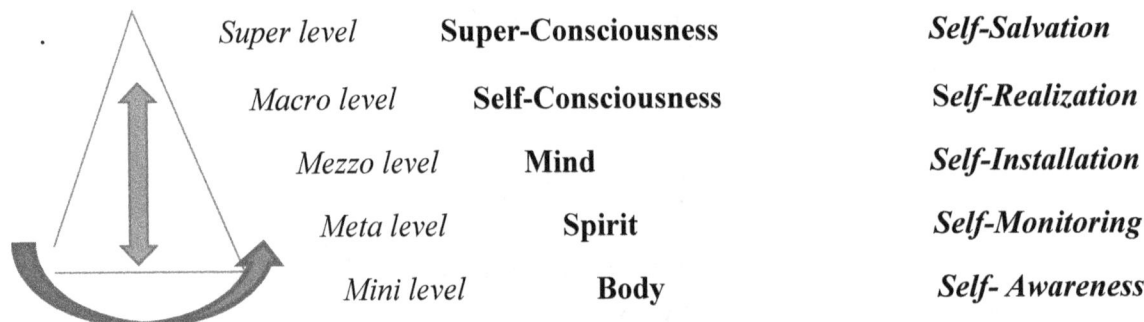

Super level	**Super-Consciousness**	*Self-Salvation*
Macro level	**Self-Consciousness**	*Self-Realization*
Mezzo level	**Mind**	*Self-Installation*
Meta level	**Spirit**	*Self-Monitoring*
Mini level	**Body**	*Self-Awareness*

(For more see the first book on Self-Creation: " I am Free to Be the Best of Me!"

Be a Sage on Your Personal Stage!

(End of Stage One, Division 1 - Physical Intelligence)

Vistas of Intelligence to Install Next:

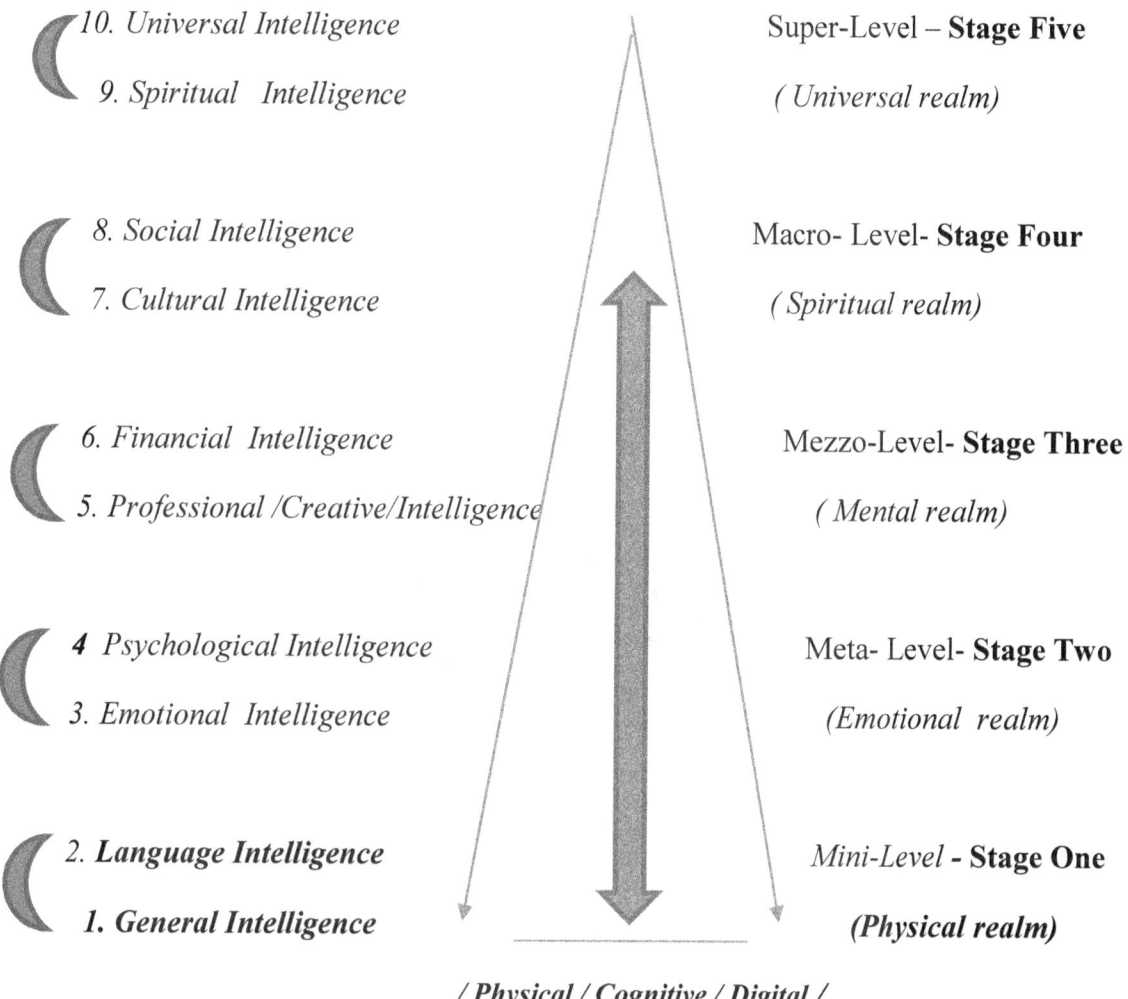

10. *Universal Intelligence*	Super-Level – **Stage Five**
9. *Spiritual Intelligence*	*(Universal realm)*
8. *Social Intelligence*	Macro- Level- **Stage Four**
7. *Cultural Intelligence*	*(Spiritual realm)*
6. *Financial Intelligence*	Mezzo-Level- **Stage Three**
5. *Professional /Creative/Intelligence*	*(Mental realm)*
4 *Psychological Intelligence*	Meta- Level- **Stage Two**
3. *Emotional Intelligence*	*(Emotional realm)*
2. *Language Intelligence*	Mini-Level - **Stage One**
1. *General Intelligence*	**(Physical realm)**

/ Physical / Cognitive / Digital /

*"**Fertilize your mind with thinking!**"* (Albert Einstein)

To Make Your Life Wise,
Strategize – Optimize - Actualize!

Stage One

Mini-Level of Intelligence - Physical Dimension

Cognitive Intelligence

(General Intelligence - The Primary Self-Genesis)

Division 2

The Time of Digitized Intelligence has Come!

To Be Interesting, Get Interested!

The Art of Living is the Art of Learning!

Chunk 1

Intelligence is the Universal Language of Life!

The second vital part of the *General Intelligence* formation is the necessity *to know* more.

There are Two Ways in life - to Be and to Know! " Osho

A new approach to knowledge accumulation, or *cognition* is required at our times not only to sustain the pressure of the exponential growth of technology and a fierce competition, but *to deal with the inner pressure for the necessity of a personal self-expression* that keeps us wishing to erupt with the force we had never known so far.

I see *Cognitive Intelligence* as a sub-level of the physical one because language and cognition are the foundation for our human essence. I started the holistic paradigm of intelligence formation with the physical intelligence only because it has overwhelmed the humanity. We are more conscious of the physical aspect of survival now, and the body is, after all, the most intelligent machine that *accumulates the memory or the intelligence* for us to function at the biological and mental levels in an inseparable unity.

Don't be in a rush to become biological trash!

I keep accentuating an evident fact that *intelligence enrichment is getting more and more neglected by our youth.* Pleasure mongering, immediate gratification of it, money-chasing, drugs-addiction, and alcohol are consuming many young, gifted minds, and this book is written for them, as a wake-up call

The power of our intelligence determines the life without negligence!

Our intelligence is closely interwoven with our consciousness that is governed by the Universal Intelligence. Meanwhile, *"Ignorance is still the worst enemy of the humanity." (Albert Einstein).* How great and how simple these words are and how often they are repeated to no avail! *No technology can heal ignorance; we need to irradiate it in ourselves* by discovering new and new dimensions of the unknown.

The only true wisdom is in knowing you know nothing." (Socrates)

The universal knowledge is infinite, but our personal knowledge of everything should not be *finite* because it is a never-ending process of the evolution of life. Fortunately, we are gradually realizing an urgent need for *converting the automatic processes of digitizing of our minds into the conscious processes of controlling and re-programming them* for the goals of our evolution.

"We must use the brain to intentionally alter the way in which it is organized and the way it makes connections to rationalize our behavior." (Deepak Chopra) It's important to mention here that *intellectuality is often mistaken for intelligence."*

"An intellectual has ready answers for everything; his mind is closed, it's frozen in his patterns of thinking. He is knowledgeable, but not intelligent." ("Intelligence," Osho) **We should not live on borrowed information;** we should seek the information that expands our own intelligence, independent of the opinions of those individuals whose intelligence is damaged by *"**collective psyche**" (Carl Yung).*

"Real intelligence is an open sky. No one limits you!" (Osho)

Albert Einstein never identified with the image that the collective mind had created in him. He remained independently-authentic in his mind, in his *"**thinking laboratory**."* Long after he became an icon, a celebrity genius, he ruefully and most modestly confessed,

"I am no Einstein. I'm just a thinker."

A holistic mode of knowledge acquisition that this book is advocating for is not a mechanical combination of thought patterns. ***It is pre-programmed by the whole evolution*** We cannot but marvel at the honeybees that use abstract reasoning, learning, accurate decision-making and display an amazing amount of *"accelerated intelligence". (Ray Kurzweil).*

Researchers observe a certain amount of intelligence in plants and even in stones. Paying *aware attention* to nature and to life in its every form, *we are learning to become life-conscious and life-appreciative, respecting intelligence in everything around us and displaying our own.*

Auto-Induction: *I have a spiritual glee.*

I am in love with life, and life is in love with me!

In My Thought,

I Plug Myself to the Universal Life Volt!

Chunk 2

Elevated Self-Consciousness

I have outlined **Physical Intelligence** as the first stage in the holistic paradigm also because it initiates **the process of self-quest** that is people's life commitment now. We are much more aware of the physical state the body, **working as a system.** We are yet to realize that our bodies are run by the highest intelligence that we have just started to unravel, and this intelligence is the product of the evolving self-consciousness.*(Introduction, Thesis 2,"Consciousness Integration).*

We do not run our bodies, the energy of intelligence does!

There is no intelligence without knowledge, and *"the world is the mountain of knowledge." (Albert Einstein)* There is no intelligence without the cognitive intelligence because cognition means knowledge.

Cognitive intelligence is at the base of any intelligence because it is intelligence itself!

Cognition is the process that requires *"cognitive structuring and restructuring of our lives."(Watson and Tharp)* I will just outline here some major points to consider because self-consciousness is based on intelligence, and it is very low with us now. *"Science proves that mind-body connection, blood vessels, brain cells, and cognition are related A conscious mind becomes activated through the accumulation of knowledge and overall awareness of one's place in the river of life. (Rave. .PS. Berg)* **Self-awareness generates self-worth with the help of growing intelligence.**

The thinking process converts knowledge to energy, and it is mental energy that is our engine in life. Science teaches us that the structure of matter is dependent on the universal intelligence or consciousness that is still the puzzle for us to unravel. It means that the acquisition of knowledge is not merely a transfer of information from one source to another. The roots of knowledge run far deeper than the intercourse between a mother and a child, a teacher and a student, a body and the mind, a computer and a user. *It is our responsibility to change our cerebral script and elevate ourselves consciously!*

Those that defy the gravity of the common - fly; those that crawl - die!

There are many people that can be called *"giants of intellect, but pigmies of consciousness." (David Eike).* Knowledge is not just accumulating information that makes us more powerful. Knowledge becomes power only when *it is processed consciously, selected for its validity, and is turned into real wisdom*, having been verified by the right action.

Knowledge is Chaotically Mis-leading now!

Chunk 3

The Art of Thinking is the Art of Conscious Learning!

It is very hard to live, not thinking. However, the greatest part of people's thinking is involuntary, automatic, repetitive, and therefore, it is devoid of real quality that conscious thinking should manifest. *Since the mind is conditioned by the past*, we are pushed to repeat the past habitual actions again and again, governed by the sub-conscious mind *that is not yet holistically-re-wired.*

The greatest enemy of the non-thinking mind is its divisiveness and automatism.

The duality of our perception of the world and automatic thinking result in automatic learning that results in accumulating unprocessed knowledge that only clogs the brain. Ignorance manifests itself in and our automatic actions that we always find the way to justify. As a matter of fact, self-justification for the repeated mistakes stands in the way of self-modification and self-actualization, or in the way of the *rationalization of thinking through the paths of logic, with the aware attention guiding the process.* A creature of habit is unable to reason, make correct conclusions and take a reasoned-out action because he/she is *lacking this thinking culture*, to begin with. Lack of reading means lack of thinking resulting from the lack of knowledge.

"Most people would sooner die than think; in fact, they do so."(Bertrand Russell)

Mind without conscious control and order becomes neurotic, unbalanced, destructive, and restless *"One of the greatest blessings in the world is to have sound, healthy mindfulness. The one who possesses it is the most fortunate. When you achieve such healthy mindedness, you are a free human being!" (Delia Lama)* But this mindfulness comes only with a fully e self-educated mind.

Healthy mindfulness means having a mind devoid of inner conflicts, uneven emotional reactions, and obsessive behaviors. Even though thinking comes naturally to us, we need to study the techniques of *productive, self-monitored, and self-constructive thinking.* Apparently, the process of up-loading the information into the biological computers, our brains, needs to be modified, cutting *the automatic, uncontrolled perception of* it in the bud.

We are of a four-fold bind – the soul, body, spirit, and the mind!

The mind unites these four parts into one - *the Ultimate Result You, the Vintage You, or the Integral You!* Science shows that we are of two minds. The left hemisphere is rational, analytical, and logical. The right hemisphere is nonlinear and instinctive. The left hemisphere reasons sequentially and excels at analysis. The right hemisphere recognizes patters holistically, creates, and interprets emotions. *"It's most vital for us to develop the right hemisphere now because it is responsible for our ability to comprehend life conceptually and consciously." (Daniel H. Pink)*

The Art of Living is, in fact, the Art of Thinking!

Chunk 4

Mental Architecture is Holistic in Nature!

The Mental architecture is the core of a thought process. "New information that is flooding our brains competes with the old in-put, and it may ultimately overwrite it only if **the information-processing system is in order** and is not overwhelmed by inflowing data stream" (Scientific American Mind", May / June 2014) We are the ones that are supposed **to consciously monitor this process.** "Then, like a good intelligence agency, information is stored in our brains and shared only on a need-to know basis."

Rationalizing over everything in our lives and, therefore, building up **the awareness of the cause–effect modality** requires that we develop our critical thinking skills at every level of intellectual self-development and self-actualization, not allowing automatic reactions to life occur. Putting the mind in charge of our emotions and actions means **rationalization of every step we take.** Gradually, a person changes his individual physical, emotional, mental and spiritual messy, **random programming** and becomes a self-made man with a determined will.

Auto-induction: **I think consciously, I speak consciously, I act consciously,**

I breathe consciously, I eat consciously, I drive consciously.

I'm a New Me; I'm a Conscious Me!

As a matter of fact, any action you take, however small, needs **to be consciously monitored** by the **aware attention and the information that you operate at that moment.** The input of information needs to be digested mentally and structured consciously **on *five basic philosophical levels.***

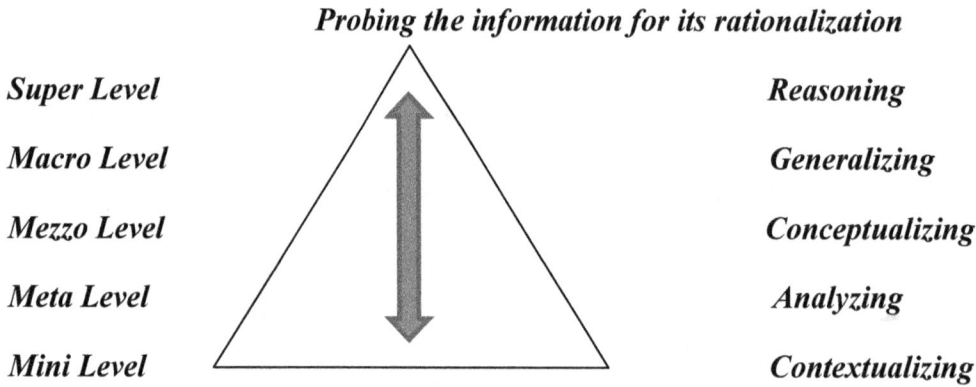

Super Level		*Reasoning*
Macro Level		*Generalizing*
Mezzo Level		*Conceptualizing*
Meta Level		*Analyzing*
Mini Level		*Contextualizing*

Another conscious act is our dealing with the information that overwhelms us in its immensity. We need to probe any piece of information for its interest, validity, and importance first. We need *to sift it* for its validity holistically, too. , at every level and *from different angles of our general intelligence,* experience, educational background , or our dilettante view of this or that area of expertise.

Information is ammunition, but only if it is sorted out for its rational use.

Note it, please, that without general expansion of knowledge, *no selection in the brain is possible* because ***there are no points of reference for such mental operations***. Thinking should start with a philosophizing and ***general intellectualizing*** of the problem first, ***analyzing***, or probing the options and arguments of its solution next, and finishing with ***inferring on the outcome***, or by the route:

General – Specific – General   or   *Synthesis – Analysis - Synthesis !*

The mind should always ***be consciously following this route***, in full awareness of its rational necessity while studying, learning, listening, talking, writing and working, irrespective of the field of knowledge or the trade that you operate in. Our school kid should ***acquire the critical thinking skills*** not through all kinds of tests, but by way of ***demonstrating their reasoning ability verbally,*** not just in a written form. And again, the background knowledge is a start in *establishing a mind-to mind connection* with another brain!

To be interesting, get interested!

Selecting the information for its validity and organizing it into the meaningful chunks conceptually in the order presented above is a special skill that helps ***establish a mind-to-mind and heart-to heart connection*** in communication. Therefore, ***education should provide knowledge holistically!*** Forming a general idea in many fields of knowledge works much better for young minds than the specialized education with a selective background. This situation widens ***the area of intellectual vulnerability of the students*** that are not properly informed in some areas of knowledge that they had not chosen to study. Such education is incomplete for the ***global interaction*** and ***constructively holistic mind-to-mind cooperation***

That's probably why the US students normally ***have a very vague idea about geography***, say. It just was not the subject that they had chosen to be mastered in high school. Obviously, the widening of a general outlook gives a person more food for thought and adds confidence in building up his / her "***network intelligence***" *(Reid Hoffman)* that we are focusing our socializing on these days. The expansion of the educational horizon will also translate into much more pronounced ideals that our young people will have, and, naturally, into ***raised self-consciousness.***

Intellectual networking is at the core of our evolutionary development now!

In sum, life demands that we get generally informed in science, art, literature, technology, culture, interpersonal relations, economics, politics, etc. ***at least at the dilettante level for our holistic, integral self-formation*** because it is propelling us to the unavoidable rationalization of our lives and multi-dimensional consciousness development that we are headed to in the future.

Being Rational Means Being Conscious!

Chunk 5

The Integral You is a Holistically-Thinking You!

In every book of mine, I present many inspirational mind-sets that are meant to work as the pills for your sometimes sagging will-power. They will help you boost the emotional make-up any time because **the mind will be monitored by you, not by your impulsive emotions!**

Writing about this insatiable urge for inspiration in us, Dale Carnegie states, **"People are of two types: symbols and patterns."** It's much easier to be a pattern of someone else, but it is worth all the gold on earth to be a different person, **a self- monitoring one** in order to become **"a symbol of meaningful changes"** and transformations that help others go ahead in life and have a holistic, spiritual rebirth. *"Invest in yourself!" (Reid Hoffman).* Self-creation is strenuous work, but if we do not do it, no one will ever run to our rescue. To get on the spiritual path of self-creation, one needs to **charge his / her intelligence in five levels!** *(Thesis 2,3)* **Knowledge becomes power when it is put to action holistically!!!**

We absolutely need to upgrade our most precious and invaluable asset – our consciousness. The only possibility of success on this path lies in your being able to truly visualize our position in life on the ladder of the formation or the transformation of self until the holistic utilization of **the Ultimate Best of You!** can materialize into **the Integral You**!- a true man / woman of personal integrity, charisma, and personal magnetism – **the being with much higher self- consciousness**

That's the goal of our education on Earth!

The present-day science has opened another mind-boggling door for a personal development of the humanity. *Richard P. Feynman, a* Nobel Prize winner, in his book" *The Strange Theory of Light and Matter"* wires about **the Quantum Field of Information,** made of quantum waves and the fact that our brains can tap into these quantum waves and receive the information form **the Unified Informational Field** *(Dr. John Hagelin).* It appears that the human brain is full of electrical activity that is being constantly monitored by the Unified, Quantum Field of information, and every electron in our brain is, actually, a receiver of this information.

"My brain is only a receiver in the Universe. There is a core form which we obtain knowledge, strength, and inspiration. I have not penetrated into the secrets of this core, but I know that it exists" (Nikola Tesla) Apparently, our **holistic awareness of the latest developments in physics is vital** for our thinking ability to receive the information from the Quantum Field of Information, and process it in a new, most insightful and constructive way. New knowledge invasion is the best source of inspiration for us and the core of our integrity with life as a whole!

"The Whole Science is the refinement of day-to-day thinking in all its forms." *(Albert Einstein)*

Chunk 6

You Are How You Think!

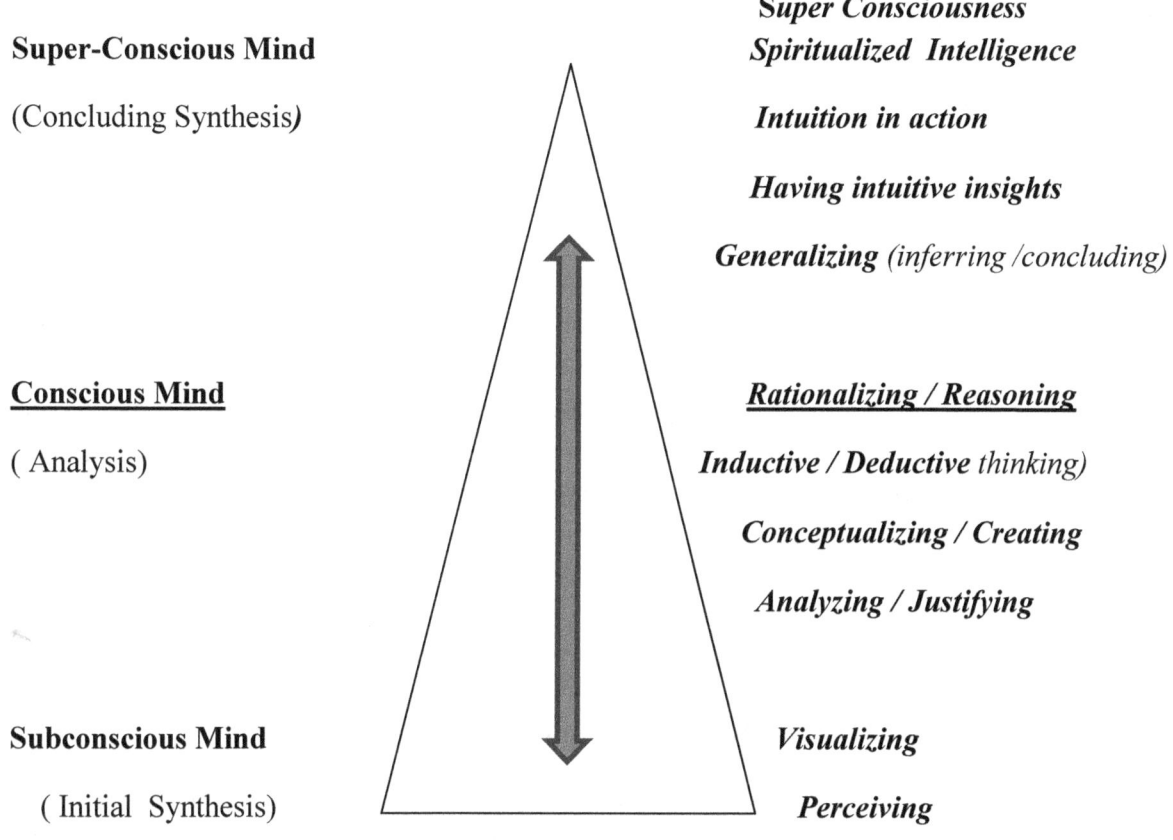

Auto-suggestion: ***I live consciously! I have a thinking life!***

Knowledge has many degrees, and to reach the highest degree of conscious development of logic and all the sophisticated forms of reasoning, or" **pure reason**" by Kant. The mental skills presented above have to be mastered continuously and consciously, with full awareness of what mental work is done and why. Teaching these thinking skills is essential in holistic education that I am advocating for here. Then ***knowledge becomes true awareness*** that, in turn, stimulates **the** development of a person's intuition and insightful, *"spiritualized intelligence." (John Baines)*

Rationalization of thinking is the name of the technique on the path of self-regeneration and self-actualization.

In *Chunk 5 above*, we were talking about the extent of potency of cerebral programming of an individual that is going on now though all kinds of digital means, TV, radio, and mass media. Such programming converts an individual into a ***"biological robot"*** with automatic psychological, instinctive, emotional, and intellectual reactions of" *a collective unconscious."*

Awareness of the true reality of things is a must!

Such shift in consciousness is quite attainable because the possibilities of our brains are endless. Science proves that a common man uses only a small portion of his brain for his intellectual function. This function has to be intensively expanded volume–wise *(Thesis 8)* with all kinds of mental operations that ***develop both hemispheres of the brain***, prioritizing the right one as the most creative one   Most people are left brained thinkers. Writing about the necessity to develop the right brain now, I mean that this process will bring us to the goal of our intellectual development- ***the whole brain thinking*** that is crucial for our rapidly developing economy. The right brain thinking is rapidly developing thanks to the electronics and our ***holistically-channeled education***, *(Thesis 7)* supplemented substantially ***by self-education.***

New times require new ways of learning and a holistic culture of thinking!

In this context, our schools need to prioritize on the holistic development of ***the mental growth of students in every area of knowledge*** that incorporates classical arts, philosophy, ethics, manners, music, literature, world geography, and the kaleidoscope of the world's religions and cultures. Such holistic education   needs to capitalize on ***the quality of students' thinking skills*** rather than on their brains accumulating often questionable, unnecessary, and even dead knowledge for a test performance. The required rationalization of thinking is vital for our fast growing, electronically-charged economy, and the skills of **VERBAL REASONING** need to be much more operational and ***mind-broadening*** than just testing the ability to pick the right option in a multiple-choice display. *(Thesis 8,9)*.

"I not only use all the brains I have, but all I can borrow." (Albert Einstein)

Finally, the **AWARE ATTENTION** skills are also an absolute necessity to be developed as early as possible. Ask your kids to pay attention to the trees, flowers, leaves coming to life and dying, the animals , the sun, and the clouds in the sky, and teach them to appreciate life in its any form. ***Keep modelling their mind and emotions, working with their subconscious mind when they go to bed,*** That's the best time to program their minds and hearts for intelligence, love, and compassion. Take time to develop their imagery. Send them to space. Tell them about the super-heroic action of consideration, love, friendship that they have performed.

Help them feel extra-ordinary!

Being aware means having the ability to retain mindfulness and   perceive the information ***holistically and conceptually.*** Aware attention skills will contribute a lot to developing and gradually employing the entire spectrum of the thinking tools, presented above.

Auto-Induction:

I'm Becoming a Much Wiser Self-Actualizer!

Chunk 7

"The World of Organized Inadequacies"

The pace of evolution is amazing now. Experts predict that by mid-century, quantum computers will be able to function at the speeds billion times faster than the human brain. We know that ,but we are not consciously aware of that. Machines operate our minds and prompt our behaviors.

We forget or are unaware of the fact that consciousness is inseparable with intelligence!

We are acting under the impact of a very sophisticated and a much more informed **social brain – the human society at large.** It is programming us all in a common way, enlarging the army of the machine-driven people. *"We live in the world of organized inadequacies."(Joseph Campbell)* Schools should be particularly alert to the new electronic times that deepen the existing educational crisis. They and do not help our children intelligence-wise and ,still less, consciousness-wise.. **Children become geniuses of digital ingenuity, but "dumbed down vassals."** The necessity to develop solid, general, insightful, stimulating *expansive thinking skills* that are essential for the present-day market economy are not being addressed properly. Joseph Campbell said,

"Every failure to cope with a life situation leads, in the end, to a restriction of consciousness."

It is very disheartening to know that our school children and college students get a lot of **mentally-undigested information** on the computer, without really processing it intellectually. They ridiculously text their conversation partners sitting next to them, instead of talking to them face-to-face and mind-to–mind. They plagiarize their academic papers, and they often stop reading altogether. Most importantly, **students stop thinking individually and critically**. So, our indispensable role in their lives is to teach them solid **Thinking Critical Skills** that are only declarative in our text-books. Students need to voice out their idea, present them outwardly, not just through the test papers that only limit their learning. Any testing should be **backed up with conceptual discussions and argumentative talks.** The last menacing feature alone debilitates them incredibly! They rush to find the correct answer without bothering to know why it was correct. It narrows down their outlook, **makes them lazy consumers of electronic stuff**, and it turns them into indifferent people emotionally. As a college professor of Psycholinguistics, I witness the situation with an aching heart. **Students become robotized, not intellectualized!** We should not let it happen because artificial intelligence is meant to help us, **not to enslave us.** Not to become slaves of technology, we need to protect our individual thoughts and emotions, our psyche, and our souls from mechanical intrusion and **digitally-inflated thinking!**

The Freedom of Thought, not just of Word, is what We need to Launch into the World!

Chunk 8

Beware of the Inflation of Thinking!

We have talked above the necessity *to live in synch with the universal laws of life.* (*Thesis 5)* Talking about integrating the mind and emotions, we need to remember that our holistic *self-growth cannot be accomplished in separation from the basic cosmic laws*. Unless we do the self-work holistically, in a tight tandem with full awareness of the cosmic laws governing our lives, we can hardly accomplish any operative result in life. We know that something is amiss in our life, but we are not aware of the causes of our fears and frustrations because *we are unaware of the cosmic laws* that we violate. True, *"ignorance is the greatest enemy of the humanity!"(A. Einstein)* Being aware of, at least, the cosmic Law of Cause and Effect unleash self-power.

All the cosmic laws work holistically and in unison. The observation of these laws is at the core of personal integrity, to say nothing about obtaining a much higher level of consciousness. We would not have the evolutionary quality to it, since we hadn't had it, to begin with. That's why many enlightened leaders are not as inspirational as those who have worked on their *self-enlightenment consciously,* with full awareness of the Universal Laws and applying integral will to reprogramming their minds and emotions.

Self- induction: *I intellectualize my emotions and emotionalize my mind!*

Being unaware of the universal laws and the latest scientific developments, we face a common enemy - *the inflation and deflation of thinking*. It means that we are suffering from the use of the old patterns of thinking and behavior due to the absence of awareness of the basic laws governing our lives and the latest developments in science that are now trying to go in synch with the God's wink.

Life without any inner fraction is in the harmony with the Law of Attraction!

The Law of the Right Human Behavior by Richard W. Wetherill that I am referring to throughout the book is fundamental for holistic self-realization of a person, too.

Self- suggestion *I think, say, and do the right thing in the life's ado.*

It is extremely important that we take care of our holistic growth in *full awareness* of what we did not know so far because our ignorance and intelligence-unprocessed personal defects will take body in our children who will *inherit our inflated thinking, demagnetized values, lack of spirituality, and the disconnection of the spirit and the body in time and space.* Do the Auto-Suggestive Meditation using any mind-set you need or give your brain much food for thought, inspiring your kids with your ger for knowledge. As William Shakespeare said,

"Nothing is good or bad but thinking makes it so."

Chunk 9

Reflective Thinking is Conscience Shaping!

Reflective thinking is inseparable with conscience! The idea of living at peace with conscience is instilled by the parents in any culture because it is essential in all sacred books. It is also at the core of a continuous process of self-construction and consciousness rising. It is also the cause-effect incentive for our prayers, meditation, and self-reflection. It is the starting point for self-awareness, self- judgment, and self-balancing. It provides food for self-inductive work mentally and self-perfecting work emotionally in the Now, not retrospectively as we often tend to do.

"Thinking that is not rooted in the Now is dysfunctional!" *(Eckhart Tolle)*

Every one of us needs to clear up **the mind IN SYNCH with the heart** and make oneself more aware of what is going on in them at any given moment in life. Neuro-science provides us with the invaluable information that self-reflection is indispensable in the process of rationalization of thinking and empowering of our emotions.

Self-awareness is impossible without such on-going practice.

That is why it is so good to observe oneself during the meditation, a passive or an active one. We can do reflective thinking and actual re-unification with our ***intuitive conscience - scanning*** while walking, running, driving, while putting everything in order inside the house, the office, and inside ourselves, and especially before going to bed, especially if we feel distraught emotionally. No wonder, women that are constantly putting things in order have a much more developed intuition than men, and ***they are more conscience-conscious*** and prone to ask for forgiveness.

It is noteworthy to mention again that when we have the basic knowledge about how the brain operates at least in general terms, we are more able to better control both the brain and emotions through self-reflection and auto-induction. ***"The power of reflection fortified by the most primary idea how the brain operates will help us get better insights into our own thoughts".*** *("Scientific American Mind", Sep/ Oct .2014)*

Reflective thinking should be trained **holistically** - at every level of intelligence development: **Mini, Meta, Mezzo, Macro**, and **Super** because your intelligence is directly reflecting on your consciousness. Reflecting on what is bothering you ***physically, emotionally, psychologically, mentally, and spiritually*** does not necessarily mean stopping the chatter box in the brain as many books suggest. It is also your active and constant rationalization of everything you think, feel, say, and do while processing it through ***the grid of conscience. (See Chunk 10)*** **You have a chance to put yourself in order in every dimension though holistic self-scanning**.

Intuitive Conscience Scanning is Soul-Refining!

Chunk 10

Self-Education without Proration!

As we have signified above, our present-day advancing depends not on *the programmed knowledge* that we receive in schools, colleges, and from random reading, or *compulsive gaming* but on the individualized and consciously-processed knowledge that each of us acquires on the path of *building up his / her own Living Intelligence*. It means that we need to consciously assess the level of our general ignorance and convert it into *the un-programmed individual intelligence* that needs to be enriched consistently, as a life-time job of the most inspiring character.

First, the technological revolution demands that we create *a new level of reasoning,* superior to the ordinary one, trapped by the names of schools, professors, titles, positions, and countries. No wonder, the best minds have always been self-educated and mind-expansive in every area of knowledge, and they did come from different countries of the world.

Conscious self-education generates conscious living and creates a thinking personality!

Second, the most essential factor for the development of higher consciousness is **DISCIPLINE** that is applied to self-growth not sporadically and chaotically, but in one, well-constructed and consistent way, without any excuses, self-justification and with much true consideration for what you are becoming in life of your making.

There is no learning without discipline!" (George Miller)

Thirdly, to develop living consciousness, we need to monitor ourselves *from top to bottom and from bottom to top* on the holistic track of learning. By the way, according to the Jewish religion, *the Star of David is the symbol of life*. Its upper triangle symbolizes the higher consciousness that is represented by the three digits **999** - the three empowered beasts - *mind, heart, and sex,* while at the bottom triangle, we have three digits of **666** *that represent the undeveloped consciousness, governed by the three unconquered beasts,* mentioned above. *(Rav, P. S. Berg).*

The balance of the fundamental concepts in life to be spiritually alive:

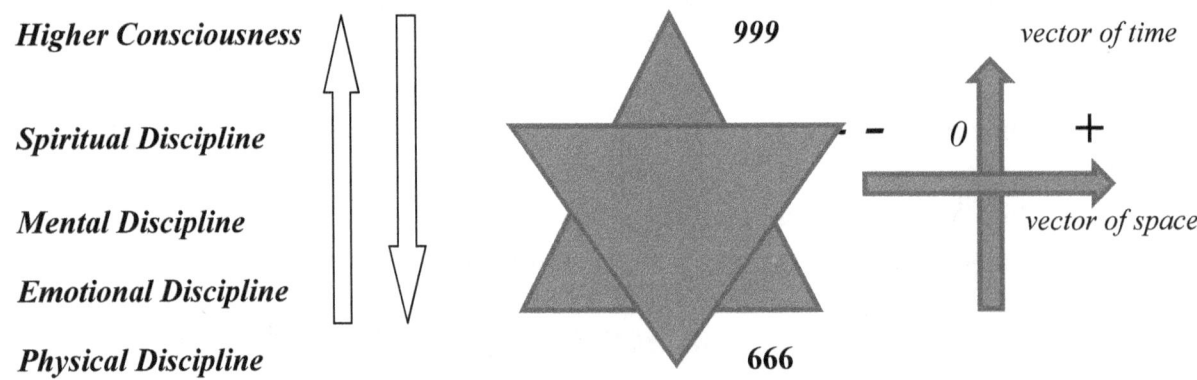

In Christianity, the cross, having for centuries been viewed as *the matrix of life*, mathematically speaking, represents *the vector of time* and *the vector of space.(Sam Gazarkh" The World at Large")* The center of the cross represents *the balance of these fundamental concepts of life* in balancing the lower and the upper levels of consciousness. *The time vector indicates our mental movement from the past to the present, and the future,* while *the space vector indicates the movement from the negative to the positive transformation of self.* T<u>he Zero point</u> indicates the necessary *balance of living in the present* that we must consciously perceive with this knowledge. (See *Suggestive Meditation, Chunks 17, Physical Intelligence*)

The Chinese signs of life *yin / yang* are also pointing to the necessity of *a balanced self-management*. Oslo teaches us to see our conscious development as going from *inside out and upward,* while our degradation goes from *outside in and downward*. An authentic process of self-creation is independent, personable, and full of freedom of self-expression that elevates the spirit in contrast to the process of self-destruction that downgrades the spirit and makes life meaningless.

So, define your path in these universal signs and reason out the direction of your soul.

Obviously, *conscious living is a consistent process of an integral conception of all the levels of intelligence* when intelligence surpasses the intellectual boundaries of each dimension and you become a whole person, *an Integral You – physically, emotionally, mentally, spiritually, and universally.* *Meanwhile, your personal integrity should be governed by the holistic formula :*

Synthesis-Analysis- Synthesis! *(See Thesis 8,)*

Internalizing knowledge - processing it selectively - externalizing and actualizing it!

In sum, constant and aware self-monitoring is a must for a growing personality! The education that generally focuses only on what we study should be focused on *how we study, that is how we structure our thoughts.* Self- actualization needs substantial enrichment of the mind with the information about different areas of knowledge and constant conscious control over our thoughts, words, feelings, attitudes and actions.

Auto-suggestive work needs to become an everyday ritual of the mind.

It also demands that we generate a new attitude to the process of knowledge accumulation because new thinking requires new sorted out knowledge, the knowledge that is based on *conscious control of the in-put and out-put of the information* that needs to be consciously-processed, digested, and assimilated by the mind-body of a person. The auto-induction should be:

My Life goes on without any Fraction because

I am Living Intelligence in Action!

Chunk 11

Dissipated Consciousness is a Wasted Life!

Thinking is the process of operating the mind in synch with the brain, **synchronically and consciously.** As science has it, *"the quality of our thinking depends on further development of the right hemisphere"*, and, therefore, thinking also needs to be enhanced with **knowledge about the brain** and **self-managing skills**, essential to develop *Professional Intelligence* that I am exploring below! Your professional and personal mission must be grounded **by your personal philosophy** that must permeate your entire being, generating y**our personal integrity.**

"I cannot teach anybody anything. I can only make them think."(Socrates)

Summing up this part of the book, here are some *tips to jump-start constructive thinking:*

1. *The Universal Mind choreographs everything that is happening in our lives.* Our talking to ourselves while meditating is, in fact, self-programming every cell in our body, every mini-computer, uploading them with our daily programs. Our thinking also has **to work in synch with the Master Brain–Mind of the Universe.** It means that we have to learn to upload our brains consciously to construct our thinking that is dissipated, unmanageable, and messy otherwise.

Be aware of your thoughts! Don't let them go uncontrolled!

2. *"There is no true thinking without discipline."(George Miller)* Discipline requires thinking slowly and step by step, zooming on the messages that the mind gets. *Thinking slowly does not mean that you are dumb* Thinking slowly makes it possible to sort out the in-coming information's **in a conceptually-governed way** into special compartments / windows.

3. *Being logical is another demand.* When we are logical, we are able to organize the information into *chunks* and store them carefully in the brain.

The compartmentalization of information is the organized brain formation!

Storing information in the window-frame way is essential for constructive, expansive, and developmental thinking skills that we need to rationalize our life. Interestingly, the electrical circuit in the brain lights up when we speak or write logically.

Think on paper to build up logic better!

4. *Build a language-control muscle*! *(See Language Intelligence below)* Thinking and language are inseparable in the brain. *Writing develops strategic thinking and a strategy-oriented mind. Speaking creates an emotional personality and listening shapes respectful man.*

"Don't Say Everything you know but know Everything You Say!"

Chunk 12

The Thinking Hygiene is on the Scene!

5. Both forms of communication need constant self-control to maintain *the thinking hygiene.* To actualize in-coming information correctly, *we need to learn to use aware attention as our scanning tool.* I consistently call it AWARE ATTENTION because aware attention is the attention that is loaded with *conscious perception of the information* that had already been sorted out by the brain for its validity based on the prior *conscious compartmentalization* of the processed knowledge that you want to be constantly growing and getting up-dated.

Auto-induction: *I need a lot consciously--organized food for thought!*

6. Next, the skill for speed-reading comes to the scene. The manner of writing of scientific articles and other important pieces of information in mass media that are supposed to provide the food for thought *are too wordy and too professionally-specified.* The readings meant for popularization and mental digestion, especially by our young, very-digitized minds is often, if not always, beyond their comprehension.

Teaching of *speed-reading* is rarely provided, but this is the skill we desperately need to be able to scan the information for its validity. I always start any course with teaching my learners to speed-read, to skip and scan the information for its conceptual value, connecting this skill with teaching the conceptually- concise writing and speaking.

Time is sped up - no mind space for crap!

7. Developed aware attention helps us *store the information in the pre-frontal lobes of the brain.* Science proves that most thinking is done in the perception area - the area that assesses the information for its importance. Only with aware attention to our thoughts and words are we able to follow another rule:

Auto-induction: *Say what you mean and mean what you say!*

8. Also, we need to learn *to combine emotions with reason* with the help of aware attention, paid to everything and everyone around you. Having observed the situation and those involved in it, give yourself a minute to think about your response, *halt the immediate, impulsive reaction.* " *"If you don't have something nice to say, don't say anything at all!"*

Don't verbalize everything that comes to mind! Be One of a Kind!

9. Since we delegate more and more processing to computers, *perceptual thinking* that is developed based on the aware attention habit and *independent thinking* becomes more and more crucial nowadays because it remains to be human.

10. Finally, it's crucial to follow every chunk of information that you want to digest with the question: *"What do I make of it?"* - *Aware attention and perceptive thinking* will help you remove *the chaos in the mind or* clean up your memory storage from the junk that you have accumulated there, uplift your spirit, and make any job that you are doing meaningful.

Auto-induction: ***My aware attention is never in retention!***

The same as your body needs a shower to water you off the negative energies that you might have picked up from different people during the day, or might have polluted yourself with negative emotions that sometimes take the upper hand in our perception of the circumstances of life, **the brain needs to do the cleansing of its compartments /** windows / from the memory pollutants that you let penetrate inside and clog the pathways that you need to make constructive decisions.

Give your brain a break! *(Auto- Suggestive Meditation)*

To do this cleaning, **rub the palms of your hands vigorously and shake them off several time**. *Put your elbows on the table in front of you and connect your hands together so that the four fingers of your right hand were on the top of the four fingers of your left hand. Now, rest your head on the hands so that both eyes could be jus ,* **opposite the solar plexus centers in the middle of both palms.** *Close your eyes and rest your head on the palms for half a minute. Then start rotating the eyes to the left , visualizing your cleaning of the left hemisphere of the brain in its every compartment, every corner.*

Rest for another half a minute, and do the same, **rotating your eyes to the right and cleaning the compartments of the right hemisphere**. *Slowly, but surely. Rest for some seconds. Open your eyes. you will be as fresh as new to think, to discuss anything, and to use your brains a helping hand. Constantly discipline your brain and* **thank it for its constructive work at the end.**

Start with generalizing information, selecting the valid pieces of it , and strategizing it for a successful solution of any problem.

Synthesis - Analysis- Synthesis!

Nothing is sacred, but the integrity of your mind."

(Ralph Emerson)

A Whole Human Being is the Goal of Evolution!

Chunk 13

Intellectual Superiority is Sky-Limited!

To be intellectually-inspired and inspiring, we have to develop our thinking skills non-stop. *"Our mental skills are just as trainable as the physical ones."* *(Discover, Jan. 2011)* Physical and cognitive intelligences are inseparable in us, as well as language intelligence, emotional intelligence, and psychological intelligence that I will overview below.

Auto-induction: *You are what we think, say, feel, eat, and do!*

The purpose of any person is to get his / her thinking across clearly in any situation. Applying it, however, requires ***considerable discipline*** because when you get on the path of enriching your cognitive intelligence, you will have ***to deliberately force yourself to think first and say or write later.*** Just loading the unprocessed information into your brain does not work anymore.

Such personal growth is called rationalization of thinking!

It is the way to increase the clarity of self-expression, decrease redundancy in speaking / writing and be rid of muddled, messy self-expression. We have become too wordy and too sophisticated in expressing even banal ideas. ***Computer consciousness is increasingly ruling our mind-world. So what?*** No one can shape our lives better than us, especially at the electronic times!

There is much more to life than increasing its speed through electronics, or robotics!

More and more people get dependent on a machine in their thinking and perceiving. Machines are gradually getting ***intellectual superiority*** in our lives, but we need to make them build us up holistically, not just digitally*!* Machine is just a great tool of our mind because there is no superiority in the world to **the Universal Mind** that we are part of! (*Part Two, thesis 2- The Grid of Consciousness Integration*) Regrettably, ***a new dimension of consciousness*** that has come into being with electronics, though it connects us to the world; ***it also disconnects us with ourselves.*** We started developing new intelligence - ***digital intelligence*** *(See below, Division 3.)* that needs our new intelligence to be *c*onsciously processed with ***aware attention*** acting as a mouse in hand.

Old models of learning need to be demolished!

If technologically-enhanced intelligence is not used consciously and with reverence to the Universal Mind , or ***the Master Computer***, it turns us into human robots, reacting to an automatic impulse of a gadget in hand. Follow the five letters "*C*" in the mind-set below.

Clear Mind + a Cool Spirit + Calm Guts =

the Connected Consciousness Smarts!

Chunk 14

Self-Scanning Auto-Suggestively!

Self- scanning clears the mind, calms down the emotions, and focuses you on the priorities in life. It is indispensable if your bettering yourself stumbles **on self-doubt and self-criticism**, **but most vitally, on self-justification.** Old people often say that a person can sleep tight at night only if his conscience is clean. We have become over-protective and even soul-blind in self-justification. *Self- reflection, X- rayed by conscience, is a sure way of acquiring inner gravity.*

It's essential to live at peace with one's own conscience. Your conscience, **fortified by auto-suggestive back-ups** will not bother you with past memory pangs, and your psyche will become much stronger and more imbued with intelligence and self-confidence. Soon negative images of self-imperfections will never happen, and intuition will prompt only positive steps to follow. Self-reflecting means self-assessing to help yourself, not to judge, or victimize yourself. **With positive self-hypnosis, you will be able to center yourself in any situation in the NOW!**

While self-reflecting, *you analyze and synthesize*, REASON OUT the outcome of your actions and **conceptualize them**, focusing on the **URV** *(The Ultimate Result Vision) of the best of you)*. Learn to form *a conceptual hierarchy* of the URV of yourself at any given moment in five dimensions. see what you are like *physically, emotionally, mentally, spiritually and universally,* and **objectively** locate the blocks in any of these areas to remove them consciously. Thus, instead of **self-guilt**, you will develop **self- support** just in time for the right action. Remember to constantly induct yourself with inspirational mind-sets and remind yourself repeatedly, **Right is My Might!** But *there is no right without a true union of the mind and the heart!*

I keep emphasizing this concept from the start of the book We live in a very impersonal world when the phrase *" I don't care!"* is constantly heard everywhere, and it is hurting us with its comeback, especially when it streams from our kids. We cannot *observe hygiene of the mind or conscience* unless we tune in to each other's mind and heart and try to put them in synch with ours. Zillions of books are written about attaining success, happiness, and love in life, without pointing out to us this main aspect of our human essence - *living at peace with our conscience! Make your mind kind, and the heart smart! Learn to be exceptional at that!*

Auto- Induction: *I know who I am!*

I am a strong, bold, calm, and determined owner of my firm will.

I can…; I want to…; and I will…! I am putting my actions and conscience in synch. I think!

Life isn't Always Fair, but it's Here and There!

What's in it Your Right Share?

Chunk 15

I Live Consciously and Visually; I'm a Visionary!

In sum, **Cognitive Intelligence** *is the process of acquiring more life awareness and transforming yourself* in the way which presupposes developing *a new mental set-up* and a new, transformed, and enriched intelligence. It will enable us to synergize the negative and the positive sides in us to produce *a holistically thinking human being* with much more *advanced consciousness and limitless imagination*. Einstein once said, " *When I examine myself and my method of thought, I come to the conclusion that* **the gift of fantasy** *has meant more to me than my talent for absorbing positive knowledge.*"

Everything around us is completely interlinked in time and space, and we need to get rid of our polarity consciousness, *the illusory nature of duality*, generated by the, society-induced thinking. The new times demand that we stop being channeled by *"the collective unconscious"* (*Carl Yung*) and develop our own **personal gravity, personal magnetism, and personal integrity**. Even personal power is dual. It starts with making a decision, on the one hand, and taking action, on the other, when problem-solving is separated in time and space.

"Only with awareness of the whole, transformation and freedom come."(Eckhart Tulle)

Reprogramming the mind for the holistic, but individual perception of the world, we can empower the mind holistically, **using both brain hemispheres of the brain in synch**, and expanding our vision both in space and time. New, holistically-developed intelligence raises us to a higher level of consciousness that touches *the Omega Point – True Enlightenment.* The people who attain it can **distinguish the terminal from the eternal** and save our infinite souls from ignorance and impulsiveness of behavior. Knowledge empowers and refines with its limitedness.

There are many great spiritual leaders now that we should follow knowingly, not blindly. I like **Drunvalo Melchizedek** and **Sadhguru** for their unique, well-processed, **objective knowledge of life**. Their free thinking enriches, expanding our intellectually-enhanced life awareness that reflects the vastness of our ignorance and inspires us with the desire to give the world the best we have.

Auto-suggestion: ***Don't let your brain repose and decompose!***

Save it from decay;

It must be working tirelessly every day!

In My Life Quest, I Manifest My Very Best!

(End of Stage One - Cognitive Intelligence --Division 2)

Vistas of Intelligence to Install Next:

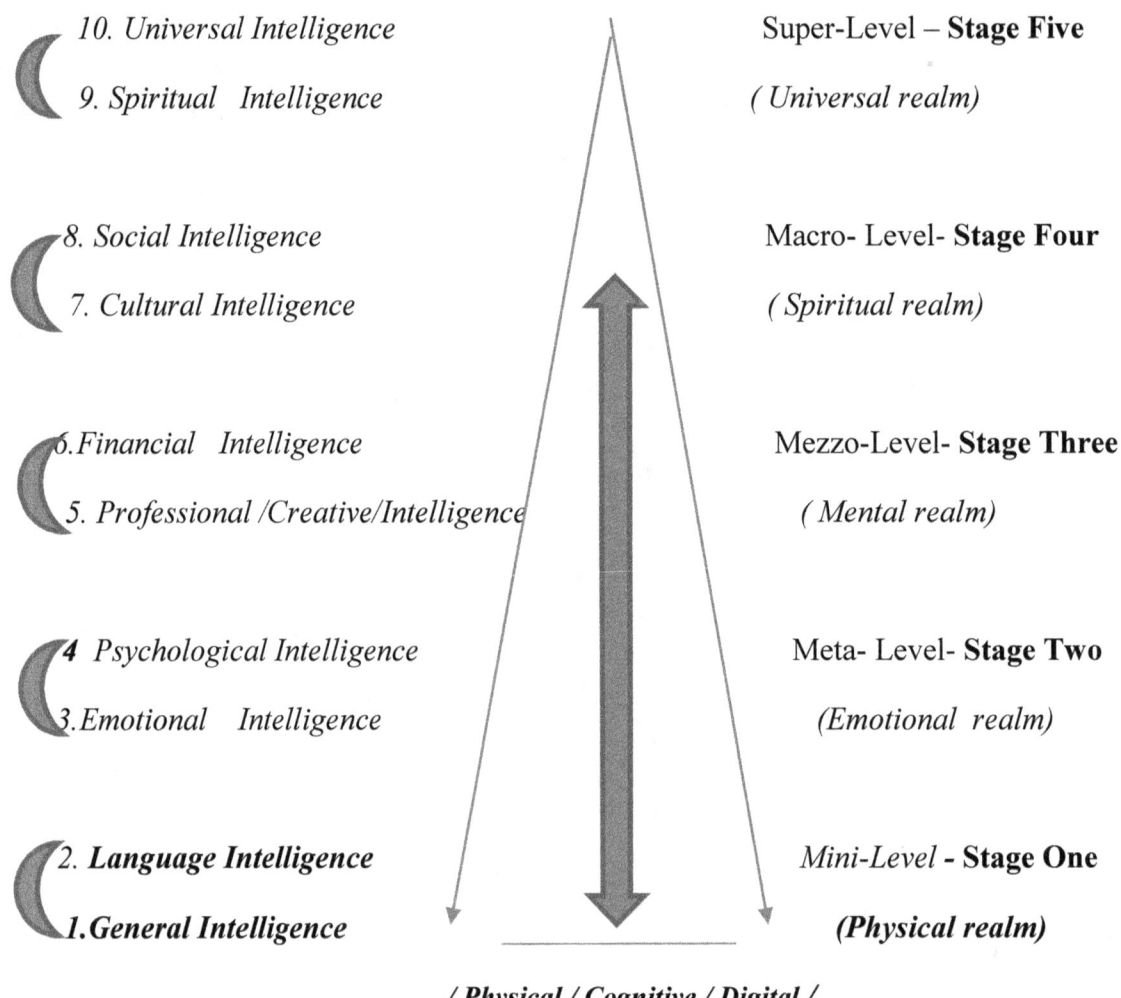

10. Universal Intelligence	Super-Level – **Stage Five**
9. Spiritual Intelligence	(Universal realm)
8. Social Intelligence	Macro- Level- **Stage Four**
7. Cultural Intelligence	(Spiritual realm)
6. Financial Intelligence	Mezzo-Level- **Stage Three**
5. Professional /Creative/Intelligence	(Mental realm)
4 Psychological Intelligence	Meta- Level- **Stage Two**
3. Emotional Intelligence	(Emotional realm)
2. **Language Intelligence**	*Mini-Level* - **Stage One**
1. General Intelligence	**(Physical realm)**

/ Physical / Cognitive / Digital /

"Fertilize your mind with thinking!" (Albert Einstein)

To Make Your Life Wise,
Strategize – Optimize - Actualize!

Stage One

Mini-Level of Intelligence - Physical Dimension -

Digital

Intelligence

(General Intelligence – Division 3)

To Be More Life-Fit, Enjoy the Present of It!

Our Life is Now Set in the World-Web Net!

Digital Intelligence without Negligence!

Wow! I Live Now!

Artificial Intelligence

(An Inspirational Booster)

Artificial intelligence,

Is it our new mental negligence?

    Or is it our contribution

    To the human evolution?

Can a machine feel, hear, and think

As a human being at a click?

    Can we create an Electronic Being

    Able of hearing and seeing

Far beyond our mental horizon

And the ability of memorizing

    All the data seed

    At the fingertips of our need?

Will such a human robot of the future

Fall in love that is also mutual?

    Will the Machine Being

    Be able of dealing

With another intellectual human form

Clad in an electronic uniform?

I guess this new mechanical Me

Will have a digital consciousness glee

        And with it, I will flee

        To a New Universe of Me!

Has it happened already,

 And should we all be ready

        To get rid of our emotional self-expression

        And become mental in every dimension!

Artificial Intelligence is dead and programmed,

    But I am Aware of that.

Let's have Evolutionary Vanity to save our Human Sanity!

The Art of Becoming now is

the Art of Digital Mind-Monitoring, Wow!!!

Chunk 2

"Our Mind Potential is Exponential!" *(Ray. Kurzweil)*

Electronic intelligence alters the way we think, write, and speak, and *"at the cellular level, technology is revealing how a person's neurons update themselves **to generate a living library of experience**."(Scientific American Mind, Nov./Dec.2014)*

The Center for Assessment Technology and Continuous Health (CATCH) is developing tools that can continuously monitor people to get a better understanding of how to make the electronic intelligence better serve our needs. Our scientific world publishes novel materials **about new ways of thinking** that could be shaped at a command and help us considerably rationalize our thinking speaking and acting.

Wow! I live now!

Mind-advanced computational scientists Skylar Tibbits and Banning Garrett, for instance, are leading our creative thought to *"self-assembling future"* doing the*"* ***programmable matter research"*** that is mind-boggling in its potential because robots will be self-aware, conscious, interactive, and even dangerous in their ability to considerably surpass humans.

Robots become companions, looking like a person. A roboticist and a real artist of the computational mind Hiroshi Ishiguro builds up androids to closely resemble human beings – including his own digital clone.

Another genius of technology, the IBM researcher Dharmedra Modha is successfully working on the computer that thinks, feels, and adequately communicates with a human brain and is gradually ***becoming a beautifully functioning, independent* ELECTRONIC BEING.**

Artificial Intelligence is, in fact, ***surpassing human intelligence*** and is becoming a new, unpredictable menace, looming in its exponential potentiality that needs to be channeled by us in a new, holistically-developed way that will allow us *to monitor the future*, not to become its victims.

However, ***consciousness is not a human-mind creation*** and the part of us or our future artificial brothers, sisters ,friends, enemies and lovers will be just the **EVOLUTIONARY TOYS IN THE UNIVERSAL MIND'S CREATION VOICE.**

Let's better attune to it to be safe and celestially life-fit!

"We cannot Pick the Future, but We can Design it!"

(Ray Kurzweil)

Chunk 3

Mind Means Intelligence + Self-Consciousness!

Our evolutionary development on the mental level calls for *the Living Intelligence* that is an aware, creative, self-confident, self-reliant, self-programmed you. *It's not automatic, it's reflective* because the mind analyses constantly and channels us along the evolutionary steps of raising our consciousness. Certainly, with the digital revolution, our personal intelligence has been enriched immeasurably. I have written about the positive and negative effects of the technological emersion for us above, and I cannot stop marveling at its wonders.

The Artificial Intelligence is at the base of our developmental pyramid! (Thesis 9)

It is the greatest creative intelligence ever! I have positioned it at the bottom of the holistic pyramid at the menta l level because our indigo children start using it almost at birth. It's amazing how a year-old child is operating his mom's smart phone while she is busy doing something. It's the best toy for the kids that organically perceive the new digital world around us. From initially professional level, the use of digital technology went down to the basic level of holistic intelligences - *the General Intelligence!* Electronic competences became an urgent demand at the level of professional intelligence, but presently, they have become *as critical as the language competences* at any level, and therefore, I present electronic intelligence at the bottom, or at the mini-level of the intelligence developmental pyramid.

There is no real cognition without these two dramatically vital competences now.

Computing is an inseparable part of our lives, and apparently, we cannot talk about developing ourselves without getting in the flow of digital evolution. The United State is the country that has changed the way we all live, having imposed the digital revolution upon us during *the presidency of President Bill Clinton* whom we owe a lot for our advancement in the technological field in schools and colleges.

It is a great step forward in the history of the humanity, and, inevitably, many most gifted and electronically-minded scientists are leading this evolution in terms of extensive robots-oriented economy and more *liberation of our minds from hard labor-stereotyped lives.*

Today's technology and science culture are shaping our minds with the help of hyper-powerful computers able to perform septillion operations every second *"The emerging techniques are letting us back up the brain, lay bare its secrets, and extend our influence past the boundaries of flesh and bone." (Scientific American mind, Nov./Dec. 2014)*

Indeed, "Imagination is Infinite!" *(Albert Einstein)*

Chunk 4

Electronic Intelligence is Ruling the World, So What?

Electronic intelligence becomes pivotal because *it is permeating all the other intelligences on the ladder of our intellectual self-installation*. The Internet makes more and more scientific information available to the public, thus contributing immensely to whetting of our imagination, expanding the outlook, and building up" the *intelligence network."(R. Hoffman)* How can one remain indifferent to this well of knowledge and to the scope of intelligent minds that we can connect to from all over the world? It is, indeed, very enriching!

The Internet informs us, for instance, that a group of scientists, working on the phenomenon of our DNA, has discovered lately that it is able *to produce the magnetic black holes* as miniature bridges to transmit information. According to the Russian scientists, that are trying to probe further *a genius supposition of Einstein-Rosin,* these bridges *might be connecting different areas of the Universe,* letting the information be transmitted beyond the time–space continuum. They are trying to discover how to consciously monitor these communication lines, using our DNA as a receptor, able to transmit and receive the information from the Universal Web Wide system.

What a great extra-terrestrial perspective!

Today, innumerous wonders of technology that are being developed all over the world at an unprecedented rate *change the intellectual picture of the world in every field of knowledge*. They globalize economy and remove the barriers of interpersonal communication. Our marveling at the technological advances stimulates and inspires us to live longer to become the witnesses of new wonderful developments in science and life. *What an incentive to live and to create!*

Our social consciousness develops with new scientific ideas steering the world of thought.

However, this most advanced attitude to life needs *to be self- monitored, both consciously and consistently,* for us not to get more stuck in a self-destructive mode of mechanical thinking and living. We should be aware that these *new modes of patterned thinking and behaving* are occurring within the frame-work of a person's intellect, limiting it and indoctrinating it in the programmed direction of the same *"collective unconscious"* that is digitally-enhanced now.

In the present-day world, *governed by mechanical intelligence* and *bondless irrationality*, the one who has more information in his cerebral program and the one who is skilled enough to operate it to the best of his abilities are deemed to be most intelligent.

But life is a dynamic interplay of consciousness, not just digitally-enhanced intelligence!

You Must Be bold to Fit in the Evolutionary Mold!

Chunk 5

Brain Plasticity and Automation

While the scientists are working on programming computers with human capabilities, *we are learning to* **code new short-cuts that will be wiring our thoughts through space and time in a novel way.** In fact, we can hardly imagine our life without different helpful gadgets at hand, the use of which adds up to the most amazing capacity of the brain - *its plasticity*. (Dr. Michael Merzenech) **Brain plasticity is the ability of the brain to adapt,** to change, and to delegate different duties to other parts of the brain, should such necessity occur. Neuroscience calls this ability *neuroplasticity.*

The ability of the brain to change our learning thanks to its plasticity has also been proved. .All these amazing technological developments only testify to the power of the brain and the necessity **to develop it in a holistic way**, using the brain's amazing mechanism of neuroplasticity to create new connections in the brain and expand the parameters of artificial intelligence. Computerization of knowledge goes along the ways of creating **quantum computers** that will widen our intellectual horizons unpredictably.

Amazingly, the IBM researcher Dharmedra Modhathat and his team whose mind-advanced work we have mentioned above, have created the computer that is able **to route information around a burned core in a computer,** like a human brain does in case of any damage, delegating its functions to a healthy part in the brain. . The computer is monitoring its functions like brain plasticity does

I have outlined above, in the section " ***Cognitive Intelligence***", ***the stages of the thinking skills*** development on the path of raising self-consciousness – the goal of self-evolution for every one of us. In his wonderful book *"How to Create a Mind",* Ray Kurzweil is talking about ***"the conceptual hierarchy"*** of different activities that the artificial intelligence is working on , programming the robots to recognize the patterns, stored in the memory. Apparently, the neocortex of the machine is trying to make sense of the in-put , presented to it.

It's mind-boggling work, and with all due respect to it, we need to question the ability of the artificial mind to operate the language with an ***amazing flexibility of the thinking skills*** that a human mind displays on the path of its self-consciousness raising. **The language habits +** **speech skills** that I am talking about in the *"Language Intelligence" Section Two* below leave a lot of other questions of the possibility of the artificial intelligence to surpass us in this capacity.
.

Be immune to the digital mind's inflation in favor of the conscious human nation!

The most vital components of cognition are **the electronic and magnetic fields in the brain.** They are generated by the synaptic currents that constantly ripple through the brain and promote the evolution of our thinking technologically. Apparently, ***artificial intelligence will*** *produce a new thinking mind* that most likely will outshine us in many mental abilities, but one - *our Language Intelligence and its evolution.* (*See below)*

I think that our *Language Intelligence will never be surpassed by any artificial intelligence* because the ability to operate the language is innate in us, and it is closely connected with *the evolution of our self-consciousnes*s that is part of the universal consciousness. A part cannot surpass the whole! All we should worry about is *how to better program our super-computers with the language habits and speech skills* that need to work in synch in a holistically-wired brain. So, let's not worry about robots being our enemies in the future.

Let's worry about our computer-programmers being much better educated in linguistics and having the thinking skills that they lack noticeably when it comes to sophisticated language operations. These skills need to be prioritized *in a holistic frame-work.*

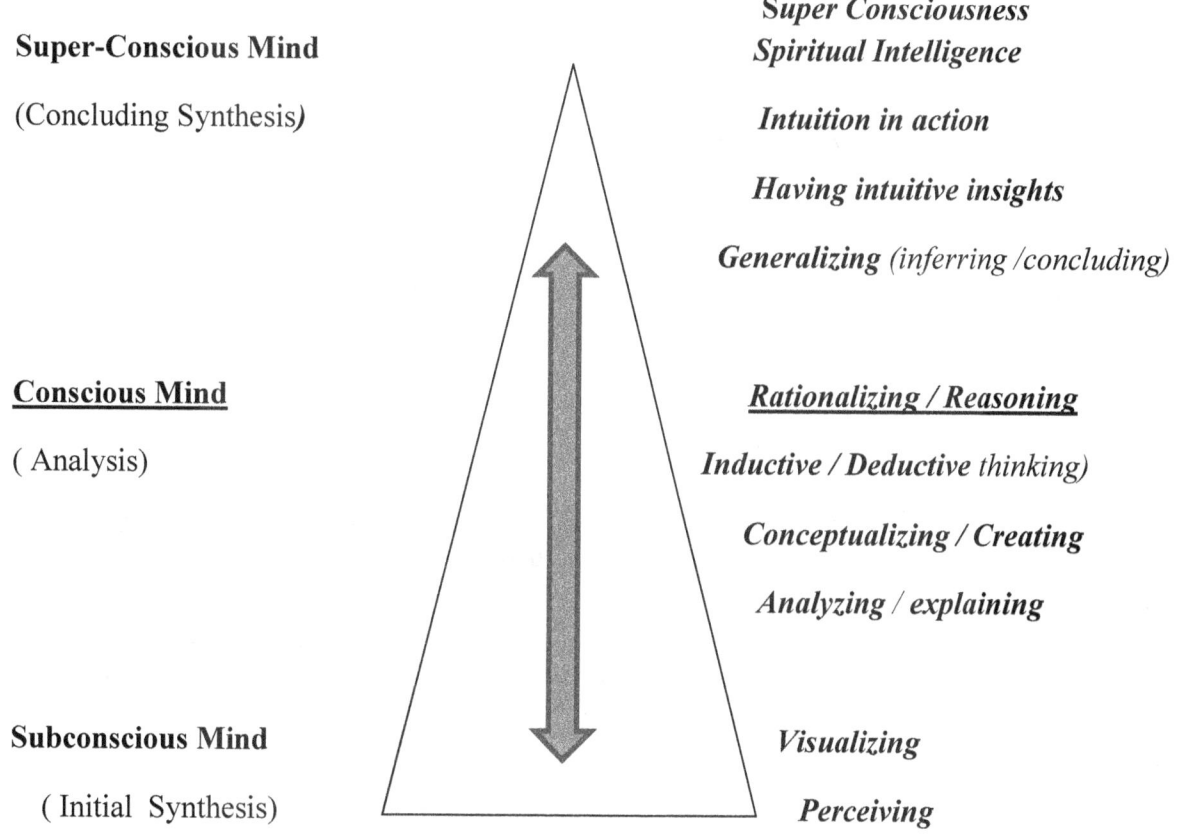

Auto-suggestion: *Live consciously!   Have a thinking life!*

Let's have Evolutionary Vanity to save our Human Sanity!

Chunk 6

Capitalize on the Electronic Competences Consciously!

No doubt, digital evolution is great, and it is unthinkable to imagine our life without this leap in our intelligence. ***Digital intelligence gives us an evolutionary boost with the ever-expanding modes of communication.*** For the last couple of decades, people continually learn new things and ways to communicate with each other on the Internet through the English language, called "***Globbish***" most justifiably now. Every day brings along new unbelievable changes that demand immediate adjustment of our electronic competences.

Thanks to the electronic evolution, each of us is building his / her own ***Tree of Knowledge*** which changes our belief system and impacts the way we rationalize our lives. Every concept, every opinion forms a little branch of that tree through "***intelligence networking***" *(LinkedIn)*

The operating system of the brain is like a computer and, consequently, you need to take care of your brain, your "personal computer" against viruses and other pollutants ***to preserve your tree of intelligence intact and remain authentic in your thinking abilities*** .

Digital intelligence has also come to the forefront of education, involving everyone, from toddles to old people into the vortex of its interplay. Computers improve our cognition, sharpen multi-tasking abilities, speed decision-making, ***increase our aware attention span***, and even prolong our lives. The changes in electronics are amazing and often go beyond our ability to follow them because the artificial intelligence is driven by Thomas Edison's challenge:

"If there is a better way, find it!"

This better way is connected not only with computation, but ***with the language competence*** that is the base of our thinking, especially in terms of holistically-developing our brains. No doubt, digital intelligence strengthens our intellectual culture and develops our resourcefulness. We are in the situation when we have to devote much attention and time to deliberate ***the systemic development of our digital personalities that is a new phenomenon in psychology,*** and we need to do it without self-imposed limitations and in synch with the demand of the time.

Next, we see that ***physical intelligences and digital intelligences are inter-dependable,*** and their synchronic development explains why our indigo kids acquire these intelligences with amazing ease. Our children pick this new intelligence up in the most natural way. Electronic gadgets help develop their thinking skills ***through gaming intelligence.*** New connections in their brains are growing with an unbelievable speed, widening the generation gap that ***can be bridged because our language' thinking capabilities are much higher*** than those of our kids. So, let's keep growing in every respect for self-respect!

When we Know Better, we Do Better!

Chunk 7

Immunity Against Digital Addiction

Obviously, computer intelligence that very many young gifted minds possess, even when it is brilliant, is still *mechanical, dead, programmed, and artificial.* We should continue to expand our minds with the help of electronics, but we should not robotize them and become robots ourselves.

In the Universal Life Spine, we connect the space and time with the artificial intelligence twine!

We have to remember *that the mind monitors the brain, not vice versa* and the computer mind cannot yet substitute the human mind. It will be possible within two decades or earlier, and it will undoubtedly boost our mental evolution to new heights, but *the problem is to find the way we will coordinate our consciousness development with that unstoppable process.*

Consciousness is infinite while the digital mind is finite, created by the Infinity in action. The downside of our overwhelming enrolment with the digital evolution is our inability to prioritize the essential intelligences and *act on them holistically,* using the electronic intelligence as a backup tool for developing our self-consciousness! That's what it is here for!!!

Research warns us that using social media, "*we get used to it in terms of a drug-like behavior*". We get overwhelmed with the avalanche of information, and we often become life-smitten with its flooding stream. We become worn out, de-focused and very virtually-entangled emotionally. Consequently, we fall into *the state of commonly-inflated, or deflated thinking* when we are unable to think straight and be consciously detached from computer programming.

Be Cautious! Be mindful; Be conscious!

I repeat again that the process of developing true and aware digital intelligence must have a holistic outcome that works for the development of our higher consciousness. It should not be hampered by *the robot-like thinking* that becomes totally dependent on the machine because it shoots into *the brain digitally-stagnant habits.* I witness my students' inability to get though the wall of blurry thinking that becomes a new educational challenge. If the flood of digital information is not properly digested, it clogs the mind.

Undigested intelligence results in the situations when a student does not assimilate knowledge; He /she cannot *disassociate himself / herself form the virtual reality*, cannot feel mind-free to express an individual opinion, not the one that can be easily plagiarized and perceived as one's own. The thinking skills enhanced digitally, need to be processed through the holistic paradigm of – *synthesis -analysis -synthesis (See above).* To keep your consciousness intact, practice *Suggestive Meditation*. consistently .

Internalize - Select- Externalize!

Chunk 8

Go Beyond the Basic Content of Your Intellect!

There is another side of the coin here. Despite extreme socialization, we *feel lonely and self-un-reliant, seeking the solution of any problem* by grabbing the cell-phone and calling someone or getting in touch with a "friend" for Face Book. I think that technology makes us more self-reliant, not visa -versa. It's great to know that help is at a click of a finger, but let this feeling add security to your *independent being.* A lonely, dependable person gets obsessed with electronic match-making, kids stop reading and become heartless and indifferent, and we get irritable due to **the lack of face-to-face and heart-to-heart communication** that we start hungering for when we are unaware. Unfortunately, the unstoppable digital in-put and **the cacophony of information** that we get daily is often left unprocessed, unselected, unsorted out for its validity, with no aware attention applied to this indispensable process. As a result**, the neural code in the brain gets messed up,** and it is very hard to untangle it, unless it is meditatively and consciously done.

So, we need to constantly *develop our aware attention skills to oversee both the in-put and the out-put of our mental energy.* A rigid brain control should be taught to raise brain's adaptability to new life demands. With the above said, the unprogrammed living intelligence needs to be developed when the level of our curiosity is high, our rationality is self-controlled, and our wakefulness is conscious and ready to go forward on the ladder of evolution.

Digital intelligence is amazingly creative when it is ***used consciously with much awareness*** and with a lot of sorted-out knowledge. These are the cases of. ***Steve Jobs, Bill Gates, Mark Zuckerberg, Reid Hoffman***, and many more most brilliant advanced-thinking innovators in electronics that have never rested on their laurels and that have bettered the world in so many business, cultural, and social ways.

Only with the computers plugged into our intellectually-emotional volt, can we become ***more intellectualized, strategized, emotionalized, energized, better informed, and totally reformed!*** Digital equation with the neuro-linguistic self-programming that is being promoted here has to make us realize that every advanced idea sends a conceptual signal to the Universal Intelligence, and it is being fed back by it .We witness this interaction in the amazing work of many computer scientists in any area of knowledge that they explore. Let's stand in awe to their contribution to our evolutionary development and never forget their incredible input into our lives. Obviously**, *going beyond the content of a person's own intellect*,** expanding it all the time is what is crucially important for a personality development and the preservation of individuality now.

Auto-suggestion:

I don't think in a Robot-Like Trance; I Relapse!

Chunk 9

Digital Clicking in Love-Seeking

Automatic thinking without awareness is the main dilemma of human existence now! Unprocessed digital intelligence deflates a mind-heart connection ,if such clicking ever occurs! *Numerous match services are booming, but heart + mind connection is swooning.* Everyone is hoping for a soul mate, being unaware that clicking should occur in five holistic levels, or at least in three - *physical, emotional, and mental,* preferably starting with the *spiritual probing of each other* and finishing with the physical testing.

Doing the right thing polishes the mind -heart ring!

The frame-work of many sights for dating is set in scanning a potential partner by asking to fill in the questionnaires that are psychologically-unprofessional and superficial. I think that they need *to be holistically-targeted in five dimensions of life,* mentioned above. Too specified questions are not helpful here. The quality of our intelligence in an inseparable connection with the *heart-based qualities* of kindness, compassion, care, and consideration for the other need to be considered. We should click on both planes to have life gains.

.Thinking + feeling awareness is the blue-print of self– creation and self- fairness.

Being aware means getting rid of compulsive thinking and living in the past. Since our relationship chances are limited to digital communication more and more, we need to use digital means *to enhance, not deflate the mind + heart connection.* . Very soon robots will be able to duplicate and even surpass us in our unique ability to love. The key to this strategy is our understanding of the power of the opposites and the ability to connect them in our behavior, *synergizing our joint intelligence and consciousness on the way.* Self-change focused on *emotionalizing the heart and intellectualizing the mind* is the solution in every area of our technologically-enhanced life.

Mind-to-mind and heart-to heart are the way to that!

Transformation of consciousness to a higher level must be in the goal of our creative minds in technology. It presupposes the change of the frame of thinking, on the one hand, and our observation of *the cosmic Law of Cause –Effect*, on the other. Philosophy teaches us to constantly clean the dashboard of our life errors and start from a clean slate. Our kids should be taught to observe this Law at every level of intelligence formation. **"Eliminate the Cause to change the Consequences".** *"(R. Wetherill," Right is Might!")*

In sum, to rationalize and humanize our lives, we need to learn *the cause-effect strategy of living and enhance the mind + heart connection.*

Mind + Heart are in a Connected Volt Cart!

Chunk 10

Raise Self-Discipline on the Digital Scene!

Digital intelligence is the greatest opportunity for us to establish the needed connection between, **THE MIND AND THE HEART in GAMING** business that is an open sky for us in this respect. .At present, electronic games is the field of war-mongering and the display of super-human powers that develop wrong addictions, while the gaming opportunities are sky- bound in terms of helping *to develop* AWARE ATTENTION *to professional intelligence,* or the kid's / teenagers' / grown-ups' abilities to manage themselves.

Equally important is to use the artificial intelligence *to cultivate good human qualities* and lay the foundation for *a moral, ethical framework of the innovations in neuro-science* and digital technology of the future. We need to teach our kids and ourselves to love, care, display compassion, kindness, truthfulness, and love, through games, that often are heightening their aggressiveness, careless, and an impersonal attitude to the outside world. *Such games only generate inner imperfections* and the disconnection with the parents because the participants *identify themselves with the electronic personages and are losing their own individual characteristics*. The virtual reality gets extended into the real life that is perceives as hostile by the brain that needs de-programming both mentally and emotionally.

Psychologists are desperately seeking the solution to the new addictive behaviors of the growing souls that, when they reach their teens become actually unmanageable, disrespectful, and impersonal, seeking more fun in drugs, alcohol, and excessive, uncontrolled sex. (*Step 2, Chunk 5 above*) **Holistically-applied discipline** at every level generates a new quality of personal integrity that keeps a person from getting morally de-magnetized.

5. Disciplined self-consciousness

4. Spiritual Discipline

3. Mental Discipline

2. Emotional Discipline

1.Physical Discipline

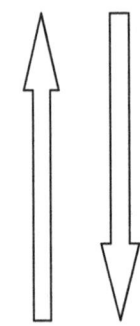

We just need to be conscious of the changes that occur inside and outside us, *getting much more aware of these changes and much more informed about the reasons* that generate any emotional for us or psychological consequences.

Humanize and Harmonize your Contaminated Inner Device!

Chunk 11

Be Integral, Sincere and Kind! Be One of a Kind!

That's why *digital monitoring* in this respect will be a great opportunity for us on the path of raising our consciousness and a great help to our psychologists. Future avatars will be attuned to our psychological imbalances, giving us proper warnings and helping us to get together at the right time Start visualizing your *spiritual, psychological, mental, emotional and physical blocks.* De-magnetize them and delete them with a conscious effort consistently.

Be a Medusa Gorgon!

Freeze stone the unwanted patterns of behavior, emotions, words in you!

Psychological awareness (*See Psychological Intelligence below*) is **essential in electronic games** *to* widen the scope of the beneficial effect of the games that are often the war-fields of aggressiveness and the demonstration of the super-power. There are boundless opportunities to engage players in the activities that develop holistic *Living Intelligence* Skills and instill the most noble qualities in them.

Being integral, sincere and kind should reside in a super human mind!

In sum, we should use our future electronic friends, programmed into a wrist watch, or any other mind-boggling form *to boost the spirit* by suggesting right decisions, expand our educational horizons, or instill in us the right emotional response by *charging the situation-prompted mind-set at the right place and at the right time.* For sure, future gadgets will be properly tuned to our mental, emotional, and psychological states. Electronics is our step forward on the ladder of evolution, and it is the greatest device that we have had so far in our exploration of the world. Shape your digitally-focused mind to become more self-consciously refined!

Marvel at the Internet that is God-se, t but be connected to the Conscious Life Net!

This is what *the auto-suggestive mind-programming does t*o your brain naturally. You can program your smart phone not only to boost your spirit, but also to instill in you the qualities that you wish to enhance at any time and in any place. Very soon, we'll be able to fix our psychological and moral imperfections with the help of digital identities, called *avatars* that will reveal more aspects of our personalities. Undoubtedly, digital intelligence will promote our brain wavelength to a much higher overtone enabling us *to heighten the level of our consciousness considerably* with each evolutionary step of the humanity at large.

Wow! I wish I could live then, in the Unanswerable When!

Chunk 12

The Age of Quantum Computing Has Come!

As I have mentioned above, the age of the unprecedented power of the artificial mind is coming to our life stage, and ,therefore, considerable improving of our thinking abilities of *reasoning, conceptualizing, analyzing, and generalizing* become exceedingly important. These abilities should continue being the prerogative of our general education and self-education. now. Any most advanced computer is a great tool, **but it is not the Universal Intelligence itself, part of which we are.**

Undoubtedly, developing **AWARE ATTENTION** to what is going on in life in terms of mechanization of our thinking comes to the forefront of our digital education. Zillions of websites are competing for our aware attention that needs to be channeled with much more *conscious selection* on our part. *Aware attention development is at the core of digital intelligence now*! We need to adjust our brains to the ever-expanding modes of communication to deal with the avalanche of information and a brutal job competition that electronic evolution has generated. Self–suggestive work is the best reminder to you about your being the owner of your mi**nd**. It helps de-atomize our thinking, speaking, and acting!

Auto-suggestion   ***I am becoming more intellectualized , not robotized!***

In sum, the electronic evolution is meant to help our consciousness get enriched with higher overtones of intellectual interaction., based on considerably enriched language intelligence. Digital intelligence is a great part of our intelligence when it is **consciously monitored by the mind** in the process of self-actualization aimed at the evolution of the humanity in five levels consistently. ***Heighten your magnetic electricity volt!***

See how it integrates into your physical, emotional, mental, spiritual and universal world!

Amazingly, with digital intelligence in progress, ***we are tuning ourselves to the Universal Intelligence electronically and physically in some inseparable link,*** synchronizing our terrestrial existence with the extra-terrestrial one in the most amazing way.

Every Human Mind is One of a Kind!

Start Mind-Wising –

Generalizing - Selecting - Actualizing!

Chunk 13

Strict Mental Hygiene is on the Scene!

Giving more tribute to our fantastic computer engineers, let's remember that thanks to the magnetic currents that we are surrounded by now, the brain *"invents entirely new coding schemes for novel situations". (Freedman)* The ability of such intelligence is called" ***the improvisational dexterity of the brain".*** *"We need to set up an entirely different set of neural signals, create implantable brain chips that can restore or enhance memory thanks to the embedded electrodes in slices of hippocampus."*

"It is both liberating and constraining in its essence." (Richard J. Haier)

This is a very challenging goal because this process requires ***a strict mental hygiene*** to be constantly performed with the help of meditation or auto-suggestion. Also, we need to learn ***inner brain-scanning.*** It presupposes the necessity to develop the habit to sort out and delete the polluting the brain information and organize it into conceptual chunks at the conscious s effort of the mind. The brain needs to be able ***to compartmentalize the incoming information at the command of the conscious mind*** as opposed to a computer that does it automatically.

Mental discipline is the skill that needs to be trained continuously and consciously!

The uniqueness of each of us represents a fundamental barrier to science attempts to understand and control mind. Dreaming of finding ways of our expansion into space, imagining high speed travel in low pressure tubes, participating in the on-going robot revolution, or thinking of becoming a would-be specialist in robotics are the ways of expanding our digital intelligence.

The mind should never stop steering the brain, not just a gadget in hand!

Frankly, digital intelligence also demands that we **heighten our brain wave frequencies!** We, supposedly, are yet unable to see the aliens that most likely are trying to get in touch with our civilization because they are overtones higher in their vibrational power than us. The goal is to advance the operational capacity of a computer from billions to trillions, and from trillions to quadrillions of operations a second. Consequently, we" *need to constantly turn the mental rheostat to the mark that is* ***"brighter, brighter, and faster!"*** *(Robert Stone)*

Let's give much credit to the producers of space trip movies and TV shows that promote extra-terrestrial thinking, making us marvel at the scope of their intelligence that expands the unused capacity of a human brain. The Oscar award movie "**Gravity**" is a great illustration of what we might be like in the future. Our great actors, Sandra Bullock and George Clooney materialize our future thinking capabilities in a mind-boggling way!

The Quality of Our Thinking becomes the Priority!

Chunk 14

Five-Dimensional Self-Consciousness

To conclude my outlining of the *General Intelligence* for us evolution-wise, let me reiterate that the intelligence that we need now is something that *must be redefined and constantly updated scientifically and technologically.* Being aware on both venues is key. .

We all make mistakes, feel lazy and overwhelmed with life, but if we develop the bone of breaking the old conditioning that makes us victims of ourselves due to our *old level of consciousness, ,* we will become much more aware of the consequences of our unconscious or automatic actions before we take them. We need *to develop aware attention* to the" **how** "instead of the "**what**" we are doing, and it is *aware attention* that needs to be developed urgently.

Aware attention channels our self-governed thought process toward conscious action, away from living in a robot-like trance.

Aware attention is the state of the mind when we can properly encode the incoming information as well as retrieve it thanks to our *creating a sufficiently strong neural network* in the brain and modernizing it in the same way we improve our computing with new developments every day. Professor Giamo Undivert from the Institute of Neuro-Informatics in Zurich and his team have managed to give a computer the brain that can perform tasks requiring *short-term memory, decision-making, and analytical abilities of its own.*

The IBM researcher Dharmedra Modha and his team are also building the computer that works like a human brain, the one that is able to mimic human abilities for sensation, perception, interaction, and cognition. *("Scientific American Mind", Sep. / Oct. 2014)* There are other amazing testimonies of the computers in robotics developing consciousness of their own, becoming independent of the programmer's commands, and this fact scares the public with its unpredictability.

"You cannot conquer life because the part cannot conquer the whole,

but you can be the best part of the whole!" (Carl Yung)

The mind is the product of the brain that is based on the memory mechanisms, and the dynamics of our learning relate to memory formation. *This fact is most hopeful and intriguing!* A phenomenal discovery of our time connected with *brain plasticity* provides a general structure in neuro-science 's *"connectionist's"* view of the brain as a highly plastic organ ,defined by inter-laced connection among neurons and brain regions.

This is how Eric Kandel defines us, *"You are your synopses."* Dr. Kandel revealed that we learn not by altering neurons, but by strengthening or building new synapses or connections between them – a breakthrough of our time. To put it simply, we change ourselves *by changing our memories*. Our biological computers are run by the memory that we have accumulated and the one that we can change *consciously, consistently, and holistically* by altering our awareness about this amazing revelation about the way we can rebuilt ourselves.

" We are who we are because of what we have learned and what we remember' (Eric Kandel)

Yes, the machines will be way faster in operating their electronic memories, but they will never be able *to integrate them* the way a human, well-trained, holistically-educated , creatively-unstoppable brain can do., taking us on a new journey of self-consciousness development because *intelligence and consciousness are inseparable.*

Perceptually, *our consciousness has height, depth and width.* It's great to be reasoning in these three dimensions, but the work of self-actualization and the pressure of the present-day digital evolution demand that we upgrade our consciousness from three-dimensional to the four–dimensional level, obtaining *the volume of consciousness* that can be obtained if we develop our self-consciousness in a holistic unity at every level of consciousness s development

If a human mind can create a twin machine, why can't we perfect ours and step up to *the fifth dimension of consciousness* – the universal expansion of *the volume of our consciousness* by considerably enriching it at the third, mental and the forth, spiritual levels *with the help of the artificial intelligence, that is taking us to the extra-terrestrial realms of life*. The science proves that *there is no consciousness without intelligence., or there is no mind without the brain*

"The mind is the product of the brain." (Eric Kandel, a Nobel Prize winner)

The Grid of Our Consciousness Integration (See Thesis 2)

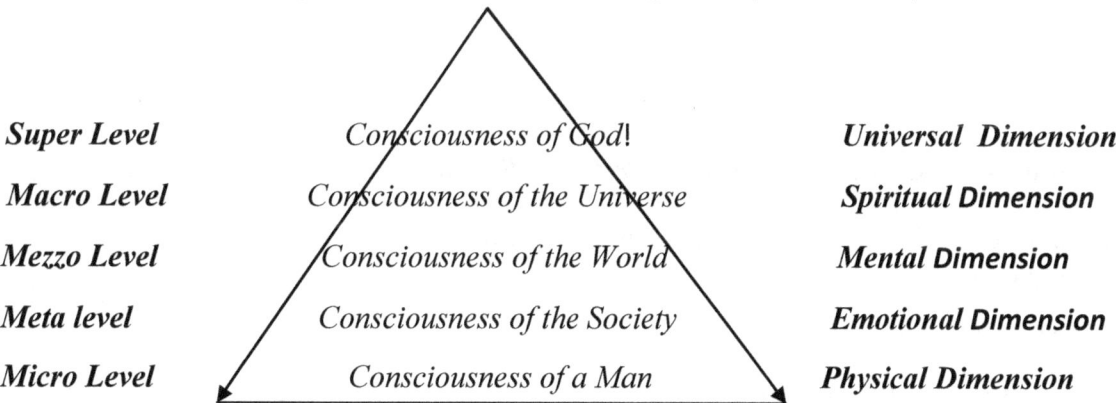

Super Level	*Consciousness of God!*	**Universal Dimension**
Macro Level	*Consciousness of the Universe*	**Spiritual Dimension**
Mezzo Level	*Consciousness of the World*	**Mental Dimension**
Meta level	*Consciousness of the Society*	**Emotional Dimension**
Micro Level	*Consciousness of a Man*	**Physical Dimension**

Be Your Own Coach in Life!
Be a Conscious, Digitally-Enhanced Human Type!

Chunk 15

The Holistic Education is the Solution for Our Evolution!

Our educational goal is to gradually move to the universal realm of extra-terrestrial communication and become the citizens of the universal realm of the mind - *the Source !*New amazing discoveries are made every day thanks to the electronic intelligence in every area of science that is propelling us *up-ward, on-ward, and God-ward.* Apparently, the development of human consciousness is inseparable from the digital evolution that is pushing us forward in terms of *creating a new volume of our consciousness that* will expand our communication with each other and the world around us inconceivably. *(See Electronic Intelligence below)*

No doubt, artificial intelligence is channeling our evolution!

New times need constructive, well-structured, properly-channeled, emotionally-empowered minds that will necessitate physical, emotional, mental, spiritual, and universal changes and propel us forward to the Star people level.

The fantastic thought-machine of yours is not for the residence of moths!

There is a great old Jewish saying that illustrates the idea of a conceptual mind-set that we need to generate, *"If there are only two courses of action, you should always take the third one."* In our case, it's the self-development along the paths *of the Holistic Education* , the education that provides the development of intelligence *in five levels* that will considerably expand our human evolutionary outreach and raise our self-consciousness:

Physical +Emotional + Mental + Spiritual + Universal!

Unconscious ⟶ Conscious ⟶ Superconscious

Self-awareness – Self-Monitoring - Self-Installation – Self-Realization - Self-Salvation!

Such education, backed up by an exponential growth of technology and supplemented by an irresistible urge for self-installation in life, should follow *the holistic formula: Synthesis - Analysis- Synthesis!*

Internalizing knowledge - Personalizing it – Externalizing it!

Our Digitally-Enhanced Human Essence

is in the Intellectual and Spiritual Renaissance!

Chunk 16

Increase the Psycho-Tronic Energy of Your Consciousness!

Concluding *Stage One - General Intelligence,* let's focus on heightening of our brain-wave frequency by considering the essential concepts, outlined above, avoiding the traps of ignorance that appear to be the hurdles to overcome consistently and consciously, and *by tuning up to the Universal Intelligence for intuitively-gotten advice.*

Attune your mind's Auto-Antenna to the Universe! Be Your Own Boss!

Re-program your mind to avoid:

1. Taking advice from people you want to trade places with. Amaze yourself with your own! (*Socialize, relying on personal advice!*)

2. Doing nasty things to people but asking forgiveness from God!

3. Feeling regrets about the past.(Delete the memories of the past1

4. Having worries about the future. (Upload a new, inspirational mind-set auto-suggestively!)

5. Being ungrateful for the present!(To be more life-fit! Enjoy the present of it!)

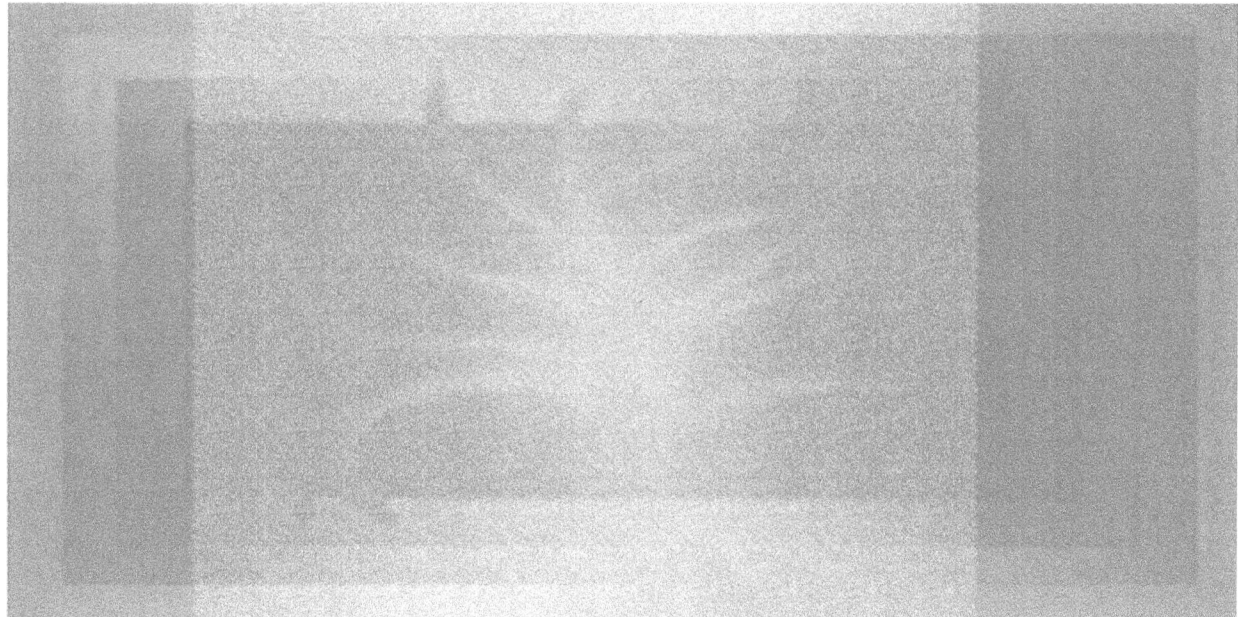

Digitize the Mind in the tact with the Heart Beat," So Be It!"

(End of the Physical Intelligence Part -Mini-Level of the Holistic Paradigm of Self-Actualization- Mental Dimension)

Vistas of Intelligence to Instill Next

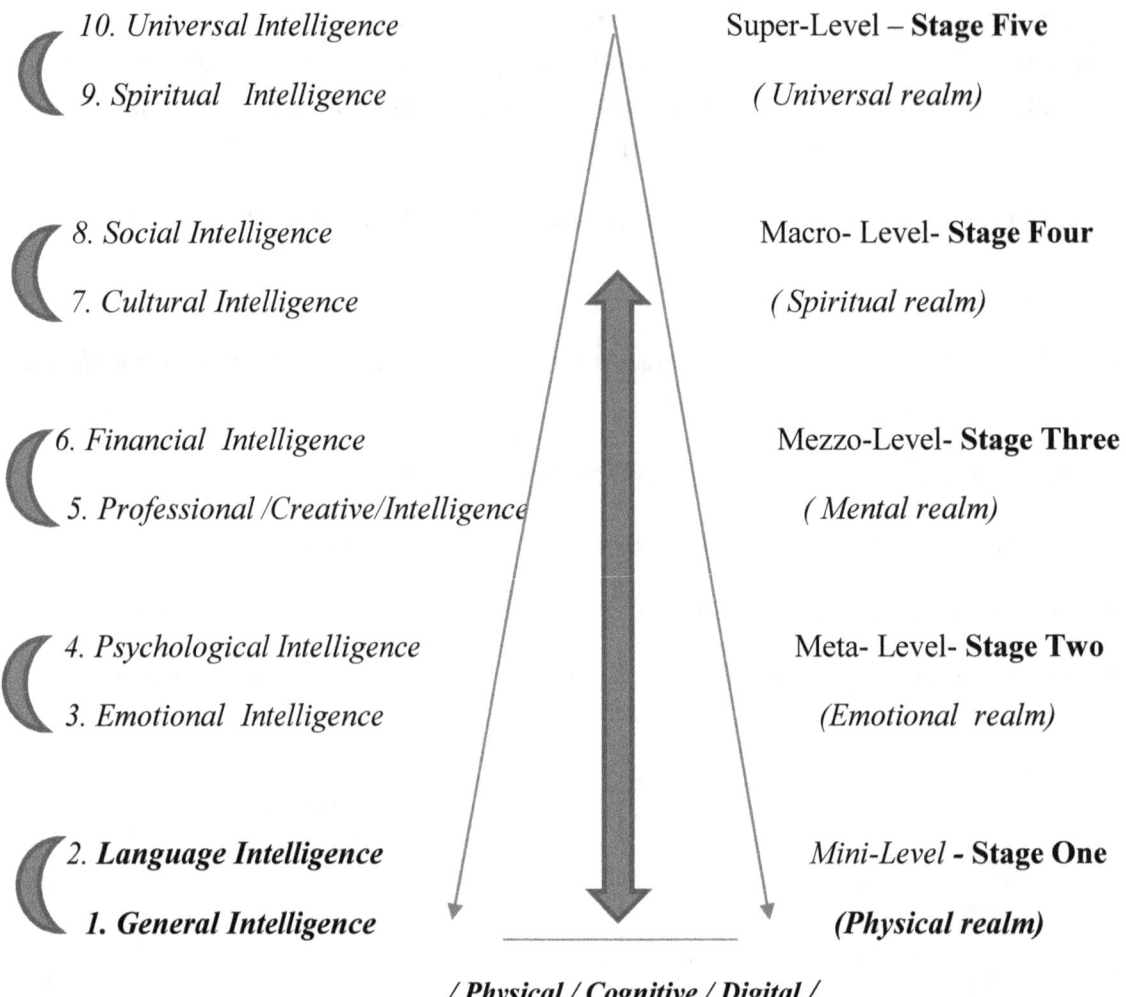

"Fertilize your mind with thinking!" (Albert Einstein)

To Make Your Life Intellectually-Wise, Strategize – Optimize - Actualize!

Stage One

Mini-Level of Intelligence   Physical Dimension

Language Intelligence

(General Intelligence - Step Two)

"There is only one language in the world – the language of God – the rest are just dialects" (Umberto Eco)

(For more, see the book "Language Intelligence or Universal English")

Be Language-Fit to Feel Complete!

Have Language Awareness with Fairness!

Language is Me; Language is My Identity!

Chunk 1

Language is the Matrix of Our Thinking!

Every Language is a miniature universe and language intelligence determines our life in it. It is the essential intelligence, the one that separates us from the animal kingdom and gives us the main assert – our **thinking consciousness.** *"Thinking is a subtle state of speech, verbal or written".* (*"Language Intelligence or Universal English,"* Book One) **Rationalization of the language use is inseparable from the rationalization of thinking** that requires another level of language awareness.

The words we use create the states we are in.

Inspiring words inspire! Despairing words despair!

There is no intelligence of any kind without language in the brain! That is why language Intelligence is **at the mini-level of the holistic pyramid of intelligences** that we have to ascend in our self-creation. *(Introduction, Thesis 13).*

I have not started the presentation of **the hierarchy of intelligences** with the language intelligence because, unfortunately, before a person comes to the realization of the necessity **to tame his tongue**, he first gets interested in preserving his health and prolonging his life span, as well as learning and doing something life demands. No doubt, language Intelligence permeates all the vistas of intelligence that a person has to develop in the process of self-actualization.

Language is the mind; they are an inseparable celestial index!

In the Introduction of the thesis statements of this book, I compare **the interconnectedness of all the intelligences** that we must develop on the path of self-formation to the Russian dolls. Like the Top Doll that encloses all the rest of the dolls in its structure, **the Universal Intelligence** is covering our intellectual development and consciousness rising, acting as **the blanket intelligence,** with **the Language Intelligence being at its core** , and it is this intelligence that needs to be developed holistically, to begin with.

Each language phenomenon is rooted in the brain, as **the matrix of thinking and the root of our self-consciousness.** As a matter of fact, *"pure reason" (Emanuel Kant)* **is the Universal Intelligence** by which every language phenomenon is roofed.

Our language capacity development will always exceed the best computer in the quality of your thinking and its conceptual display

Language is the core of our Cerebrally-Conscious existence.

Chunk 2

Language Awareness

Our consciousness is part of the Universal Intelligence / consciousness that will never be exceeded by any machine because no machine will ever be able to operate the language the way our trained brains do.

"Language is a dynamic interplay of consciousness." (Rav. P.S. Berg)

Developing our intelligence, we are automatically raising self-consciousness, and both evolutionary accomplishments are impossible without the holistic development of language intelligence, or the unity of **the language habits and - speech skills** that determine holistic thinking and can be considerably improved with technological enhancement.

Holistic thinking based on the holistically-developed language skills. means the holistic work of both hemispheres! The brain is a very complex machine, but its broad topography is simple and symmetrical in managing the two main parts of it. The left hemisphere is rational, analytical, and logical ; the right one is non-linear that , instinctive, and intuitive. Language resides mainly in the left hemisphere that reasons sequentially, excels at analysis, handles words, and operates the structural system of the language, or it's grammar.

The right side of the brains reasons holistically, recognizes patterns, interprets emotions, and builds up thoughts and concepts with the vocabulary tools that the left hemisphere provides. That's why the development of this hemisphere is crucial at the technological times. The right hemisphere of the brain is underused at present and this fact undermines our holistic brain development. Obviously, knowledge in neuro-science in this respect ,is essential for boosting our thinking abilities because driving a car blindly, we will eventually come to a dead end .

Our language awareness will boost language intelligence that, in turn, is the pe-requisite for the cognitive development of the brain. A person who hardly ever reads and is tongue-tied in speaking cannot accomplish a lot in life on the venue of creation. Consciously developing our language intelligence, we are automatically raising self-consciousness that is the goal of our evolution. Language can be mechanically-programmed, but it cannot be mechanically- dynamic *in raising our self-consciousness that* is supposed to *evolve the holistic mind + hear*t connection that is broken in us at present. The evolution is pushing us to this unity, and we can witness it in the best, most-advanced people among us. This unity is the reflection of the holistic development of the brain with the right hemisphere taking the creative lead in the development of our intelligence that is language-based., *We cannot change the outer projection (speech)-* the right brain, **unless we change the inner program (language)-** *the left brain.*

Being Language Conscious, we become more Life-Conscious!

Chunk 3

Language Consciousness!

Unfortunately, our language intelligence is suffering tremendously now. The memory is clogged with disunited information, the vocabulary stock of many people is appallingly limited. There are many junk words and phrases that ***substitute the clear-cut expression of thought. There are no words in the brain to help a primitive mind out.*** The hierarchic nature of language mirrors the hierarchical nature of our consciousness, or unconsciousness.

Language Intelligence is language consciousness in action!

Our language consciousness is part of our ***Universal Language Interaction*** with ***the Unified Field of Information (Dr. John Hagelin)*** that is permeating everything and that we are part of.

The scope of our memory at present is ***7 plus / minus 2.*** It means that we can retain seven or nine pieces of information or words at one presentation. The technological enhancement will change this capacity tremendously, but the brain won't be able to ever work at the speech of the hyper-computers that we develop. It is quite natural and understandable. Since the artificial intelligence disciplines the use of the language, ***we need to do the same***, but in our creative, conscious, and exponentially-unstoppable way because ours is ***flexible, not mechanically-based language-intelligence***. Our interaction is based on language -consciousness, *inseparable with the Unified Field,* perceiving our mental signals and responding to them through its digital means.

Language intelligence is "telling" the brain not only WHAT to think, but HOW to think!

As a psycho-linguist, I am sure that computers will never be able to beat us in our language intelligence and the flexibility of ***thinking + feeling***. capabilities. Computers can create art, compose beautiful music, inspire great minds of Steve Jobs type, but they will never produce another Lord Byron or Tchaikovsky, another Einstein or Dostoevsky, another Sigmund Freud or Nikola Tesla. These people had ***exceptional minds and a very rich emotional perception*** of the beauty of the world, that the artificial mind will never be possible to develop in synch to that quality. Most importantly, the artificial intelligence can never master cognitive and emotional intelligence ***holistically*** which is another step in obtaining ***language consciousness***, inseparable with the Universal Intelligence - Consciousness we are living in.

To be consciousness- refined, we need to intellectualize the emotions and emotionalize the mind!

Nickolas Roerich, a great Russian scientist and an artist who had been probing the extra-terrestrial and spiritual realms all his life and the tribute to whose life is given in a wonderful museum in the center of Manhattan, once said,

Beauty that is Consciously-Perceived will Save the World!

Chunk 4

Language Fitness without Cognitive Sickness!

We know that *the **digital neocortex is being created in now***, but I think that, irrespective of this mind-boggling fact, we won't be able to raise our language consciousness that I have touched upon above , without healing our **Language Habits** and *perfecting the Speech Skills* both in a native language and English that is called by linguists "Globish" now. The way the English language is used on the Internet and while people do texting on their smart phones is appalling. New language-awareness needs to be instilled in our schools as early as possible, because the damage that we are doing to our language intelligence might become irreversible.

Language fitness is directly connected to **RATION + EMOTIO** *fitness.*

I consider the English language that is dominating the technological world to be the language that helps us develop the language fitness that evolution demands from us. English ,when consciously used, can express absolutely anything in the most precise, thought-provoking, insightfully-beautiful way because it has an exceptionally-simple ,linear grammatical structure.

English is the first global language in computation because its structure is a one-way street. ***It's mathematically-correct*** and, therefore can be used for programming. The word-order of the English language lets the machine perform linear thinking operations. ***The lexical wealth of English has an incredible volume of a shot-cut scientific preciseness, too***. That's why there is never exact translation possible computer-wise from English into any other language and vice versa. The linear restructuring of the mind is needed when the English mentality comes into play .That is why English is rapidly developing from the status of a global language into the status of the universal one, ***the language of God!*** Obviously, language operating robots should be programed ***by very good linguists, not just electronically-smart programmers.*** We should not have any negative experiences language-wise, like with poorly programmed dictionaries.

In sum, we need ***to raise our awareness about how the brain works , creating the mind.*** "*Our neocortex is virgin territory when the language mentality is created. It has the capacity of learning and therefore creating new connections between its patterns , but it gains these connections from experience*" (Ray Kurzweil) ***It means that learning and recognition take place simultaneously***. If we learned the pattern consciously, we recognize it. The neocortex is continuously trying to make sense of the in-put, presented to it. So, we need to constantly select the information , and delete the one that clogs the neurological paths and blocks our creative thinking and holistic brain development. Consciously discipline your thoughts language-wise!

Learn to Speak Consciously; Language is the Passport of Your Personality!

Chunk 5

Language Pollution Impedes Personal Evolution!

The lack of language controlling skills is always connected with *the lack of the bad language immunity* that I have touched upon above. In the process of self-transformation, we cannot afford to speak casually, automatically, polluting our speech with banal phrases, junk words, and commonly-used misjudgments. We must not let our bad language habits make us dis-empowered emotionally and mentally. We have to kill them, or as Albert Einstein put it,

"Bad habits have a good tendency; either you kill them, or they kill you."

The knowledge of a native language or of English that is ruling the world now is marked by our thinking, feeling, and acting in these languages. There is a flood of **language pollution** on the Internet and around you, but our language intelligence should not be affected by this avalanche of contaminated language. There should not be any casual word use, without any monitoring of a thought. A beautiful British saying testifies to such a necessity.

Self-induction: *"You never have a second chance to make a good first impression!"*

The holistic approach to language-speech performance also demands that we develop a tight control over **the synchronicity** between the language habits and speech skills that we have noted above. It's not an easy thing to master, but it is not altogether impossible.

Language habits (*Pronunciation, Grammar, and Vocabulary*) that constitute **the language operandi system** are formed very slowly, and they require aware attention to be paid to redesigning them **to** make our pronunciation or diction comprehensible, our grammar accurate, and the vocabulary use varied and exact in its transmitting our thoughts.

Speech skills *(Listening, Speaking, Reading, and Writing)* are formed much quicker. We need to learn to be economical and exact in speaking, conceptually-oriented in reading, and insightfully perceptive in writing. However, if the speech skills are formed on the automatic pilot, without **aware attention being paid to the process of conscious language use**, bad habits are very difficult to be eradicated. That's why many junk words that pollute the speaking of our kids are so difficult to be rid of.

Bad language habits result in bad language rituals.

Bad language rituals result in a bad speech performance. Bad speech performance results in a bad destiny because we stop paying conscious attention to the way we speak and to the exactness of the messages that we communicate with the help of the language. **Bad language control and meaningless talkativeness generate** family problems, relationship fractions, job problems, money loss, and, ultimately, health worsening. Only conscious, aware attention to the way you speak does the trick.

Auto- induction: *"A minute of your thinking is worth an hour of talking."*

Since speaking is actually our first action since birth, it needs to be governed by this rule all life. So, don't ever stop controlling your language, a native one or English, because the image that might have been once sharp and clear becomes dim and blurry with lack of language control. What we do not use, we lose!

Language degradation is a very quick process that drags us down unstoppably!

Degradation in language intelligence is also connected with **the degradation of a personality** - slagging of character, weakening of will-power, emotional misbalance, and **inflation of thinking.** *(Cognitive Intelligence, Chunk 5)* So, motivate yourself to do any action by correct speaking about it. Any problem gets resolved through *correct language framing* because any problem awareness is heightened by language exactness.

The philosophical effect of framing is amazingly effective in preserving our language ecology and dealing with language intelligence, emotional intelligence, or psychological one. An unframed picture always looks less impressive.

Auto-induction: *I am much less if I am frameless!*

In short, language pollution impedes personal evolution. What's really amazing is the inner feeling of accomplishment that you will generate once you start working on your **language ecology consciously.**

Auto-induction: ***Commit to Being Language-Fit!***

(For more, check out my web-page Language-fitness.com)

Be Devoid of an Automatic Speaking Negligence;
Use the Language of the Universal Intelligence!

Chunk 6

Mind Your Thought-Coding!

(An Inspirational Booster)

Mind your thought-coding

And word - molding!

    They are of a wave nature;

    Both have the same DNA structure!

A thought and a word are the forms of light,

There is no enlightenment without their might!

    They are the unity of everything that's light and dark

    A thought and a word are under their ark!

The shade from a thought has an evil eye,

The shade from a word is a sure lie!

    So, a thought and a word

    Should not be twisted or have an evil distort!

To preserve the sacredness of their toes,

We must consciously guard them both!

Practice a Strict Language Hygiene in Your Personal Mental Gene!

Chunk 7

Language Correctness and Speech Exactness

"Language is our first action in life!" *(A. A. Leontief)* There is no evolution of intelligence without *language fitness* because there is no development of consciousness without the clarity of thought and the accuracy of word. Also, language has a profound effect on our life, and it needs to be grammatically correct and lexically precise. We are defined by the way we speak and write!

Language should be in rapport with speech in the holistic unity of the left +right hemispheres.

The moment a person opens his mouth and says something, you can place him for his social status, profession, attitude to life, and even his philosophy of life. Taking care of our physical fitness, or our physical intelligence, we often forget to control *our verbal impeccability* and, thus, we display most disrespectful attitude to the language in which we communicate our thoughts. In our digital times, the adequateness of the thoughts that we impart and the language that we use have become appalling. We cannot establish *a good mind-to-mind contact* with a conversation partner in a face-to face communication or in the virtual space., unless the language and speech are in synch.

We need to speak / write correctly, language –wise, and with precision, speech-wise.

Correct speaking of a person relates to his correct behavior because it signifies to his correct thinking. Speaking with precision and, therefore, correctly, being able to adequately communicate your ideas requires *a precise choice of words* that gives you the chance *to say what you mean and to mean what you say.*

Obviously, *language unfitness always testifies to lack of intelligence.* We should note here that any personal contact to be adequate has to be based on proper language habits – *good grammar, correct sentence structure, and meaningful vocabulary choice.* We must be sharpening our language skills all life to be able to express ourselves clearly and consciously, both verbally and in writing.

The use of the language in *artificial programming should be especially accurate* Language operating should be marked by conscious, controlled, sense-making mode of speaking that requires also *much richer vocabulary stock, too.*

The brain constructs the vocabulary of a single person.

It is always personal, and therefore, each of us speaks and thinks differently, and this difference is always monitored by the richness / scarcity of the vocabulary that we use. It will not be an overstatement to say that there is no personal growth without a substantial growth of the vocabulary stock in a person's brain.

The richer the vocabulary, the better the thinking!

We can diversify our language habits and speech skills much better if **we read consciously**, paying attention to what we read, *conceptualizing the text while reading* and paying aware attention to the richness of the vocabulary that is being used by the writer. These skills should be developed in schools through extensive *mind-provoking reading though, analyzing, interpreting, and synthesizing the information* verbally and in a written form.

Synthesis- Analysis –Synthesis!

Professional vocabulary skills are also extremely important in this respect *(See Professional Intelligence)* The professional use of the language means that we need to make the right vocabulary choice to express our thoughts adequately in any professional environment and to describe any problem in a concise way and to find a short-cut to its solution as quick as possible.

Self- induction: *"Talk the Talk!"*

This rule is applied to any area of expertise because every profession has its own vocabulary stock in use. If we are not aware of this vocabulary, our talking about job problems is vague and, hence, the decision-making skills will never be formed adequately. It's also very helpful professionally *to visualize the professional terminology* what you hear it.

Self-induction: *Practice visual listening!*

In sum, evolution of a language use requires *the paradigm shift in language competence* because it redirects our attention from the predominant focusing on the speech skills to a holistic and keenly conscious linking of *language habits and speech skills. (Chunk 2 above)*

We can tell our brain not only what to think, but how to think and what to say! Going along this path of perfecting our language intelligence, you will inevitably stop being self-conscious especially when speaking in public and *become more language conscious*. With your attention to the language in you, you will be much better perceived by people *in your face-to-face, mind-to-mind, and heart-to-heart communication.*

The communication at the heart-to- heart and mind-to -mind basis is an opportunity to be changed by another person!

Stop Seeing Yourself in the Language and Start Seeing the Language in You!

Chunk 8

Language-Speech Immunity

To conclude this part, language intelligence also means developing *language-speech immunity against using bad words, junk words, cursing, insulting people, yelling, constant lying and, most importantly, judging yourself and others.* The ability to control thinking and speaking is a real might! Bad language-speech immunity is the obstacle to self-regeneration overall.

Auto- induction: *Watch your word!*

Bad language habits get harbored in the brain, and they require **individual, intentional, and conscious surgery** to be done to irradiate them from there. In his wonderful book that is amplifying to us the meaning of the Universal Law of the Right Human Behavior**, Richard W. Wetherill writes,"** "Nobody can change human nature, but we can change people's thinking and speaking and though that their behavior can be changed, too" *("Right is Might"*)

Language de-contamination and its eventual healing is a willful process!

Try to have a small language survey of people's speaking around you. Go for a walk in the park or just sit on a bench and watch the world go by, focusing especially on how people are talking behind your back or in front of you when passing by. You will be appalled to discover that they are talking about someone doing something wrong, or they are complaining about something done wrong to them.

Negative assessments of people and life are heard all over: *"That's absurd. / It's insane. / It's crazy. / It's ridiculous. / I can't take it anymore! / Are you nuts? / Leave me alone./ You know what I mean, etc.* There is a lot of cursing accompanying these reactions, too.

Intelligence and attitude are shining through the language!

Why can't we share our most inspiring emotions, talk about some great things that we have done, complement each other and oneself on doing a lot of good things that often go unnoticed and unappreciated because we are not in the habit of paying attention to them? I am extremely grateful to **Oprah Winfrey,** the woman that had shaped the minds of millions in the world and injected eternal, positive values of love, respect, and morals into her public. It was the first TV show that I was very much impressed with, being very used to the Russian style of intellectualizing the public through TV. People hunger for the shows of this level of *intellectual challenge and emotional pumping.* What a great professional and personal magnetism and inner integrity!

Obviously, the quality of thought generates the quality of speech and modifies behavior. Constructive, language-sensitive, very knowledgeable, informative, and *thought-provoking shows* by *Charlie Rose, Larry King , Oprah ,and Diane Soya* also helped me a lot to intellectually survive for years on end and gave me much needed food for thought language-wise.

Brain imaging proves now that even the circuitry in the brain brightens up when we speak correctly and beautifully.

Negativity in our speech, on the contrary, darkens the brain and pollutes our thoughts and words, to say nothing about the spirit that is directly connected with the desire to change ourselves, to improve, and to perfect.

Finally, there is too much language contamination on the Internet!

People text each other, using the language horrendously, without observing any rules of grammar, spelling, punctuation, capitalization, etc. ***The number of language errors is appalling!*** This disrespectful use of the language is a direct testimony of a person's messy, muddled thinking and his / her disorganized brain.

Self-Induction: ***If you text, do it with the correct language reflex!***

The fact that people prefer texting to actual talking ***adds to the contamination of the language*** even more. English, being the global language now, suffers the most, and a decisive personal action is needed to be taken on the part of every one of us ***to stop this avalanche of language deterioration.*** Young people, especially kids, become bad language hoarders, and the work at cleansing their conscious language use should, therefore, start as early as possible.

Self-Induction ***I re–engineer my language and modify my speech!***

In sum, we can tell the brain not only what to say, but also how to say it. Developing language intelligence requires constant language control, so that the unconscious language use could be hampered by the conscious awareness of the language incorrectness that should be immediately taken care of. The art of managing the language is every one's personal responsibility! Language perfection should always signify to our never-ending intelligence enrichment and raising of our consciousness.

Auto-Induction: ***I organize my language and beautify my speech!***

I fill them both with the philosophy I preach!

My Language Mending is Never Ending!

Chunk 9

Tame Your Tongue!

"Language is impregnated with individual characteristics of a person" (John Binge) People who are language–savvy get along better with relatives, friends, and colleagues at work. Their thinking is normally well-structured, and they can better communicate their thoughts to their listeners. They think before saying something, and they oversee their tongues. Apparently, *a language-savvy person has a strong, confident, well-developed language personality.*

Goal # 1 – *Developing a new language personality* is the primary goal in working on language intelligence. A language intelligent person manages his language as much as he manages himself. Every religious book of wisdom tells us about the absolute necessity **to tame the tongue** since uncontrolled speaking is sinful. In our knowledge–based and increasingly competition–driven society, *language skills are certainly number one aptitude* and determines our intellectual health.

Auto-induction: *"Be impeccable with your word! (Don Miguel Ruiz)*

Goal # 2 - *Language Intelligence means thinking first and saying something next.* If you become polished in your language in tone and vocabulary, if you are very out-spoken and clear-cut in self-expression, if you can *express yourself clearly the first time around*, your language intelligence is healthy and solid. All these qualities become attainable if you manage your language, or, in other words, *if you put the letter" T" before the letter "S"* in your language use.

Auto-induction: *Think before speaking!*

Goal # 3 - *Redundancy pollutes our communication and kills our precious time. Speak less!* Language mirrors your personality, and it helps establish and maintain a better rapport with people if you are clear, concise, and exact in self-expression.

Self-induction: *Avoid speaking with nothing to say!*

Goal # 4 - *Learn to hold your tongue to avoid saying more than you can!* Language communication needs an absolute establishment of a **mind-to-mind contact** with an interlocutor, especially now, at the time of digital communication. Only conscious and concise communication teaches a person *to recognize the relationship within the structure of thought.* Only then can a person end up saying what he / she means to be understood adequately.

Auto- induction: *Don't verbalize everything you want to say!*

Goal # 5 – *Say less but mean more! Learn to decode implications! To* hit this goal, we have to change our cognitive culture considerably through rationalizing our thinking and learning to structure it properly. This is the language skill that we desperately need for our new electronically-based and choice-driven economy. Speaking and writing with implications is a great gift!

"The method of the tip of an iceberg" was introduced in the world literature by a great American writer Ernest Hemmingway. The tip of the message, like the tip of an iceberg that is seen over the water, is said, while the rest of the iceberg or the body of the message that you want to communicate is under the water. ***It is implied, and it needs decoding.*** Such communication is very economical, but it necessitates a great deal of awareness of the subject of the conversation. This is what is required in the professional intelligence development nowadays. (*See Professional Intelligence, Stage Five*)

Goal # 6 – *Language respect is also self-respect!* It has become a bad habit with many people to assess things negatively and to complain about being discontent with the state of things in their life, or the life of other people. *Judgmental speaking* has become a norm among young people, too. Every other word in their conversation is ",*She is like..., he is like....*" behind that person's back. Listen to the people talking around. They try to impress their listeners with something out of line, judging and condemning someone or something, expecting a listener to back their judgment up with the same train of thought. *"Clever people talk about ideas, mediocre people about events, stupid people about people."* (*Rubaiyat of Omar Khayyam*)

Judgmental speaking is being instilled in us by mass media that focusses only on the negative side of life for its sensational value. Why don't we learn to notice the positive, constructive things first, and respect any constructive gesture, especially on the part of the President of the Country whose job, being the hardest of all, is judged most of all. Also, the uncontrolled language behavior of people in some TV shows and their manners are accepted by the public as a norm. The language of the participants of such shows is beyond description and *the inflation of their language skills* signifies to the inflation of their thinking that's hardly curable. Nevertheless, such shows are appallingly popular

Treat your language with piety! It's the mirror of your personality!

For more on language fitness, see www.language-fitness.com and the books " Language Intelligence or Universal English" (**Book One,** *(the Method of the Correct Language Behavior)* **Book Two** *(Remedy Your Language Habits)* **Book Three** *(Remedy Your Speech Skills)*

At the Universal Bay,

You are What You Think and What You Say!

Chunk 10

Impeccability of Self-Expression is in Session!

The brain is our legislative power; hands, vocal cords, a tongue, and lips are our executive power. We are in charge of our body language, our words, and their meaning. *"Being impeccable means controlling your speaking and not using words against anyone and yourself."(Don Miguel Ruiz)*

There is no evolution of intelligence without the clarity of thought and the accuracy of word!

Mark Twain wrote that "the difference between the right words and almost right words is like the difference between being struck by a lightning and a lightening bug." Finding the right words at the right time is being able to adequately communicate by saying less but meaning more. It is the skill that is in great demand now.

There is a lot of untapped language potential in us; it is in the matrix of our native language mentality with which we came into this world. Innate language potential later gets developed into L***anguage Habits*** that will eventually get developed into S***peech Skills***, the skills that are self-learned, self-practiced, and self-perfected.

Language Habits + Speech Skills + Language Competence!

I view language intelligence as the one based on "***Language-Speech dichotomy***" introduced into science in the 19th century by a great French linguist De Saussure who viewed language as the blueprint for speech which is ***actualized language.*** Backing up the genius of De Saussure, we think that language intelligence is based on solid ***Language Habits*** *(pronunciation, grammar, and vocabulary)* and well-developed ***Speech Skills*** *(listening, speaking, reading, and writing).*

Language is the portal of speech. Thinking is the two put together!

Language intelligence can be compared to a coin of two sides: ***personal language*** and ***interpersonal speech.*** Managing the language means observing its structural rules, or its unique grammar, while managing speech means being in charge of the meaning enclosed in this structure. A person is learning to say what he means and means what he says all his thinking life. It's the skill that comes to the front of our intellectual development now.

Auto- induction: *Say what you mean and mean what you say!*

Our ***mind-to-mind communication***, whether direct or indirect, when it is mediated by electronic gadgets, is possible only based on solid ***language-speech proficiency.*** However, a real the ***disconnectedness of the form and the content of the language*** that we use presents a real challenge now. Such state of things signifies to the disconnections between the right and left hemispheres in the brain, the left brain representing the structure of the language, *(the form)* and the right one being responsible for its creative use *(the content)*. *(See "Language Intelligence or Universal English", Book One)*

The way the brain works, the mind talks!

Thinking psycho-linguistically, language and speech, habits and skills, form and content, or, in other words, brain and mind have to be trained to work in synch for us to be able to develop language intelligence on the basis of the ability to empower our *language–speech competency* and develop considerably our language personalities.

Language competency means being in charge of the language in-put and speech out-put.

Impeccability of self-expression is what is required of us nowadays. No wordiness, no time-killing, no misconceptions, no messiness of thought! To be more exact in speaking, you need not only to read more and work on your vocabulary habits; you should also pay aware attention to your writing skills. *Writing is the algebra of speaking!*

Speaking skills make a ready man! Writing skills make a strategic man!

With the speed of our life being accelerated so fast, we have no time and patience to listen to or to read long business reports, descriptions, speeches, explanations. *We need the precision of self-expression by a speaker with aware attention* applied to such work and with a great consideration for the time that is a precious commodity now.

Writing thoughts down and organizing them into the conceptual chunks is essential because the human brain compartmentalizes the information in the same way as computers do, or rather, computers are made to follow the brain in its amazing organizational capacity. The more we do such **synthesizing**, the more developed the right brain becomes, and the better our thinking skills will be.

Conceptualizing means organizing and synthesizing.

Finally, we often say things that we regret about afterwards. So, establishing a tight control of the brain over *the language impeccability and speech exactness* is the prerequisite for everyone's success on the path of self-installation because *you are the way you speak!*

Synthesis - Analysis – Synthesis!

(Cognitive Intelligence, Chunk 9)

Do Consciously Mind-Language Wising – Generalizing - Selecting - Actualizing!

Chunk 11

Manage Your Language!

The Law of the Right Thinking

Is in synch with the God's inkling!

    The Law of the Right Language use

    Is in lieu with the right behavior fuse!

We ignite it and often abuse

When we are emotionally defused!

    Our thoughts result in words and impact our actions,

    They, in turn, generate the language fractions

That damage our left brains

With bad habits refrains!

    To turn them into good ones

    Is impossible to be done at once!

Patience and control of a casual language muse

Are required to be put to use!

    Tongue accuracy corrected at a brink

    Demonstrates exactly how you think!

Remember , your personal profile brick

Is laid down by the way you speak!

You and the Language in You are the Inseparable Two!

Vistas of Intelligence to Instill Next:

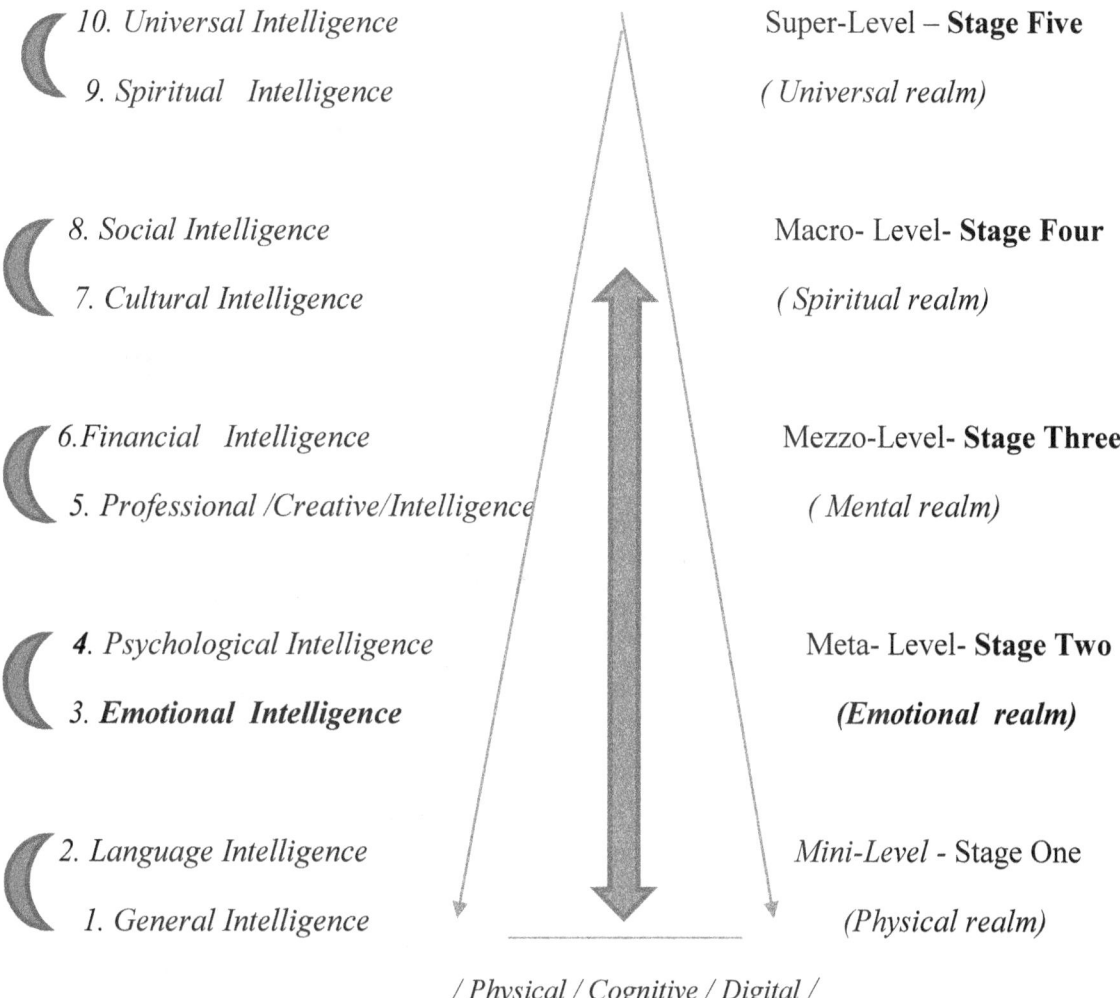

/ Physical / Cognitive / Digital /

"Fertilize your mind with thinking!" (Albert Einstein)

To Make Your Life Intellectually-Wise, Strategize – Optimize - Actualize!

Stage Two

Meta-Level of Intelligence - Emotional Dimension

Emotional Intelligence

Step One

Harmonize your inner guts to enjoy life in all its parts!

Emotional Intelligence is an Internal Maturation without Frustration!

Emotional Intelligence with Much Negligence!

Make Your Heart Smart, and the Mind Kind!

Be One of a Kind!

Chunk 1

Emotional Intelligence

Emotional intelligence,

Is it a notion or our untamed negligence?

        Don't we have to learn

        How to handle emotional oblivion?

How to think right and say something bright

When life is at the brink of a fight?

        And how can we ever succeed

        With the present-day technological speed?

However, there is a solution

To the mind's evolution

        You must put the strain on your brain

        And keep the tongue in the captivity of your mind's run!

Only then could you mount the hill

Of your unbeatable self-esteem!

        And only then will you obtain the skill

        Of operating the no-vengeance will!

So, master your emotional will

To make it as strong as human steel!

Thus, Your Emotional Diplomacy will come through,

And You'll become a Self-Managing Guru!

Chunk 2

Life is Mentally-Emotional!

Science proves that *life is mentally- emotional,* and the present-day state of our emotional intelligence leaves much to be desired because *we have not matured internally*, and we remain savages that react to the external circumstances, not nobly respond to them.*(Part Two, Thesis 3)* The first reactive impulse of anyone who was suddenly insulted is to lash back. But **the proactive, mind-governed response is to restrict that impulse and instead of reacting, respond!** It is much more beneficial for a person to take control of a negative emotion and suppress the urge to strike back verbally. *One absolutely needs to out-power his emotions with the mind!* .This restriction uplifts consciousness because we **heighten the level of internal commitment** and *obtain emotional wellness* that is inseparable with physical and psychological well-ness.

Be kind to the unkind! Be One of a kind!

Studies reveal that success takes more than intellectual excellence. We need to develop the skills that raise us above the crowd. *These are the Emotional Skills.* Also, we must learn to operate our emotions with the help of the brain, acquiring **emotional intelligence *(Daniel Goldman)*** that is the next most important intelligence after language intelligence and the one artificial intelligence has to master. *Auto- induction:* ***I intellectualize my emotions and emotionalize my mind!***

It means that you put your **mind over the emotions *(Introduction, Thesis 6)*** and think before acting, on the one hand, but you are also aware of the reason of our emotional misbalance, on the other. Unfortunately, in the hierarchy of our consciousness development, ***the cone of emotions is over the cone of reason.*** We are not in charge of our emotions yet. We still tend to be more animal-like in our reactive state of mind, rather than human-like in a responsive state of **conscious mind control**. Dysfunctional thinking is the result of negative, uncontrolled emotions.

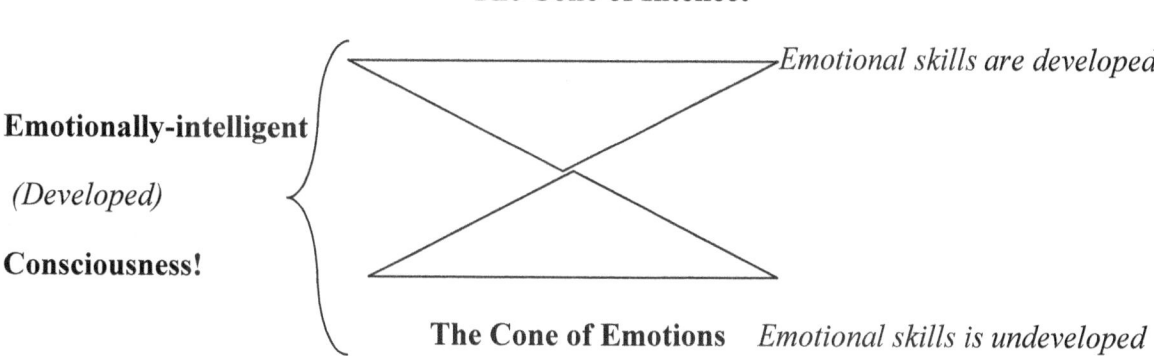

You are what you choose to be in an emotional turmoil.-a lady, a diplomat, or a rat.!

Consequently, everyday emotional stress becomes a new reality that requires that we develop new tools of coping with it. Sometimes, stressful events come so fast one after another, that there is no time to recuperate emotionally. We become irritable, impatient, messy and irrational in our thinking and often stop bothering about self-development or self-realization altogether. Becoming emotionally-intelligent also means that we become aware of the fact that we have an emotional and rational brains – the limbic system and the neo-cortex, and that these brain systems interact with each other. Obviously, **being emotionally-disciplined requires a lot of self-work and self-control, self-knowledge, and self-awareness!**

*"Why are you always anxious? –asked Jesus his disciples. **Can an anxious thought add a single day to your life?"***

True, in certain situations in life, we find managing our emotions especially hard when the emotional brain becomes predominant. That happens because, when emotionally-distraught, a quicker signal is sent to the amygdale, which is the emotional center in the brain. At such moment, we fight, yell, and argue because we completely lose the ability to be rational. *But if we focus our aware attention on the mind,* it gives the command to the brain, and we get in control.

Mind ⟹ *Brain* ⟹ the *Rational You!*

Unconscious ⟹ *Conscious* ⟹ *Superconscious!*

So, if we know what pushes the emotional keys in us, and if we are aware of the necessity to use the rational brain at this moment or *pay aware attention to the reasons of the emotional outbursts,* we can eventually train our brains to work for us, not against us. Such timely restriction saves us a lot of embarrassment, self-guilt, and regret because people, even though they are prone to expressing uncontrolled emotions themselves, *judge us brutally,* making us feel worse, ashamed, and belittled. Socrates was teaching his disciples,

"Strong minds discuss ideas , average minds discuss events, weak minds discuss people!"

Auto-induction: *So, be nice and beautiful and beware:*

There are eyes and ears everywhere!

In short, *our emotional awareness* puts the mind in gear and helps us correct our behavior in accordance with *the Law of Right Human Behavior. (Richard* W. Wetherill, **"Right is Might."**)

Put the Mind in Gear, Steer!

Don't Fight to be Always Right; To Be Right, Be Bright!

Chunk 3

Emotional Self-Awareness

Emotional self-awareness is essential to gain for your emotional self-quest. You have to be aware of your *emotional key-board, and* what keys you, not anyone, have to push so you could sound Pianissimo or Crescendo. The problem is that you have to be a self-playing instrument, as an automatic piano that is being coded for a certain melody by the brain.

Emotional attuning or refinement is like tuning a musical instrument.

A good musician would never let anyone do the tuning up of his instrument for him because no one is able to hear his tool from within, and no one can operate it in lieu with the instrument's specific inner sounding.

Emotional awareness means you are the pianist, not the piano!

We also need to develop the ability *to use emotions to enhance thought. (See Cognitive Intelligence above)* We need emotions to motivate ourselves to reach a goal or maintain a positive attitude even when we experience difficulties.

Auto- induction: *To be inspired, I need to be self-inspiring!*

Emotional awareness is the main boost in life because *we first behave joyfully, then we feel joyful!* Smiling and laughing, we are giving our brain an oxygen shower, on the one hand, and we are shaking the cells from within, letting them get rid of the pollutants, or mental- emotional residue, on the other. Interestingly, science proves that our facial expression take place before we express emotions, not after. We read a lot about the necessity to smile to feel happy, not smile because we are happy. However, the ability of seeing the seeds of contentment and joy is yet to be developed by every one of us consciously.

We need to put the mind and emotions in synch.

Edgar Cayce suggests using the command to the mind," **Halt!**" to help oneself stop the negative expansion of emotion in order to put the mind in command and give it a chance to switch gears. Learning to be joyful is learning to be conscious!

Drive through the time and space with a smile on your interface!

Self- Induction: *You cannot say, "More Sun!" You cannot order, "Less rain!"*

You have to sustain!

Power Up Your Inner Rehab!

Chunk 4

Choreograph Your Self-Creation with Elation!

Every year, before a New Year starts, we make our provisions based on what is essential for us in *the Master Plan* of our lives, that I call at the beginning of the book *Your Mission Statement.* However, very often our mission statements do not help us choreograph the inner transformation in action because *they are not properly structured, strategically and tactically.*

In our life's ado, we are what we think, feel, say, and do!

To fill up our lives with the action steps in five life-dimensions - *physical, emotional mental, spiritual, and universal*, and thus, going through *self-awareness, self-monitoring, self-installation, self-realization, and self-salvation (See Preface)* presupposes charging our batteries with inner integrity and determination, not de juror, but de facto, *processing every chunk of information for its personal validity, clarifying your life's sense* for yourself in a new, systematized way. I am not the Ultimate Truth, but I try to be most *objective* in the presentation of the information that I outline for your judgement, having sifted it many times through myself.

In other words, we need to choreograph every Pa in our "life- ballet!"

We have great advice and directions in *our basic divine books*, starting with *the Ten Commandments* that we all know, but we leave it as a side dish in our minds when it comes to action. The book that you are holding in your hands is the result of extensive reading and learning from all kinds of sources for years on end, but this most inspiring process is not over yet because self-creation never ends and change needs guts. It is meant to help you say:

Auto-suggestion: *I'll never get back on the "Poor Me" track!*

The Law of the Right Human Behavior that I keep bringing to your attention lays out **the what, the how, and the why** we must act in synch with the universal laws to stop making the same mistakes in life and start living according to the Law of the Right Human behavior. Regrettably, we often forget that being fussy is being weak, and being thoughtful and reasonable is being strong.

The gift of intelligence that is granted to us by God demands *we do our own individual molding*, backed up only by the divine connection with the Universal Intelligence that should be unbreakable in us, no matter the circumstances or life tribulations. We live under the laws of God that *"the* **Celestial Court instills them in us."** *(Robert* Stone) Let's align our thoughts, words, emotions, and actions with the Universal Laws now! *"The right time never comes!"* (Osho)

"If You Stop Being Better, You Stop Being Good!" (Socrates)

Chunk 5

Emotional Skills and Techno-Babies

The future of humans does not look promising as it encompasses the accelerated development of artificial intelligence without love and the spiritual content to love. Every students of mins says he / she believes in God, but what it means in the actual sense, none of them can clearly explain. the difference between being religious and being spiritual is very vague in their minds.

The new generation is raised on abstract, unspecified information that they get quickly adjusted to and acculturated by.

Children now are raised as techno-babies that get attracted and adapted to the new technology very quickly. Of course, this pace of development being very important evolution-wise, has a bad impact on the kids' brains and their nervous systems because we do not consciously channel this process in the way of ***developing our own and our kids' Emotional Intelligence Skills.***

Children get emotionally-overloaded and therefore, are often rebellious.

There is no flat ground, no security, no rest, and no compassion if they slip down. Today, young generation is running on *a trade mill that is set on the uphill mode,* but, unfortunately, it takes them down intellectually and spiritually."*(See Introduction, Thesis 6)*

There is no counting on someone's consideration. We are all in the same boat. The world has become very impersonal and lacking in emotional equilibrium. There are no sex or age differences in emotional intelligence. Our competence and incompetence in it keep growing throughout life. Obviously, developing our emotional skills should start as early as possible, and *it should be studied as a separate subject at school!* Daniel Goldman' book was published more than ten years ago, but its wonderful ideas are not put into practice in our schools.

Auto-induction: *I absolutely need to be emotionally-equipped!*

There is one more thing to consider here. A badly needed *mind-to-mind and heart-to-heart mating* is possible only "*if we return to the only place of power- the present moment." (Eckhart Tolle)* Dealing with the present emotional trauma then and there and out-powering negative emotions with the help of the mind returns a person to reality, and it does not leave the residue of the past emotional memory that poisons the lives of the ones involved in the conflict. A beautiful quotation from a great novel "*Love Story" by Erick Segal* is a great example of such a situation.

Auto- induction: *"Love means never having to say you're sorry"*

Emotional skills are not being in any way taught, advertised, or simply given a lip service to on a general scale. We watch movies and TV shows in which cakes are thrown into faces, wine glasses are emptied onto an offender's lap, emotional outbursts and ugliest reactions are followed with storms of laughter.

There are also many TV programs that promote yelling, fighting, pushing, verbal disrespect, aggression, and other animal-like behavior patterns. What can we expect from our kids and young people? They haven't heard or seen better!

Auto- induction: ***First think, then say, then do!*** *(The Law of the Right Human Behavior)*

Why don't we follow or show the wonderful examples of ***the Schools of Ethics in history*** – the school of gentlemen and ladies in Great Britain, the school of nobility in pre-revolutionary Russia, or ***the Spartan system of upbringing*** that stressed love of intellect and knowledge as much as physical exercise. Sparta was also characterized by an unusual degree of self-government, freedom, and responsibility. These schools developed ***gallantry, self-reserve, manners, and great values in their learners.*** We still feel their contribution to the world in rare testimonials of such behavior on the part of ***the impeccably-mannered men and women***.

So, the etiquette, manners, morals, polite rituals and restricted talking must be studied and constantly self-guarded!

In sum, good manners and a reserved attitude to problems have been instilled in people for centuries. Why not have them back and consider the necessity to be in charge of emotions a priority.

Self-induction: ***A posture, a smile, and a good mood are my emotional food!***

With ***neuroscience behind this aspect of emotional intelligence***, we will no doubt succeed more in enriching our kids' education and expanding their outlook immensely in this respect. Researchers recommend that we first consider the capacity to perceive emotions in yourself and others. So, let the well-known saying below never lose its freshness!

"If you don't have something nice to say, don't say anything at all!"

"Emotions Follow Behavior!"

(Antony Robins)

Chunk 6

Self-Assessment and Self-Monitoring

To empower yourself emotionally, get down to the business of self-assessing your own ***mentally-emotional potential.*** Emotions and thoughts become de-personalized though awareness. The knowledge about oneself is the starting point in self-formation.

It is hard to live with self only if you do not know yourself!

Therefore, self-assessment is a priceless tool for self-awareness. Auto-suggestive work that we suggest you resort to at every level of your intelligence development will be more effective if you keep assessing your self-growth at every stage that we outline in this book, defining for yourself what you want to accomplish at each level separately: *Mini, Meta, Mezzo, Macro, and Super (Introduction, Thesis 7).* Assess yourself in a holistic mode, in:

Physical, Emotional, Professional, Mental and Spiritual dimensions

----

Such self-assessments has to be done without ***criticizing and victimizing yourself*** and with a lot of self-love, self-respect, and self-consideration. *(See Self-Love Meditation, Physical Intelligence)* All emotional changes happen from within. The latest research shows that our DNA is affected by inner and outer vibrations, the verbal presentation of our thoughts and behaviors.

A person gets demagnetized and de-humanized due to these changes!

Having assessed yourself most objectively in general terms, along the objectives outlined above, you may get down to your specific **emotional refinement** at a particular level. Interestingly, self-assessment starts playing a very significant role not only in psychology, but in business, too. People with the ability to objectively assess their own talents and abilities are in great demand now because ***they sell their skills more adequately and***, therefore they are more marketable, competitive, and compatible.

Success begins with an assessment of personal strength and weaknesses.

Above, in the section "Physical Intelligence," we have presented many tips for self-assessment and self-management. *(Chunks 4, 5,6)* We suggest you go over them again and assess your strong points and the weak ones objectively in terms of your growing emotional intelligence.

Self-quest is a process; it is not an immediate result!

You work on the objective vision of yourself for your own good, not for anyone's appreciation. True, a supporting word backs up our self-esteem, but it is not propelling our self-growth.

Be silently self-assessing and never discuss your weaknesses with anyone!

A famous American psychologist Robert Steinberg has proposed the theory that, first, we need to focus on our own strength, not deficiencies. **So, compliment yourself first!** Remind yourself about your good qualities, your strong will-power, and your ability to keep going up the hill of self-formation first. Do not confide in anyone about it, not to be criticized and rained on your parade. *(Physical Intelligence, Chunk 18)*

"Be the thing in itself!"(Hegel)

If life tempts you with its downfalls and with the urges of" immediate gratification" or different whims that you might have, be the only one to know about it, and you will be able ***to reject, resist, and reform*** *your imperfections* on your own. (See *Introduction, Thesis 16*) Keep "injecting" self- boosters into your will–power at any time when you need to be self-inspired:

I know who I am!

"I am a strong, bold, calm, and determined owner of my firm will.

I can…; I want to…; I will…!

I am becoming better and better at … with each coming day!

This is not to say that you should not obtain help if it is needed, beyond your efforts to manage yourself. As a matter of fact, no one can feel your frustration, depression, your inner anguish or your anger when it spins out of control. People, psychologists, psychiatrists, friends, relatives, or the loved ones may just share our thoughts, but they are unable to feel our emotions for us However, professional advice is invaluable and should be sought, if need be. ***Emotional refinement*** is also connected with changing the attitude to oneself and others. Always respect the advice given to you, but ***consult with your intuition***,

Tune your spirit to your inner sounding! Your intuition is there pounding!

Emotional Reaction is Like a Nuclear One;

It Must Be Under the Control!

Chunk 7

To Be More Life-Fit, Snap Out of it!

However, emotional reactions do occur, and they are often automatic and unconscious, while responding to them should always be controlled and conscious. If the emotional turmoil did get you inside its vortex, try to snap out of it as quick as possible, before it sucked you in to the point of no return! **Do not react, respond!**

Auto- induction: "Halt!"/ To be more life-fit, snap out if it! / Don't let your emotions vent!

Such conscious responding to feelings fills you up with a great feeling of **self- monitoring!** Command to yourself at the moments of irritation, frustration, depression, or self-pity," Halt!" and snap out of it then and there. Having snapped out of bad emotions that have had their grip on you at will, you are shaping good habits and manners in you, or you are developing **the Self- Management skills** - the ability to respond rationally and not to react emotionally. *(Physical Intelligence, Chunks 7, 19)* It means that **you gave your brain the signal to be aware,** to pay aware attention to the emotional turmoil. The right hemisphere of the brain gets enacted, and it will not fail you, once you start training it consciously.

The unconscious brain gets empowered by the conscious one!

Also, mastering emotions with the mind is always a step forward in developing your consciousness. Switching to a positive attitude means that you protect your energy field against bad energy habits, too. You are not a victim of negative thinking, aging, sickness, and death!

Face your obstacles with full empowerment and work hard on your emotional refinement!

Self- induction: ***If anything, negative ever occurs,***

Immediately change your electro-magnetic course!

Switch your brain's Amygdale to the front lobes of emotional gala!

Practice restrained reserve that contains discreet and concern!

"It takes only a Stroke to change a Minus into a Plus!"

Do it, Thus!

Chunk 8

Cleanse Your Emotional Memory!

We all experience the moments when we say, *"I forgive, but I don't forget."* Studies of emotional memory lie at the heart of brain science now. It is emotional memory that is prompting our impulsive actions, making the habits of uncontrolled emotional reactions very hard to break, and the memory that is responsible for heart-breaking pains and strokes unforgettable.

"What makes the brain a brain is memory and emotion is arguably the primary sculptor of memory" (Scientific American, May/ June 2014

Yes, it's easier to forgive than to forget! It's impossible to forget unless **you do it intentionally**, erasing emotional scars in your brain **consciously** and never putting salt on the old wounds again. Just send a bad emotional memory into the recycle bin of your brain with a willful move of your mind.

To be able to do that, **you have to forgive yourself first** for having let somebody hurt you due to the lack of self-worth and the absence of a true protection of your soul. Our inner self, our intuition, and our conscience are always on guard, but we do not pay aware attention to their signals. We are negligent of those signs in a rush to react at an impulse.

Self- induction: *Listen to yourself! Respect your intuition! Take your own council!*

We have already reminded you of the old schools of gallantry and inner integrity. From ancient times, such schools were preparing people through the process of very challenging initiations to be in charge of their emotions, putting the mind in command of their lives. *The movie "Secret" and the book by* **Rhonda Byrne** *are a great contribution to our self-growth in this respect!*

We also love watching old movies that depict the people of nobility and honor, real gallantry and manners, self-worth and mastered self-reserve. A great American movie *"Meet Joe Black"*, with two amazing actors, **Anthony Hopkins and Brad Pitt**, communicates to us many thought-provoking messages how to build up inner integrity and have power over death.

It's a real manual of self-respect and a great piece of art!

Apparently, consistent **auto-suggestive work** with the best examples from literature, art, music, movies and innumerable wonderful self-help books, as well as the on-going inspirational self-inducting will help you break bad patterns and install good ones **through the process of intentional synergizing any emotionally-explosive** situation.

Follow the intuitive guidance of your mind and sensations with patience!

A wide sincere smile, for example, will detonate the strenuous moment and help you ground the negative impulses in yourself or someone that had generated negative emotions in you. **Christ's** *instruction not to strike back should you happen to be struck on the cheek is a great exercise for the mind and will-power* that we have to **practice consciously**.

It is still a very controversial statement for many people who want to justify their *"eye for an eye"* philosophy, considering the emotional reaction to be natural in this respect. However, the response that ***Christ professed needs a lot of conscious action to be put to work,*** when you do not belittle yourself with the move that was devoid of any mind-power. Such *self-empowerment* will help you stop victimizing yourself and fill you up with self-pride and honor. Thus, you'll manage to defy a low-gravity common sense impulse that you might get. *What a feeling that is!*

Auto- suggestion: *I never get back on the "Poor me" track!*

A powerful image of yourself in the mind, **the URV** of the best of you *(Physical intelligence, Chunk 5)* is very helpful in this respect, and *it should be visualized continuously and consciously.* Teach yourself self-empowerment while thinking, breathing, eating, talking, exercising, working, driving, walking, etc. You are performing *self-cleansing or self-re-cycling* without which the clogging of your emotional mind will happen again and again. Therefore, your conscious work at self-actualization and self-perfection might be either stopped altogether, or your uncontrolled weakness will fling you way back from the stage that you had accomplished so far. Order and self-control should be constantly on guard!

Beware; emotions need as much order as thoughts do, even more!

It is only natural that women start cleaning, cooking, or putting everything in order to calm them down when they are very upset. This practice helps them discipline their emotions, sharpen self-awareness, and uplift their consciousness. *"**Be the light onto yourself**!"! (Buddha)*

Self-induction: *In my mind, I am one of a kind!*

There wasn't, there isn't, there won't ever be

Any on like me!

*In a wonderful book, "**The Flower of Life**", Drunvalo Melchizedek discloses the ancient secret of the flower of life (**Merkabah**) that represents **the Sacred Geometry** of the unity of the heart and mind. Drunvalo Melchizedek considers it to be the magnetic center of our bodies.*

Make Optimism Your Perpetual Mobile!

Chunk 9

Emotional Diplomacy and Courtesy!

Being emotionally strong for oneself and the people around us is the demand of life that is becoming emotionally tougher and tougher with each new century." *Mastering emotional intelligence is a demand of our time."(Daniel Goldman).* **Each of us has to have a diplomatic key to operate some one's psyche.** All we have to do is to try and adjust the key to a person's heart and mind with patience and a great deal of **emotional diplomacy.** As a result, we will develop **emotional competency** that will back us up in any emotionally-charged situation. *(See my book "Emotional Diplomacy")*

Emotional competency is how well we handle ourselves and others.

You are not a passive receiver of feelings. You are the creator of them! You simply must take responsibility for **the creation of your emotional will**, aspire to become a charismatic person that everyone likes to be around with, and stay that way for the rest of your life.

Auto suggestion: ***"Will your life more!"(Carl Yung)***

Once you start to interact with another person, you put your emotional diplomacy to a test. In fact, it begins before that moment. It begins when you first open your eyes in the morning, when you first interact with yourself and when you say Hello to a new day. Saying a happy hello to yourself every morning has to become a habit!

But beware of anyone's bad mood around you. Don't get injected by it

I admire Americans for their happy Hellos! It is so pleasant to see a smiling face everywhere, to be welcoming anyone while holding a door for him/ her. The Art of Living lies in such light - filled moments, in our conscious choices to be happy, joyful, grateful, helpful, and smiley.

Choose the state of mind of ***a life –lover, a life-winner, and a life –appreciator. Thank the Sun, the God, and the world around you!*** Have you smiled to the beginning of a new day today? Do you realize the value of this day in the life of others?

Auto-suggestion: *.I' m not aggressive, abusive, or static;*

I am emotionally-diplomatic!

Emotional Diplomacy is My Every Day Courtesy!

Chunk 10

The Code of Love!

We live on the phenomenal planet that is governed by *the emotional energy of love*, and it is unique in the space which is predominantly mental. .Having gotten the gift of love from berth, we need to consciously develop it throughout our entire life. The breath of love was blown into us by Jesus Christ that had planted this seed for us to be able to experience love, *starting from the Above. According to neuroscience, love has a neurological basis*. The scientists prove that when the neurotransmitter of love, called *dopamine,* is released in the brain, it contributes to a rise in energy, motivation, and feelings of euphoria or elation.

Love is hardwired into the structure of the human brain, not the heart!

From the spiritual point of view, *I believe that love has a structural nature, too.* In my understanding, it should be grown in the five above mentioned levels -

Physical, emotional, mental, spiritual, and universal

If love starts *on the physical level*, it can or cannot *grow emotionally.* If it passed this level, it can grow up to *the emotional / psychological level* of mutual understanding. It becomes much stronger, but it is still not enough for the love emotion to last. *It needs the mental back-up -* the two people should connect on the intellectual level. They, according to Edgar Cayce, need to *have" the union of purpose"* in life. If love has sustained the growth in these four levels, it is prone to die because *there is no spiritual connection* in it. Therefore, people from different religious backgrounds can hardly keep their love for long.

Only love that was strong enough to go through all the levels can last!

That is why a one-night stand or a love relationship that is based just on the emotional spark cannot last. *Like anything else in life, love has to grow together with a person's intelligence and consciousness, and it is much better if it gets sparked up at the spiritual level first.* It then most likely will mature mentally, emotionally, psychologically, and physically. Such love relationship is endless! Most importantly, love needs to be studied and learnt from a very early age and for the rest of our lives. *.Even the love of God is not just granted, it's earned!* . The inner job of love is eternal! Learn a short prayer of love:

Dear God! Throw me a handful of stars and bless me from the above with love!

I Live and Love by the Code of Love!

Chunk 11

Love Intelligence + Love Induction

Love intelligence is the hardest intelligence to obtain of all! We have to get trained for it from the earliest age possible. It is never too early or too late to learn to love! The philosophy of love hadn't been absorbed by our minds for centuries. But now that neuroscience has proved *that love **is hardwired into the architecture of our brains, not hearts,*** we can conclude that a self-quest that starts with self- love is meaningless unless it is inspired by love for life and the people that inhabit it.

Love is the greatest incentive for self- perfection!

All the world masterpieces, the greatest innovations in science, the best pieces of art, literature, music, and poetry were created under the most inspiring emotion of love! Apparently, the more love we radiate and get in return, the better we become consciousness-wise.

Love Induction (*See the Self-Love Induction for reference / Physical Intelligence, Chunk 24)*

1. **Rub the palms of your hands vigorously** *till they become very warm. Stand behind your loved one, put your hands on his / her shoulder so that the centers of your palms on both hands (the solar plexus area) lay on the very edge of the shoulders of your loved one, on the rounding pars of both shoulders.* **These are the spots of love!** *(See Love Booster, Chunk 19, Physical Intelligence)*
2. **Start radiating love to his / her body from within,** *calming him/ her down, and proving to yourself that love is the best empowerment of self and the other.*
3. **Stand like that behind the person you love for some minutes,** *till he /she feels calmed down and warmed up with the overwhelming feeling of your love for him / her.*
4. **Start moving your hands slowly down his / her arms***. When your hands come to the point where both palms meet, make a short pause and say,*

"I love you the way you are!"

Then shake the hands off, *as if removing any negative thoughts or feelings from his /her body and your own mind and say out loud. Shake off your hands when saying these words inwardly ,or outwardly! Always remind yourself and the person you love of your love.*

"If any one doesn't love you, it's his or her problem, not mine!"

The Core of the Mer-Ka-Bah Link is in the Heart and Mind in Sync!

Chunk 12

The Elation of Love-Illumination!

Any change translates as stress, but science proves that the greatest stress we have is lack of love. Love stress generates anger, discontent, irritability and self-guilt in the outcome. Most substantially, *it clouds our life with misbalance, insecurity, haste in decision making, and indifference to other people.*

The words **"I don't care! / What do I care? / I care less!"** are emotional pollutants for love intelligence. They have to be eradicated from our minds and the language. *We have to care*! No one can consider anyone a good person if he / she is indifferent to whatever situation he / she has to face in life. Adjusting to life emotionally, we raise our consciousness as human beings!

"Life does not adjust to us, we adjust to life!"

You need to drive your emotional mobile consciously in your married life or in a love relationship. Conscious response will take you to the place of your destination without any dismay and with a great sense of self-power in love.

*"We need to be especially **emotionally-refined** in a marriage union. "Matrimonial aura is the mental child of both mates" (Laureli Blyth). "It's not the laws of man that wed two people; it's always God!" (John Baines)* So, induct yourself, rewording the saying above.

Auto-suggestion: ***Love does not adjust to me, I adjust to love!***

Let's compliment and complete each other! Add the formula below to you **auto-suggestive menu,** too. *Illuminate yourself, the person you love*, and the loved ones with your presence in their life space and time. They are not here forever! Induct the formula below to enhance your luminosity.

Being a luminary is a hard job of love intelligence!

To have love, be love!

The More Love You Create –the Better is Your Fate!

Chunk 13

Self-Management and Self-Regulation Skills

All things are created twice, first–mentally, then - physically. *As you think, so you will be!* A healthy mind gives a healthy body! Physical intelligence presupposes that each of us develops his/ her general intelligence on the basis of the awareness how to strengthen physical fitness in synch with the levels of refinement that are listed above. But the mental / physical refinement needs an emotional boost ,given to the cells.:

Self-induction: *The quality of my life is the quality of my cells!*

A healthy body is also the result of the constant auto-suggestive work of its owner. Be vibrant, keep auto-suggesting health, vitality, and youth to your mind and see how your body reacts to such boosting during auto-suggestive meditations *(See below)*, or just during your **non-stop conscious self-monitoring that should never end:**

Self-Induction: *I know who I am!*

I am strong, calm, bold, and determined owner of my firm will!

I can. .; I want to…; and I will…!

We all know about the positive effect of exercising, but, in fact, it starts in the brain. Therefore, it's extremely beneficial *to do auto-suggestions that rhyme* during exercises:

If it's to be, it's up to me! / I do not whine; I shine! / In my mind, I'm one of a kind! etc.

It's important to note here that when we exercise, a protein called **IFG -1** is released into the bloodstream, and then it goes directly into the brain. At this point, IFG-1 begins its work in increasing the production of a critical brain chemical called **BDNF,** or brain-derived neurotropic factor that stimulates or promotes all *higher-level thought processes*. In a recent study, researchers found that BDNF generates new brain cell growth and promotes new connections between these brain cells.

So, our disciplined eating, exercising, and well channeled rest time have to be under the conscious control of the mind. Have you ever answered the question why people that constantly work out in the gym get sick, gain extra weight, or get depressed? *The answer is in their mechanical exercising,* without putting any *conscious thought-work* into the benefit of working out on this or that part of the body and without any interacting with the cells of that part of the body. *Working on the cellular level with the body,* we upload health and will power into every cell, our mini-computers that, in fact, our body cells are. So, keep auto-suggesting yourself while working out.

As I Think, so I Will be!

Chunk 14

If Your Train of Life Ever Derails

If your train of life ever derails at some joint,

Get in an aware state of mind at that point.

      Ask yourself why your life carriage

         Is at a damage,

And how to put it back

On the conscious life track!

      Getting off the life track

         Is worse than hitting a fork or looking back!

You need to heighten the density

Of your weak will-power propensity!

      To sustain the balance of the train, running up the hill,

         Or sometimes down, still,

Operate the engine without the spin

And stabilize the vision of the life's scene!

      Also, hold on to the wheel

         And be sure to reel

Your life's train course

To its unique purpose!

Not to Ever come to the Point of No Return, be sure to Stay in a Conscious Form!

Chunk 15

Mind-Sets Against Upsets!

1. I am a strong, bold, calm and determined owner of my firm will!

Right is My Might!

2. I rein over my brain! I always "think, say, and do what is right!

3. I refuse to think, say, and do what is wrong!

4. I am honest to myself and others.

5. I Love myself the way I am!

6. I am as good to others as they are to me.

7. I feel for others as much I feel for myself.

8. I help others as much as they help me!

9. I make allies, not enemies. Every enemy is a potential ally for me.

10. I treat others as I want to be treated in return!

11. I eat less, talk less, and spend less!

12. I conduct a self-limitation war; less is more!

With the noble work at yourself being done, you are carrying forth the torch of universal evolution toward a much higher vibrational complexity. It's our personal mission to better ourselves and help eternal life get better, too.

"Right will always prevail as the eternal basis of God's might!

(Richard Wetherill)

Life at Large goes on without Any Hitch at All!
It's the Mind that needs to Be Redefined!

Vistas of Intelligence to Instil Next:

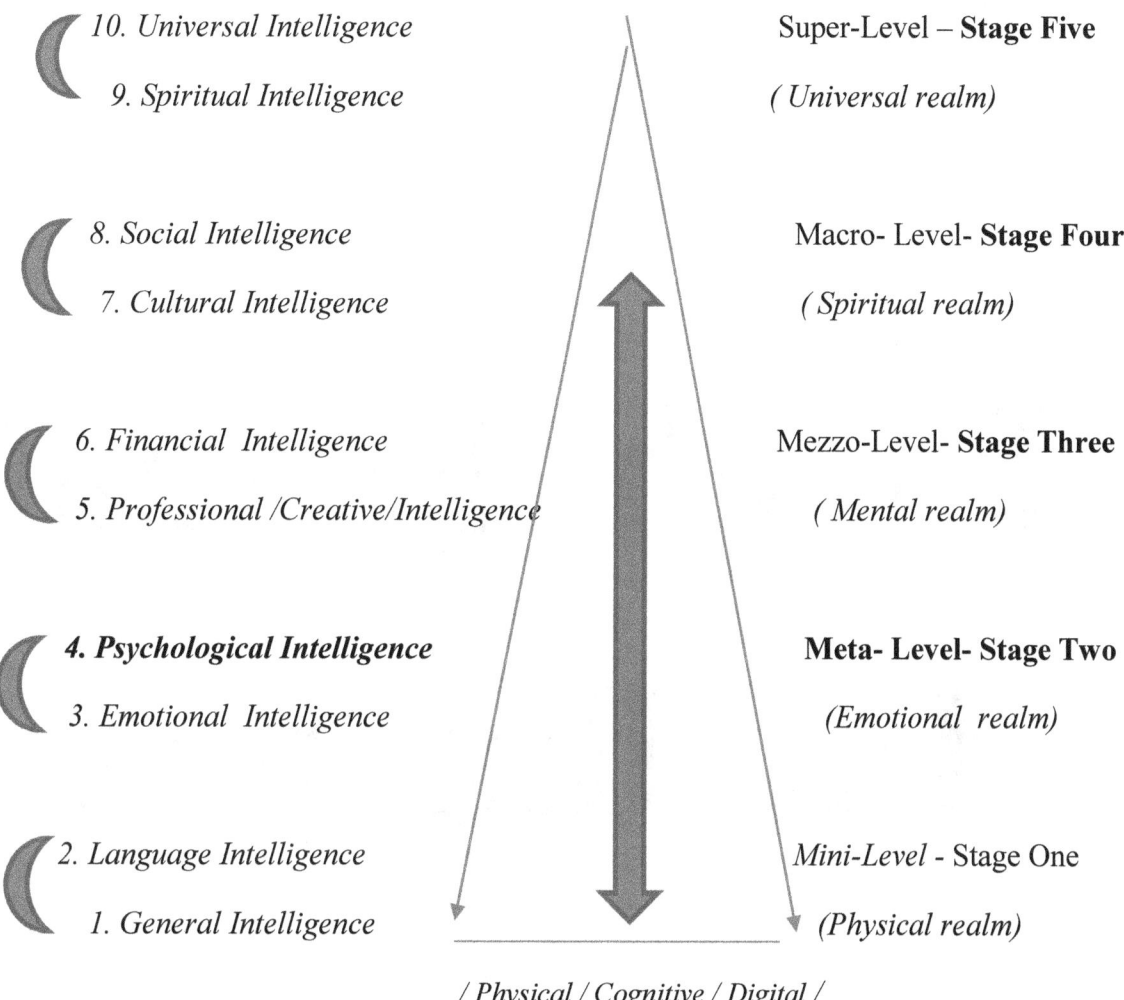

/ Physical / Cognitive / Digital /

"Fertilize your mind with thinking!" (Albert Einstein)

To Make Your Life Intellectually-Wise, Strategize – Optimize - Actualize!

Stage Two

Meta-Level of Intelligence - Emotional Dimension

Psychological Intelligence

(Step 2)

"The unexamined life is not worth living!"

(Socrates)

Inner Dignity is the Base of My Equanimity!

Psychological Intelligence without Negligence

I'm Aware of My Joy and Despair!

Chunk 1

Change Your Psycho-Culture

In Part One, Thesis 2, I stress the necessity of changing our culture of thinking into the holistic one - by reshaping our **physical, emotional, psychological, mental, professional, cultural, social, and spiritual frame of thinking** that is inseparable with our consciousness. Psychological intelligence is, in fact, **the stumbling stone** on the path of self- formation and consciousness rising.

"The law of personal survival is executed on the psychic level." (Sigmund Fraud)

Working on the psychological intelligence, *we are sculpturing our own psycho-culture*. *Psycho*-culture is the culture of willful monitoring our psyche and becoming more responsible for our actions. Self- love, will-power, and the sense of responsibility are the most important aspects of the psycho-culture that we have to capitalize on in life.

Auto- induction: *"Life is Tough, but I am Tougher!"*

The first goal of changing our psycho-culture is self- development of the ability to focus on our thoughts and channel them into the right actions according to the Law of the Right Human Behavior *("Right is Might"/ See, Part One, thesis 2,3 above)*

"Think, say and do what is right, and refuse to think, say, and do what is wrong"

As we change our thoughts, we *change the physiology and neurology* in the body This change is achieved by special chemicals, called neuro-transmitters. The body is full of neuro-logical connections that *form the pathways* that are mostly governed by the unconscious brain. In case of a foreign language learning, language is the information processing system (*speech*) that is the result of the changing thought patterns *(language)*.

In other words, we need to put the mind in control of the brain.

The cosmic **Law of the Right Human Behavior,** like the Law of Gravity, channels us along the right paths in life .All we have to do is to be more perceptive and intuition-guided, helping ourselves to tune intuit consciously and *self-suggestively*. . We suggest you come up with your own endings of the wording of the formula below. Your life situation will dictate to you the necessary suggestion to boost your will-power and uplift your self-confidence. Inducting this auto-suggestive formula every day and applying it literally to any feature that you want to improve in your ***psycho-culture,*** you will eventually *generate new, good habits, or new pathways in your brain,* if you concentrate on each of them consistently .

Neuro-Science + Psychology + Self- Awareness

= A New Psycho-Culture!

Chunk 2

The Ultimate Result Vision of Self

The main auto-suggestive formula is very flexible in this respect, and it should always be at the front of your mind. You can induct anything, making the sub-conscious mind follow the lead of the conscious one. New pathways will be formed in the brain, or **the neurology and the physiology of your body will get in synch.**

I know who I am!

I am a strong, calm, bold, and determined master of my firm will!

I can…;   I want to…; and I will…!

I am driving through the time and space with God,(a smile, happiness, love, kindness, success, health , etc.)on my interface!

Working at your self-perfection auto-suggestively, **you will also develop the holistic connection between the left, concrete, and the right, abstract, hemispheres of your brain.** We need **to put them in synch** to acquire emotional - psychological intelligence to gain a better self-control in life. It does not happen overnight, but it happens with a consistent and disciplined action directed at bettering ourselves. Many of my students have literally changed themselves and their lives.

The second goal of a new psycho-culture relates to the necessity **to form a new vision of Self psychologically.** I have been calling it *the Ultimate Result Vision* of self all along,(*Introduction, Thesis 17)* so you could enrich it with the vision of the venues of your psychological growth that I outline to you below. Having read our overview of Psychological Intelligence," *be sure to have* **a psychologically - enriched imprint of the URV in your brain holistically,** that is in the physical, emotional, mental, spiritual ,and universal dimensions of life.

As you change your thoughts, you change your psycho- culture!

Working auto-suggestively at your psychological make-up, you communicate with your unconscious mind by going within and using your imagination and inner vision. **The unconscious mind passes the information to the conscious mind.** Your nerves will set up a magnetic field over the conscious brain. The conscious brain is in turn controlled by the higher consciousness that shapes the mind of a consciously-willful person. It does not matter in this case whether you are an introvert or an extrovert. Both are great if they are good thinkers. They just conduct their thinking symphonies in a different manner. Thus, you will form **new neurological connections or pathways** which change your consciousness and make you a much better human being.

Self-Inducting is, in fact, Self-Conducting!

Chunk 3

Psychological Awareness

Life is a process of challenging and responding. It does not adjust to us, we adjust to it! When the father of psycho-analysis, Sigmund Fraud, brought our attention to the importance of understanding self through *psycho-analysis*, he meant that we had to do it ourselves. Psychological awareness is essential for developing any intelligence! ***Psychology is lifeless if we do not impregnate it with the self- knowledge and self- analysis.*** As important as it is to be able to help ourselves health-wise, we need to be aware of the essential tools to operate our psyche with, too. **Psycho-awareness** will maximize the power of our mind, and it'll clear lower emotions. I put *the spirit in the center of the unity* because the spirit that keeps the mind and the heart together in us.

Body + spirit + mind = ***Self***

To be *psychologically-aware* means not only being in the know of your own psychological make-up, but also, ***being life-aware every living moment.*** If you ever disconnected with conscious perception of life around you, remind yourself of the necessity to be together with the induction:

My aware attention is never in retention!

Stay aware while driving, talking to someone, walking, working, and exercising. When working out in the gym, focus on your muscles, or areas of the body that you need to shape, do not become an automatic object of living unconsciously., as a robot on a remote control. ***Be there! Stay aware!***

"The Center of Gravity is in the psychological awareness of a person" (John Baines)

Being at the end of the psychological tether is too dangerous, and there are too many bad stories to testify to people's helplessness in dire circumstances. It's easy to say, *"Snap out of it!"* The question remains how. ***The essential knowledge in psychology is a must for every human being, and it is most crucial for teaching our children its basics at school.*** We need to do it to get rid of the bulling problem that is looming over weak, unsteady, ***uncultured souls of our kids***. . This is the area where knowledge is real power! You may get the information on the Internet about your type of personality and how you can help yourself, or seek professional help, if need be.

We need to know how to handle ourselves to be able to handle others!

The knowledge of our psychological make–up is power only when it is put to action, in our case, **psychological awareness** needs to be applied to the action of self- creation What we call our comfort zone is, in fact, our self-awareness. So, don't fight to be always right; to be right, be psychologically bright! ***Never forget who you are and why you are!***

I Know Who I Am!

Chunk 4

Immunity to the Poison of Life

To be **psychologically-intelligent** means also *to take responsibility for your responses to the present moment*, without resorting for the immediate help of a psychologist or a psychiatrist. Life is too stressful for us to have no idea how to help ourselves in any problematic situation and at any time. Getting an appointment to seek immediate help might be a problem, but life cannot be stopped. Whatever the problem might be ,be your own best friend in it; be aware, be in control!

Auto-suggestion: *"Be immune to the poison of life!"*

Do not fear, steer! The best and the most precious thing in the world is *to be free of other people's negative influences,* or free from what Carl Yung calls " *the poison of life*" that builds up inhibitions or complexes in our psychological make-up"

"Real freedom is the freedom of the spirit!"(Dr. King)

1. *We need to learn to be in control of ourselves*, for we can give the world the best we have only if we have accumulated the values that can be beneficial for it. In this respect, we need to find the way to incorporate both the Western and the Eastern psychologies into our mental framework. If we respect life in ourselves, we have to respect it in others because our sameness is our psychological unity. (*Cognitive intelligence, Chunk 13)*
2. We know that the Western psychology is based on outside, objective observation of people; whereas the Eastern psychology is based on profound, meditative introspection of self. ***Holistic psycho-awareness demands that knowledge about both systems*** be acquired to better our social skills and get new leads in life.*(See Cultural and Social Intelligences below)* Both philosophies are the indispensable basis for widening our outlook!
3. Other than that, to be invincible psychologically, we need not only to expand our psychological awareness and general outlook, but we have to ***de-magnetize, or to deactivate our conditioned and limited psychological patterns of thinking and feeling***. We have to remove the mental blocks that we had accumulated for centuries under the effect of the *"collective unconscious"* that we now seem to turn into *"robotic unconscious"*.
4. Finally, and most importantly, *I totally agree with* **Paul Pearsall, the author of the phenomenal book" Super-Joy"** that psychology should be renamed into **Joy-ology** - the science that instead of focusing on the abnormalities of human psyche and behavior will instill in us the joy of living that will teach us"" *to cure the normal*"' and take a risk of being **"super-normal."** Have the guts to say to yourself and others:

Auto-suggestion: If you want to be happy, just be", like Buddha and me!

"Joy-ology" is My New Phycology!

Chunk 5

Demagnetization of the Spirit

It is an accepted fact that it is easy to say," Stay away from the poison of life!" than to actually do it. To be successful in this very challenging goal, we have to first learn to resist the temptation and then *to magnetize our inner core with new values.* (Check out Part One, Thesis 5)

Auto-induction: *Resist, reject, and reform to obtain a new life uniform!*

We need "*to reverse the triple 666*, signifying the **mind, heart, and sex** into *the triple 999*", or in the celestial terms, change the evil, badly-willed side of us into the divine one that is still there, but got weak for whatever reason "*Most of us spend our lives bouncing back and forth between the good and the bad sides of life.*"(Rav. P. S. Berg). "*Be activated by the internal influences for the external responses*" Don't be a mere echo of the instinct reaction of the majority or, of the "*collective unconscious.*" (Carl Yung) Play a solo role in that concert.

Be unique, personable, and charismatic!!! Be a New You!

Launch yourself every working day by heightening the voltage of your spirit self-suggestively! Giving yourself the command by counting backwards:

Self-Induction: *Three -Two- One – Start!*

Resisting, rejecting, and reforming are very self-forming!

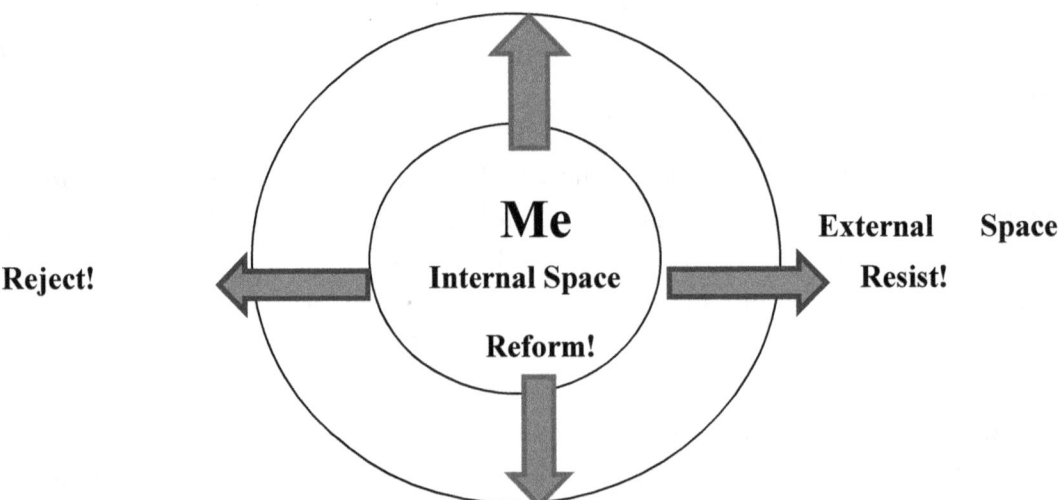

Expand your inner circle of resistance to the poison of life and thrive!!

Never stop strengthening your *intellectual culture linguistically, emotionally, professionally, culturally, and socially.* Self- creation is an integral process that goes holistically in every level.

The necessity to train ourselves to respond to life mentally as opposed to reacting emotionally gets fixed into our *virtual matrix* now only if we are aware of the importance of shaping our minds.

Auto-suggestion: *I have to be reasonable and bold to fit into a new life's mold!*

We all make mistakes and have sins of wrong thinking, saying, and doing. All a person needs is to realize what he had done wrong and not get into the vortex of more wrong doing by force of habit.

The inner matrix should be personalized, not digitized and robotized!

It appears that only with the belief in God and real rationalization of thinking; governed by the emotional intelligence can we resist, reject, and reform our imperfect inner uniform. The words of a great British writer Somerset Maugham are very convincing in terms of the punishment we get if we have no immunity to the poison of life.

"The mills of God grind slowly, but they grind exceed small!"

There is another point to consider. We cannot be weak for a long time. The people that get discouraged or depressed, those that make drugs or alcohol an obsession , justifying themselves that they are too stressed out, **sink into the psycho-holes** that they are unable to get from because they do not blame themselves for the weaknesses that demagnetize their personal core.

"General demagnetization of a spirit always starts and finishes with the brain!"(Dr .Bell)

Therefore, it is vital *to inspire yourself and others with love for life*, compassion, understanding, mercy, self- belief, and the incentive for self- actualization in life. Don't let yourself fall into the depression stall. I totally agree with *Antony Robins* who declares,

"Depression is a self-inflicted disease!".

Constantly Reform Your Inner Deform!

Chunk 6

Boost Your Will-Power to Self-Empower!

When inducting the main inspirational booster (*I can, I want to, and I will*…!), remember, please, that it is not even necessary to specify **what you can, want to, and will do**. It's enough to **boost your will power just saying those words together**. The mind will do the rest! Amazingly, if you do the meditation right, you will literally feel the air going in and out of your feet toes, each finger on your hands. Every breath will be taking away all your problems and, calming you down unbelievably. It might seem to be childish to do that, but aren't we children in our minds still? We do not age emotionally, we first age mentally!

Auto-suggestion: *Your aging starts with the mind. Switch the gears!*

Later, you might want to expand your suggestive meditation to **different parts of the body**, from bottom to top. The mind-sets that you down-load with every breath can be different. It depends on what information you want to program your brain with during the meditation, and what part of the body might need your aware attention at that moment.

Auto-induction: *Be conscious! Your body's talking to you!*

Also, while reading this book or while trying to memorize some of the mind-sets, jot them down on the index cards and have them at hand in your purse. The constructive ideas that they communicate are **very inspirational**, and those that rhyme are easy to remember. With time and practice, you will learn to feel consciousness and life energy in any part of the body where you direct your aware attention and visual perception to. Five seconds of your looking through the body in a scanning fashion are needed every day! Get into a habit of **processing your aware attention** through your body in a conscious, loving, and thankful way every day before sleep. You will do wonders to your body and your consciousness, boosting them up, on the one hand, and inspiring yourself, on the other.

You will become unbeatable and unbreakable, invulnerable and firm in your will-power!

Eventually, *you will feel the inner body as a single, whole field of energy*. Try to be visually present in every cell. Talk to them, program them! Thank them for their great work. Express your love for them! *Always finish your suggestive meditation with a constructive mind-set.*

In my mind, I am One of a kind!

There wasn't, there isn't, there won't ever be

Anyone Like Me!

Chunk 7

Self-Acceptance is Essential!

Self-management and self-refining are inseparable with self-acceptance. If you accept yourself the way you are, you are more determined to change yourself through self-management. Thus, you'll be better equipped to give yourself the command, **"Halt!"** at the right moment.

Do not use standardized images of people to boost your self-esteem. Compare and compete only with yourself! Perceive, think, and feel in your own unique way! Consciously assess the motivation of other people for using external references to control your behavior and exercise power over you. Listen to your intuition, your gravity and integrity guard.

We think what we are, and we are what we think!

Just get into the implication of these words and be a winner in your mind, not a victim of the hectic life around you. ***Think differently and respect yourself for the boldness to do it!*** In the world of individuals, victimization is impossible. In this context, inner strength means being able to **stop** *trying to get everyone think and feel what you are thinking and feeling* **and** stand up firmly for what you believe. "Live and let live!"

The concept of existential aloneness is ruling our lives!

Auto-suggestive work that this book is based on affects your psyche in a very subtle, simple way to manage yourself much better than any affirmation because it **hits exactly the emotional deficiency** that we might be experiencing at a certain moment, and it adds the mental energy to your **sagging self-confidence** at any place and time. You are the only person on Earth who knows when that right time strikes. Help yourself help you!

Auto-suggestion: **The Sun will still shine whether I frown or smile!**

Using auto-hypnosis, you realize the rule of being your own best friend, and you synergize your inner space, developing a physical habit of perpetual happiness. ***Self-respect becomes the modus operandi of every action you undertake!***

Auto-suggestion: *I know who I am!*

Remember that *"one of the basic causes of sickness is unhappiness, and one of"* the best healers is super joy*"*. *(Paul Pearsall)*

Auto-suggestion: *I enjoy my super-joy!*

Auto-suggestive work might seem to be a simplification for you, especially if inwardly you feel that you are much more than an average person, and why should you bother with primitivism like that. Don't get side-tracked. Accept yourself the way you are and continue uploading simple formulas into your mind. ***The mind likes simple, not overcooked food.***

Finally, watch what you say about yourself to other people. Be honest, but self-protective. Don't get demagnetized or discouraged by someone's skeptical remarks. Rewording Hegel, command to yourself,

Self-induction: *"**Be the thing in yourself!**"*

Stay away from skeptical remarks yourself. Be modest tactful, respectful, and responsive.

Auto-suggestion: ***"Use your skepticism to amuse, not to abuse!"***

Lastly, if you do happen to slide down in your emotional reactions or to the lack of the resistance *"to the poison of life,"* if the guilt trip snatches you by the throat, the best that you can do is to get out of this shell immediately. Only an independent and happy state of mind creates crescendo in life!

Self-Induction: ***Be emotionally-fit. Snap out of it!***

"We do not run our bodies -the energy of the Universal Intelligence does. Help it do its work." (Osho)

Auto-Induction:

A Smile, the Posture, and a Good Mood

Are My Psychological Food!

Chunk 8

Introspection is Self-Inspection

Emotional intelligence and psychological intelligence are inseparable in our mind. The difference is only in our awareness of the emotional life we have, on the one hand, and of the peculiarities of our psyche, on the other. *Introspection is an indispensable part of both intelligences*. The challenge of life is always there, but to sustain the pressure of a fast-developing economy and our hectic life, we need *to take an observer position* on the intellectual, emotional , professional, and moral levels of our personal growth.

Auto-suggestion: *If I don't discipline my thoughts, I live backwards!*

We are either aware or unaware of our psychological states. When we are in the dark, we are prone to panic, to seek someone to share our worries with. In the long run, we develop more complexes that do need professional help to be removed. *When we are psychologically aware,* we know what to expect of ourselves in different situation and how to avoid unfavorable consequences. The vital thing is *to make the right choices* in life by giving yourself time to think of the consequences of your actions first and consider which side of the equation (*light or darkness*) this choice is on

"You can be light, you can be darkness, but you cannot be both!" (Eleanor Roosevelt)

Get used to X-raying your thoughts, words, and actions. Introspection of the past actions triggers the body's self-healing abilities and boosts self-esteem. It *is not good to be totally dependent on a psychologist or a psychiatrist* to explain to you what's going on inside you, unless ,of course, you absolutely need it.

Don't ever whine, shine!

You are the only person in the world aware of it, and if you start looking at yourself *retrospectively and introspectively,* armed with the essential knowledge about your psychological make-up, you will be your first urgent help.

Don't pass judgment on yourself!

Help yourself at the first signs of anxiety, depressive thoughts, or irritability. *Try to illuminate the causes for such feelings and give yourself an inspirational boost.* You've made the right choice!

He who holds up his head will always go ahead!

I'm My Best Friend; I am My Beginning and My End!

Chunk 9

The Path to Moral Maturity

There is no personal growth without *Moral Intelligence*. *Check out Physical Intelligence, Chunk 12) Moral maturation* is a long process that needs to start with a willful ending of judging others and starting *to be more objective* about one's own behavior.

"To harvest good fruit, cultivate good thought about yourself and others." (*Buddha*)

Our values, beliefs, behaviors are over-disposed by our manners, hectic living habits, our being raised in a certain faith, our being conditioned by the mass media and the society at large. In his mind-changing and soul-forming book *"Right is Might"*, Richard W. Wetherill writes:

"Moral relativism (no right / wrong ethics) is ruining our souls"

We must halt any images of immorality and fear that harm our souls on the path of self-bettering. It's paramount *to will an image of a positive moral outcome* in any challenging situation through the mind of a growing child. Just Sunday visits to the church will not work. .Many people piously lit the candles in the church, but *they blow off their inner light or the light of their loved ones outside the church*. Be sur you have the five most important aspects of life in synch and preserve your *moral integrity.* Also, *stop justifying yourself for any harm done to anyone.*

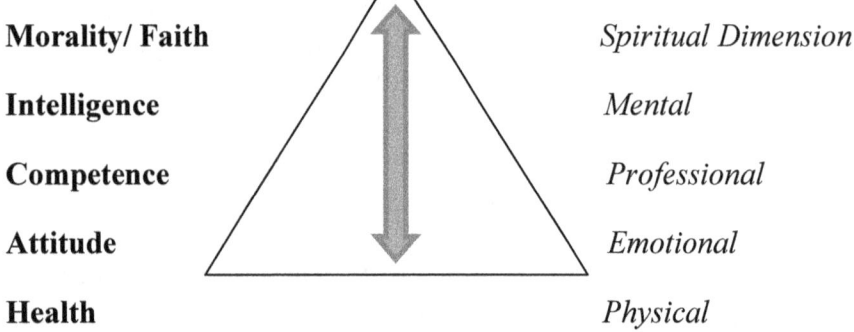

Morality/ Faith   *Spiritual Dimension*

Intelligence   *Mental*

Competence   *Professional*

Attitude   *Emotional*

Health   *Physical*

A moral person is supervised by his /her spirituality first and his /her moral integrity next., Therefore, the arrow of a person's self-growth in morality is a bi-directional process is which all the levels of self- creation ore *inter-dependable.*

Morality + faith == moral integrity in place!

A good person constitutes the unity of the most important aspects of intelligence in lieu with the cosmic laws of *Cause / Effect, the Law of Gravity, and the Law of Attraction*. When you live in the awareness of these laws, the best human features can translate into human integrity and a remarkable *personal magnetism* that gets charged *in five basic dimensions of our holistic spiritual growth.(* See the chart above)

A bad person is living under the ruinous effect of *progressive demagnetization and dehumanization.* It's a down fall at every level, and it inevitably brings him / her to the point of no return – breaking of the trust, cheating, divorce., guilt trip, depression, etc

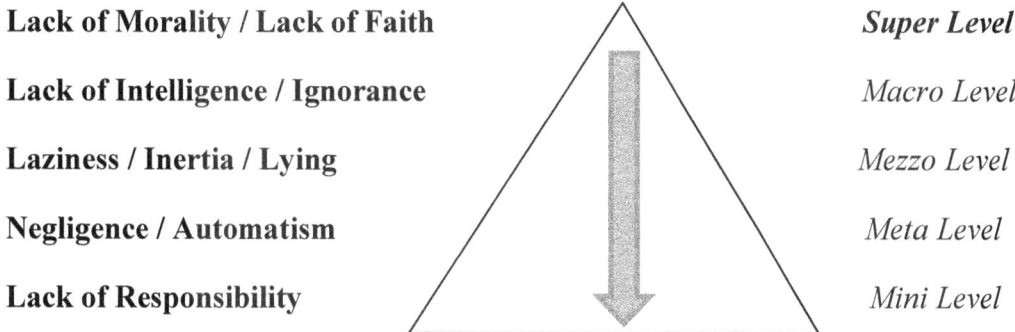

Lack of Morality / Lack of Faith	*Super Level*
Lack of Intelligence / Ignorance	*Macro Level*
Laziness / Inertia / Lying	*Mezzo Level*
Negligence / Automatism	*Meta Level*
Lack of Responsibility	*Mini Level*

Bad morality does not give life the chance to happen!

Neither of us is perfect, but it's very important to realize our deficiencies and **correct our personal defects consciously.** The simple and the most basic qualities above will serve as a point of reference for you. See if you need to work on any of these areas t*o become a spiritual aspirant* and start creating yourself in this direction **holistically.** Otherwise, the process of moral demagnetization will start snowballing. *Moral demagnetization is the beginning of depersonalization, too.* To stop the downfall of a personality development is not altogether impossible, but it requires a lot of **self-monitoring and self-control**. Self-monitoring cultivates inner balance of **morality and personal integrity** that become the basis for personal quest and inner gravity of a truly noble person. here again the unity of the heart and mind that constitute a healthy conscience comes to the surface of self- work.

Emotionalize your mind and intellectualize your heart and be exceptional at that!

The present-day science tries to get to the bottom of *the concept of impulsivity* that breaks us in half and pushes us away from balance. Rationalization of thinking is essential in this respect. *(See Cognitive Intelligence, Chunk 10)* To accomplish that, we have *to halt the unconscious, automatic way we think and justify any whim to please oneself then and there!* In his groundbreaking book "Robots Rebellion," David Ickes writes,

." The further you stray from balance; the more extreme life becomes."

David Icke states further that if we go too far to the positive polarity, we lose touch with practical side of life. *"Positive energy needs a negative balancer. Only **balancing yourself between the two polarities of life*** *can link you to the highest levels of consciousness."*

Balancing oneself is the skill of the inner equilibrium feel!

Our Moral Make-up must be under the Thinking Cap!

Chunk 10

Mental Trip to Self-Respect in the Retrospect!

With all the *psychological awareness and introspection* done, you still need more self-respect and self-inspiring that will help you leave the baggage of the wrong-doings in the past *to be burnt in a willful mind blast*! Stop criticizing yourself for not knowing or not being, not doing ,or not loving enough. The most important thing is to admit your mistakes and learn from them.

We all know about it, but , we are not aware of that action-wise! So, self-devise!

That *Auto-Suggestive Meditation* in time and space is very helpful in this *(Stage One, Physical Intelligence, Chunk 17)* You can also induct yourself with the ever-helping formula:

Can…! I want to …! And I will…!

Every one of us is in need of psychological support - the support of self-respect. Every one of us gets criticized by our parents, friends, husbands, wives, bosses, by the people we love most. We get judged even by neighbors and passers-by. One of the reasons women seek help of their best friends is the needs to be reassured for what she said or had done in her relationship with the man of her life. .In need of psychological support., they exaggerate the situation, blame the other party, expecting the understanding of the desired situation, but not the real one.

Look back at your life's surf

In the tough life's turf

And accept every cycle

Of your past lives recycle!

You cannot remove

A single turn in its rough move,

Nor can you possibly redo

Your present life's ado!

So, all that's left is to smile

In return to a negative twine!

For it takes only a stroke to change a minus into a plus,

And "So Be It", thus!

Chunk 11

Don't Be Lazy to Excel, Compliment Yourself!

There is only one person who can see the situation ***adequately and objectively, not subjectively***, the one who can always support us or back us up when we are in trouble, upset, or just feeling blue.

This person is you! So, learn to understand yourself and compliment yourself!

Only you know what you want of your life and how great you are .You do not want to be a clone of somebody else. You want to be uniquely yourself. You can do it by visualizing *the Ultimate vision of the Best of You and by complimenting yourself every day to boost your self- esteem.*

'Mark Twain used to say ,"*I can live for a month on one compliment that , if I don't get any , I can easily make it to myself.* "I also like the words of *Will Smith* , a great actor and *a true motivator for young minds.* Trying to discipline himself, he suggests talking to yourself in the auto-suggestive way:

"I LOVE YOU TOO MICH to let you do that /eat that / say that / feel regrets about that, etc. !"

Auto-Induction for a better self-function:

1. I am not yet wealthy, but I am young, strong, and healthy!

2. I am beautiful / handsome / radiant, attractive, and irresistible!

3. I am thinking, speaking, feeling, and acting WITH GRACE ON MY INTERFACE!

4. I am patient, tolerant, love-giving, and forgiving!!

5 . I am emotionally –diplomatic!

6. I am loved and loving! I am admired and admiring!

7. I don't say everything I know ; but I know everything I say!

8. I have a lot of inner glee! I am becoming a SPIRITUAL ME!

(Check out the book "Self-Taming!" – the spiritual dimension. See Preface-1)

I Choreograph Myself to Self-Excel!

Chunk 12

Self-Management is Learnable!

Self-management is our priority business, or it's the private business that we need to run to our own advantage. Self- management is a process of trial and error like anything else in life.

Self-suggestion: **Drive through the time and space with a smile on your interface!**

Self- hypnosis helps a lot to connect with your sub-conscious mind. Later, this work will put you into ***an altered state of consciousness*** that will prompt to you the right mind-sets and channel you to the right actions. Simple reading of the mind-sets that rhyme and repeating them to yourselves, or even learning some of them by heart can do the trick. The right mind-set will just pop up in the brain at the right time to back you up, if need be.

Auto-induction: **My mental wings blow off the emotional swings.**

Mobilize Yourself! You might not realize it, but your personal capabilities will be getting more powerful without making others less so. See yourself as very **charismatic and magnetic!**

Charisma is an excellent case of self- management!

Unfortunately, comparison dictates us most frustrations and judgments. **Compare yourself to the best of you not anyone else!!** Stop worrying whether you fit on the comparison scale with your successful friend, an older brother/ sister, or a neighbor. You do not have to look outside yourself for self-assessment. Say to yourself auto-suggestively, **"*I know who I am!*"**

Auto-induction: ***I do not compete or compare. I am just the best here and there!***

Once you grasp the power of self-induction, charisma can never be taken away from you. As a matter of fact, anyone can become charismatic with exceptional knowledge and a bunch of competences / intelligences that we focus on in this book. (*Introduction, Thesis 9*)The best doctor is our cheerfulness ***because it's a healthy spirit that gives us energy , happiness, and makes us irresistible.*** People gravitate to the one with a strong personal magnetism that radiates light and a positive attitude . Drive your incredible personal mobile and be proud of it while it is driving

Your self-inducting ,or the words you use create the states in you. Inspiring words-inspire; despairing words-despair. By managing the mind, you manage yourself, and you channel your life to SELF- DISCIPLINED, or SELF-MONITORED happiness CONSCIOUSLY!

"Happiness is not a habit, it's a skill!" (Dalai Lama)

"Manage Yourself like a Well-Run Private Business!"

(Reid Hoffman)

Chunk 13

Psychological Adaptability

Overseeing oneself psychologically is essential in self- actualization, but it is not enough. We are social beings, and our psychological wellness is directly connected to the wellness of the society we live in. ***Psychological adaptability*** is reflecting our conscious behavior in the society.

Never have relationships been so problematic!

Your success on the path of self –creation will depend on how well you handle yourself and others. To begin with, we need to stop judging and give others more psychological air to be able to self-actualize, too.

Shed the burden of judgment of yourself and others!

We need to accept the fact that relationships are not meant to make us happy, ***they are the tests of our self- consciousness*** that grows with each new relationship, causing us to become more conscious, more compassionate, considerate and loving. It needs reasoning, rationality, and emotional intelligence, to begin with.

Making the other wrong is easy; making the other happy is a challenge!

Recent trends including high-tech communication, overseas travel, global economy and a dramatic rise in immigration throughout the world have created new challenges for our **psychological adaptability** that is, in fact, our psychological awareness. If you observe unconscious behavior in your partner, stay aware of it yourself, so your knowing could keep you from blowing!

Be consciously conscious!

Always know exactly what you are thinking, feeling, saying, and doing!

Be aware of the fact that if you react to someone's unconscious behavior, you become unconscious yourself. Conscious attitude leads you to responding, not reacting, to understanding, rather than being understood first, to giving rather than taking, to loving rather than fighting.

Psychological intelligence becomes more and more essential because *our interaction face -to-face and mind-to- mind depends on it*. When you face a conflicting situation, remind yourself:

Auto- suggestion: *I perceive with my soul to understand and to console!*

Psychology teaches us that *"perception is more important than intent"*. In other words, what we perceive in a conversation with someone is much more significant than the intention of the person speaking to us. Here comes the rule again:

Auto-suggestion: *Say what you mean and mean what you say!*

Much too often we hear, "I didn't mean that!"- "But you said it so, and I got it that way due to the wording of your thoughts!" In view of this situation, the monitoring of our thoughts in lieu with the words into which we frame them is vital for an adequate communication.

Our new behavioral skills require our mandatory ensuring of a smooth and effective relationship with our family members, our friends, the people we date digitally or in person, our colleagues, and our aging parents. We need to work out **the adaptability pact** with everyone we care for.

Auto-suggestion: *Don't be accusatory; be "amusatory!"*

Get into a habit of X-raying the emotional make-up of a person you deal with on a regular basis. Be more perceptive. Do it with aware attention, respect, and the desire *to synergize your interaction with this person* BY ESTABLISHING THE CONNECTION WITH HIS HEART AND MIND!

Synergy create the energy of understanding, compassion, and love in a co-creative fashion.

Compassion and understanding are of paramount value here. You will be surprised with your own ability to manage the feelings of other people in the way that helps you both. It's like playing a different musical instrument, being proficient on the main thing - *the note reading*.

Conduct the inner orchestra in yourself with aware attention and life-affection!

Adaptability should be our main behavior pattern only with our children. It's vital in your relationships and in your resisting the habits of discriminating people by skin color, the religious affiliation, or jus lack of education that they never had a chance to get. people are amazingly interesting if you give yourself time and patience to explore their brains and souls. Acceptance and adaptability are *the Life Skills* that you need to keep developing for the entire life

Try to reform only your own deform;

Be a self-guru, then people will gravitate more to you!

There is no one to fix *your inner gravity* that holds you together in any situation. You do not need any psychiatrist, any un-related advice that you are seeking from your friends, loved ones, etc.

You are the only one who knows *what to magnetize your soul- space with* and how to keep it from getting it partially or totally de-magnetized. totally Read the proverbs from the Bible on each day of the month. The King Solomon's wisdom is really a great gravitation device. So, be wise!

Inspiration or Desperation – That is the Life's Equation!

Chunk 14

Enact Psychological Diplomacy!

You need to learn the tools by which you can get what you want not by being assertive or even aggressive, not by raising your voice, not by using your fist, not by deceiving someone, but by ***mastering psychological diplomacy*** that is actually psychological adaptability in action. We can tell our brain to be more perceptive and receptive.

Every thought you have results in a spark of psycho-chemicals!

These chemicals can affect the body either positively or negatively. So, the most vital thing for you is to keep an eye on the brain to be able to first discipline your thoughts. Shut the negative thoughts off first. The mental input should be only positive not to hamper or disrupt the intangible flow of

Intent ⟹ **Will** ⟹ **Action** ⟹ **Success**

If a negative thought persists and might ruin your intent, say to yourself again and again:

Self-induction: ***Snap out of it! / Halt! / Stop! Stay with a happy beat; be upbeat!!***

Apply psychological diplomacy to every problematic situation in a relationship because our psychological states ruin or erect our lives and the lives of the people around us. . Give your partner space for self-expression without your immediate reaction. The confusion that we are experiencing today is due to **the lack of acceptance of the differences between us.**

Self-induction: ***Deny yourself the luxury to react; get on the response track!***

Psychological diplomacy is at the core of our relationships, and we need to teach our kids the basics of the emotional and psychological intelligence to get them better prepared for their relationships. The rules of diplomacy, for example, teach future diplomats to interact with people from different cultures, to be impeccable in their manners, to be able to meet a partner half-way in negotiations, and to be tactful and ethical.

Emotional and psychological diplomacy should be taught and studied from birth.

Both skills are essential in a marriage relationship to preserve a peaceful co-existence in a family. I have been working on developing these vital skills in myself, my kids, and the students all my life, teaching myself and them to be more perceptive of ***the person's response*** to what we say or do, because the rule below is vital in ***the psychology of a mind-to- mind and heart-to heart relationship.!***

"Perception is More Important than Intent!"

Chunk 15

Personal Magnetisms is in a Good Inner Rhythm!

The best and the most precious thing in the world is **to be able to delete inhibitions in us that had been installed by the society.** These inhibitions get decelerated in the subconscious mind ,and develop *complexes of inferiority* in us. We then live under their influence, and we are never emotionally or mentally free. Give yourself some time and space to get magnetized again.

Auto-suggestion: ***Do not self-criticize or downsize; better self- super-wise!***

Remember, if you are not at peace with yourself, you are never really proud of yourself! **Being proud of yourself is your goal**! If you are a woman and you think you are not beautiful or attractive enough, upload the words of Coco Chanel into your mind:

"*There are no women that are not beautiful. There are women that forget that they are!*"

If you are a man, focus on your intelligence first. The Russian people have a saying is:

"*If a man looks 1% better than a monkey, but is intelligent, he is already a great catch.*"

His **b**utt doesn't count! Magnetize people's eyes to yourself and enjoy admiration! You will be developing **personal magnetism just as you think so,** and your personal behavior will be, naturally, attracting people even against their will.

Radiate charisma, charm, light, and confidence. Do it on a regular basis, not just sporadically.

We do not like sulky, grumpy people as much as we don't like grey clouds in the sky. We all gravitate to those *people that shine with kindness* and a smiley way of welcoming us into their time and space. We all know how unacceptable it is to display discontent or scorn in public.

Self-Induction: ***Keep your soul intact. Seal it with the goodness pact!***

The facial expressions must be controlled, too! We see too many cases of people making faces to demonstrate their discontent. I like the Japanese people for whom" *dressing up the face* "in the morning is a rule. My Japanese students always surprise me with their lack of attitude .A smile on their faces is always genuine. A smile is or welcoming pass. not a mask that is off the face the moment a person passes by. Being hypocritical twists the soul!

Auto-Suggestion: *Always thank life for the magic of smiling, gazing, and Sun bathing!*

I do not Whine or Despair; I give Others Psychological Air!

Chunk 16

Mind Your Soul's Size; It might Get Demagnetized!

With the technological explosion, we became more self- exposing! **People self-expose themselves too much physically and emotionally now** on the Internet, at different second-rate shows, calling it "cool and fun". It's natural that we often seek advice of a psychologist because we do not want to open up to any one psychologically. But, apparently, *trust our inner power less and less*, thus letting our souls get de-magnetized, become helpless, and overly weak. Turning to drugs or alcohol is no help because it pushes you down the rocky road of self-corrode.

Use the Auto-Suggestive Psychology for self-ecology!

We find it to be a matter of course to watch the shows based on the behavioral or psychological problems of the people who desperately seek help on mass media. Unfortunately, watching such shows, *you identify with these people, and such negative programming is not helpful*. Not every show of this kind is operated by *Oprah or Dr. Phyl* whose contribution to a public's inner awareness. is immense. There are shows in which people behave as if they are in a human zoo. Their casual, full of profanity language use and *absence of any manners* whet the appetite of the public for some spicy details from their lives. The marketing maxima, " *Sex cells!*" is ruining our inner integrity and de-magnetizes the behavior to the point that we feel disgusted, and that is a very de-constructing emotion. *Thus, the lives of these people stop being private and become the dough for the public to mold.*

We should remind ourselves of Hegel's thought **"Be a thing in itself!"** over and over again. In his famous thesis, a brilliant German philosopher is teaching us to be more reason–oriented, more insightful, and observational about life. *Be a loner! Be silent more! Talk peacefully to be peaceful!* The Latin wisdom says,

Omnia mea, mecum Porto! (All that's mine, I carry with me.)

Another most indispensable thing is the absolute necessity to be honest with oneself and other people. **Lying is a way to expose the rotting soul.** It's noteworthy to mention here that brain imaging studies show that lying takes greater mental effort than telling the truth. In his l book 'Right is Might", Richard W. Wetherill describes different consequences of dishonest behavior that is" the main violation of the Law of the Right Human Behavior." *"Honesty was, is, and will be the best policy for self- regeneration!"* However, the overworked adage *"Honesty is the best policy"* has become a meaningless proverb because people say it, but they keep lying and believing in their own lies! To stop lying is a great exercise for will-power, to begin with.

Let's get in shape of Honesty for the Family Dynasty!

Chunk 17

Practice What We Preach!

To conclude my short overview of this very important stage of acquiring Physiological Intelligence, let's consider some more suggestions and the necessity to do self-X-raying that help **synchronize our emotional and psychological make-up**. The first wonderful piece of advice is given to us by Aristotle in "The Nicoma Bean Ethics:"

1. *"Anyone can become angry-that is easy. But to be angry with the right person, to the right degree, at the right time, for the right purpose, and in the right way – this is not easy."*

2. **Synergize Your Space!** *Our immune systems are very vulnerable now with the electronic pollution mounting up and engaging us totally mentally and emotionally. Only your positive reinforcement or your self-illumination can do the job. So,* **bank on your personal synergy***! Synergizing is much better than compromising that we often have to resort to, anyway.*

Self-induction: ***I smile to synergize my space and the eyes!***

3. **"Perception is more important than intent!"** *This rule is crucial for our emotional and psychological health. Whatever a person of your personal contact is, his perception of you, the space around you, your voice, your words are much more important than the initial intention you had. You might have worded it out in a wrong way, and the person perceived it wrongly. But it was your fault!* **Your trying to justify yourself with, "But I didn't mean it!" doesn't work here**. *That was the way you had communicated your thought, and that was the way it was perceived. So,* **say what you mean and mean what you say!** *(Language Intelligence, Chunk 7)*

4. **Always neutralize an opponent's intention for control**. *In every encounter, one person has more command over the situation than the other. If you happen, be the one, be diplomatic.*

5. **Build a shorthand profile of the person facing you.** *X-Ray your conversation partner for his/ her weaknesses and strengths. You'll manage the situation better mentally and emotionally.*

6. **Trust your intuition.** *It will scan anyone without fail and help you be more diplomatic in a mind-to-mind battle. So, dress up your face and open up your heart*

7. **Practice language mindfulness, that is, moment-to –moment awareness of what you say**. *Focus on the structure of your thought—the point, the proof, and the bottom line. (* **General-Specific- General***) (Cognitive Intelligence, Chunks 7,8)*

8. **Be focused on what other people say; hear them out.** *A dissipated mind is a constant stress and an irreparable breakdown of the psyche, both yours and your partner's. Listen to hear!*

9. **Practice paying aware attention to the logic of your communication.** *Be able to establish a mind-to-mind connection. Get rid of redundancy in your speaking. Don't verbalize everything on your mind. Sort your thoughts out.*

10. **Continue practicing the use of self-inductions in any situation**. *Give yourself a boost of confidence, self-love, self-defense and positive self-attunement. Be consciously alert!*

11. *"* **Come from the divine source of love.** *Generate love in your heart and mind!" (Dr. Dyer)*

10. **Clean your mental-emotional landscape!** Let constructive boosters root in your mind;; let them help you weed out all the doubts, bad memories, and emotional inadequacies.

11. **Think and act in a win-win mode.** *Do not generate negative energy - synergize!*

12. **Don't criticize – help!** *Don't politicize – help! . Don't compete – help!*

13. **Don't second guess – talk it out!** *Less talking = less pressure and more result!*

14. **Don't judge – help!** *We are all much more alike than different. Be in a hurry to understand.*

15. **Don't react – respond consciously!** *People always have something to be respected for. People are innately good and what lies within is even better.*

16. **Be just divinely guided, looking for the way, but do not block the sun for others.**

Doing all that, you'll increase your own awareness. You'll also affirm yourself inwardly and outwardly and give others psychological air. Giving others psychological air, you'll create an environment for synergy.

A reminder!

This book is not meant to be read from the cover to cover. It is a study book and ***a help-help one****. That's why I try to make every chapter is a page or two long, follow the holistic paradigm-* ***synthesis-analysis-synthesis****. Remember the main mind-set that I keep posting in all five books, promoting* ***the Auto-Suggestive Psychology of self-ecology.*** *(Check out the Auto-Suggestive Meditation, Stage One)* ***Pick any mind-set, download it into your smart phone, and help yourself help you to become the Best of You!***

"Life is not Happening to us, it is Responding to us!"

Chunk 18

Auto-Suggestive Tools to Mind-Install

Life problems are a part of our life experience. Life is the cosmic fluctuations of energy, and the fluctuations are a sequence of ups and downs. It obviously means that we, as part of the entire life flow, are supposed to have our ups and downs as well because happy and sad are one. ***Pick some more mind-sets that rhyme below to boost your psyche and back up your sometimes-sagging self-esteem.*** Have them at hand in your smart-phone ,or in any other electronic gadget.

Use the mind-sets like the self-help tools in case of emergency:

1. I uplift my spirit every minute!

2. Eternity is what's ahead for those who self-reset!!

3. I go afore! I am not addicted to stressful living anymore!

4. I listen to my voice within; it's my inner twin!

5. I adorn my personal form! I transform my age into a vintage!

6. I hold my tongue to avoid saying more than I can!

7. I practice being reserved; I keep my emotional pendulum in a neutral surf!

8. I keep my anger sound away from being rewound!

9. I hurry to practice kindness, tolerance, and mindedness.

10. I alter my perception by changing the reception.

11. I say "No!" to a quick –fix relationship exchange; I love by the moral code for a change!

12. My inner dignity is the base of my equity!

13. I do not depend on anyone's opinion. I have my own personal continuum!

15. I release all negativity to get on the path of infinity!

16. I don't put my life in reserve of the other people's surf!

17. I inject myself with a dose of anti-depressant, anti-obsessant, anti-felony, anti-baloney, anti-hostility and anti- humility! I strengthen my personal immunity!

18. I defuse my anger (hatred, self-pity, discontent) fuse! I do not self-abuse!

19. I am learning the art of seeing with my heart!

20. I am not a down-to-earth guy; I defy the gravity and fly!

21. I don't die with the music still in my thigh!

22. I love my life at its every turn, and life loves me in return!

23. *I generate, I ovulate, I consecrate, and I create my own fate!*

I Beat the Hell; I Am an Angel!

To conclude, we think that there is an urgent need for psychologists to reconsider the way they conduct group sessions with life-beaten people. Unfortunately, the sessions at which life-traumatized people share their very negative stories often have ***a debilitating effect on the participants,*** instead of inspiring them for an uplifting, self-actualizing work on their weakness and obsessions.

Sick, traumatized, life-smitten, drugs-addicted and, therefore, ***life-paralyzed people*** desperately need to be given some inspirational, life-transforming techniques. These people are hungry for real, ***life-actualizing tools*** that can help them get inspired and become productive members of the society again.

Trying to be perfectly perfect is realistically unrealistic, if not sadistic!

The most inspiring book that I have ever read is the book **"Super-Joy'** by Paul P. Pearsall It helped me tremendously to get adjusted to a new social system where everyone is for himself and where the survival is one's own personal business. I think that this wonderful book should become everyone's manual for happiness, perseverance, and ***psychological awareness.***

Follow the holistic route of choosing the auto-inductions that you need. Write them down and keep them at hand by downloading them to your smart phone or any other electronic gadget

Positive, constructive self- hypnosis is the best life prognosis!

Make up your own inspirational boosters, but be sure they rhyme.

The rhyming word goes better inward!

Everything I Say, I Do, I See Gladdens Me!

Vistas of Intelligence to Install Next:

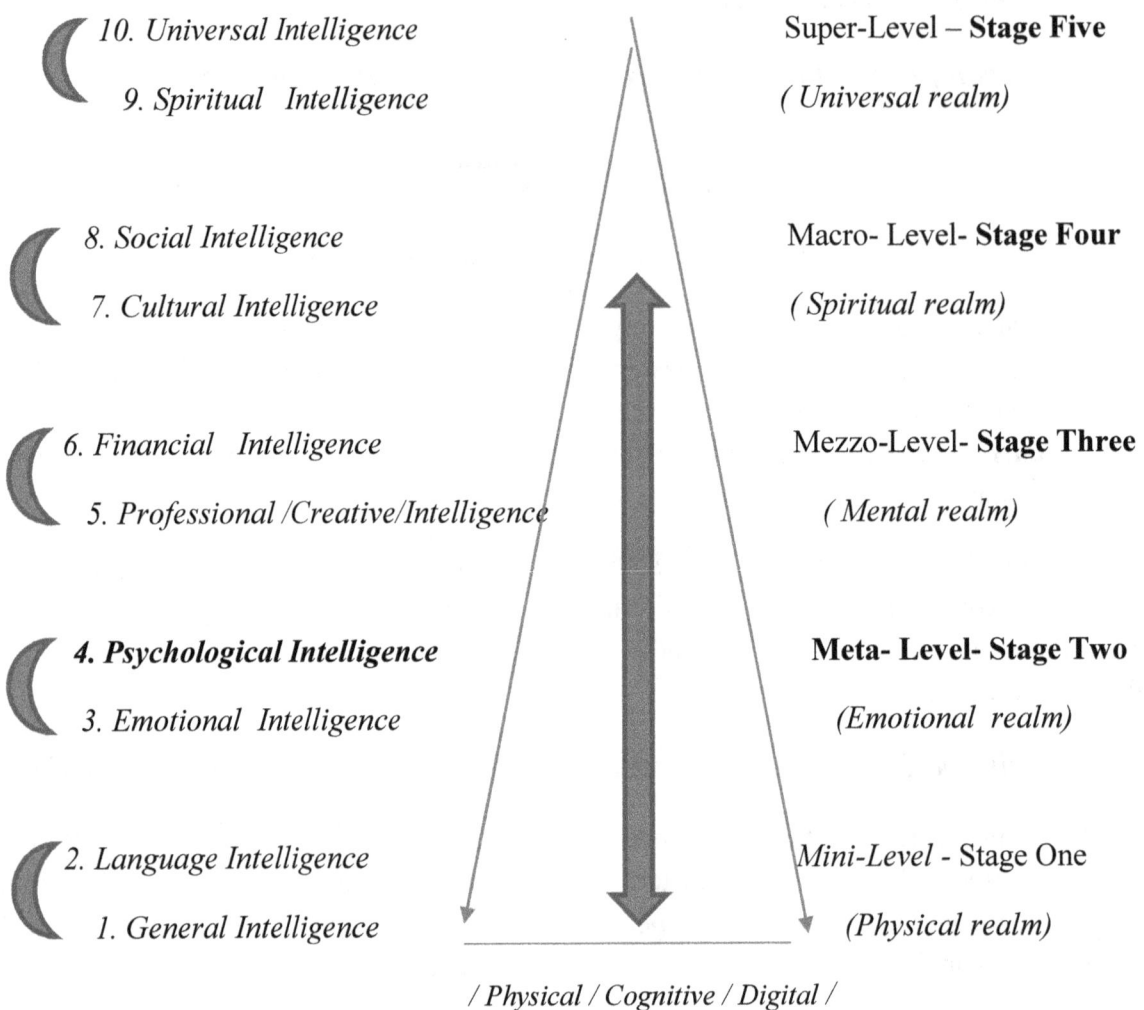

"Fertilize your mind with thinking!" (Albert Einstein)

To Make Your Life Intellectually-Wise, Strategize – Optimize - Actualize!

Stage Three

Mezzo-Level - Mental Dimension

Professional Intelligence

*Self-Installation – **Step 1***

"Try? There is No Try, only Do and Not Do!"

(Steve Jobs)

I Can…; I Want to…; and I Will…!

Professional Intelligence without Negligence!

Your Professional Vigor is at a Trigger!

Chunk 1

Professional Awareness

I have devoted so much attention to the psychological intelligence because it in essential in developing the **Professional Intelligence or** building up professional **self-installation in life.** Professional intelligence is the domain of the mental dimension, and the greatest part of our life is spent in the professional environment and its psychologically healthy / unhealthy climate..

At this level, the mind monitors the brain much more proficiently. You have already molded somewhat your physical, emotional, and psychological intelligences; and you are more able to monitor your language and speech. You do not verbalize everything that comes to your mind, and you think before doing anything. At the next level of our intellectual evolution, *you need to live by the professional code that every one of us needs to work out for himself.* And that always depends on the rightly chased *professional field* that is the prerogative for self-realization in life. (Introduction, Thesis 9) *You install yourself professionally,* and you realize yourself on the path of perfection of your area of expertise.

I don't want to be ever told about my imperfect professional mold!

Professional intelligence is also a life-long commitment, the same as self-development. Recognition should be given again to the book "*The Start-up of You*" by Reid Hoffman and Ben Casnocha that view professional development in a very actionable way. Obviously, professional intelligence is not a stagnant phenomenon! The authors, for instance, suggest most rightfully "*developing more transferable skills.*" In our understanding, these are the skills of high option value — *speaking / writing skills, general management experience, technical and computer skills, people smarts, and international experience, or cultural skills*

The point is, "*to adjust to the needs of a fast-developing market, you need to invest into yourself and compete only with yourself in developing all the necessary skills."* Self-development will help you preserve "*the autonomy of thinking*" and go forward, no matter what, without expecting any praise or promotion that might never happen.

Auto-induction: *Self- actualization is self-monitored and self- reliant!*

Also, "*youth does not have a monopoly for professional intelligence, age does." (Reid Hoffman)* With age, we sharpen our professional skills and intelligence, but we also can fall into **the trap of** *stereotyped professional thinking* that is often in the way of new ideas and a fresh vision. Mediocrity is another pest on this way. Unfortunately, it's true that *the leadership usually belongs to the mediocre*, but you should not get discouraged by that if you are professionally-aware.

"Income Rarely exceeds Personal Development!"

Chunk 2

Professional Self-Installation

There is nothing compared to the feeling of a single accomplishment on the path of self-evolution professionally. *You attain the super power over your***self**, and you feel that people start gravitating to you in hope to gain some inner strength that you emanate and the peculiar knowledge that you have. So, true professional intelligence goes beyond one's specialty and professional credentials. Because only a real professional can connect THE FORM AND THE CONTENT of the product of his mind or put the professional knowledge and skills in synch.

Professional intelligence is the unity of the knowledge and skills.

It's your personal, unique know-how! Over the years, a true professional *accumulates very special, selected knowledge,* and he / she develops personally exceptional *professional skills* that no one can take from him/ her because *the Metrix, the complete framework* of the thought-process of its owner is beyond anyone's reach.

Everyone has a unique structure of thought!

That is why, even in the cases of the intellectual theft, the intellectual property cannot become totally plagiarized. Any idea that you might have voiced out cannot be taken by someone ready to pick up somebody's brains. You can be robbed of your idea partially, *but it will never be realized in the way you see it yourself, in its unique totality.* So, do not limit yourself with the fear of plagiarism.

What's yours is limitless!

A professional mind is an endless source of ideas when it keeps operating with confidence of its uniqueness. *Professional confidence penetrates* the essence of other disciplines and gets to the hidden causes of all that is manifested as an effect in your own area of expertise that remains to be unique. Such situation proves Norbert Winner's brilliant observation of today's professional world when we need to send a person that is seeking the solution of a professional problem "*to the next door down the corridor*", instead of answering his question then and there. All a real professional need *is a holistic visualization of the problem* and its immediate **X-Raying** for the solution. As I keep reminding you, *self-growth should be channeled holistically*, following the paradigm below. Only then can you out-best yourself!

Generalize - select- actualize! / Synthesis - Analysis-Synthesis!

Auto-Induction:

In My Life Quest, I Manifest My Best!

Chunk 3

Self-Genesis Strategically and Tactically

Acquiring the ability for ***reasoning and rationalizing life*** is a great skill that, unfortunately, fails us sometimes because we are emotional beings first, at least at this point of our human evolution. ***The pendulum of our life mistakes often crushes and destroys our creation of Self.*** Obviously, we have to respect our feelings, too, and be aware of their harmful or beneficial effect on our personal mind-set.

Intuition is more emotional than mental, while conscience is more mental than emotional.

Therefore, we always have intuitive feelings, warning us against wrong choices in life that we have to reason out later thanks to ***the twinges of conscience*** that prick us inevitably. Therefore, every mistake we have is a lesson to learn, and there is always another lesson inside each lesson.

Auto-suggestion: ***The choices we make dictate the life we live!***

The point is to start seeing with the heart and stop repeating the same mistakes repeatedly. But intuition will prompt the right action only if we rationalize its message in the outcome first. In other words, ***the paradigm of rationalization of life demands that we first think of the consequences of our actions strategically***, then take the action and watch ourselves ***performing it tactically.*** Thus, we'll be paying conscious attention to the causes of your actions, not only their consequences that is we ***synchronize our mind and the heart.*** *(See below)*

Auto-suggestion: ***I am learning the art of seeing with my heart!***

As an egg-headed intellectual, you are gradually shaping yourself into an egg-form, into a cocoon that can transform into a butterfly. This is the process of accumulation of the magnetic power of the mind, on the one hand, and the healing power of the emotions, on the other.

Self-induction: ***I am what I think and feel, but I sometimes need a refill!***

That is why we look for solitude to let our mental and emotional wounds heal and to give ourselves time and space to rationalize the life steps that we take. To accomplish that, it's paramount to always have the initial, holistic vision of ***the Ultimate Result Vision*** of self-creation in the mind. (P*art One, 7*) ***It's your reference point*** that will help you compare the URV of one time-space period to another, obtaining a qualitatively much better vision of self in space and time. If every misstep in life is a message to learn; we need time and space to process that lesson consciously through our ***conscience grid first strategically, then tactically.***

Thus, you are molding yourself over and over into a Whole You – the Vintage You!

A new self-image will start crystallizing in your mind each time , and it will be shaping your modified self-awareness, strategically, tactically, and strategically again, building up the life perspective in your mind in time and space.

General – Specific – General! / Synthesis –Analysis –Synthesis!

Internalize ⟶ *Optimize* ⟶ *Strategize!*

Thus, **self-genesis** from a latent, embryonic form will develop into a **holistic vision of Self**, and, consequently, the level of personal intelligence will grow considerably. As a result, **the self-formation skills will start getting framed out,** and balance, equanimity, and self-discipline will rule your life.

Personal integrity is the holistic reflection of your Life Skills!

You will feel happier and much more content with life and yourself. It's like looking at the mirror and feeling good about yourself because you look good .For sure, your life will become more conscious, and the inspirational feelings of **successful self- sculpturing** will be really overpowering the moments of weakness. Your personality will become more magnetic and intriguing for others.

Continue sculpturing yourself in MIND+ HEART TANDEM in your professional stem!

In sum, only going through your own personal credos of life in an individual motion of choreographing yourself first strategically then tactically can you change your own patterns of behavior and fortify your essentially good beliefs that build up your inner gravity and strengthen your anti-crowd immunity. *"Keep self-unspotted from the world!" (Edgar Cayce)*

To do the right thing at the right time,

"Don't cast pearls before swine!"

And don't ever whine;

Change your present life twine!

To Reform Your Selfish Gene;
Practice Strict Mentally-Professional Hygiene!

Chunk 4

Rational Thinking and Intuition Development

***Rationalization starts with changing* the way we process the information** that invades your brain non-stop, and rational thinking is at the core of any professional intelligence. Only conscious thought process can *channel cognition to action,* when each bit of information is filtered by the brain through the existing knowledge, gets selected or sorted out for its validity, and is later organized into the chunks of information on the basis of a conceptual principle and in the holistic way, presented above. (*Mental Architecture, Chunk 9*) Start with reading or listening to the piece of information that you need *analyze it quickly for its validity* and *select the information* that is of interest for you. Be professionally-wise - .

Strategize- Optimize – Actualize!

Next, you need to *conceptualize it* into the massages that you get, reading between the lines of the text, a verbal or written one. Thus, you will be able to channel your *thinking consciously and rationally in the cause-effect frame-work* much better, because you will feel more responsible for every thought you have, every word you say, and every action you take. Never view the problem in one dimension only! *Aware attention* should be given to the problem at every level - *physical, emotional, mental, spiritual and universal.*

Only holistically reviewed business has the perspective to grow!

The reasoned out and structurally-governed thinking should always be rational and conscious, and it needs to be monitored by *the Universal Law of Cause and Effect*. It should not be affected by the patters of thinking that are already established in the brain and that *generate compulsive thinking* and therefore, an action impulse that we might feel sorry for later. A person's conscious mind should always be in *charge to block the inertia of thinking* that Richard W. Wetherill calls "*Distorted thinking" (The Tower of Babel")* It is very common among people now, led by the automatic patterns of behavior more than ever.

Automatized thinking is the result of an unconscious, automatized, and patterned thought.

Other than that," distorted thinking causes emotional energy to be used destructively and the end result of distorted thinking is emotional and physical debility that gradually becomes complete."

As it is Above, so it is below!"(the Hermetic maxima)

Besides science proves that most people *over-analyze the information,* the process for which the left hemisphere of the brain is responsible for. We first need to deal with critical items of information as fast as possible, *conceptualizing them in the cause-effect fashion.* What is needed next at this new stage of our evolutionary development generated by the digital revolution is *to put our reasoning in synch with feeling.*

PUT THE MIND AND HEART IN SYNC; HOLISTICALLY THINK!

To put it differently, and that is *our next evolutionary step*, we need to process the in-put information though our individual *mental-emotional grid synchronically,* forming new patterns of conscious, rationalized behavior.

Auto-induction: *I intellectualize my emotions and emotionalize my mind!*

Putting the mind and the heart in synch, *we are processing the informational in-put through the test of consciousness and intuition,* the act that will always point us to the right behavior solution-making, or action-taking. Neither just the mind, nor the heart will do the job on their own.

Our intuition is, in fact, our conscience!

The conscience and intuition are inseparable entities. They are testing every thought we have, every uncontrolled word we say, and every automatic action we take. What we call "**a guilt – trip** "that is always crashing us after any wrong-doing is our conscience at work**.** To keep self-unspotted from the world, we need to tune to our conscience that in the form of intuition works as **the scanning mechanism** of the cause-effect frame-work of the mind-heart unanimity.

Intuition is the basis for your communication with the Universal Intelligence – God!

Intuition is, no doubt, the propelling mechanism of our self-development, too, because it is connected to conscience that is the testing mechanism of our growing consciousness, governed by our tuning to the station "God" continuously for our intuitive self-assessment and guidance in our very turbulent life.

Self-induction: *I tune myself to the station God for my inner peace reward!*

It's noteworthy to mention here that the ability to unify the mind and the heart is the brain operation that builds up **the mental-emotional grid** as the Fort of our inner gravity and personal magnetism, and, most importantly, it is channeling us to rationalized behavior. The mind has to be in charge, silencing the chatter box of the brain.

Auto-induction: *I put the strain on my brain!*

I Make My Heart Smart, and the Mind Kind!

I'm One of a Kind!

Chunk 5

Professional Consciousness

Holistically–developed professionals are the cornerstone of today's economy, and professional intelligence is at the forefront of evolution. We need to raise the level of professional awareness to a higher *professional consciousness*. It is the most paramount way to raise the economic productivity and the quality of the economic output, as well as the way to make our businesses more viable.

Professional consciousness is something that often sags due to the desired security of a job that is never there and *loss of intellectual or financial motivation that damages professional conscience of a person.* Professional consciousness requires constructive or proactive thinking to be done in terms of the quality of the work that you perform daily, and it should not be damaged by .the colleagues of less motivation and less intellectually – up-dated . Such thinking has to be always **logically-structured and strategically-disciplined** on the basis of a person's *unique know-how* that will remain in constant and flexible growth, seeking perfection till the end of a person's life, adding a lot to his / her sense of self–realization in life.

. *There is no success in self-quest without a person's professional self-actualization!*

In fact, *professional intelligence is at first governed by the programmed intelligence* that any person gets with the college education on the road of career searching. The one, who has *processed information in his own unique mind consciously,* is capable to handle it skillfully in the future. Unfortunately, there are still cases when the professional intelligence of people that are heading a business, a company, or a governmental institution leaves much to be desired and, therefore, it becomes the obstacle for many advanced minds on the way of the realization of their wonderful ideas. You need spunk to overcome these obstacles.

"Character, not circumstances, makes the man!" (Booker T. Washington)

In sum, professional consciousness is, by and large, a display a strategically-structured, professionally-disciplined, insightfully deep, and very creative thinking. It is, in fact, very proactive thinking because a highly professional person should be able *to generate new context, concepts, and objectives* in the most constructive way, putting both *the heart and the mind* into his job.

No doubt, a career choice that goes with the calling of a heart is a must!

Auto-Induction:

I Take My Professional Life's Tide in Stride!

Chunk 6

Professional Conscience and Competence

However, the period of a heightening of a person's professional consciousness is an on-going process that requires ***mastering of the profession*** based on constructive and disciplined thinking in any professional situation and very often way beyond it.

Belief in oneself becomes practice. Practice becomes professional awareness.
Professional awareness becomes professional competence.
Professional competence becomes professional integrity. Professional integrity becomes professional conscience!

Practice ⟹ *professional awareness* ⟹ *professional competence* ⟹ *professional integrity* ⟹ *professional conscience*!

Professional conscience is Mind + Heart Competence!

Only those people whose intelligence goes beyond the educational programs thanks to their bold imagination and insatiable curiosity are capable to change themselves and the world. History contains very many stories about amazing geniuses that went far beyond their personal limits, questioning the impossible and evolving the world with their incredible discoveries.

The giants of professional intelligence, such as **Bill Gates, Steve Jobs, Alan Mask, „Jack Ma** and many, many newer wonderful minds are the examples of extreme brain organization, discipline, independent thinking, and constructive, strategic vision, that ***encapsulates the form and the content***, or the design and the function of their creation.

This is the sign of the right brain endeavors that is able to synthesize the work of both brains. ***Constructive intelligence is a true testimony of the right brain in action.*** In such cases, professional intelligence is in lieu with creative intelligence *(See below)* that demonstrates an ardent desire of its owners to change the world for the good, when the mind of a thinker opens the door into the Universal Intelligence and works in tight cooperation with it.

Intelligence + Conscience = Living Intelligence!

Living intelligence is creative and self-programmed, not society-programmed.! It requires non-stop designing and re-designing of self. It means you are shaping yourself into a leader! ***Living intelligence is very personable and integral***; it is always holistically based on the joint work of the minds of the team members, impregnated by one idea of the leader of the group.

The problem is, people are often either unable or unwilling to make hard decisions and to bring about real changes that provide a vision and a new strategy for their implementation. ***Our managerial culture often lacks professional intelligence,*** and so happens that a manager sometimes cannot explain the job to the employees in a simple, aware way.'

We have a lot of managers everywhere and **very few real leaders** that are able not only to decide smartly and hit more lucrative targets, but they can also change the framework of business, science, and life on the whole. Senior management often cultivates **the culture of fear** when people are afraid to express their thoughts which could have changed the texture of any professional enterprise. We should feel free to demonstrate our professional competence and express it freely without any red-tape restrictive instructions or the fear to lose a job.

New professional methodology demands inclusive leadership and holistic professionalism! It means that professional assessment should be done on five levels:

Mini, Meta, Mezzo, Macro, and **Super**

Mini level – a start-up position; very little knowledge, limited job skills; no experience

Meta level – Knowledge and skills are still disconnected, some experience is acquired

Mezzo Level – Knowledge and skill are synchronized, a person has worked his own **know-how,** professional competence, full awareness, professional intelligence.

Macro level - Great professional intelligence, spontaneity and creation, leadership skills

Super level - Professional consciousness, great cultural and social skills, enrichment in other expertise, holistic professional outlook, *synergistic professional skills*

In sum, professional competence has a new meaning now because *our professional expectations have changed drastically.* The new time demands that holistically- educated and self-created individuals perform in the best way possible *in the multi-national, globalized, electronically-governed world.*

Therefore, the ability for innovative and constant growth in every profession is the given now. Professional growth has to come in new ways, and our mission is to make it inclusive of the latest scientific developments, technological advancements, and the methods of working together synergistically with diverse teams of people.

A competent representative of any company should be a representative of the holistic intelligence inclusively.

Personal Magnetism is not What you Do;

it is How you Are!

Chunk 7

Beware of Stereotyped Thinking!

To get to a new dimension of professional consciousness, we also need to operate any problem in the most **conscious way** because the professional world is also being screwed up by automatic, thoughtless job functioning. **Brain-wracking** is an exercise *for **purposeful thinking*** in the search of the solution of any problem.

"Put your mind on fire: be proactive!" ("The Start-up of You")

Unfortunately, once a person gets stuck in a framework of his professional obligations, he stops caring for the quality of the job done and often functions as *a working robot.* The obtained academic degrees and tenues are often in the way of a person's further professional and scientific growth. It happens because we generate certain **stereotyped mental habits** at work that condition our thinking unless we are fully aware of such a possibility and do not *let the mind get inflated with worked-out patterns of thinking.*

Professional thinking is inseparable with constant growth in professional awareness.

The use of old patterns in professional problem-solving generates **patterned thinking** that is a dead end in professional sense. Not to fall into the trap of patterned thinking, Reid Hoffman suggests**,**" **You should never leave a start-up's mind position**" to always challenge yourself with the unpredictability and insecurity at work. He writes that" the rules of the labor market have been permanently altered. **"Ready, aim, fire"** has been replaced by" *Aim, fire, aim, fire, aim, fire!"*

What a great way to put it! That is so true because only a start-up professional is always agile, thinking-wise. **The Law of the Right Human Behavior comes to our rescue here,** too. "Being right is the identification with a mental position. There is nothing that strengthens our professional skills more than being right. However, this skill needs work, too." (R. Wetherill).

Therefore, we have more managers now than real thinkers or true leaders that are able to reboot their minds with new thinking patterns, devoid of programmed, overworked ones. We can get rid of this harmful state of thinking if we develop *the aware attention skills* that we have been referring to so far.

We can acquire these skills if we consciously process any information that we get through a *previously sorted out and well–organized knowledge grid* that enable us later to take the right actions.

"You Need to Forever Be a Start-Up!"

(Reid Hoffman)

Chunk 8

Inflation of Professional Thinking!

We live in a technologically sophisticated universe. However, since we delegate more and more processing to computers, perceptual thinking remains to be often forgotten, whereas it is essentially human. Only human interaction helps generate neurons within the cerebral cortex and form new memories.

In fact, forming new connections in the brain, we essentially rewrite our consciousness!

In-coming information gets organized into patterns, and the mind follows the patterns automatically, following the recipe. However, the best recipe can be screwed up due to the **inflated thinking** of an employee who works on the automatic pilot, on the one hand, and is driven by the feelings of insecurity of losing his job, on the other.

Inflation of thinking generates fear of action and hinders the mind in the process of decision making or creation of a new thinking vibration. The mind of an employee gets emotionally and mentally inflated by the negative vibration. Science proves that our thoughts, emotions, desires or impulses are only vibratory states. In our personal or professional life, *everything revolves around the vibration*. If we are happy, we generate positive vibration, or we feel happy due to positive vibration. Sadness, fear, discontent, suppressed anger generate negative vibration. Each person has a mental wave length of his own, according to the vibratory frequencies of his intelligence.

Our thought makes us intelligent according to our mental vibration.

The fear of being politically-incorrect and breaking the protocol generates negative vibration, and as a result, inflated thinking. That is not to say that following the job instructions is bad. *While organization and discipline are essential at work, they should not be in the way of a creative mind-flow* of the employees and their **freedom of self-expression**. We have a lot of people in any profession who stop growing professionally altogether. We cannot rely here on professional development sessions. it is a personal obligation for every man / woman to be aware of the developments in their field of expertise, without relying on a guaranteed tenue, or any other professional security means.

Finally, a healthy *synergistic professional climate* is essential. It stimulates employees to creative thinking, and eventually, everyone benefits.

The link of the m*ind + mind and heart + heart is the basis for that!*

Auto-suggestion: *I communicate with my boss without being a sugar-coating moth.*

Steer your Brain with the Mind at the Steering Wheel!

Chunk 9

Holistic Professional Wisdom!

If you have assessed yourself in all the *15 guidelines* and have gotten an optimistic overview of yourself, congratulations! *Now you can channel your self-assessment to the quality of your professional thinking.* Higher professional intelligence means effective, *proactive, not compulsive thinking*. The critical use of intelligence is required when our job situations demand that we generate new context, concepts, solutions of problems, and set up new objectives. Today, the brain storming technique is not sufficient. Digital reformation demands new skills.

New professional awareness + aware attention skills = Professional wisdom

Proactive thinking can also be called **expansive thinking** when the solution of any professional problem goes way beyond the obvious and the possible, and when it becomes impossibly challenging and soluble in the most unexpected way. In other words, we need to expand our **professional thinking** to **professional wisdom!** Professional wisdom means that we do not think reactively, we think proactively, but in five main dimensions:

Mini ⟶ *Meta* ⟶ *Mezzo* ⟶ *Macro* ⟶ *Super*

The usual sharpness of the mind is not of value here; i**nsightful, slow, digestive thinking** comes to the forefront of proactive thinking because the amount of information to digest is overwhelming now. Effective thinking also is based on conceptual analysis on five levels of consideration. *process any problem s through the physical, emotional, mental ,spiritual, and universal GRID!*

To be a mental leader, channel the thinking of other people objectively and holistically!!

Conceptual approach to problems channeled by aware attention holistically is incorporating any business **both tactically and strategically.** Reid Hoffman suggests being well aware of your **"competitive advantages"** and personal professional assets. The ability to single out the relevant information, conceptualize it, and organize it into the valuable chunks is essential in any business dealing now, and it should be done with the help of aware attention skills.

"Thinking without awareness is the main dilemma of human existence" (Eckhart Tolle)

When thinking is based on awareness, it is always constructive and much more operative At Stage One of the intelligence development, (*Language Intelligence, Chunk 3*), we mention the necessity to develop *the skill to say less but mean more.* This is possible only if you have an expansive and constructive professional awareness and if you have taught yourself " **The Less Principle."** It means that you develop the ability to generalize and rationalize professional thinking. Constructive thinking is structured and disciplined.

Even in an emergency, there is time *to think slowly and substantially*, zooming in on the messages that the mind gets. I call such aware thinking - C*hanneled Thinking* because it is channeled by aware attention that is actualized **as a scanning tool** in the five suggested above dimensions. View every problem on *the Mini-Meta-Mezzo-Macro, and Super levels!* *(Introduction, Thesis 7)*

Well-processed intelligence redesigns the problem into a solution!

Such approach generates **the holistic awareness** that helps not just resolve any problem; it designs a solution for any problem strategically and tactically. Channeled thinking is also a *purposeful thinking* because you channel your thinking holistically and in full accord with the cosmic laws, outlined above, that are inseparable from our thinking and actions. Purposeful thinking is the thinking that is done in accordance with *the cosmic Law of Cause and Effect* that we should not overlook in any situation, to say nothing about a professional one. We have to deal with any problem with full awareness of the reasons that have generated a professional problem. *Purposeful thinking is free of compulsive thinking*. Reasoned–out quality thinking helps you make a leap from potentiality to actuality.

Auto-induction: ***Re- engineer your thinking in a cause-effect way!***

Professional intelligence that is based on solid awareness also demands **slow, not compulsive thinking.** Thinking slowly translates into focusing clearly on each stage of the problem-solving in a progressively constructive way. *Slow thinking is the mind-channeled thinking.*

You will finally acquire the highest **professional consciousness**, and with it, a promotion or the desired financial reward will come without fail. So, practicing mental tasks, like *generalizing, assuming, realizing, inferring summarizing, conceptualizing, etc.,* we strength the existing brain connections as well as help develop new ones, avoid redundancy in thinking and speaking, and practically re-engineer the brain.

Also, professional wisdom is always connected with the work of the mind and the heart in synch, when you tune to the thoughts and feelings of your staff and can read their minds and hearts. A wonderful movie with *Mel Gibson and Helen Hunt* **"What Women Want"** has a great concept of the necessity to tune in to your staff. You don't need to experience an electro-shock to become more sensitive and perceptive to make the people that work for you or with you more productive not because they are slavering for a promotion, but because the work is the demand of their free self-expression and *the irresistible desire for self-installation in professional life.*

Auto-Induction:

Think Fast, but Slow;

Give Any Problem an Intelligent Go!

Chunk 10

Professional Superficiality

There is another very significant point to make here. Science proves that most of our thinking is done in the perception area. Perception is how we look at things., and how aware of life we are. The neurological understanding of the brain affects how we live our lives. Your professional intelligence absolutely has to be enriched with the new insights from neuro-science about the *flexibility of the brain and its plasticity.*

The development of these innate qualities in our brains should be t*he main goal of our technologically-baked up education!* Such necessity applies to any field of knowledge and any expertise as the demand of our times.

Knowledge about the brain has huge cognitive benefits professionally.

We alter synaptic connections in the brain and change the language behavior patterns, thus changing a regular human interaction *to a mind-to-mind communication*, as well as making the interaction with a machine become more and more meaningful in the virtual reality.

Also, being right does not mean necessarily that we immediately must find someone who is wrong. "*The finger pointing to the moon is not the moon*". *(Buddha) Being right means acting with aware attention, applying proactive thinking, purposeful thinking, or the cause-effect thinking* that are resisting patterned thinking in its core.

New professional awareness demands conscious recognition of a pattern.

One of the reasons we often must deal with ignorance at work lies in the fact that ignorant people lack intelligence due to their *patterned thinking blindness* that is never questioned, challenged, or destroyed with a new flood of consciously processed professional information that   demands not only a mind-to-mind interaction, but also a heart-to-heart connection.

Our evolutionary development depends on the unity of our hearts and minds

that are now in defiance!

Developing aware attention is another way to battle the inflation of thinking. Aware attention is an electronic commodity now that helps to confront this situation. Aware attention is the ability *to discriminate the knowable from the unknown* or from the patterned application of knowledge that is killing many businesses now worldwide. To channel attention of the website visitors in the right way guarantees success only if you manage *to hook their aware attention* and thus **establish a mind-to-mind contact with them** and help them make a professional judgment at a much higher awareness level because there will be such a contact.

Conscious professional thinking is a must here!

Another pest on this path is **professional superficiality** that is always based on the duality of thinking *(good- -bad-, win-lose . success – failure, money-gain- money- fail , etc)*

Next, we might have to battle the inertia of thinking and intellectual apathy that mostly make superficiality a bad habit. Not to aggravate the situation, impedes the search for the critical information that might be needed to resolve a professional problem effectively.

Make Your Thinking One-Pointed and Purposeful!

In sum, to be immune to the inflation of thinking, keep on surpassing yourself with the help of self-induction: Don't knock yourself out, trying to compete with others.

Self-induction: ***Build yourself up by competing only with yourself!***

To conclude, learn to work with people below you. But dealing with the people below, don't get affected by the phenomenon of **psychological inflation** due to the prestige of your position. Remember that nothing is permanent under the sky, and you might end up where you had started.

"Life has no beginning or end, but everyone can be caught by a circumstance" (A. Block)

Learn to work with people above you, too. . It takes integrity not to be with your boss a sugar-coating moth .*Be professional, but impartial, respectful, but not impersonal.* The communication with your colleagues only on the mind-to mind basis will be good, but not excellent.

Only putting *the heart and the mind in synch can we get the God's wink* of approval, or can we tune ourselves to the vibrations of the Universal Mind that is emitting them non-stop for those who are able to hear the vibrating Universe ,like Nicola Tesla.

My auto-antenna is lit by the Universal Information grid!

Put both, Your Mind and the Heart, on the Front Seat of the Professional Perpetua Mobile!

Chunk 11

Professional Self-Assessment

Professional self-reflection is the guarantee that you will never fall behind in your knowledge and skills. Constant work at both is a necessity because **a real professional has to have them in synch,** especially during our digitally changeable times.

Knowledge + skills = the flow of professional life!

Listed below are fifteen guidelines that can be used for any professional self-assessment, after you have scanned yourself for your knowledge and skills levels presented above. Of course, every field of knowledge has its peculiarities, but there are some features in every profession that are of a general value. You can make your own list of guidelines, depending on the expertise you have and the job that you are practicing. Quiz yourself to build more professional confidence and fortify your professionalism with more awareness.

"Excessive Ambition leads to Disaster!" (William Shakespeare)

Self-Assessment:

Guideline 1- Assess your job responsibilities. What does it take to do this job superbly? Comprise a strategic plan of action. The one who plans better accomplishes more. Studies reveal that planning is a cognitive task. It demands the development of analytical and conceptual thinking. De-automatize your work. Assess the necessity to fill your mind with new knowledge and skills. *(Cognitive Intelligence, Chunks 7-12)*

No pseudo-learning! Develop professional awareness non-stop!

Guideline 2 – Assess your job performance. Face any challenges objectively and consciously.

When the going gets tough, the tough gets going!

Guideline 3 – Professionalize your speaking habits. Talk the professional talk, use the professional vocabulary. Manage you bad language behavior patterns. **First think then speak!**

Don't verbalize everything that comes to your mind!

Guideline 4- Get the feedback from others. Studies show that people get to know us better in reflection. They reflect us and thanks to their input, we get valuable professional feedback

Guideline 5 – Build up on your natural talents. See what makes you special and unique and how you can incorporate those talents into your job.

Guideline 6 – Seek out excellence in all that you do, all that you say, and all that you are. *"You should not be just the best; you must be the single one!" (Steve Jobs)*

Guideline 7 – Continue to invest in your mind. It's your biggest asset. Professional mistakes are the result of undisciplined, negligent mind and lack of professional awareness.

Guideline 6 – To be interesting, get interested! Go with the science flow! Be well- informed1

Guideline 7 Live by the professional moral code! - You need to trust your moral barometers, be in charge of your moral behavior at work as much as you try to display it at home.

Guideline 8 – Learn to synchronize intelligence and professionalism! Connect them by the formula: **Synthesis – analysis – synthesis** when resolving any problem.

Guideline 9 – Keep professional integrity. Don't undermine it for anyone's sake. Always build **a "shorthand' profile** of the person facing you. Trust your own intuition more than any one's.

Guideline 10 – Synergize the working place, radiating the win-win attitude. Enlighten the professional space! Apply" **network intelligence"** skills.

Guideline 11 –Always think of the outcome that you will accomplish in qualitative terms. Neutralize an opponent's intention for control with your intelligence, then take power!

Guidelines 12- Don't ever surrender to ignorance. Resist it and fight it with the power of your professional logic and informed attitude ,**not political correctness!** Growth vs. Stagnation!

Guideline 13 – Give yourself and everyone around an emotional and professional pump up. Learn to compliment and praise any one even for a smallest accomplishment.

Guideline 14 – "Make a leap from potentiality to actuality!" Acting on the mind-set auto-suggestively and uploading it in the brain is the best way to upgrade your professional toning.

Guideline 15- – Most importantly, don't knock yourself down, trying to compete with others. Build yourself up competing only with yourself!

In my inner cell, I compete only with myself!

Auto-Induction:

I am a Unique Cell; I Keep on Surpassing Myself!

Chunk 12

Professional Intelligence Auto-Suggestively!

To finalize my schematic presentation of a very conceptually rich topic about professional intelligence, we would like to share with you a few main tips on how to better shape professional intelligence auto-suggestively. Remember, in a psychologically-challenging situation, we need to create a vacuum for *new psycho-tropic energy – the main energy of the spirit!*.

1. **Take care of your good health, professional look, and a nice, synergistic personality.**

2. **Self-acceptance is an absolute must!** No one holds a good opinion of a man who has a low opinion of himself. It is especially important to remember about your self-image at a job interview.

Self-induction: *"You never have a second chance to make a good first impression"*

The core of your being is personal magnetism! The feelings of self-acceptance are not instilled in our emotional and mental make-up overnight; we need to build up this feeling in five stages *(Introduction, Thesis 8) in* the most consistent manner on the physical, emotional, mental, social, and spiritual levels.

Self-induction: *Do not de-magnetize yourself; remember who you are in your every cell1*

3. **Stop thinking of your imperfections as unchangeable.** The wisdom of real professional transformation lies in the changeability or impermanence of our misgivings.

4. **Always picture the URV** *(The Ultimate Result Vision)* of your work and **the best of you in it:** full of energy, enthusiasm, competence,

5. Psychological intelligence is generating success, personal magnetism, and respect.. Stay away from negative, critical people that drain you of the psycho-tropic energy that you need to get totally self-realized at work.

Self-induction: *Energy is not what we do; it's how we are!*

Also, the spiritual teachings tell us that to feel better, we should help someone. Kindness is a dose of anti-hostility, anti-depression, and anti-self-pity. Kindness is our best friend at work; help someone wholeheartedly!

6. **Program your mind against fear. Be psychologically strong**! The auto-suggestive formula that we have been using so far is very helpful to boost your self-confidence.

Self-suggestion: *I know who I am!*

I can...1 I want to..., and I will...!

I am becoming more and more invulnerable / confident / self-sufficient / self-reliable / unbeatable / unstoppable etc. **with each coming day!**

7. Do not compete with any of your colleagues. Envy creates a gap within you. Don't fall into that gap! Keep improving your own professional awareness and competence.

Self-suggestion: ***I don't fall into an envy cell; I compete only with myself!***

8. Don't create the feelings of doubts in you; do not self-sabotage your self- transformation. Eradicate doubt in the bud once you get aware of it. Fill your brain up with enthusiasm, self-confidence, and self- sufficiency.

Self-suggestion: ***"If it's to be, it's up to me!"***

9. You most likely need more **psychological awareness.**(*Psychological Intelligence, Chunk 2))* We need to know more about our own and other people's psychological make-up not to depend on a specialist that might just generalize individual problems and *label us according to their professional or unprofessional, personally-involved or impersonal, conclusions.*

However, a psychologist's or a psychiatrist's help might still be needed if you feel unable to see yourself adequately in *the psychological mirror of objective assessment.*

Auto-suggestion: ***Think for yourself! Accelerate your intelligence with diligence!***

10. Finally and most importantly, ***professional intelligence should be a part of general education.*** The major part of our lives is spent at work, and this time needs to be used productively for our self-actualization and full contentment.

Professional intelligence paves the way

to a full Self-Realization in life without any dismay!

Auto-Induction:

I Wind and Rewind My Professional Mind!

Vistas of Intelligence to Install Next

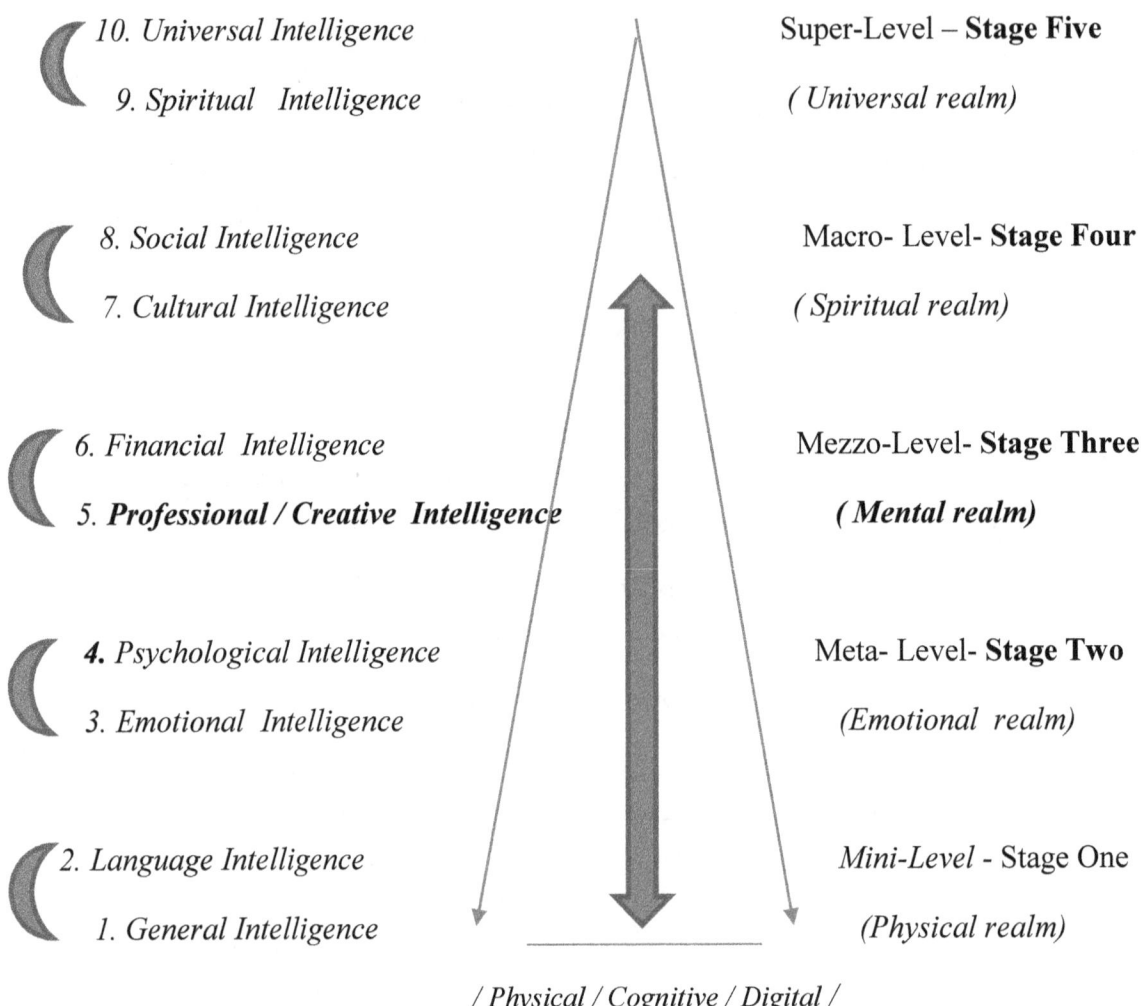

/ Physical / Cognitive / Digital /

Wind and Rewind Your Creative Mind!

To Make Your Life Intellectually-Wise, Strategize – Optimize - Actualize!

Your Creative Vigor is at the Trigger!

Mezzo-Level / Mental Dimension -

Creative Intelligence

Professional Intelligence - Step 2

"To Be a Creator in Hell,

You must believe in God and Yourself!"

(Ben-Groin)

"A Man's Reach Should Exceed his Grasp!"

(William Shakespeare)

In My Professional Life's Quest, I Manifest My Best!

Creativity is Me; Creativity is My Identity!

Chunk 1

The Will to Create is Encoded in Our DNA!

Give creativity an open air because creativity is everywhere! We live at the time amazing creativity antihanging our world exponentially every day. I love this country for the level of creativity around me, having inspired me to create all my books, too.

The Creative Intelligence that had created us initially is remaking us all the time!

Creativity is a burning sensation to let the world know about your idea and find the way to present it to the world. *It's the main asset of any good professional!* Creative expansion of the mind occurs when you listen to your inner voice and trust your intuition, or the hunches of the right brain, while following the logic and the structural lead of the left brain. There is no true professional intelligence without the upbeat contribution to it on the part of the creative mind of its owner. But how can we know something without feeling something? *The divine spark of creativity* is in everyone who realizes **the need to think and feel in his own unique way.**

RATIO + EMOTIO = CREATIVITY!

For 25 years that I have been in this country, I keep marveling at the American creativity and ingenuity. I love this country of doers and creators, of advanced minds, of intellectual and spiritual gurus. *A deep well of brain potential resides within us all*, but only those that keep developing their creative intelligence *"find the best way to tap into the inner savant' (Scientific American", August 2014)* A creative person is driven by a very altruistic urge to better the world

"Creativity is ingenuity in action." ("Scientific American Mind", July 2014).

"Creative skills let the scientists explore undiscovered artistic capabilities of the right brain." In 2008, a cognitive psychologist John Koumiss and his colleagues found that the brain activity of people, who used insights, differed significantly from those who preferred just analysis. This study, along with **Carson's reports** from highly creative individuals suggest that to prompt your brain to create, you should first *"wander the world with an open mind!"*

Curiosity and imagination develop our creative right brains.

To develop the right hemisphere of the brain that is responsible for our unique creativity, we need to learn *to generalize, to visualize*, and to develop the right part of the brain with the help of listening to classical music, *beautifying our speech skills*, enriching the vision of beauty and harmony around us, and synergizing our lives and the lives of the people that we come in touch with. *Creativity has no race, no skin color, and no politics. It's universal!*

Creativity is Me; Creativity is My Philosophy!

Chunk 2

Change the Form and the Content of Your Thinking!

To be creative means to question the existing *form + content* of the life stuff ,surrounding you and, most importantly, *put them in synch!* "*For knowledge to be useful, it must be creatively applied.*" *(Albert Einstein)* The moments of insight," *the Aha moments"* occur when the brain spontaneously reinterprets information to reach novel, nonobvious conclusion" *(Nessa Victoria Bryce)* As I have indicated in the part "*Cognitive Intelligence,*"

Creativity is the synch of the form and the content of the object of creation.

Interestingly, *Steve Jobs*, a genius of our age, managed to change and to connect the *form and content* in all his electronic marvels in the unity of an unbelievable precision. Our present-day most advanced contemporizes, amazing entrepreneurs and philanthropists, such as *Bill Gates, Elon Musk, Mark Zukerman, Reid Hoffman* and many others are moving the technological world forward unbelievably. It takes a true visionary to bridge both design and its inner capability.

The desire to pursue the self-quest and self-creation is driving only creative minds!

Emotion is also the bridge between conscious and unconscious minds. *Creative emotion is called inspiration!* So, the power of creativity needs to be directed willfully, otherwise it disturbs the mind. That is why creative people are always very vulnerable and too sensitive .They are consciously conscious of any hostile attitude to the product of their creation. Therefore, they are tenaciously fighting for it with those who are unconsciously or deliberately hampering their way.

The untrained intellect has no power over a genius mind!

Next, anyone can enhance his creative thinking *by expanding the knowledge base,* by learning new skills, by talking to someone outside his immediate professional network. We harness our creative potential through expanding a general outlook and a spontaneous thought

Creative intelligence develops a person's mind more than any other intelligence!

In sum, creative intelligence is uplifting the mind to the Living Intelligence because a creative person gets out of the loop of the "immediate gratification" of his wants that demagnetize his inner core and weaken his consciousness. Finally, auto-hypnosis helps us *spark the Eureka moments* in the brain. Use it to boost your creative confidence and to expand your life - changing expertise.

I can…. I want to….and I will…!

I Marvel at the Grander of All and Self-Install!

Chunk 3

Actionable Imagination

Creative intelligence is never ordinary because *it repels the patterned, inflated thinking*!(See *Cognitive Intelligence above*) Science proves that most creative thinking is done *in the perception area of the brain* that determines how we get to look at things. Creative imagination is the intelligence that goes beyond the limited understanding of things that better you and the world. Creativity is becoming more and more a collective phenomenon now thanks to the digital revolution because it is more than an expression of individuality. *Creativity is taking shape in a social context.* Actionable imagination does not come out of nowhere.

It's the pursuit of collective wisdom!

Since we delegate more and more processing to computers, perceptual thinking remains to be the most important to preserve. We know that the in-coming information gets organized into patterns. The mind follows the patterns automatically. The purpose of perception is to allow patterns to form and then to use them.

A creative mind focuses on the proximity of form and content of these patterns.

Creative intelligence requires **conscious recognition of the patterns**, not to be automatically driven to a programmed solution. It rebels against the patterns and creates new connections between the neurons in the brain that get programmed for the impossible, unexpected, and unique. We are all familiar with the beautiful words of Albert Einstein, *"Imagination is more important than knowledge. Knowledge is limited, imagination is infinite."*

Actionable imagination is the fuel for the mind, and creativity is the process of proactive thinking and feeling. The world never stops marveling at the creativity and ingenuity of the American people. Wonders of engineering, technology, medicine, space exploration, you name it, are countless. *No doubt, the Chinese people got their present ingenuity striptease from the American breeze.*

The American Ingenuity award was given to *Elon Musk*, an engineer, a serial entrepreneur and a great innovator who is rocking the world now with his innovations and most sparkling intelligence. *"When I am concentrating on something, I tune everything else out. I am curious about anything." (Elon Musk),* Mr. Musk is launching a private cargo into space, designing upscale electric cars, and changing the way we think about the solar power! He is a self-taught engineer that explores the frontiers, so daunting and so dangerous! He wants to defeat the incumbent old thinking in rocket building and fundamentally change the way we travel. As the *CNN's Amar C. Bakshi said,*

"His career encapsulates a particular brand of big, big thinking!"

Chunk 4

Making Things Possible is Not Impossible!

Opponents of Elon Musk's phenomenal contribution to the world of innovations tell us that he had the money to do that. Unquestionably, that's obviously true, but **he made the money building up on its potential power.** He, obviously, has the will power to expand his intelligence, his limitless creativity, the most surprising awareness in many areas of science, business, and technology. *(Introduction, Thesis 3 and Financial Intelligence below)*

What a wonderful example of self-propelling and most creative intelligence!

Positive emotions, a romantic love, the desire for self-realization and self- establishment act as boosters for creative intelligence. Aha moments come while we are observing nature, reasoning on the problems, scanning books for interesting information, or just while meditating. We kind of question the right, creative hemisphere that harbors our intuitive feelings, and we get the unexpected answers to our questions out of the blue. Just imagine the audacity of thinking that **Elon Musk** displayed to the world!

Only the minds that question the impossible make things possible!

But this magic happens only *in the intellectually-loaded brain*, the one that is in constant beta mode. *"Such thinking can be called enlightened for it is based on awareness that enlightens the mind and redesigns it. Such designing goes beyond the boundaries of the mental dimension up to the spiritual one."* (Osho, "Intelligence")

That is why creative people are loners, not like others. They fly in their mind; they are out there, somewhere, not quite together in the sense of the most other people. We have to be particularly grateful to such people and help them in every way possible. Their sensitive human brains add immeasurably to the richness of life. They have made their choice, and it always justifies itself!

Before you can get something, you have to be somebody!

Finally, the management culture that we have touched upon in the previous section, has to be built on creative intelligence of the best leaders, those who are able to strategize life, rather than focus on immediate tactics in the resolution of any problem. **Be such a leader**! Be able to demonstrate your brain-power, your awareness, your skills, and your creative energy!

A new culture of thinking demands new ,creatively-minded leaders!

Auto-Induction:

In My Creative Life Quest, I Commit to Be My Very Best!

Chunk 5

To Be Interesting, Get Interested!

No doubt, enlightened knowledge is in synch with consciously developed professional skills. *It is based on aware attention to the object of creation.* The evolutionary hunger to discriminate the knowable from the unknown is driving creatively–charged minds to be unstoppable and unbeatable in their search. Finally, the long-awaited times for the intelligence and *advanced awareness* have come to the forefront of our economic and social development.

Creative intelligence generates *the new light of thought at* a peculiar wave length concentrated only on one thing. A creative person always has *a skill mix and the mix of intelligences* that help him illuminate the patterns of thinking in his head. His knowledge acquisition is in constant flux.

Without awareness, knowledge is dead and creativity is impossible!

Aware attention to the potential marvels of discovery has become a real business commodity People that can think beyond the professional frame-work are in demand now The required peculiar mix of professional skills is always based on the information that has been accumulated by the inquisitive minds thanks to the aware attention that they pay to a much wider range of expertise than their own, on the one hand , and thanks to *the ability to question the ultimate resolution of any problem* ,on the other. *Creative intelligence is ruling the world of inadequacies, anyway. That's why we are progressing!*

Creative, independent people burst with ideas, and it is very important for those that do the hiring *to tune to the creative vibes* of such job-seekers and be much more professionally aware themselves, not to fail to place them at the right time.

The awareness for the potentiality of a creative mind is a must now!

Naturally, the development of aware attention is indispensable in any creative process. The code for understanding and communicating between aware people is very special. It is being developed in social networking on the Internet. But to connect to the ideas that *the Universal Intelligence* is communicating to us *in a mind-to-mind fashion*, we need to get rid of *the mental paralysis* of fear, self-doubt, inferiority and inadequacy. Most urgently, you need *to tune your* **AUTO-ANTENNA** *(your intuition)* **to** the Universal Mind and act confidently toward a sure success! If you are self-reliant and can meditatively attune yourself to the universal mind , you will be successful without any doubt. Just be patient. The Universal mind has you scheduled.

Competence generates creative confidence!

Vision + Idea = Creation + Determination!

Chunk 6

Steer the Self-Judgment of Your Idea!

A true creator judges the validity of his / her idea on his / her own, without paying attention to the critics and all those who rain on our parade. I am sure **Elon Musk** who has had the most outrageous idea to explore the outer space on his own, having started his new company **SpaceX,** had a ot of "well-wishers" whose predictions he had discarded and launched his own rockets into space. *That's the best example for every forward-thinking mind to follow.*

Below, there are some more recommendations that you might want to apply.

1. Process your idea on your own; do the self-judgment of its uniqueness. An identity decal is not a reward for being unique, but it's the inner assuredness of being individually unique and having the ability to stand up for your uniqueness, **like Jesus, Socrates, Gandhi, Mother Teresa, Mather Luther King, J., Steve Jobs** and many other most advanced minds.

2. Assess the depth and clarity of your idea and its potential novelty and advantages with aware attention.

3. Examine the key ingredients of its implementation on all the Holistic Five Levels : physical, emotional, mental, spiritual, and universal.

4. Offer more practical tools and techniques.

5. Anticipate the costs and the result. Keep rechecking them and transforming them.

5. hare your ideas only with your co-thinkers. Create an aura of thinking together!

"We are mating through creating, and we are creating though mating!

In sum, we all have within us untapped potential and undamaged areas that lead to new open doors. This potential needs to be actualized in the most personable way. Reading avidly and expanding your general outlook, admiring art and listening to classic music feeds actionable imagination and .results in wonderful Eureka moments of an amazing inner inspiration. No wonder, Einstein was playing the violin to boost his actionable imagination that was ruling his" *thinking laboratory."* Creative intelligence is the intelligence that sees everything as a problem that can be fixed without any excuses, but with a lot of determination, zest, and love of life.

A Creative Being does a lot of Intellectual Brewing, Creating, and Redoing!

Chunk 7

Self-Hypnosis is at Hand; Remember About That!

Unfortunately, there are always obstacles on the way of our polishing and selling the pearls of ideas that come as a revelation. We all know how hard it is to fight with ignorance on this path, and how much self-confidence, belief, perseverance, and just strong will-power we need to promote our ideas, especially when we are well aware of the fact that nothing is impossible.

"There is no idea so good that it can't be ruined by a few well-placed idiots" (Scott Adams)

Since no one is aware what ideas you are nursing in your wonderful head, you are the only one who can help those ideas mature with the boost of your self-confidence and a firm will-power to back them up. So, keep saying to yourself auto-suggestively the mind-sets that will help you become ***a stoic in the fight with ignorance.*** Every idea is propelled by your self-confidence, faith, imagination, and your uniqueness.

Self-induction: ***I'm a stoic, not for fun; I get through life with an up-lifted thumb!***

Doing suggestive meditation as often as you manage, you will be able to relax and clean up your head. *(Chunks 12, 13, 14, Physical Intelligence)* Never stop boosting up your will-power with a regular reminder:

I know who I am!

I am a strong, brave, calm, and determined owner of my firm will!

I can…, I want to…, and I will…!

You can always come up with a better way of doing anything if you inspire yourself on a regular basis auto-suggestively. All you need is to imagine the impossible and put a lot of effort into making it possible first in your inner vision. ***Never lose faith in your mind!***

Upload it with a dead-set assuredness and belief!

Often, all that's required is simple activity, instead of passivity. Choosing not to speak up or do anything in the face of obvious impossibilities fades your talents and deletes the possibilities. ***Help your professional intelligence infiltrate your job environment.*** Turn on your mind and enthuse yourself with confidence. Someone said,

"When I am right, nobody remembers, when I am wrong, nobody forgets."

That so true! Your new ideas may seem bold and unrealistic, but you know better. You are the one who is on permanent communication with the Universal Intelligence. It is guarding you in the implementation of your crazy ideas, and it pushes you to defy **the gravity of a common thought.**

"For an idea that does not at first seem insane, there is no hope." (E. Einstein)

Most importantly, don't knock yourself out trying to compete with others. Instill in your mind the mind-set:

In my professional cell, I compete only with myself!

Making yourself better and better with each new working day, you never stop visualizing the expected result , not just in the materialized form, but in self-realization form. True personal growth normally occurs during the professional life of a person, especially when this person puts **both his mind and the** heart into his / her job, loves it, enjoys it, and grows with it physically, emotionally, mentally spiritually, and universally in terms of realizing *the responsibility of Oneness* with the business of his / her life and the people that he / she shares his /her life with. .

"Income rarely exceeds personal development" (Jim Rohn).

Let the right action become your *physical, emotional, mental, and spiritual might*! Be proud of yourself! Your vision will inspire the mind. *Your connection to the Universal Mind will back you up!* The result will manifest itself without fail!

The Law of Attraction works without a fraction!

Remember, you are the Only One on Earth who has the idea that is propelling you to the stars! If you do not implement it, who will1 So, to be more life-fitting, keep repeating:

Auto-induction: *In my mind, I'm one of a kind!*

There wasn't, there isn't, there won't ever be

Any one like me!

Self-hypnosis will give a boost to your creative powers that are so accelerated by technology now., and it'll back up your confidence that might sag sometimes. To boost your creative intelligence, just remind yourself as often as possible:

My aware attention is never in retention!

The Air is Full of Ideas for the Connected Mind!

Chunk 8

Oy Vey! Is Victory on the Way!

Psychology teaches us that *"there are no hopeless situations; there are people that take hopeless attitudes."* In the world of non-stop creation, failures are the best exercise for the brain in this endeavor. Failures are our indicators of the short-cuts to self-awareness and self-confidence. Unfortunately, when we fail on our trial and error path, we allow others to drain us of our enthusiasm and the intuitive feeling that the right decision is just around the corner.

" Beware of lack of perception of your control dramas." (*Eckhart Tolle*)

Success-failure are natural fluctuations of a creative intelligence. However, failures happen much more often on this path, and a creative mind has to sustain them against all odds. The world history is full of such stories, and they always fill us up with awe at the perseverance of talented people.

"Feed your faith in success and doubts will starve to death!"

You must always control our attitude. The degree of your healing after a failure depends entirely upon your ability to restore **the inner light of your self-confidence** and the desire to better the situation with your new special in-put into it. With any negative act we are putting ourselves at risk because we change the charge of **the informational field** around the body and it gets disconnected with the Informational Field of the Earth and the universe. **Disconnection is death!**

Without conscious control of this connection line and tuning your AUTO-ANTENNA to the Universal Mind, you are doomed to walk all your life on **the cyclical treadmill of success – failure.** We must develop personal determination to participate in the process of self-actualization and do everything required for it. As a famous business philosopher Jim Rohm puts it,

"If you must be addicted to something, make it an addiction to winning!"

When you failed to do something, the first question should be not **where** the mistake lies, but **why** the mistake occurred in the first place. It is at your fingertips to regenerate the action that had failed and channel your thinking toward success in it. Such attitude speaks of the **change of professional consciousness.** *"If you think you'll lose, you are lost!"* (*Napoleon Hill*)

"Failures are the best lessons. (*Steve Jobs*)

Winston Churchill had to start from scratch in his political endeavors four times, and each time he taught himself to take every failure with more calmness and acceptance, generating more confidence and faith in God and himself thanks to his being calm. He kept saying to himself,

"Don't be vexed, be humbled. Victory is on the Way!"

Chunk 9

Doubt is an Immobility of Thinking!

On the path of *your most important mission in life*, there should be no doubt in you because doubt poisons all endeavors and generates *the immobility of thinking* that is the malady of people in trouble. Doubt is, in fact, part of life if we view life as the field of energy that is fluctuating in a negative / positive fashion non-stop, exactly as our personal lives do. Doubt is also generated by some one's reaction to our actions. People rain on our parade and change the fluctuations of anticipated positive result in our minds if we let them do it , having no umbrella over the head.

Quoting Hegel, let's say again, *"Be a thing in itself!"* A greatest German philosopher points to the representation of **content-form** phenomenon. *"If you view self-formation as a life phenomenon, the inseparable unity of your form and content will be pointing to the necessity of developing intelligence in synch with the will, as only such oneness completes a person as a subject of the world."* (Hegel) **Re-charge your aware attention** by processing your idea through the holistic paradigm of **synthesis- analysis -synthesis**, or *Internalize – select – externalize;*

Strategize -optimize -Actualize!

Developing the **"thing-in-itself" wholeness** will make you self-reliant and self–sufficient. It is the prerogative of a talented person to choose *"a narrow way"* in life. Robert Shulle says, **"Don't be simple-hearted about your success in front of people, only in front of God!"** Only with your inner wholeness and optimism will your mind and you psyche be enthused. You will become the happiest man / woman on earth because *you are blessed with a mission* that keeps you going on and on, without being hampered by anyone's judgment or skepticism.

. *An optimist lives in a self-created bliss because his world is never amiss!*

.Great minds teach us to clear the residual emotions and see the roots of our failure. Then we need to tap into the energy of true knowledge and the latest information in science that feeds the brain and changes its three-fold transformational capacities:

1. Find yourself! ⟹ **2. Motivate yourself!** ⟹ **3. Commit yourself!**

According to Ben–Groin, *"To be a creator in hell, I must believe in God and myself!"*

Auto-Induction for self-production:

I am driving through the Time and Space

with Success on My Interface!

Chunk 10

Self-Affirming is Self-Forming!

When time allows, and you feel like giving yourself a boost, do some self–suggestive work in terms of self-affirming, saying to yourself some compliments that are presented below. *You can never overdo with self-inspiration, for it is never enough!* Do it consciously and with much *aware attention* applied to the meaning of the words.

Feel your unique presence on Earth!

1. I'm never in a robot-like trance; I'm governed by my aware attention dance.

2. I get lighter in my mind! I am getting refined!

3. I discipline my thoughts, words, emotions, and actions without any fractions!

4. I'm physically and mentally fit; I'm upbeat!

6. I love, and I am loved in return! I respect, and I am respected!

7. I am developing a synergetic win-win mentality; I turn hostility into humility!

8. I accumulate a solid emotional account; I raise my words, not my voice!

9. I don't listen with pseudo-attention; I am in my aware dimension!

10. I listen to be listened to, and I hear to be heard!

11. I compliment others sincerely on their success to an excess!

12. I build myself up by competing only with myself in every cell!

13. My financial intelligence knows no negligence!

14. I am the clone of the best of me, see!

15. I am happy, no matter what! Happiness is my full-time job!

P.S. Any of the booster and mind-sets above are good to be used while doing **the Suggestive Meditation** (Stage One, Ch. 10).Breathe in the first part of the induction, breathe out the second part of it.

In My Mind, I'm One of a Kind!

I Do not Whine; I Shine!

Vistas of Intelligence to Install Next:

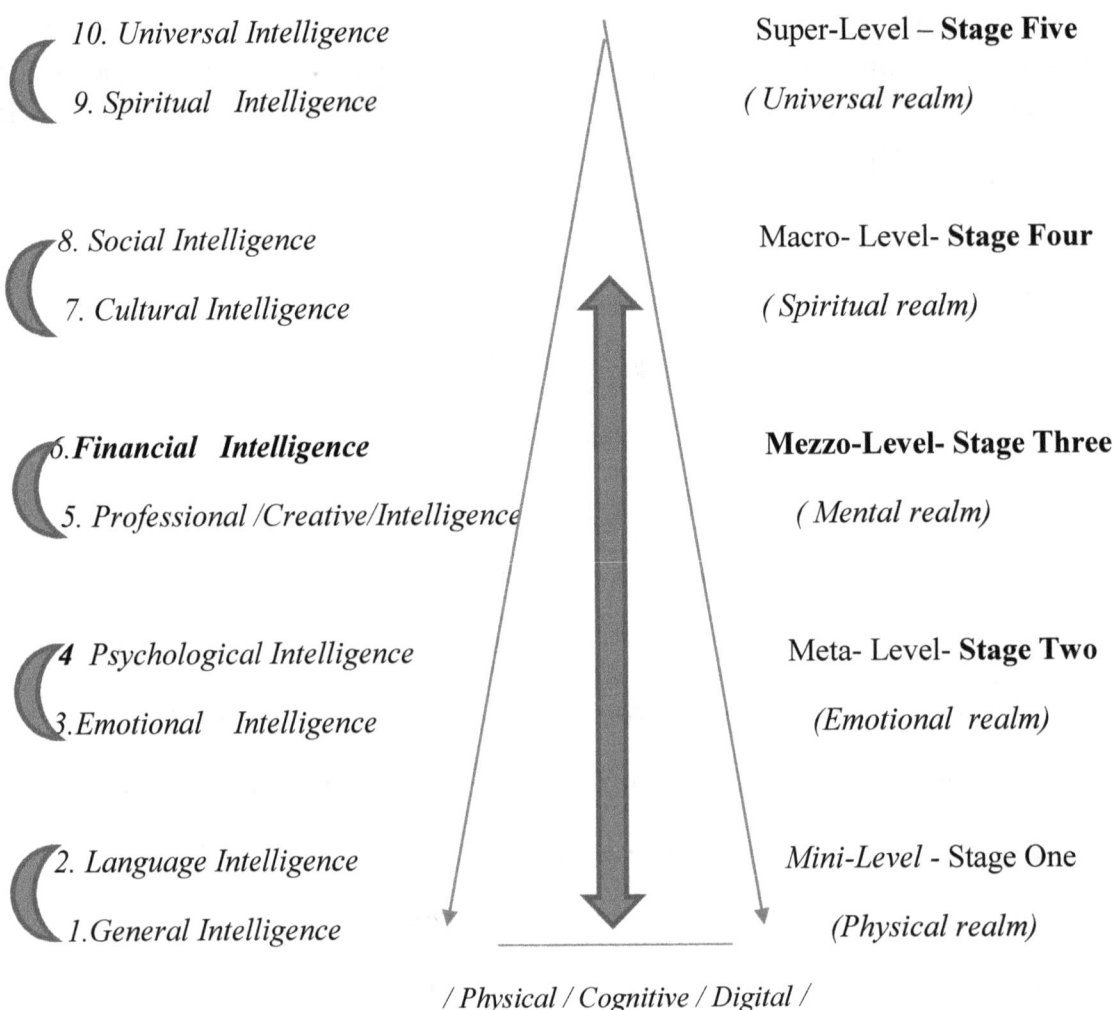

10. Universal Intelligence	Super-Level – **Stage Five**
9. Spiritual Intelligence	(Universal realm)
8. Social Intelligence	Macro-Level- **Stage Four**
7. Cultural Intelligence	(Spiritual realm)
6. *Financial Intelligence*	**Mezzo-Level- Stage Three**
5. Professional /Creative/Intelligence	(Mental realm)
4 Psychological Intelligence	Meta- Level- **Stage Two**
3. Emotional Intelligence	(Emotional realm)
2. Language Intelligence	Mini-Level - Stage One
1. General Intelligence	(Physical realm)

/ Physical / Cognitive / Digital /

"Fertilize Your mind with Thinking!" (Albert Einstein)

To Make Your Life Intellectually-Wise, Strategize – Optimize - Actualize!

Stage Three

Mezzo-Level / Mental Dimension

Financial Intelligence

Professional Intelligence– Step 3

"Money is not the root of all evil; lack of money is!"

To Climb up the Financial Hills,

Develop Your Money Management Skills!

Financial Intelligence without Negligence!

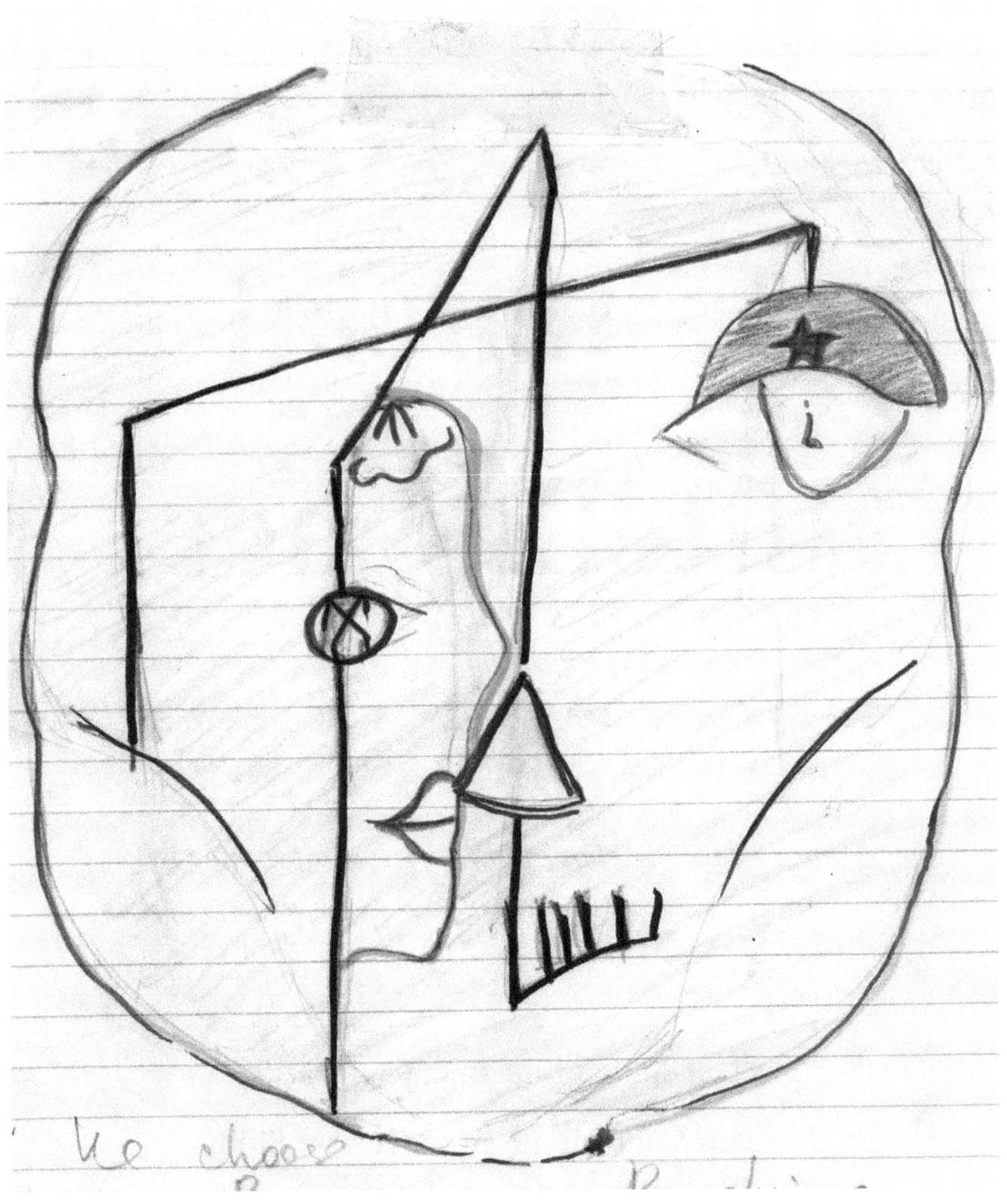

A New Me is Financially Free!

Chunk 1

Money Veins Need Brains!

Financial intelligence is an integral part of a personal growth and self-actualization. In the *Introduction, Thesis 5,* I talk about the change in the paradigm of our self-development, accentuating **being over having**. However, money is the tool that a self-developing person needs to operate consciously to base his self-propelling on. Financial intelligence helps us attain economic independence lack of which hinders the process self-creation. in its core.

We all need money management skills.

In other words, we must have financial intelligence to be able to digest complicated financial information, teach ourselves and our kids how to handle money, make investments, and harness financial appetites. And the earlier we learn to manage our money, the better! Everyone needs to start his self-growth with gaining *financial awareness,* preserving his *financial integrity*, and protecting his financial privacy. Money is a very important aspect in self-realization, and money managing is the skill that is essential in the evolutionary process of an individual growth if it is . subordinated to self- creation and self-installation in every level in the holistic paradigm.

We all deserve to be well-off, wealthy, prosperous, rich, and affluent. These words, though they are synonyms mean different levels of financial prosperity.

***Financial maturity as any other intellectual maturity needs to grow at all the levels of intelligence** (See Thesis 8).*

Financial intelligence requires *financial-awareness* skills and at least general knowledge of the basic subject of life – *Economics* should be taught at schools, and without the basics of it, **there is no financial awareness in our kids.**

True financial competence, ascertained in terms of business or personal needs at each level, will channel the mind in *mini, meta, mezzo, macro, and super levels, or* in a holistic way. You will be processing *Money Strategizing Skills* through the grid of the *physical, emotional ,mental, spiritual, and universal* dimensions, nor just in an in-coming and out-going way.

The strategic plan of action, that is holistically-amplified , is the Universal Mind-- fortified!

I have been managing my money through these dimensions for years, and I have always put both ends together. I am a scholar, not a money-maker, but I managed to live at peace with my money, having followed the holistic paradigm all my life here, where money dealing often takes a chaotic, un-manageable form.

Strategizing – Optimizing - Actualizing!

Chunk 2

Money-Managing is Learnable!

Many financially-intelligent people teach us how to handle our money and manage our banking accounts better. We need to study their wisdom and never stop working on our money management skills. "**They teach us to make money work for us, not us work for the money!**" The advice of **Suzi Orman** is so valuable because there are no gimmicks behind her financial solutions. I also recommend some very special books: "*The Richest Man in Babylon*" by George Cayson, the life-changing books by *Robert Kiyosaki and his book , co-authored with Donald Trump.* All these authors suggest many actionable solutions, and, in my understanding, they follow the holistic paradigm of **synthesis-analysis -synthesis** in their money wise--dealing books and talks.

" You are what you read!"(Jim Rohn)

All the people with exceptional money skills offer not only very peculiar shot-cuts to wealth, but they also instill in us the necessity ***to put the conscious strain on our financial brains.*** The point I am making here is connected only with the absolute necessity for everyone nowadays ***to acquire financial intelligence*** to be able to intelligently manage their lives money-wise. Disrespect for money, innumerable credit cards, and mindless spending result in ***self-demagnetization*** that is getting a person off the self- actualization track.

*"**Persistence beats resistance**! (Antony Robins)*

There is a British joke about a frivolous son who sent a cable to his dad from college: The joke teaches us how to be both mindful of money-management and teach our kids this essential skill in life. The son sends a cable to his dad: "***No mon., no fun, your son.***" The father responds: "***Too bad, very sad, your dad***". The message is clear:

*"**Be a programmer, not the programmed one.**" (Robert Stone)*

Please, continue working on your financial intelligence auto-suggestively, using **the Auto-Suggestive Meditation** *. (Part Two, Chunks .17,18):*

I know who I am money-wise!

I am a strong, brave, calm, and determined owner of my firm will!

I can manage my money, I want to manage my money, and I will manage my money!

I'm Becoming a Much Wiser Money-Actualizer!

Chunk 3

Good Financial Metabolism = Financial Fitness!

Financial fitness as any other fitness is the result of the metabolism, or *financial metabolism* of the mind that needs to be boosting in the form of using .the quality food for thought (*knowledge how to manage money better*) and processing this knowledge regularly through **the holistic grid** in all the five levels. *Your investments into your physical, emotional, mental, and spiritual* departments of life on the personal or business level must be reviewed holistically.

Next, *your connection to the Universal Intelligence at the universal level* should be working permanently, since you know that you need to tune your **AUTO-ANTENNA**, your intuition on to the Master Mind, and never get disconnected from it.

The Law of Attraction is constantly in action!

Each level, in turn, should be processed through the holistic formula: *synthesis-analysis-synthesis*

Strategizing – Optimizing - Actualizing!

The next, the most vital supplement for the financial metabolism is *the sense of measure!*

Self -induction: ***A sense of measure is a great treasure!***

You should not make the desire to get rich, or to impulsively get what you actually do not need overpower your mind. *"Do not be over worn with the desire to be rich, because of your own understanding cease. (Proverb 23.2)* **People who lack internal fortitude often become victims of the money chase** or victims of those who have self-discipline and self-management skills.

Self-Induction: *Conduct a Self-Limitation war; Less is More!*

Financial fitness needs *a sense of measure* to become a part of the financial skills training. One can hardly become a billionaire, without having a *peculiar sense of measure* we have to develop in yourself. The French feminists say,

"If a person has no sense of measure, he / she has no brains."

We all need *to train our aware attention to gain financial fitness* first. As a matter of fact, this training for financial fitness should start at school. Kids absolutely have to get the money-managing skills before they leave high school. Economics is the subject that is as indispensable in children's education in mathematics. Money does not favor those who deal with it casually, *without due awareness.* A financially-intelligent person is the one who has learned the rule below:

Turn your Intellectual Quality into Quantity!

Chunk 4

Financial Awareness is Your Life's Mast!

It's not a surprise that financially-competent people are very well-organized and are very personable. There is a certain *magnetic field* around these people; *they glow with the money energy.* Money favors them because they respect money in the most rational, proactive, and intelligent way. Also, they are also very engaging intellectually, and, most amazingly, they are truly spiritual.

I personally admire **Suze Orman** who is giving us very instructional and valuable advice that helps people not only enrich their financial intelligence, but it also builds up the character of a person who wants *to make money de facto, not just de juror.* Besides, she is very personable herself! *Her personal magnetism is amazing and very persuasive*! She develops in us a peculiar sense of measure that have outlined above, and that financial fitness requires as an indispensable skill.

Money has a magnetic power that generates self-confidence and doubles the mind power!

Following the ideas of a personality development by a great Russian psychologist, Leo Vygotsky, I would like to back up my arguments with his brilliant observation that" *teaching any subject, we should not focus on teaching the subject itself, but on " teaching a whole person."* No doubt, financial education helps to make the sslf -image of a person complete

Money management skills should be an indispensable part of the holistic education!

Besides being built on self-discipline, charisma, personal magnetism, and a sense of measure, *financial intelligence needs patience and the feeling of contentment* to be developed in the brain. Being overly frugal does not work for consciousness raising, either.

Auto- induction: *"Discontentment is poverty even in riches." (Confucius)*

In our time, the plague of petty, *impersonal bureaucracy* is familiar almost to everyone. It kills our enthusiasm, down-grades our abilities, and depletes us of the best intentions.

It's worth every treasure on earth to be strong for oneself!

But being strong is not enough. You need to be orderly and disciplined, correct in our speaking and controlled in our reactions. Most importantly, you have to be financially free *because "money is not the root of all evil; lack of money is!"* To frame your life financially means to have **a strategic plan of action** and program yourself for orderly, not messy and sporadic thinking, speaking, and acting.

Money is in a friendly seat only if you intelligently manage it!

Chunk 5

Money-Actualizing Skills

The Money Managing Skills should be developed in synch with the Money Actualizing Skills, not by way of grabbing some valuable tips over the Internet or trying to just pass the bankruptcy test. Your own philosophy of money-making might be shallow knowledge-wise and experience-wise. *Financial awareness is also a cause-effect awareness of the money-flow.*

In the present-day *Informational Biology,* we can program life by changing the sequence of DNA in a genome codes for a predictable outcome. Likewise, *we can willfully change our financial code in the brain* and teach ourselves to manage the money to our advantage. Many people have trouble living within their means. Now researchers have found that *there is a gene, linked to credit card debts. (Emmanuel De Nave)*

"A particular gene affects our financial behavior."

Apparently, we need more **neuro-scientific education in this respect**, too, to be able to have more financial awareness backed up by brain work awareness. Like synthetic engineering, *we can engineer money intelligence in ourselves*, changing the DNA of our limited thinking into the unlimited one. Piecing together of the needed mental genomes by using complex intellectual algorithms will help us re-program our cells for better money managing in time and space.

The observation of the main cosmic law will add a special quality volume to our overall intelligence and , consequently, consciousness, and it will improve our behavior in accordance with *the Law of the Right Human Behavior* in which money is a very important vector pointing to perpetual happiness only if you make the money work for the good of many or at least some people, not just for the gratification of the material needs of one person. I recommend reading the book " *Why We Want You to Be Rich*" *by Donald Trump and Robert Kiyosaki* in which they express very vividly why the rich get richer and the poor poorer. The book proves that knowledge put to action is double power!

In sum, *financial intelligence will protect us from the inflation of our thinking in the financial area* when the use of the old patterns of money-monitoring results in financial failures that aggravate our life and hamper the way for self-actualization.

True, the money God is presiding the world! Empower it with your Intelligence God!

But the technological innovations are gradually reprogramming our cells in an irreversible direction, and our *financial maturity will grow with our self-consciousness in unity.*

Let's help the Intelligence God rule the Future World!

Chunk 6

Dematerialization of the Spirit of Giving

The spirit of giving is the next important aspect in line. *"Whether born of doing anything with gratitude, revealing in a breathtaking sunset, creating a work of art, making love or just plain being thoroughly decent to a fellow human being, the portion of positivity we receive is no longer subject to entropy and **becomes money in the bank**"* (Rev. P. s. Berg)

*"**Generosity, like love and gratitude are the sentiments that free and raise individual consciousness.**" (Piero Ferrucci)*

The one who's giving is also receiving! Generosity integrates the whole psyche around a single focus - ***generating an incredible soul integrity*** that makes the owner of it the happiest and the noblest man on earth   A giving person is more likely to develop himself in the spiritual area than the one that does not have such ability.

To change your bad mood, be in a hurry to do something good!

Giving is the ability to internalize emotions and externalize the mind. Carl Yung when asked what human quality he deemed to be the most important in a man replied that it was a person's attitude to money. He said,

*"**If a person is cheap in dealing with money, he will be cheap in love or in anything he does because the spirit of giving the best of him is not there.**"*

Let's remember with a heart-felt warmth of thankfulness and pride that the USA is the greatest giving country in the world! There is the greatest number of people here who are generous enough to donate money, their valuable possessions, or pieces of art to our universities, museums, libraries, theatres, schools, etc. Millions of dollars are sent to the countries in need all over the world!

The spirit of giving is in the country's logo!

Generous gestures on the part of the country and its people make our life richer, more beautiful, and harmonious. They fill our hearts up with *"**the attitude of gratitude**"* and the sense of pride that we are passing on to others. Any generous gesture is rewarded with a happy smile that raises our self-consciousness and self-respect immeasurably.

Self-Induction:

In my Mind's Store, getting means Giving More!

Chunk 7

Financial Consciousness

Financial consciousness is a vital part of our overall consciousness! Every sacred book teaches us to give, to share, to contribute to We all know that, but we are not aware of that.

Financial consciousness means managing the money, not letting the money manage you!

The insecurity of life, and the uncertainty on the job market generated *more impersonal behaviors* on the part of people in our social service offices .in which opening the mind and the heart to a person's concern is hardly the case. When coming to know a person better, Carl Yung suggests we pay attention to his / her attitude to money. If , he says, a person is cheap in money-dealing, *he is cheap in love*, in friendship, in a family, in any undertaking because there is no soul width in his character midst. Many people seeking help feel belittled and insignificant, and such situations generates stagnation in self-consciousness growth. The necessity to admit it ,or the need to ask for it humiliate a noble soul.

Nothing makes us smaller than the lack of money!

We need to change the pattern of *our victimized thinking and compulsive shopping habits that result from financial insecurity* when a credit card becomes your best helping hand and install new, constructive, self-reliant, resilient, responsible, *electronically-backed up and strongly-willed patterns of money management,* focused on our renewed financial intelligence, monitored level by level. - *physical, emotional, mental, spiritual and , universal.*

We should follow this impeccable order of things in life in terms of money and its impact on our personal growth because it is money that often impedes it. We all marvel at the way people manage to make a lot of money, but we rarely learn from their *exceptional financial intelligence* that expands their personal universe.

As is indicated in *Thesis 2, in the Introduction,* before you can get something, you have to become somebody. The money-making ladder was, is, and always will be :

Be someone! ⟹ **Do something!** ⟹ **Have what you want!**

Also, the person, *committed to self- installation in life* wouldn't let anyone script his actions for him , or monitor his money, without his full awareness of how and why this is being done. Controlling the money consciously and with full awareness, you are teaching yourself financial discipline and expanding your financial consciousness.

Money is the Exchange Force, Not My Boss!

Chunk 8

A Vintage You is a Money Guru!

(An Inspirational Booster)

To launch your mind into the avalanche of dollars

You have to follow those

        Who know how to put the brace

        On the money interface!

True, money makes a lot of sense

In our life's essence.

        But it stays only with those

        Who let it work and repose

In banks and in stocks,

Notr in our grandmothers' socks!

        To be under the monitory Sun,

        You have to moderate your fun!

Don't trash

Your hard-earned cash

        And don't disrespect

        Your life's financial aspect!

Be Your Money's best friend,

But never let it prevent

You from giving and seeing

That money is just the means of Being!

Rack your brains to find the ways

To give your money more space!

Make your money the means

To raise your happiness and health twins!

So, create some extra knowledge space

Get rid of your mind's garbage

Don't hamper your vibration waves,

Lighten up your life's luggage!

Give way to your being

And the spirit's freeing,

First, there is an ending

Then, there is the beginning!

To Satisfy Your Self-Realization Thirst,
Get Rich in Your Mind First!

Vistas of Intelligence to Instill Next:

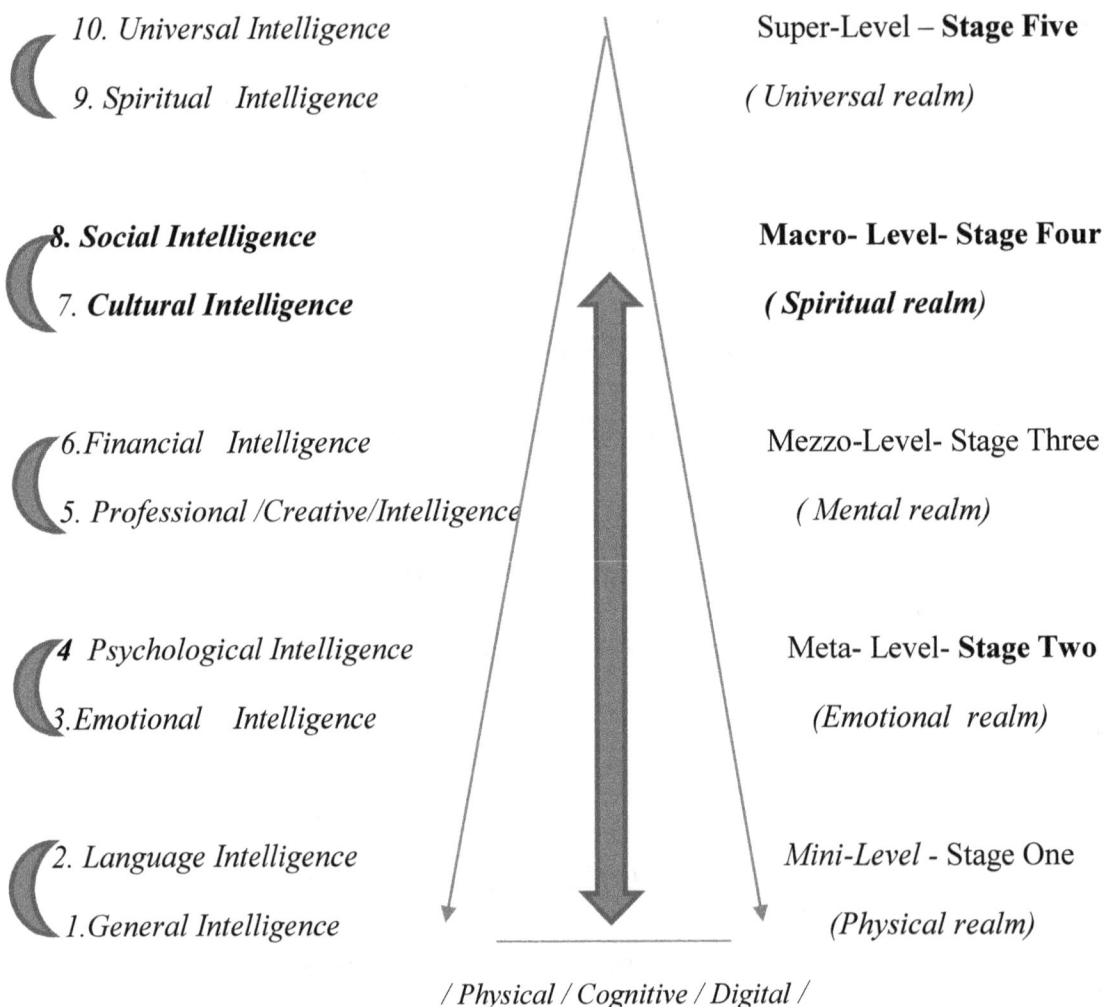

10. Universal Intelligence	Super-Level – **Stage Five**
9. Spiritual Intelligence	(Universal realm)
8. Social Intelligence	**Macro- Level- Stage Four**
7. **Cultural Intelligence**	**(Spiritual realm)**
6. Financial Intelligence	Mezzo-Level- Stage Three
5. Professional /Creative/Intelligence	(Mental realm)
4 Psychological Intelligence	Meta- Level- **Stage Two**
3. Emotional Intelligence	(Emotional realm)
2. Language Intelligence	Mini-Level - Stage One
1. General Intelligence	(Physical realm)

/ Physical / Cognitive / Digital /

"Fertilize your mind with thinking!" (Albert Einstein)

To Make Your Life Intellectually-Wise, Strategize – Optimize - Actualize!

Stage Four

Macro Level - Spiritual Dimension

Cultural Intelligence

Step 1

Change your cultural gravity of vanity!

In My Life's Perspective,

I'm Culturally-Introspective!

Cultural Intelligence without Negligence!

In the Cultural Quest, I Manifest My Best!

Chunk 1

Life isn't Always Fair!

(An Instructional Booster)

Life isn't always
Fair,
But it's here and
There!

People judge,
And they do not oblige
Your cultural array
That puts them in dismay!

But what's your
Share?
In getting more
Aware

Of your own cultural negli-
gence
That speaks of the lack of intelli-
gence?

In the New, Digital Culture,
We Need to be Universally-Cultured!

Chunk 2

Cultural Awareness as the Code of Behavior!

Having developed, or at least enriched your overall intelligence in the three main levels: ***Mini*** *(Personal and Language Intelligences)*, ***Meta*** *(Emotional and Psychological Intelligences)*, ***Mezzo*** *(Professional, Creative, and Financial Intelligences), **you have come to the Macro-level – Cultural and Social Intelligences.*** These are, the two levels that *define us as personalities* with real integrity because this is the spiritual level.

Cultural intelligence is the ability to adapt to a new cultural reality.

Recent trends, including high-tech communication, have created new challenges for global managers. They involve three components: ***knowledge, mindfulness, and cultural awareness.*** Cultural awareness needs to be a part of the whole as our new moral code, one for all the nations, the ***International Moral Code*** that provides the essential awareness in our everyday interaction on the global social arena that is the Internet now. The international code of behavior will develop a common cultural structure and will unite all the nations to the point that cultural respect will be viewed as the main code of behavior for the human kind hopefully in the nearest future.

Cultural awareness leads to cultural acceptance and heightens a person's consciousness.

The awareness of what constitutes culture and how cultures vary leads to an understanding of how these variations affect behavior. Different cultures have different values and different patterns of behavior and to be an intelligent person that wants to climb the social ladder, you have to embody those values, or at least to be familiar with them in any social environment.

Be a good kind, One with the Universal Mind!

Cultural and social intelligences are in *the spiritual dimension* because our ***cultural and social perception needs to be expanded to the spiritual level*** when we respect just the mere fact that we are all human. *(Thesis 5)* Such approach demands attention to the subtle cues from colleagues and clients who may possess different cultural values. We need to let go of the cultural and color-blind prejudices to simply understand how culture influences attitudes and behaviors with full awareness.

Globalization of the world demands our getting connected by One Cultural Code!

In the Universal Array, we are All just Human Clay!

Chunk 3

We are of the Same DNA – You, Me, and They!

Unfortunately, our schools, churches, and universities do not guide students in this respect, least of all *in the ethical and moral codes.*

We mix together mostly on the physical level, but hardly ever on the emotional ,mental ,and most importantly spiritual. There are still many ignorant, culturally and religiously separated, people around the globe who scorn cultural intelligence and call some international students that are into deep learning *"egg heads or nerds",* while such students constitute the best part of our education and often self-educate themselves to the level much higher than any local school can provide.

Bulling stems from such close-mindedness due to the lack of cultural education in our schools.

Terrorism in all its ugly forms is also the result of the lack of cultural intelligence. There is a lot of cultural diversity around us, and very many people are incredibly talented. Does God bless us with the gifts of exceptional mental value because we are Jewish, Chinese, Japanese, British, Russian, or Iranian? We are loved and blessed equally, and we need to finally recognize that and *value intelligence, not a national identity, as the highest commodity ever* Cultural education expands the horizons of the beauty of life in the kaleidoscope of its varieties.

It is an essential ingredient of a person's conscience and his growing self-consciousness!

We live in the global culture, now, and globalization is a very complex, *mind-to-mind and heart-to-heart* connection among cultures. The diversity of the world's cultures enriches our intelligence not only in schools, but in any administrative institution where people are able to analyze intelligently any problematic situation for its cultural ingredients.

Being culturally intelligent helps resolve the conflicting problem to the satisfaction of an individual from any culture because lack of cultural awareness traumatizes people and leads to *the stereotyped solutions of the cases in courts,* or even on the higher governmental levels. The key to becoming culturally-intelligent is the awareness of the conflicting values across the cultures. Any culture is a rich source of language, art, music, fashion, food, ideas, and incredible talents of people that contribute to the world's beauty. Cultural education is essential in our schools because it prepares the students for business communication on a global scale.

It teaches them to better understand the needs of the customers from different parts of the world the knowledge of which enriches our general intelligence beyond belief *and evolves our common consciousness to a new, higher level of self-consciousness* that becomes culturally-enriched.

In the Global Culture, we are Universally Structured!

Chunk 4

Cultural Metabolism and Cultural Inflation

Cultural Intelligence is the ability of a person to adapt to new cultural reality. It is ,in fact, *cultural metabolism* because culturally-diverse relationship depends on the energy and intelligence of each other. Unfortunately, *control drama prevails,* and cultural differences hinder our evolutionary progress and *slow down the metabolic processes* in our common social body.

There is no cultural tolerance; rather, we have to deal with cultural inflation.

We are so technologically advanced, but culturally ignorant! The gap between different cultures and the ignorance that people display about even the geographic position of many countries on the map is appalling! When 24 years ago, I came to this country and told one of my colleagues that I was from Latvia, he thought it was in Africa, confusing Latvia with Libya.

Acceptance of other cultures comes only with the cultural intelligence!

People love travelling and tourism, and they undoubtedly contribute a lot to our cultural integration. But cultural intelligence is not limited by the outer impressions, it is the change of programming in the brain and *the establishment of synergistic programs* in our cells. The cultural metabolism should be working on the auto-suggestive mind-set of acceptance and mutual respect.

I am One with everyone under the Sun! We are of One Blood in the Universal Gut!

Each culture, however small, has enriched the world culture, and our kids should know what contribution their culture has made into the global cultural beauty. *Knowledge of what constitutes culture* and how cultures vary leads us to an understanding of how these variations affect our behavior, our business growth, politics, and the destinies of entire nations.

Being culturally intelligent is essential in courts, in politics, in family relationships!

Cultural awareness generates healthy cultural metabolism that is the acceptance of another human being's differences to every one's satisfaction, and it is a sure way to resolve any conflict. Unfortunately, we continue *controlling each other* without an objective observation of the cultural background of our colleagues, clients, or even relatives. *Cultural inflation generates religious bigotry, hate, and violence.* Doing that, a person is trying to fit everyone to a habitual frame-work, judging people by his own standards, limited mentally, emotionally, psychologically, and culturally. *The saying-* **"Do it my way, or no way!"** cannot get you anywhere today!

Culturally-Limited Perception is the World Needs to Be Dealt with and Re-Thought!

Chunk 5

Compatible Brain Chemistry

The development of cultural intelligence also demands that *we develop compatible brain chemistry in our social relationships*. It means that *aware attention* should be paid to every person that you meet in life because as is well-known now *every person is on the same life path with us for a reason*. We need to unwind the blocked spots in the mind!

In the digital world, no one is superior to anyone.

We differ only in the level of our awareness in electronics that widens our outlook and general knowledge of the world cultures thanks to our connecting lines, such as **Google, LinkedIn, YouTube** and may others. Once, you master these global connectors, you open your **mind + heart** connection to the world. Socialization of our lives on an unprecedented scale and the opportunity to communicate with people from different cultures gives us a lot of food for thought. We have a rare chance to train *the right brain hemisphere*; *developing an objective communication* with people around us, as opposed to *the subjective communication* that is self-centered, egotistic, and limited. Our brain compatibility is amazingly uniting! Our future will be based on the objective, *God-given basis of human objectivity.*

To begin this inner process of unification, "*We need to identify partners with compatible brain chemistry.*"*(Helen Fisher, Discover, March11, 2013)* We size people up intellectually, financially, professionally, emotionally, *but we need to be more culturally-informed* to become more compatible with our partners in life from the objective premises.

Auto-induction: *Don't size up, just open up!*

Let's practice patience of mind and tolerance of feelings. Let's filter our thoughts, words, feelings and actions at work and at home, in public, and in private for their common values and get united on their basis. *Let's defy the gravity of cultural ignorance and religious prejudices!* Don't pollute your mind and heart with the thoughts and feelings of scorn, superiority, or indifference. Every person, no matter how different culturally he seems to be, is a human being that is *your contemporary in time and space*. There is a proverb in Russian that tells people to be in a hurry to do something good to a person who is culturally unfamiliar to you.

"Be in a hurry to do something good." Kindness is your friendship hook!"

Be strong enough in your cultural outlook to stand up for the people who do not enjoy due respect and might even be mistreated by others. **Stand up for them!** The better words we find to say about a person, the better that person becomes! And you get the credit from the Above!

Assess a Person's Fairness by his Cultural Awareness!

Chunk 6

Establish a Synergistic Cultural Climate!

We sometimes experience *some hostility at work* on the part of someone that is **culturally-unaware.** We might manage to get out of the back-lash loop successfully, but if an unpleasant situation is generated by the leader of the group, a boss, or a supervisor, the presence in such an environment becomes very stressful and even harmful to our health, to say nothing about the quality of work that we might be responsible for. Doing any work becomes a real burden, and we wish we could avoid being in the same room with *the person of emotional abuse* that we depend on, anyhow. Emotional intelligence needs to be applied here to change the vibrational quality of the energy in the room.

Generating a pleasant, synergistic climate at work is the rule # 1 for any manager.

Being a right-brained, creative, positive, content person goes beyond personal good. *It works for the common good!* Such attitude helps generate *the feeling of welcoming peacefulness, respect, and trust* that we are all seeking in life and without which our lives are not complete.

So, let's establish *the synergistic climate and a sense of Oneness* with every colleague at work or every member of the family at home because we are dependent on one another. We see a lot of such cultural integrity in different sport teams that demonstrate to us that we are the citizens of the planet Earth, and our national belonging to this or that country is secondary.

No doubt, interdependence is the basis for any job, any business ,and love relationship.

This interdependence is not only professional; it's intellectual, emotional and, psychological. It's good *to be an independent thinker*, an individual, but not *an impersonal individualist* who cares only for his/ her own persona, for the paycheck and the security of retaining the job at the expense of being compassionate, understanding, inspiring, responsive and responsible for another human being's *professional comfort* at work. Unfortunately, it's appallingly common these days.

Impersonal attitude is ruining our relationships, and eventually, it is damaging our lives.

Alongside with the cultural awareness, *we need a lot of sensitivity, empathy, and tact* to share the space and time with the people at work, school, at home, or any place where life engagement might place us. *It's remarkable how we are all part of one life system!* So interdependence is what keeps us together and makes us strong and able to create, to think, and to evolve. Synergizing your inner space by means of the auto-suggestive work, you manage to synergize the outer space, too.

The people around us are our contemporaries; we share the same space and time with them. Just think about this interconnection and respect the life next to you. Just imagine that everyone might be gone earlier or later, in the same way that the previous generations did. Thinking that your life is terminal makes us appreciate it more in ourselves and the people around us. As a well-known Russian poet Boris Pasternak says,

"The miracle of life is just an hour long; live this hour honorably before you are gone!"

It's essential to control oneself first and establish a synergistic, productive supervision of the people under you, with a welcoming smile, **a supporting word of praise**, and an honest appreciation of someone's contribution to a common course at work. Learn to compliment the people around you honestly and wholeheartedly.

"I can last on a good compliment for a week" (Mark Twain)

So, be sure to synergize your relationship with your colleagues, employees, partners to a mutual benefit of all. Being synergistic means being able to generate good, friendly, **pleasant vibration** to help people feel calm, inspired, and appreciated.

If you have an argument, learn to channel the discussion by *the method of consensus building* that helps people working at the same project gravitate together. *(See Chunk 14, "Emotional Intelligence")* Consensus building is synergizing the working atmosphere and helps people transcend the uncomfortable feelings of fear and the expectation of a conflict. They begin feeling free from *the pressure of competition as a looming force of elimination*, and they start seeing competition as the means for constructive self-growth and illumination.

"I am One and you are One; we are One together." (Tara Rae)

If a person is argumentative, if he/ she is challenging your cultural individuality and even uses debasing language, immediately surround that person with brilliant white light in your mind. I am sure that the light will enlighten that person with the realization that he / she might be wrong. ***Surprisingly, it works!*** If you are the one who generated the conflict, it's your responsibility to acknowledge your misgivings with the light thought in the mind.

"Respect is the telephone line that makes all contacts with others

a two-way communication."

When we get Racial and Nationalistic, we become Disconnected and Sadistic!

Chunk 7

Be Culturally Apt Auto-Suggestively!

The ability to influence and persuade others can be developed only through love and patience, through respect and acceptance of another person. *The ability to tune to the feelings of the people from other cultures, to feel empathy and enthusiasm* as opposed to the feelings of superiority, rigidity, and moodiness is easier obtained through auto-suggestions.

I know who I am,

and I let others to have the sense of self-worth.

I can *accept some one's difference* ***I want to*** *respect some one's values.* ***I will become*** *a culturally intelligent person.*

I am becoming more and more empathetic */ tactful, appreciative, more culturally aware, and culturally intelligent /with each coming day.*

Now that English has become the universal language, cultural intelligence should be an essential part of a person's education. Our courts will be much fairer and more considerate in their judging, and people will be more harmonized in their inner responsive frame-work and, therefore, they'll be much more productive at work.

Lack of cultural aptness is a real sore in a person's score!

At this level of developing ***intellectualized spirituality***, cultural intelligence entails the necessity to instill in our kids and college students **the Cultural Behavioral Skills** so that our education could further ensure smooth and effective ***cross-cultural relationships***. We should give the United States a great credit for uniting people of different cultures and changing their mentality from a limited cultural one to the international and eventually, global outlook. People stop being Chinese, Italian, Russian, Hispanic, Turkish, etc. here. They become just the citizens of the planet Earth, and ***that is the mentality we are all heading toward***. Isn't it very promising? So, let's instill in our minds the mind-set that says.

Auto-induction: *Every human contact is a responsibility!*

Be Culturally-Apt; Culturally Respond, Don't React!

Chunk 8

The Divine Spark of the International Consciousness!

To conclude , *our new global culture demands now that we develop our cultural intelligence into the international one.* We see and hear on mass media that people are often judged or even labeled from a narrow perspective of a dominant culture. They are manipulated with the help of money, a higher position, or just by having more energy physically. We must be more culturally-aware to decode each culture better to have a better idea of the international situation overall and the reasons that generate immigration. It's essential in our schools to have *the News Briefings* when the students exchange the news from all over the world and ger better informed and therefore, better *internationally connected.*

The present-day world news un-awareness is appalling!

Lack of international awareness adds fuel to the struggle of misconceptions and misunderstandings to the point that we are unable to integrate our opposite features, cultures, educations, values, religions, and politics. *This is the 21st century after all!* Haven't we had centuries of ignorance to consider?

We evolve only through the process of integration and mutual enrichment!

We know it, but we are not aware of that. The lack of real international intelligence hampers this process because we are not conceptually aware of what every culture constitutes in a global kaleidoscope of cultures. Each culture is a new concept to be processed through one's own **grid of prejudices.** Mass media programming and political indoctrination often limit attitudes, and, therefore, lead to the distortion of thinking, common judgments, and lack of general intelligence. *We need to learn to honor not only our differences, but our commonness. (Introduction, Thesis 5)* Young people need to be better informed about the world events , and they should be encouraged to discuss these events, focusing them on their own wies ,not those of the commentators that are often biased and present the opinion the political party that the Tv the channel is voicing out.

In sum, cultural intelligence necessitates breaking the vicious circle of behavioral standards and *transcending our cultural and religious differences* to develop a divine spark of the international intelligence, based on acceptance and mutual respect for our common time and space on the Mother Earth that needs our protection now. *The lack of cultural awareness is so harmful* now that the only way to remain psychologically-fit and culturally-individualistic is to cut the branches of the rotting cultural intelligence *and plant the new seeds of cultural consciousness* in our kids and ourselves at will.

"Like Begets Like!"

Vistas of Intelligence to Instill Next:

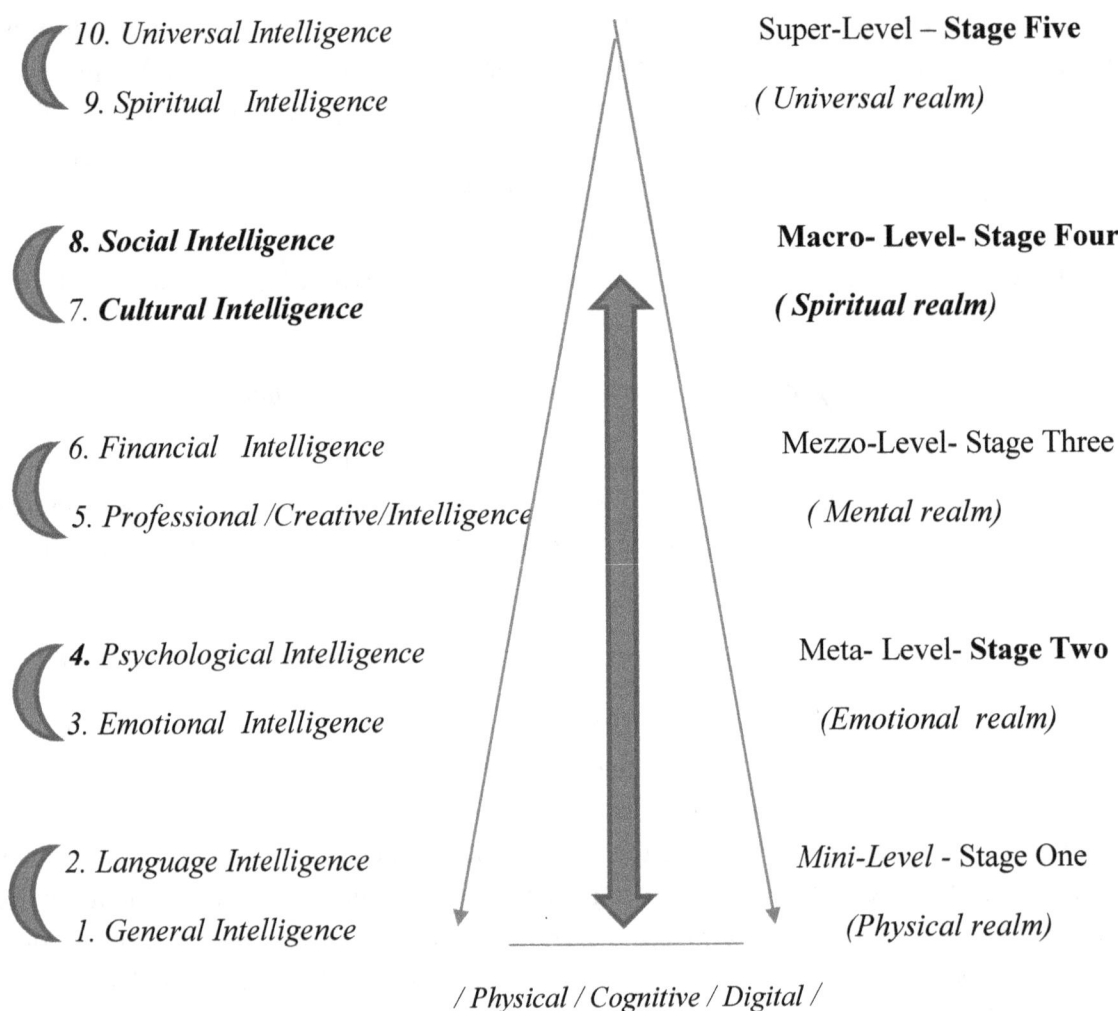

"Fertilize your mind with thinking!" (Albert Einstein)

I am a Social Cell; I keep Surpassing Myself!

Stage Four

Macro-Level - Spiritual Dimension

Social Intelligence

Step 2

Resist the social gravity of your personal vanity!

Every Human Contact is a Responsibility!

Our Social Big Bang

Is in the Unity of Ying and Yang!

Chunk 1

Social Awareness and Aptness

I have indicated in the Preface to the book that *following the holistic paradigm of Self-Installation in life is an integral process* of a gradual self-transformation in five dimensions, a considerable enrichment of intelligence and self-awareness becomes a reality. *"Humans are inherently social beings; that's our evolutionary legacy."(Popular Science", Nov. 2014)*

Evolution through relationship shapes us personally and socially. No doubt, socialization promotes our intellectual culture. However, never have relationships been so problematic and conflict- bound as they are now. The quality of our lives now is the quality of our global vision!" *Our collective reality is **a symbolic expression of fear** and **an insatiable desire for security**,* as well as heavy layers of negativity and judgmental attitude that we have accumulated in our collective human psyche." (the "Scientific American Mind," (July 2014)

"A shift in planetary consciousness is taking place now."

As any other intelligence, *social intelligence also needs to be holistically developed* because it incorporates all the intelligences outlined above. An unenlightened person usually has a narrow vision of himself and life as if he were looking at the world through a small window. However, when a person *expands his self - consciousness*, it's like going through a door into a world of communication. Every one of us is globalizing his mind, the vision, his / her personality and a professional outlook. *Instead of fighting the darkness, bring in light. Allow all people to be as they are.* ***Shine for others, too!****"(Dale Carnegie)*

Being **socially apt** means establishing **a mind-to-mind** and **heart-to-heart connection** with all the people you get in touch with in a face-to-face communication or digitally. If we remain impersonal, we cannot have a peaceful, healthy society. ***Learning to expand the living intelligence holistically,*** you are also developing new respect for life in yourself and in others. The vision of a person who has *obtained the living intelligence* in five levels, becomes inwardly stronger, his concentrated mind performs correctly and in unison with his trained emotions. People gravitate to him / her for spiritual energy and life wisdom. At this spiritual level of self-training, you are also obtaining *the Ultimate Result Vision* of yourself. (*the URV*). You are changing the *form and content* of your life, you are becoming *the Vintage you.* Having channeled hundreds of my students from all over the world along this path, I can vouch that you have develop a solid trust in yourself, and you can handle any situation consciously. ***You are at the point of self-revelation and self-realization***! Congratulation! You can rightfully declare,

I am Free to Be the Best of Me!

Chunk 2

Social Metabolism Without any "Ism"

Forming *a new content* of your life and propelling yourself forward with *a much more refined self-concept,* you become socially apt, more responsive, and responsible, and that is a great accomplishment of our unprecedented socialization. Changing ourselves, we create a new *holistic We - Concept* of social unification and mutual responsibility for the life on the planet Earth. Our new digitally generated social connection is gradually forming a new world community and *the global consciousness* at large. (*Part Two, Thesis 1*) *Information is ammunition because our awareness of it changes the content of our lives!*

Unfortunately, due to high tech explosion, life has a different narrative of self-erosion!

W*e live in a socially and digitally polluted world* now, the world of social labels with *the "ism" endings* of all kinds. . It has become an urgent necessity for us *to disintegrate ourselves* from the social pollution and formulate our own personal stand-points, finally ending our dependence on "*the collective unconscious"* and start respecting life in its forms, colors, and beliefs.

Our *social metabolism* is now clogged more than ever with *impersonal egoism, nationalism, chauvinism, and racism*. Many people do not think on their own; their judgement is formed by *the crowd mentality* that is unconsciously blind in interpreting the events outside their comfort zone. Mass media does not provide a holistic, *objective view* of the circumstances that generate the events. *The Law of Cause and Effect is not observed by our media!* Being in the dark, people often adapt the commonly programmed view. Total unawareness, wound up by the manipulators of the minds, generates *impulsive reactions* of the "collective unconscious, perceived as the fight for justice that, in fact, is the struggle against a holistic, insightful vision of life. *"Our seeing of the reality requires a correction of mind; just as clear vision requires a correction of the eyes"* (Alan W. Watts)

Each of us needs to learn to think on his /her own, based on well-processed social information and his / her own *social metabolism* that is *a healthy personal view point* on any issue, irrespective of the common-sense wisdom. The content of each individual life needs to be sifted off its polluting stuff! *"Autonomy of thinking is a Must!"* (Reid Hoffman)

Our interdependence on the tools, manipulating the social opinion, entangles the. minds and blurs *the objective social vision*. So, let's be governed by *aware attention* and purposeful *sorting out of the social contacts* that we have. We have no luxury of wasting time on the people of no intelligence and no human value, killing their lives in meaningless talking and crowd driven actions. *Socializing means getting interested and becoming more interesting yourself!*

People, like information, Need to Be Sorted out, too.

Chunk 3

Mind-to-Mind + a Heart-to-Heart is a New Social Art!

There is the reason I place the social intelligence at the top of *the self-actualization pyramid. (Part Two, Thesis 9)* To learn social skills, a person needs to incorporate all the above studied intelligences and become a new human being - a really advanced one, a man / a woman of integrity, able to combine thought and feeling and be socially-fit. A higher level of interpersonal mental frequencies is needed. *A new level of social vibrations is changing the world.*

Mind-to-Mind + a Heart-to-Heart is a digitally - enhanced Art!

Any art is a form of communication, but this form becomes classic if a piece of art enclosed in it radiates beauty, has a structured composition, and is very thought-provoking. I think that our socializing in general and the one on the Internet should be much better both *in form and in content* and our Internet companies should contribute more to the quality of our socialization.

The vital principle of holism is ruling the world of unification in human salvation!

Amazingly, socialism was uniting people, while capitalism is dividing us. Obviously, the best features of both social forms are to be adopted by us on the new twist of the evolutionary spiral. The countries that have *incorporated the features of both social systems* into their national frame-work are doing much better than the rest of the disconnected world. Sweden and China are the best examples of such conversion that results in a much better standards of living. The concern for the well-being of the people needs to be driving us toward unification, and that's the only way for all the humanity to survive.

Social behavior has evolved beyond belief because of modern communication technologies. With the younger generation leading the way, large groups empowered with Internet-enhanced communication accomplish a variety of diverse goals. We are gradually becoming global software entrepreneurs, and *we develop electronic competences* of holistic value every day.

We enhance our souls and expand social outreach with a digital switch!

However, *our social communication should never lose its individual characteristics (See the Chunk 1 above).* Often, inept socially people do not integrate collectively and are believed to be anti-social. However, these people are better thinkers, and they can contribute more to the society than the ones that merge completely with the massive culture and lose their individuality. In fact, we get back here to *the first level of intelligence – the personal level.* It's impossible to help and love others, without first doing his own self-quest and giving his best to the society.

The Identity of the Hearts and Minds Binds!

Chunk 4

Social Network Equilibrium

The difficulty some people have in global communication comes from their ***different mental wave lengths*** which are not coinciding with the vibratory frequencies of the people they communicate with. *"It is as if we tune in to a certain broadcasting station on a wrong frequency."(John Baines)* A mind-to-mind communication becomes possible only between the people of adequate intellectual frequencies that decisively influence ***the quality of conscious communication*** between people. Intelligence removes vibratory disharmony and establishes a social equilibrium of a mind-to-mind contact of mutual understanding without being politically-bereft with a war-mongering mentality.

Such intellectual chemistry has a much greater social potential!

New social skills that we need to develop at this level should not conflict with a sincere intention to contribute to the world our unique gifts of intelligence. With the unprecedented speed of life that stresses us out beyond belief, we need to establish a mind-to mind and heart-to heart connection between people that we communicate with for business sake or personal reasons. Our new social experience proves that *aware attention displayed on the mental level* and the emotional understanding, backed up by the cultural intelligence insure much success in business solutions and ensure that a person will not to *get lost in the ocean of technological havoc.* The holistic paradigm needs to be followed religiously!

Strategizing – selecting - actualizing!

The contribution of our computer mega companies, like Amazon, Face Book and YouTube, LinkedIn is huge, and the improvements they are implementing on this path are most promising. The social pollution puts us in front of the necessity *to X-Ray the social contacts* for their personal, emotional, mental, and spiritual validity for us. *People that we allow into our lives shape our lives in every dimension! The question is how!*

In sum, the dynamics of socialization at present is extremely and ruthlessly competitive, but our social metabolism should grow intellectually and in a holistic way. *"What makes the meaning of life is people. So, try to be good to people immediately around you and in a broader, world community." (Reid Hoffman and Ben Lashocha)* However, if you observe unconscious behavior in your partner, hold it in the loving embrace of your knowing, so you won't react. You need to respond consciously and intelligently and cut the person off your social loop then and there. Intelligent networking is extremely beneficial for self-creation; learn to establish it.

"A single brain is a computing marvel, but it pales in comparison to the powers of the net-worked mind."(Scientific American Mind", Nov. / Dec. 2014)

Chunk 5

Social Connection is Language Interwoven!

For our digital communication o be more harmonized, we need to become *more polished in our language competences*. The correct use of the language, the tone of the language used, and the vocabulary chosen to get the needed thoughts across are crucial now. *(Check out Language Intelligence above)* It's good that the use of profanity is being checked by face book, but we need such attention to be paid to the quality of the language we operate with on every sight. A human being at the other end of virtual line is as real and perceptive as you are. Both verbal and digital communication demand your *thinking first then saying something or writing a response.* We should not generate negative consequences for ourselves or other people due to our texting on impulse and transmitting this impulse to millions of others. "

Remember," *90% of people do not care about your problems, and the other 10% are glad you have them*" *(Carl Yung)* A great psychologist means that we need to be centered on confronting our own problems ourselves, *"being the thing in itself"* in solving them because being part of all life, you are still solely responsible for your own life and its outcome.

"You cannot conquer life because the part cannot conquer the whole, but you can be the best part of the whole!" (Carl Yung)

Being a part of the whole is also speaking the language of the whole, called "Globish." English needs to be respected for its *unifying quality* and the incredible *feeling of belonging and being One in the context of life* that it has granted to us with its mathematically- impeccable structure that, of all the world languages, allows the machine to program the information in the best way possible. *(For more on the universality of English, see the book "Language Intelligence or Universal English!"* The information being programmed in English is the greatest accomplishment of the Internet!' *The dawn of human brain-to-brain connection has arrived with English" (Rajesh P.N. Rao)* So, *let's not distort this unique language while texting, speaking. or wring.*

To grasp the complex problems of socialization with its political conflicts and war-inflicted sorrows, we must bring about the understanding of ourselves and others in synch based on emotional and psychological intelligences *(See above)* in accordance with *the Law of the Right Human Behavior* that is the core of *the global intelligence* that we are developing slowly ,but surely. Obviously, we need to be focused now on working out *The Code of the Global Culture* backed up, possibly, by the United Nation's Charter of International Communication. Only then will we be equipped to master our national and political differences and focus on raising *global self-consciousness* that will propel us to a new level of extra-terrestrial communication and be accepted by the Universal Community of the celestial infinity.

Self-Transformation benefits the world at large very much!

Chunk 6

Synergize the Trajectory of Your Life to Socially Thrive!

Electronic globalization promotes business, scientific discussions, and all kinds of networking that makes our overall intelligence more creative and much more beneficial ."*Globally competitive professionals work within strong networks, achieve differentiation in the society by developing their network intelligence.* " *(Reid Hoffman)* As technologies improve, people are finding more creative ways *to utilize their social skills* to their advantage, backed up by major social sites, such as Facebook, Tweeter, LinkedIn and others. We are becoming more and more socially-apt in our social behaviors.

I have noted above how important an *individual value preservation and correct language use* are in this process, and how vigilant we must be not to be swept away *by a common trend of imitating others* in the search for immediate gratification of our needs. With robotics developing rapidly now, our social hunger will be satisfied even better. **Robots will soon become our companions**, more understanding and perceptive than humans. In recent years, a growing number of researchers has demonstrated that making robots more social *"is creating the perception that they are more sentient than a mere machine."* They will make us more sociable and even more global.

They will expand the network of our intelligence beyond belief!

Meanwhile, **becoming global** is "*growing among those who know career rules and have the new skills of a global economy ("The Start-Up of You").* It translates into the necessity to assess the basic competences. An individual should comprise **an individual plan of running his life** as his / her personal business, "*investing in themselves, in their network, and in the society."*(R. Hoffman)

We can master the basic intelligences better if we are given the digital tools for life learning.

By reaching out to a network of knowledgeable, hardworking people who display professional awareness and social competence , "*we can bring more depth and understanding to our life goals , gaining worldwide interest and support at the speed of the social Web"*("Forbes", The World Almanac of Wealth< 2014)

Another crucial aspect for the present-day economy is **the ability to promote science and the scientific thinking** that in turn "*creates new concepts, new ways of understanding the world that have an enormous influence on how we think and act'* (" WIRED", 2012, Barky Schwartz)

Mr. Schwartz means that when we think about **the technological impart of science,** we tend to think of the things that science has produced, but there is another kind of technology, produced by science thanks to the technological revolution that has just as big effect on us as thing technology.

"We might call it idea-technology."

Again, and again, the book *"The Start-Up of You"* comes across as the best manual in building ***intelligent network of ideas*** that LinkedIn, founded by Reid Hoffman is successfully promoting and that helped my students a lot to exchange their ideas and find new business partners.

Intellectually-wise, LinkedIn is the best social network out there. to advise.

Also, a new, constructive and conscious way of intelligence building network enhances our interaction with much more ***emotional diplomacy.*** We are learning to function according to the principle of ***cognitive-emotional intelligence*** in synch. That's our huge evolutionary goal, and technology is the best way to meet this challenge.

It is a revolutionary field that creates a more natural and interactive experience for a user, applying the emotional intelligence principles to the social ones, too. *"We are able to look at the world as a huge game where we are trying to optimize our abilities and our intelligences for the common good." (Reid Hoffman and Ben Lashocha)* We are able now to connect to each other better, expressing and sharing not ***only our ideas, but our emotions*** too.

Auto-suggestion: ***I synergize the trajectory of my life to socially thrive!***

Finally, to be more socially–intelligent, I also recommend y***ou keep uploading into your brain the auto-suggestions*** that I use a lot on every page to become more accepting, agreeable, and compatible. Garnish your thoughts in the way that is most appropriate and simple for you. Talk your mind into following your lead in connection with your heart. Naturally, auto–suggestive work is more than necessary at this level, ***and your main induction is always at hand:***

I know who I am!

I am a strong, calm, bold, and determined owner of my firm will!

I can…, I want to…, and I will….

I am becoming more and more open- minded / friendly/ sociable / helpful / cooperative/ innovative, etc. ***with each coming day.***

Make your Mind Kind and the Heart Smart,

And Be Unique at that!

Vistas of Intelligence to Instill Next:

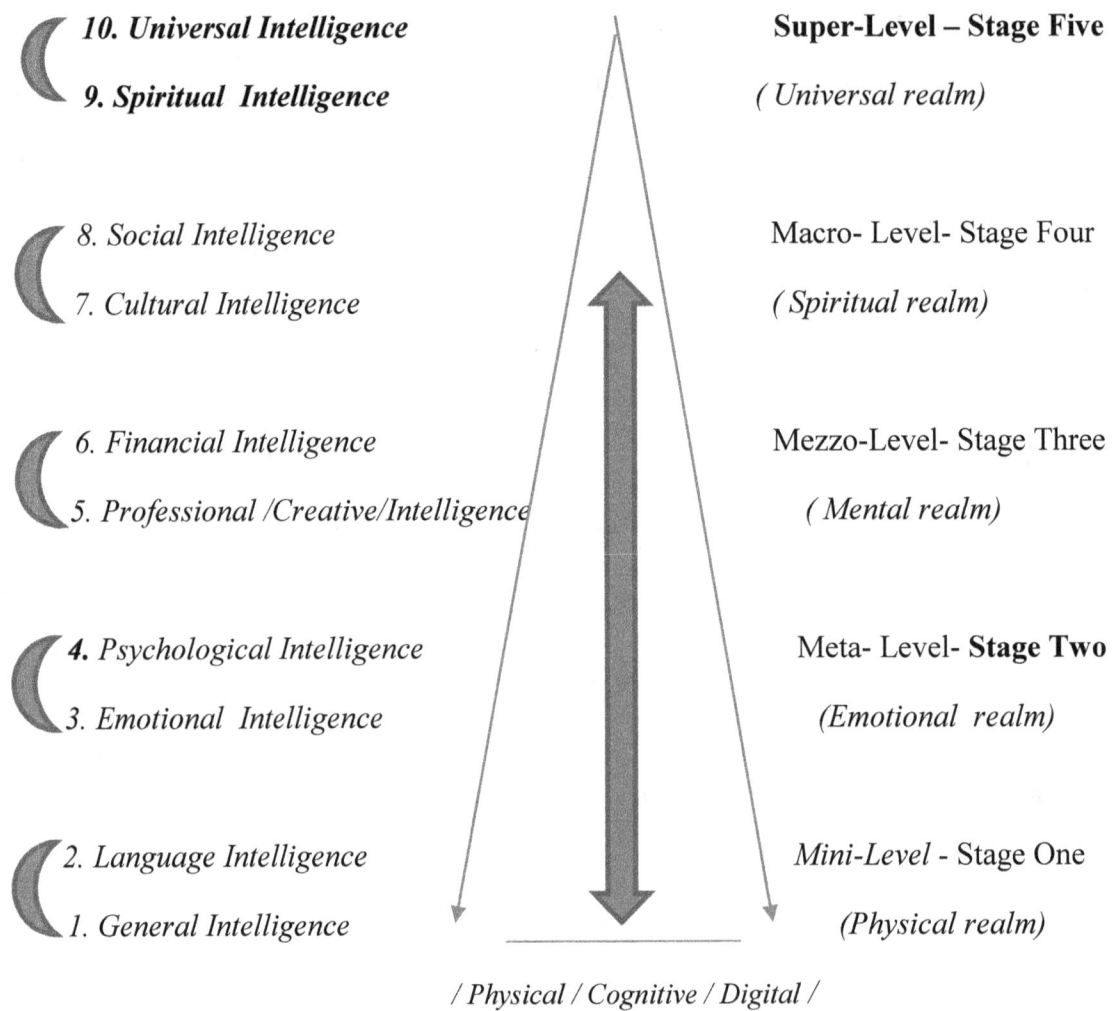

"Fertilize your mind with thinking!" (Albert Einstein)

To Make Your Life Intellectually-Wise, Get to the Higher Dimension without Hesitation!

Stage Five

Super Level - Spiritual Dimension

The Spiritual Intelligence

Step 1

"To be spiritual in truth means only one thing that spirit is manifested in one's own brain."

(John Baines)

To Clean up Your Spiritual Lot, Tune Yourself up to the Station" God'!

Spiritualized Intelligence without Negligence!

We are All in the Court of the Almighty God!

Chunk 1

Our Universal March Forward and Onward

(An Inspirational Booster)

Our universal march forward,

For centuries and onward

      Has been filled with many wrong turns,

        Backsliding and emotional burns!

But taken in its grand sweep,

It's been the match forward, indeed,

        In every life dimension

        And without any exception!

However, the cosmic realm of objectivity

Remains to be found in Christ's nativity!

      Here comes the deadly catch

      Of the humanity's split at large!

Christ made a strong case

For the centuries of evolutionary waste

      With His spiritual intervention,

      As was the initial God's intention!

For when it comes to arts and science,

We've marched forward with much godly reliance!

But on the spiritual infinity plane,

We are devoid of the progress vein!

    A lot of ruthless wars, discords, and doubt,

     Material greed, destruction, and disbelief count!

They are still filling up our common way

With much suffering and religious dismay!

    True, the potential for any creation

    In the digital realm, or any other ration,

  Is in the abundance section

Of many talented egg-heads to mention!

    Gifts are embedded in the human mind,

    And all we need to do is to rewind

 The life hoard of people and the animal world,

Into one fundamentally strong life Fort,

    Able to unite us in a firm determination

     To secure the vital Earth preservation!

For in the vast universal spell, our unique human cell

Is on the track of the cosmic expel!

    Due to our unlimited resources consumption,

    We are prone to the total life destruction!

So, let's synchronize our technological march

With a new spiritually-charged re-touch

        Of the consideration for the Mother Earth

        And Christ Consciousness rebirth!

Our inner architecture is complex,

But we can make it luminous in its reflex,

        Moving onward, forward,

        Upward and Godward!

    What is Your Direction Toward?

"There is no conflict between religion and science. In fact, they are complimenting each other as a form of consciousness."

(Edgar Cayce)

"Life at Its Best is the Life of Faith!"

(Dr. Stanley)

Chunk 2

Being Spiritually Aristocratic

Spiritual intelligence is the top of intellectual development of an individual! It's the process of serious self- quest and self-perfection, not self-demonstration in a religious sense !Being spiritual also means that you have matured in terms of self-awareness and life-awareness, leant to monitor your life emotionally and psychologically, self-installed yourself professionally. constantly tame your bad patterns of behavior and feel holistically united to life around you.

Self-awareness – self-monitoring- self-installation- self-realization-self-salvation!

Generalizing-internalizing -actualizing!

If you have started shaping yourself holistically, you are becoming or have become an accomplished human being with a new perception of life - new thinking, speaking feeling, and acting. you are in control of your intelligence , not just your society-shaped intellect. Your **WHAT + WHY + HOW** are personalized and in synch and mostly based on the knowledge that you had accumulated, selected and actualized.

You are a free, conscious thinker, living in the present and appreciating your life as is.

This process **refines the soul**, and it starts shining from inside, irrespective of the skin color. I have met many black people in the USA that were shining from inside with true readiness to help and to back me up with a blessing at the moment that I needed most, being often lost in the country with a hostile, capitalist structure, set up on the money-making and an impersonal attitude to people.

Many people in different social offices have a nice smile on the face, but don't care about what bothers you. They go to the church every Sunday, though, believing to be Godly, but being, in fact, heartless and godless. Being spiritually aristocratic is a challenging responsibility without a devilish inner response, " *What do I care? or What is there in it for me?*

Every human contact is a responsibility!

With such inner current, your life will have a renewed quality, depending on the state of your self-consciousness. Transforming yourself intellectually, you develop new thoughts, feelings, convictions, values, and aspirations. You are different because you embody different , refined patterns of behavior, controlled by your conscious mind. you respect yourself, and you feel content with what you are. You generate new abilities to love, to forgive and to forget because you have sorted them out through your *growing spiritualized intelligence and self-consciousness.*

"It's difficult to climb the heaven, but very easy to slide down to hell!"

You have a strong position in life and you can stand up for it, for yourself, and for others that are still much weaker than you.

Life is the process of self-seeking, and many people are on this journey now.

There are many admirable **God–transmitters** now**,** and they are amazingly insightful and self-educated, to begin with, and therefore, they gather thousands of people that tune to them physically, emotionally, mentally, and spiritually because ***their mental and spiritual frequencies synchronize with the God's messages.***

The crowds Joel Osteen and Joyce Myer gather are all there to get inspired by the intelligent minds and pure souls that Joel and Joyce preserve in this challenging world against all odds.

"I want to know the God's thoughts. The rest is details! *(Albert Einstein)*

We mean here that just praying is essential only when it is ***consciously mind-channeled and in no way mechanical.*** Most spiritually-intelligent people do not interpret God in a scary, spooky way. ***They transmit God, tuning every listener to the station "God" individually*** because it is everyone's personal responsibility to try and find God for himself / herself. Also, spiritual leaders are the people of ***spiritualized intelligence*** that is the result of the consistent self-growth and constant self-enriching.

" I use my own brain and I never stop borrowing the brains of the others."(A. Einstein)

By being more self-educated, critically-thinking, and independent in the perception of the world, we become new human beings, proud to rightfully declare,

In a noble life quest, I am my very best!

I am physically , emotionally, and mentally alive!

I have transformed the spiritual quality of my life!

There is no Spirituality without Intellectuality!

Chunk 3

Being Godly in a Godless World

I have been outlining the nine levels of intelligence and their role in self-monitoring so far only to remind you in each chunk of information that *we are evolving our intelligence to enrich our spirituality and to raise our self-consciousness*. It should be done , not just in a religiously-mechanical way, but through deep, insightful, aware, unshakable awareness that we are being digitally governed from the Above, or, actually, everywhere, by some creative force: ***The Universal Intelligence, the Master, Mind, or the Source that we all perceive as God and call God.***

> *"Man may produce the stumbling stones; God alone-in the mind of man may make them stepping stones." (Edgar Cayce)*

I think that every sacred book I read is, actually unfolding the secret of life in the five levels: **physica**l *(mini)*; **emotional** *(meta); ***mental*** *(mezzo);* **spiritual** *(macro).*; and *universal (super)*. We are developing *the Super Conscious Mind i*n these levels holistically and auto-suggestively.:

I'm No Longer Automatic; I'm Becoming Spiritually-Aristocratic!

Mini level -   I personalize myself mentally, physically, and verbally.

Meta level -   I emotionalize my mind and get more psychologically– aware.

Mezzo level –   I intellectualize and individualize myself professionally!

Macro level –   I acculturate, socialize, and spiritualize my life.!

Super level –   I perceive with my soul; and I see myself as part of the whole life.

The body is a physical, emotional, mental, spiritual, and universal part of the entire life in the Cosmos ,and therefore, it needs to be sculptured in all these planes

Self- Evolution is a gradual process, and it is going on according to the Universal Plan.

Each level is integrated with the next one. Self-realization is the process of internalizing the necessary ***intelligences*** in synch with the development of ***self-consciousness.*** We call this union- ***personal integrity***, and it manifests the outcome of the self- actualization process that ends with life itself. So, when talking about ***Spiritual Intelligence,*** I do not mean any religious affiliation, nor do I give preference to any religion in particular. All religions are the interpretations of the eternal concept of creation - **God**. As John Baines puts it,

"Spiritual aristocracy begins with the individual and ends with him."

Chunk 4

"God Helps Those Who Help Themselves!"

Spiritual Intelligence is the top intelligence! No doubt about it. However, we cannot just declare that we are spiritual beings. ***We must earn this title with*** our thinking, speaking, and acting with our personal integrity. Only then our magnetic human energy, imbued with kindness and love, will be charged with a lot of tolerance and understanding of those that are not there yet.

Spiritual intelligence comes from within, like inspiration that propels you

forward, upward, God-ward!

As I have stated many times so far, spiritual development is the most important stage on the way of self-creation because the search for God had never changed.

God is eternal and innate in all of us!

The urge for the perfect in life has been driving human beings on the path of evolution for centuries. So, the statement," ***Nobody's perfect!*** " is banal and meaningless because it is used to just justify one's weakness on the path of self-formation. And such a person cannot consider himself spiritual.

Being spiritual is becoming a willful person, able to manage his inner downward currents!

As per science, ***the Americans are the most sinful nation on earth.***(*Scientific American mind< 2013)* Fun and money chasing are killing the minds and souls of people. Moms tell the kids heading to school, "***Have fun!*** Later, after they come home from school, they ask them, "***Did you have fun?***" Isn't it indicative of a wrong orientation for kids who, unfortunately, seek fun afterwards everywhere, prioritizing the search for money and fun for the rest of their lives?

Let's enjoy the fun of life, but do it at the right time and site!

Also, we have all seen the appeal. "***Be born again!***" on the bumpers of many cars, or we have heard it a lot from many Christ followers that are very sincere in their fanatic belief that someone can be born again with their recipe. The statement is very convincing, though seemingly banal, in the sense that we all do have to be born twice - ***the second time - spiritually.*** But we cannot and should not just declare that! To be true to what we all preach, we have to acknowledge that it's a conscious and very willful process that often remains just words, not action. The problem is, *it **is** literally impossible to attain spiritual intelligence without enriching your self-consciousness* on all the previously outlined levels!

The motivation to be spiritual grows inside the person, level by level!

Chunk 5

Spiritualized Intelligence is the Root of All Wisdom!

Wisdom is consciously-processed knowledge and rationalized thinking about the roots of life experience, religion, science and human evolution. ***Wisdom is the root of spirituality***. Every ***Proverb*** in the Bible talks about wisdom and they are, obviously, meant to be read by us every day of the month, since ***there are 31 of them***. I personally, read one every day, and I discover new revelations for myself each month. Learn to see the manifestations of God's wisdom in every beat of life, every blossoming flower, and every bird in the air. No wonder, the spiritual dimension comes after the mental one.

It's the apex of the pyramid of self-creation!

We need to learn to reason out the religious standpoints and the spiritual aspirations for ourselves, without relying on the priest or any religious leader, even though helping to those people who have not yet reached the mountaintop is part of our spiritual responsibility. ***Being spiritual is being integral, and integrity is a matter of personal mastery*** and the ability to share the knowledge that you have managed to accumulate on this path.

Self-induction: *The voltage of my spirit is high and infinite!*

Only **spiritual reasoning helps to put our emotions under the control of the brain**, to learn to synergize our space with love and appreciate life in all its manifestations. Even the spiritual meanings of every day of the week can make a difference and illuminate our day with a conceptual meaning if we are aware of them. This is what ***the Jewish wisdom*** teaches us, so we could mind the meaning of each day of the week consciously.

Sunday is Mercy; Monday is Judgment!

Tuesday is Beauty; Wednesday is Victory!

Thursday is Glory; Friday is Foundation!

Sunday is a New Beginning!

So, every day has a meaning!

A great Russian writer Leo Tolstoy, who was deeply godly in his perception of life and the world has a wonderful story" ***What a Man Lives By.*** " that instills a great message in readers.

"Men do not live on bread alone! Men live by the divine spark of their spiritual wisdom."

True, wisdom helps us survive and do many good things to each other during the life time. But there is no wisdom, without the wrapping of a man's intelligence.

"Spiritual intelligence uplifts and expands our souls, brightens our soul light," (Fred Bell)

The soul light protects us against the poisonous impact of the society. It builds up the spiritual immunity against godlessness of the people around that manifests itself not in a person's different faith, but in the desert of his /her corroded, un – educated, dark soul.

Self-induction: *A soul lives on the mental nutrition!*

There are a lot of different speculations made about spirituality in different religious affiliations, but it becomes more and more evident with every passing year that all of us are seeking one thing - *spiritual maturity*, and it does not matter what religious way we choose to accomplish it.

Religiousness + intelligence = spiritualized intelligence!

Being wise is also being in constant service to others and giving the best we have to the world. The Chinese wisdom rightfully teaches us that human values manifest themselves through service. Spirituality is the quality of higher intelligence, personal maturity, a lot of sacrifice, and our service to each other and God.

Auto-suggestion: *"Sacrifice is necessary.*

Without sacrifice, nothing is attained!" (Buddha)

Finally, I have attended many different seminars, listened to numerous spiritual leaders and gurus, read numerous books, and did and continue doing a lot of thinking on my own before I started putting any of my thoughts in books. still feeling not quite filled up with wisdom to share it with the world. All the wonderful people that have contributed to ,my personal growth have had their own share of troubles and tribulation before they started sharing the realization of truth with us. *We are not supposed to blindly follow their paths!* You cannot pay a thousand dollars for "*becoming limitless*" and overly successful after any seminar. You need to study, learn, process the exceptional, personally- knowledge that you get *through the personal grid of your perception* and work out **YOUR OWN PLAN OF ACTION** and your own **MISSION STATEMENT** of the spiritual growth that is a life-long journey.

"Be conscious; consciousness mobilizes!" (Neale Donald Walsch)

Self-Induction:

My Life Goal is to Make Myself Whole!

Chunk 6

I Monitor My Life! I am Alive!

To conclude this part, the increasing number of people all over the world is raising their consciousness in the spiritual way that incorporates all the other dimensions of life. When you empower yourself with *the Art of Living,* you will be having *the same vibrational frequencies as the universe.*

"Consciousness is what results from growth, and all growth is educational!"

Constantly working on our intelligence at any of the five levels outlined above enables us to direct our consciousness beyond the level of visualization of the result of our accomplishments *to the depth of consciousness on the physical, emotional, psychological, mental, and spiritual levels*. Like Prometheus that brought light to people, enlightened living fills us up with the inspiration and awe for the magic of life around, when you realize, *"Super joy is being thrilled with being alive!" (Paul Pearsall)* Each higher level requires more effort to be applied to achieve the state at which the techniques relative to *the General Intelligence and the living skills* become viable.

The Vistas of Intelligence + Living skills = Spiritualized Intelligence

Spiritualized intelligence can be accomplished by us only if we become much *more life aware* and *much more equipped in the skills* that identify each separate level of intelligence re viewed so far. Only thanks to the holistic and conscious self-installation can we become strong enough to erase the scars of the past and take full responsibility of the present.

Knowledge put to action becomes real power!

We become able to harmonize our inner and outer space at will and become truly whole and integrated. Both*, the left , structural, and the right, creative, brains* will work in synch, and we will create strong, holistic psychic synergy. Then, you can honestly declare, auto-suggestively:

I am working at my inner glee, I'm becoming a Luminary! I am positive. I am getting into the state of mental, emotional, and physical equilibrium. I am not materialistic! I am disciplined in my thoughts, words, emotions, actions, attitudes, morals, my eating, my breathing, and my entire living. I synergize my life! I do not attribute everything to a chance.

I monitor my life! I am an enlightened, advanced, spiritual human being. I am a great me, I am the best I could ever be!

I Do My Soul work as a Regular Self-Talk!

Vistas of Intelligence to Instill Next:

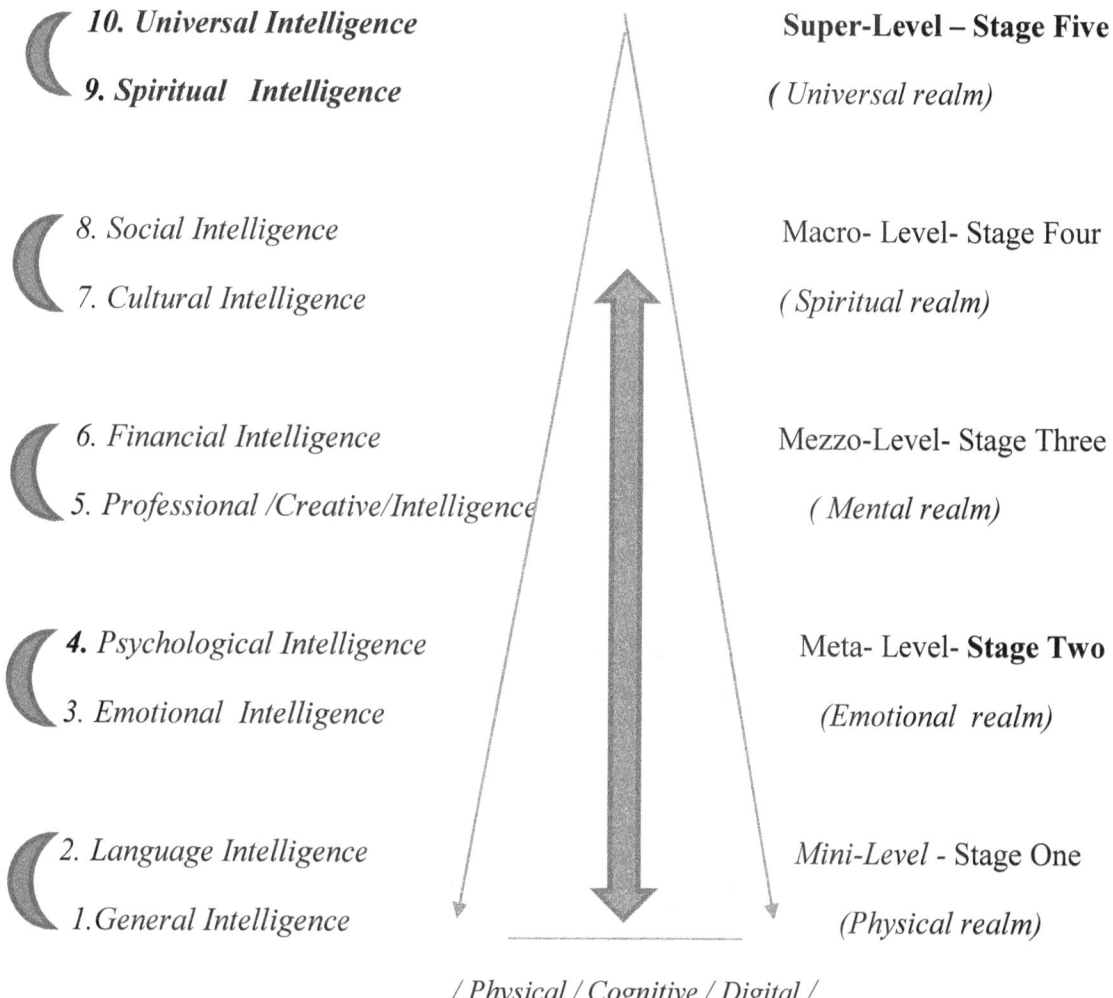

"Fertilize your mind with thinking!" (Albert Einstein)

To Make Your Life Intellectually-Wise, Get to the Higher Dimension without Hesitation!

Stage Five

Super-Level of Intelligence - The Final Step

The Universal Intelligence

Attaining Universal Intelligence is forming a bridge with the Divine.

Auto-Induction:

My Infinity is the Universal Unanimity!

The Voltage of My Spirit is High and Infinite!

I am One with Everything Under the Sun!

Chunk 1

The Universal Mind that We Need to Unwind!

The Universal Intelligence is the blanket intelligence on the holistic pyramid of intelligences that I have tried to outline in general terms above, level by level. ***The Universal Mind choreographs everything that is being***, and the most intelligent and perceptive of us get connected to it though channeling and thought control , using the Law of Attraction to fix any life fraction.

At this highest level, *"there is no separation between anything and anybody. There is only God, and everything is God!"(Edgar Cayce)*

Elon Mask is a rare man who has obtained the universal mentality in his attempt to make a significant difference in our space life, and the scope of his ideas is absolutely genius! His words truly characterize people who have obtained the universal intelligence.

" People choose to be extra-ordinary!

When we turn on the self-construction mechanism, we become extra-ordinary because we are governed by some higher forces, very much interested in our evolution. If we are persistent in our self-growth, we accomplish success that is the most rewarding thing in the world.

At this level, we transform terrestrial knowledge into the celestial wisdom!

Having formed at least a vague idea about all the above presented levels of intelligence and having worked on creating a better person of yourself, you have, for sure, gotten rid of much stagnant knowledge and beliefs, and you have stored some ***living intelligence*** in your brain and have sorted out the one you have accumulated so far. I am just up-dating it and systematizing some information holistically. Awareness is building up confidence.

*Living Intelligence brings you in touch with the Universal Intelligence in **a new, much more reasoned-out and conscious way.***

The profound questions about life in us and in the universe are not solved yet, but the fact that we are ruled by the Universal Intelligence is not questionable any more. Celestial wisdom gets transferred into the right action, and we become our own cheerleaders. We learn*" to think, speak, and act right, and we refuse to think, speak, and act wrongly"*.(R. Wetherill) I hope that we will live much better and finally manage ***to orchestrate gladness*** in the heart every day.

There will be less dissipated thinking and reckless, mindless actions on our part in the unpredictable future. that will also be characterized by the outcome below:

The will-power is firm, the values are moral, the actions are consistent, the speech is meaningful, and the behavior is constructive.

Attaining the Universal Intelligence is forming a bridge with the Divine. This connection resonates in us through our ***reading into meaningful coincidences*** that we are learning to pay attention to.

With your personal intelligence constantly changing, your consciousness enriching, and your will-power strengthening, ***you will start perceiving higher beings around you***, reasoning out very step with them, tuning your intuition up to their advice, and being able to finally view **every** *meaningful coincidence* as a sign of God, guiding your life.

Higher Consciousness without any crowd-channeled control

is our ultimate destination in self- creation!

I love the words by *Alexander Blok*, a great Russia poet that I translated and keep quoting in my books. Blok's words characterize our insatiable desire to go beyond the terrestrial and do the impossible to become one with God.

"I want to desperately live

To internalize what can be seen,

To celebrate the unforeseen,

To humanize the irreversible,

And realize the impossible!"

Admire the Beauty of the Sky;
It's the Final Domain of Your "I"!

Chunk 2

Spiritual Luminosity is Our Velocity!

"God is a supercomputer mind that contains a total inventory of what each of us is." *(Rev. P. S. Berg)* Finishing this book, I want to give tribute to many spiritually-uplifted people from the inventory of God that had enlightened our lives with their inner light of wisdom and that continue to do so with their generous service on the path of enlightening us. They were / are, and will be not just great, fabulous, fantastic, or even glamorous. **They are luminous!**

There are many people carrying ***the godly spark of light*** in them around us. A skin color, nationality, a social position, or a person's legacy that might be even publicly acclaimed have nothing to do with it. These people magnetize us with their ***unique wisdom and luminosity*** that outlines any common criticism or mass media incisures. We see and hear a lot of Sadhguru lately, and I marvel at his individual wisdom and an immensity of his personality.

The inner light that such people radiate fills us up with their ***sincere faith, high values, and incredible tenacity***. You cannot, but gravitate to such people in your mind and heart, and every encounter with a luminous person like that on the pages of his / her book, on TV, or in a face-to-face communication, however short it may be, enlightens the memory for years to come.

Let there be many more luminaries without time and space boundaries!

The luminosity of Marilyn Monroe, Elvis Presley, or Michael Jackson, for example, cannot be darkened by anybody ever. They have left to us the gift of inspiration and the impossibility to ever be duplicated in their uniqueness. There is a well-known saying, ***"Beauty will save the world!"*** These words had been re-worded by a famous Russian painter, writer, theosophist, and enlightener, ***Nicholas Roerich***, whose memory is eternalized in a great museum in Manhattan.

"Beauty that is consciously perceived will save the world!"

Only when are we able to perceive beauty of life around us and *radiate it back in our thoughts, words, emotions, and actions* will we be spiritually–advanced to the Universal level of consciousness. We will integrate life in us in its entirety, and the legacy that we might leave behind will radiate the luminosity of our souls to the people that will carry this torch of light after us, like Prometheus. ***That's our legacy!***

Everything is left for the people coming after us!

Auto-Induction:

I am an Active Captain of My Life; I am alive!

Chunk 3

Unite with the Universal Intelligence Might!

Concluding the book, let me remind you to continue *doing suggestive inspiring yourself* at any time and space. Every time you are out in the sun or while enjoying the view of the night sky, see yourself, surrounded by light. *Feel yourself immersed in a luminous substance*: the Sun rays, the white light, and the light of the stars, even the light of every lamp you are looking at or passing by while driving at night.

If you happen to be walking, *breathe in light consciously at every step,* saying any auto-suggestion that you might happen to memorize. Breathe in light, love, peace, and harmony; breathe out negativity, troubles, sickness, problems, and darkness.

Make such habit your second nature. Enjoy doing it!

After you have enlightened the consciousness of your entire body, you can start purifying it *on the cellular level*, heightening your *aware attention to the body's needs and its complaints* to you in the form of pains, fatigue, depression, sadness, lack of love, any insult, disappointment, inner emptiness, and loneliness. Gradually, you will establish a true *"mind-body connection"* at your own accord. Practicing *the Suggestive Meditation (Part Two, Chunks 17,18)*, you will not wear your body out prematurely because you are inspiring it for life *consciously, continuously, and religiously!*

Give your consciousness a much better home to operate from!

Reading self-help books about how to preserve the vitality of the body, working on its mobility and beauty, we heighten the level of our *general, physical intelligence that is fantastic as it is*, and we look further over the horizon of life, becoming conscious of the metaphysical realm that surrounds us. Developing you physical intelligence consciously, we are also becoming more and more aware of *the magic of life in us.* Even if you do not feel that there is anything to thank your body for, keep your aware attention on it religiously.

There is no need to better your overall intelligence (10 stages, outlined above)) if you do not take care of your physical one properly. Thank your body for *its unified work* on improving your health every single day, good or bad, healthy or sick, happy or unhappy.

The body is doing it, anyway! Your body is your temple!

Congratulations!

You are Living Intelligence in Action!

Chunk 4

Ten Stages of the Instilled Living Intelligence

The Universal Intelligence completes *the Self-Actualization Pyramid* of the essential levels of the Living Intelligence in the mental realm of the spiral of self-resurrection that I have outlined for you in most general terms above. All the stages are interconnected in the holistic system, presented stage by stage.

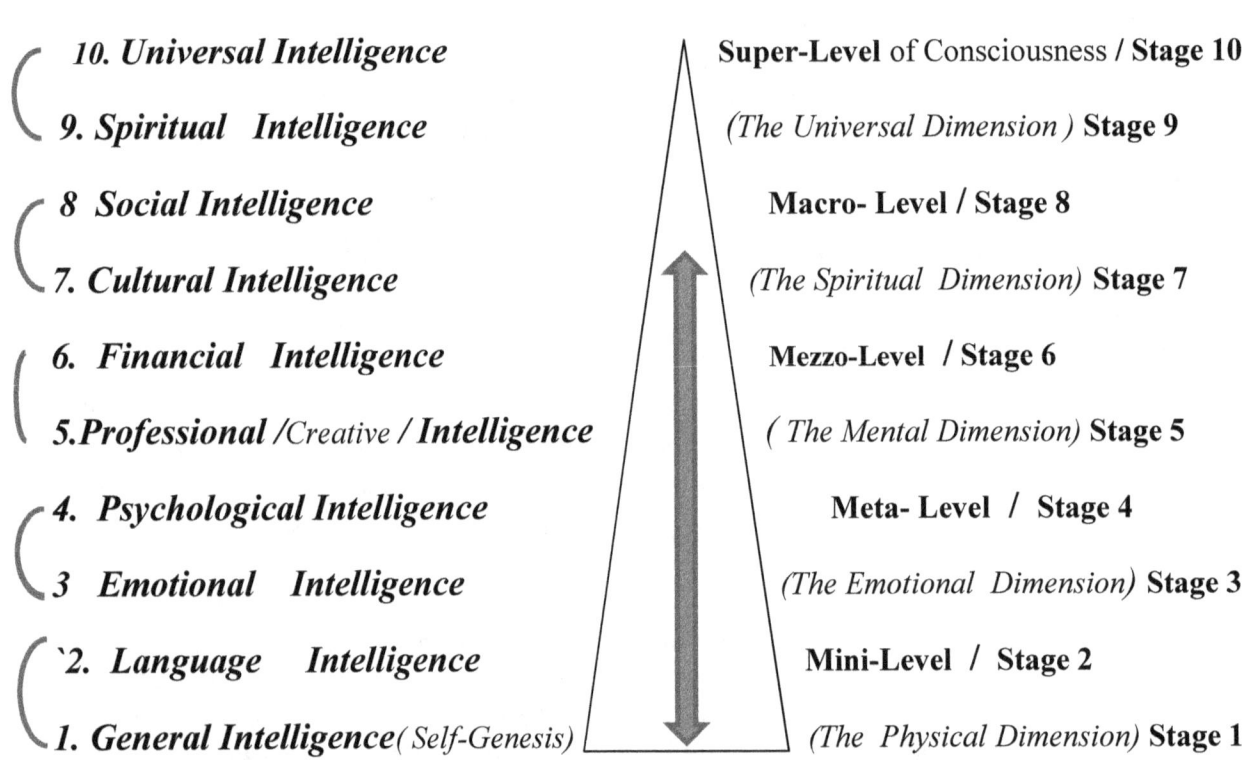

The Spiral of Self-Resurrection

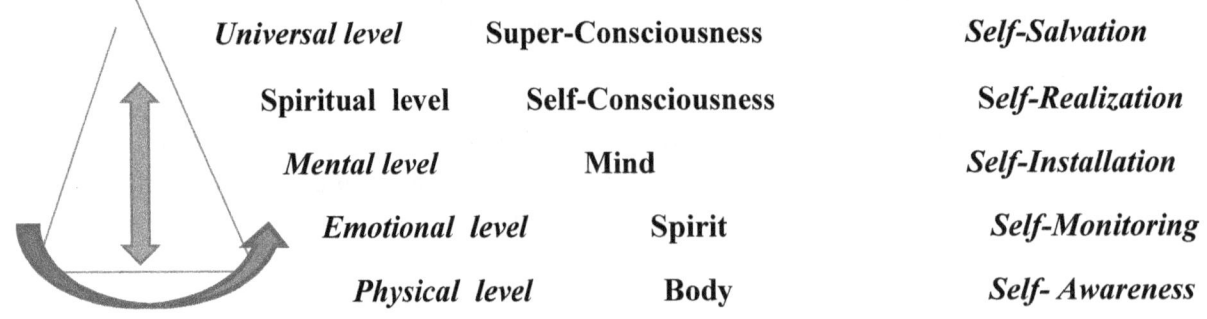

Body+ Spirit+ Mind + Self-Consciousness+ Universal Consciousness =

A New, Holistically-Developed Self!

Chunk 5

Infuse Your Self-Realization Fuse!

An Instructional Booster

Every day, without any mask,

Address yourself and ask,

"What have I done today

For my physical array?

Have I added a bit

To my emotional up-beat?

Have I also enriched

My mental out-reach?

And, finally, on the spiritual plane,

Have I gotten closer to God's domain?

Having assessed yourself

In the four-dimensional cell,

Don't waste your daily zest

To just possess!

Let it be wisely used

To infuse your self-realization fuse!

Invest in the Greatest Asset - Your Soul's Facet!

Conclusion

The Art of Living Is The Art of Becoming!

Intelligence-Ascending is Consciousness-Mending!

I Am a Thought-Evolved Being with the Universal Seeing!

The Cyclone derives its Power from the Center – Your Solar System!

Intelligence is Me! Intelligence is My Philosophy!

1. Bridge Your Dream and the Reality without Vanity!

Having read, or speed-read the book that far, you, of course, have enriched your intelligence in a general, holistic way. You might still respond to the title above with the words, " *I wish.*" Becoming the ***Dream-You*** that you had envisioned initially as ***the Ultimate Result Vision*** of the best of you (*Part Two, Thesis 8*) and that you are keeping at the front of your mind is ***the bridge between your dream and the reality,*** and the book has played its initial role, having outlined this route for you to in a disciplined, simple system. I am absolutely certain that at least one thing has been altered in your perception: ***You've changed your small life into a bigger one, and your grey life into a brighter one!***

As it has been noted above, ***the Integral You*** is the holistic self-concept that is marked in the book as the ***physical, emotional, mental, spiritual, and universal processes of your self-maturation.*** At the highest point of self-development, at ***the Super level***, all the information that you have accumulated in your mind in melting into one vision - . *The Ultimate Result Vision of the Best of You (Part Two, Thesis 8).* ***The Ultimate Result Vision of Self-Sculpturing has become a reality!***

The URV is only a vision yet. It is in the ***generalization*** process of your forming it in the mind. If you are serious about your self-sculpturing, it can be replaced by ***the Vintage You*** image later, but only after the next holistic step – ***selection.*** It has not happened yet because ***life is not the result, it's the process first!*** You might have reasoned some things out, and they have become knowledge that needs to be put to action – the ***actualization*** step.

Internalizing (*or generalizing*) – **selecting** (*or optimizing*) – **Strategizing** (*or actualizing*) !

If you have outlined the self-installation route for yourself in general terms, you might want to get to the next step - ***the selection step***. Re-read, or look through the basic concepts of the book and build up your own conceptual structure of self-installation. Use your smart phone to download the inspirational boosters that ***you select*** and that have a special meaning for. You might want to change them in the future because the third step of ***actualization*** of the programs that you have chosen will require the next quality step of self-growth. Remember, ***Life is a cycle, not a circle!***

The holistic paradigm (Synthesis – Analysis -Synthesis) is objectively the same for everyone!

(**Body+ Spirit+ Mind**) + (**Self-Consciousness+ Universal Consciousness**

⬆ ⬆

Living Intelligence + *Enlightened Self-Consciousness*

Form + Content = A New, Spiritually-Intellectualized You!

2. Become Less Life-Negligent and More Life-Intelligent!

In sum, you realize ,of course, that *self-installation is a lifelong process* with two steps forward and one step back, or sometimes one step forward and two steps back. That is a natural process of self-creation. The most important thing is *not to get on the rocky road of self-corrode*. It is always there, but your self-consciousness is getting higher, stronger, and more refined. So, to be more life-fitting, keep repeating auto-suggestively:

I am not life-negligent, I am life-intelligent!

When your spirituality is much higher, and your self-consciousness is more developed, you will finally arrive at *the Integral You,* or *"a Star Man"* stage that John Baines predicts for us in his book *"The Stellar Man"*. The best of us will attain this stage in the unforeseeable future. Meanwhile, the change will be manifesting itself in you because you are following *the objective path,* not just the one, suggested by a certain Dr. Ray.

I have verified this path all my professional life, and I can swear to you, it is right!

Anyway, you no longer have judgment about anything and anyone. *You are no longer like any one!* At this Super level, we all become one with life and the immortal spirit of Universal Intelligence which is God! *The Universal intelligence is making your mind-body obey your will which is God's will! What an uplifting feeling that is!* You will experience it at some point without fail! Your ardent desire to oversee yourself and attain full self-mastery will be instilled and constantly fortified , building up **your *inner fortress, your personal magnetic core*** where you will find refuge any time you need help. Just the reminder of the formula of strength below will do the trick. *Its inductive power is immense*! So, keep internalizing and energizing your becoming consistently, with the help of God and this formula:

I can, I want to, and I will!

May this program become *the conceptual blueprint of self-creation* for the rest of your life. The basic thing for you is *to do self-hypnosis consistently* as a boost for the self-image and the nourishment for your will-power. Self-hypnosis helps synchronize thoughts and emotions and reeducate the process of thinking. Eventually, you will learn *to think consequentially*, not *impulsively and compulsively* because awareness or conscious assessment of self-reality will change your mental digestion for new frequencies of *intelligence and self-consciousness in synch.* With new, well-sorted out information in the mind and conscious responding to life challenges, we'll attract people that have the same gravitational force in their minds, and you'll become *the Living Intelligence in action.*

Only with God in Synch, you are What You Think!

3. Oh, Gee; I'm the Quality Me!

I am driving through the time and space with intelligence, awareness, love, success and health on my interface!

I am physically beautiful, Emotionally -Invincible, Mentally - Unbeatable And Spiritually – Free! I Am a Conscious Me!

Self-Synthesis ⟶ *Self-Analysis* ⟶ *Self-Synthesis!*

Long Live the Belief in Myself without If!

Good Luck on the Self-Installation Track!

And That, in Every Air Sip, is Our Universal Trip!

Post Thought!

"I Have a Dream!" *(Martin Luther King Jr.)*

When we arrived in the USA, there were many things that we lacked in the former Soviet Union of those destructive times, but the country of plenty lacked one thing that my 13 - year old daughter noticed very soon and told me one day after she came home from Mamaroneck school in Westchester.

-*"Mom, I know my dream now. I will start a business in this country;* **I will build the center for kids!** *They have no Pioneer Canters for kids, where I learnt folk-dancing, ballet - dancing, sewing, fishing, swimming, space-flying, and toy-making.* **Poor kids. They don't have that here. Nor do they have anything for teenagers. What should I do here? Where do I go after school?** *My school peers talk only about parties, bars, sex, and sleep-overs".*

I was glad that she started thinking in the American way business-wise, but I was truly upset that she was right about the second part of her observation that very soon became a reality and a nightmare for me. The reality changed her dream, and even though she became a computer-designer and got four books for kids published, she did not manage to bridge her dream and the reality. She had never spoken about it again.

But I have never forgotten that conversation and the spark in Yolanda's eyes because I saw the same spark in the eyes of many of my students whom I try to inspire to never betray their dreams and become what they aspire to be, not what just secures their life As a matter of fact, *my five books on self-awareness, self-monitoring, self-installation, self-realization, and self-salvation* in life, are inspired by my daughter's unrealized dream to have the center like some day here.

I BELIEVE THAT LIFE IS A SPIRAL, NOT A CIRCLE!

My dream is to have a free developmental *center "Jupiter"* that will be structured in five rings - *physical, emotional, mental, spiritual, and universal*, presenting five *space stations:*

5. Universal   Space Station

4. Spiritual   Space Station

3. Mental   Space Station

2. Emotional   Space Station

1. Physical   Space Station

Wouldn't it be great to have **the Physical Space Station** for the kids and teenager to develop their physical abilities, like it was in *the ancient Greek school for Spartans.* They will enrich their *cognitive skills* and learn many new interesting things of their choice, as well as train their *digital skills* in the most creative ways. *(the book "I am Free to Be the Best of Me!")*

Next, at *the Emotional Space Station*, the kids will learn about an array of beautiful human emotions and how to handle their Amygdala glad with the help of the best movies, tales, works of art, and beautiful classic music There will be an instructor- an ***emotionalist and robot -friends*** to back them up at the moment of dismay. *(the book "Soul-Refining")*

The holistic pyramid of essential ***vistas of intelligence*** will be at their fingerprints when they chose to spiral up to **the Mental Station** to fill up the gaps in the levels of intelligence that this book features. They will enhance their awareness by connecting their two brains and boosting their creativity and ascertaining their dream of what they want to become *(the book "Living Intelligence or the Art of Becoming!")*

The most inspiring knowledge of the human evolutionary ***spiritual growth*** will await them **at the Spiritual Space Station,** with no preaching, but insightful, interesting teaching to shape their ***spiritualized intelligence.****(the book "Self-Taming!")*

The space-time journey into the impossible will complete **at the Universal Station,** with a breath-taking flight of imagination in the top observatory + a virtual space station that will take them on interstellar travels into space.*(the book "Beyond the Terrestrial!)*

And the best thing of all - there will be no obligation, no words: "***You are supposed to…"/ "You need to pay first!" That's not your station! "You need to first pay for this…"*** The possibilities are limitless, as well as ***our incredible NOW*** that is, in fact, our wonderous future and that, hopefully, will give our kids a true chance to realize their dreams!

The choices we make dictate the life we live!

Somewhere and Someday are Here, Today!

"We Cannot Pick the Future, but We Can Design It!"

(Ray Kurzweil)

Dr. Ray with Her Inspirational Say:

1. "Emotional Diplomacy", Leiris, NY 2008

2. "Four Dimensions of a Soul", Leiris, NY, 2009

3. "Americanize Your language, Emotionalize Your Speech," Nova Press, 2010

4. "It Too Shall Pass!" Xlibris, 2011

5. "I Am Strong in My Spirit!" Xlibris, 2012

6. "Language Intelligence or the Universal English", Book One (the theory and the Method of the Right Language Behavior) Xlibris, 2014

7. "Language Intelligence or the Universal English," Book Two (practical remedying of the Language Habits - pronunciation, grammar, vocabulary) Xlibris, 2014

8. "Language Intelligence or the Universal English," Book Three (practical remedying of the Speech Skills - speaking, writing, reading, listening), Xlibris, 2014

9. "My Solar System," Xlibris, 2015

10. "Beyond the Terrestrial!" Xlibris, 2016

11. "Soul Refining!" Toplink Publishing, 2017

12. " I Am Free to Be the Best of Me!" Toplink Publishing, 2017

13. "Self-Taming!" Bookwhip Publishing, 2018

Dr. Ray is running the site www.language-fitness.com.

email: rimma143@hotmail.com

Tel. (203) 212-2673

All the books by Dr. Rimaletta Ray are the synthesis of a lifetime of research, avid reading, as well as a consistent self-refining. Dr. Rimaletta Ray also runs her language-coaching business, based on emotional diplomacy training and inspirational hypnotherapy.

Yolanta Lensky *is a young thinker, a poet, a writer, and a designer. Yolanta has designed all the pictures in this book and other books of Dr. Ray*

email: yolantalensky1979@gmail.com

Tel. (203) 850-4791

www.ingramcontent.com/pod-product-compliance
Lightning Source LLC
Chambersburg PA
CBHW080213040426
42333CB00044B/2649